TRANSPACIFIC REBALANCING

NEMIR A KIRDAR

Transpacific Rebalancing

Implications for Trade and Economic Growth

BARRY P. BOSWORTH
MASAHIRO KAWAI
editors

ASIAN DEVELOPMENT BANK INSTITUTE
Tokyo

BROOKINGS INSTITUTION PRESS
Washington, D.C.

ASIAN DEVELOPMENT BANK INSTITUTE
Kasumigaseki Building 8F, 3-2-5 Kasumigaseki, Chiyoda-ku
Tokyo 100-6008 Japan
www.adbi.org

THE BROOKINGS INSTITUTION
1775 Massachusetts Avenue, N.W., Washington, D.C. 20036
www.brookings.edu

Library of Congress Cataloging-in-Publication data
Transpacific rebalancing : implications for trade and economic growth / Barry P. Bosworth and
Masahiro Kawai, editors.
    pages   cm
    "[Published in collaboration with] Asian Development Bank Institute, Tokyo."
    Includes bibliographical references and index.
    ISBN 978-0-8157-2260-1 (pbk. : alk. paper) — ISBN 978-0-8157-2261-8 (e-book) 1. Balance
of payments—Pacific Area. 2. Balance of payments—Asia. 3. Balance of payments—United
States. 4. Balance of trade—Pacific Area. 5. Balance of trade—Asia. 6. Balance of trade—
United States. 7. Pacific Area—Economic policy—21st century. 8. Asia—Economic policy—
21st century. 9. United States—Economic policy—21st century. I. Bosworth, Barry, 1942–
editor. II. Kawai, Masahiro, 1947–editor. III. Eichengreen, Barry J. Exchange rates and global
rebalancing. Container of (work):
    HG3883.P16T73 2014
    382'.17091823—dc23   2014036715

9 8 7 6 5 4 3 2 1

Printed on acid-free paper

Typeset in Adobe Garamond

Composition by Circle Graphics
Columbia, Maryland

Contents

Preface

This book takes up the important subject of how to rebalance transpacific trade in the aftermath of the global financial crisis of 2007–09. Large current account imbalances built up in the period leading up to the crisis. This payments imbalance was driven by the U.S. current account deficit, on one hand, and by current account surpluses, mainly Japan's and, more recently, the People's Republic of China's, on the other. The global imbalance peaked in 2006, when the United States had a current account deficit of 6 percent of its GDP.

There has been intense debate about the extent to which development of the global payments imbalance directly contributed to the development of the global financial crisis. Many in the West take the view that the global payments imbalance was the primary cause of the global financial crisis. However, many in Asia disagree with this view and instead point to policy mistakes made in the United States and Europe as the primary cause of the crisis. This debate has not yet been resolved.

Nonetheless, it is commonly agreed that a large global payments imbalance is unsustainable. The global financial crisis forced adjustments to transpacific payments imbalances, but in a disruptive way, accompanied by a sharp contraction of economic activity and rising unemployment. This is clearly not a desirable way of reducing imbalances. In addition, almost all governments—including U.S. and Asian governments—expanded fiscal deficits, which will eventually have to be unwound once private sector--led economic recovery is firmly in place.

From a medium-term perspective, various structural policy measures will be needed to ensure that this rebalancing process promotes growth in both regions in a sustainable way. Transpacific rebalancing should not simply mean a reduction of current account imbalances; it should mean achievement of stable, sustainable growth with domestic and external balance. It is from this perspective that the Asian Development Bank Institute and the Brookings Institution developed a joint research project to examine factors that could achieve balanced, sustainable growth in the United States and Asia and the policy implications of these adjustments in both regions. The original conference took place in March 2010, but several chapters were subsequently revised.

This book focuses on several issues, including the appropriate level of domestic savings-investment imbalance, the scope for structural policy measures to affect these imbalances, and the magnitude of exchange-rate changes required to switch the allocation of demand between domestic and foreign sources and the allocation of supply between tradable and nontradable outputs. Of course, the specific issues confronting the countries on both sides of the Pacific could be different.

For the U.S. side, a key issue is how a more balanced current account can be restored and stable and sustainable economic growth thereby achieved. A lingering question is whether U.S. consumers will revert to their previous pattern of low savings once the economy recovers and, relatedly, what policy measures would be needed to prevent this recurrence. A further question is the expected trend growth rate of the U.S. economy going forward. It is also important to identify the impact of unwinding the expansionary fiscal policy on the adjustment processes both in the United States and in Asia. The contribution of exchange-rate adjustment to rebalancing demand and supply needs to be considered as well.

Turning to Japan, although the current account is shrinking and is expected to be subdued owing to aging and low household savings, its prospective trend growth rate is low. Not only has growth been heavily dependent on exports in recent years, but the labor force is declining, owing to the advanced stage of population aging. Consumption growth also has been stagnant. As in many other Asian nations, the greatest potential for raising productivity in Japan lies in the services sector, where productivity levels are still low relative to manufacturing. Despite a program of deregulation, many regulations, restrictions, and inefficiencies remain, raising costs of operation in services such as health care. Another key challenge for Japan is to connect its economy with those of emerging Asia and to benefit from its dynamism, which requires further opening of the Japanese markets. A priority list for deregulation, liberalization, and industry promotion needs to be developed to revive economic activity. The adoption of growth-oriented polices as part of the Abenomics program is a welcome development, but it is still too early to assess long-term impacts.

The main challenge for the People's Republic of China is to reduce dependence on net exports—especially to U.S. and European markets—for economic growth. This chiefly involves dismantling current incentive structures that bias production toward enterprises and exports. In addition, Japan and the Asian tiger economies are increasingly using China as their export platform targeted at U.S. and European markets, implying that collective efforts may be needed among the Asian economies to reduce China's current account surpluses. Another challenge is to find ways to expand the share of household income and consumption in GDP and obtain a greater contribution to growth from this segment.

Export-dependent Asian tiger economies suffered most from the abrupt shrinkage of external demand since the share of manufacturing trade in GDP was high. If export-led growth—targeted at U.S. and European markets—is hampered, what are the choices for their economic growth? Perhaps, for small open economies such as Hong Kong and Singapore, international trade is a key part of growth, and there is only limited scope for domestic demand–led growth. Taipei,China is likely to deepen integration with the Chinese economy. The Republic of Korea does not have a large current account surplus, and its challenge is similar to Japan's: how to promote domestic demand in an aging society while improving productivity in the services sector.

The Association of Southeast Asian Nations (ASEAN) has an economy whose size is comparable to India's and should therefore be considered an economic powerhouse in Asia. Like the rest of export-reliant economies, some ASEAN countries—such as Malaysia and Thailand—also suffered from shrinking external demand. The association may need to reconsider its export-dependent development strategy to cope with changes in U.S. and European markets and neighboring Asian economies' development paths. Unlike the Asian tigers, a few ASEAN member countries—such as Indonesia and Viet Nam—have relatively large potential domestic demand. A fundamental issue is whether ASEAN members can continue the outward-oriented growth strategy that has been so successful or will have to shift their development strategy toward domestic demand. These countries should focus on promoting investment, through improvements in investment climates and promotion of public infrastructure investment.

At first blush India seems not relevant to issues of transpacific rebalancing because the country does not have the surpluses that other Asian economies have. However, India can provide a model for other Asian economies aiming to rebalance growth since it has a relatively low ratio of exports to GDP and also has a high contribution to growth from the services sector. The reasons for the relative success of the services sector in India need to be assessed, and policy lessons should be developed for East Asian economies. At the same time, India has a huge internal market, which is still ill served owing to the lack of developed infrastructure for transport and distribution networks.

Finally, there is a need to explore cooperative mechanisms to effect a smooth adjustment in the U.S. and Asian economies. This could include a discussion of the roles of both intra-Asian economic and financial cooperation and transpacific economic cooperation.

TRANSPACIFIC REBALANCING

1

Overview of Issues, Challenges, and Policy Directions

BARRY P. BOSWORTH AND MASAHIRO KAWAI

The global financial crisis has provided vivid evidence of an interconnected world economy. A financial meltdown that began in the United States quickly spread to Europe, and both regions entered into a severe economic downturn. The disruption ultimately radiated throughout the rest of the world through its repressive effects on trade flows. The magnitude and breadth of the recession demonstrated the strength of the global linkages and the need for a coordination of national policies to achieve a complete recovery.

The world economy is emerging from that recession, but the pace of recovery varies greatly across the major regions. Most emerging market economies have returned to growth rates close to those in the precrisis period. Their financial systems were not significantly damaged in the crisis, and the restoration of global trade has returned them to the precrisis situation; growth is slower than before but remains strong, and their most pressing concern is inflation. However, the high-income countries of Europe, Japan, and the United States were more severely impacted, and they remain mired in more difficult circumstances. This is particularly notable in the eurozone economies. The recovery of their financial sectors remains incomplete; they are plagued by excess capacity that suppresses domestic investment and by high unemployment and low inflation. In high-income economies, the effort to stimulate their aggregate demand during the crisis left them with large fiscal imbalances.

The global recession occurred at a time of large external imbalances in the global economy. In an open trading system, individual countries should not expect nor desire to maintain persistent surpluses or deficits in their external trade balances. But large continual deficits by individual countries do raise concerns about the sustainability of their ever-growing debt burdens. And, if the countries are large and their financial liabilities are liquid, they raise the threat of disruptive adjustments that cause systemic problems for the world economy. Similarly, large enduring surpluses at undervalued exchange rates raise concerns about the accumulation of low-return reserves and difficulties for the operation of monetary policy. Thus there was considerable concern that a pattern of large offsetting trade imbalances might raise a systemic threat to the world economy. Although external trade imbalances were not the primary cause of the financial crisis of 2008–09, many believe that they were an important contributing factor.

The disruption of financial markets, the collapse of global trade, and the unemployment concerns of the Great Recession temporarily shifted the focus of policy away from the issue of external imbalances. Global imbalances have shrunk, but an examination of the underlying causes suggests that much of the improvement is likely to prove temporary. The magnitude of the fall in trade was much greater than expected from past recessions, and some of that could be traced to large swings in commodity prices rather than the volume of trade. In addition, the synchronous nature of a financial crisis triggered by events in the world's two largest economies, the United States and Europe, led to a greater-than-normal fall in exports and imports. Furthermore, equiproportional reductions in exports and imports lessened the imbalances for the large surplus (People's Republic of China, or PRC) and deficit (United States) countries. Thus there is an expectation that recovery of the global economy will bring with it a reemergence of large imbalances.

On the other hand, some changes in the underlying pattern of saving and investment in the United States and East Asia suggest that portions of the rebalancing may prove to be more permanent. Private saving has surged in the United States, and, given the magnitudes of capacity overhang, residential and business investments are unlikely to recover for the foreseeable future. At present, those factors have been more than offset by the magnitude of increase in government dissaving, but a reduction of the budget deficit, even though gradual, would imply a substantial improvement in the saving-investment balance within the United States. Similarly, the PRC's current account surplus has remained well below pre-crisis levels, and there has been an accelerated growth of domestic demand, particularly fixed investment.

In any case, there has been some change in the perspective and concern with the current account imbalances. Before the financial crisis, the focus was on the sustainability of a world of large external imbalances, a fear that the growing cost of the U.S. indebtedness in particular would ultimately prompt a correction that could be disruptive to the global economy as a whole. After the crisis, the concern has been with the implications of a two-tier economic recovery: rapid growth in the emerging markets and sluggish growth or even stagnation in the high-income economies. Particularly in the United States, a reduction in trade deficits—through an expansion in exports—is perceived as critical to achieving economic recovery. The absolute size of the imbalances has fallen, but in part for the wrong reason, as lower incomes in the United States have suppressed the demand for imports. A second important development has been the emergence at the 2009 Pittsburg summit of the G-20 group of countries as the central governance forum for the world economy. In its statements and the pledges of its members, the G-20 has clearly recognized the importance of coordinated actions to reduce imbalances in global trade flows.

Defining the Problem

The determinants of the current account are embedded within an interdependent system in which the external balance is driven by a combination of domestic and foreign factors. There are two principal perspectives on the current account. From the domestic side, the current account is equal to national saving less domestic investment, but from the external side, it is also equal to exports minus imports plus net income earned abroad. Thus the current account is defined by two identities: $CA = S - I$ and $CA = X - M + NFI$, where CA is the current account balance, S is national saving, I is investment, X and M are exports and imports of goods and services, and NFI is the net factor income from abroad. One of the major sources of debate over the determinants of the current account in a specific instance is the extent to which it is driven by foreign versus domestic factors, but because the identities hold from both perspectives, outcomes are a reflection of both domestic and foreign economic developments. Since individual countries are part of a system in which they export to and import from a much larger global economy, their own specific balance is likely to be dominated by their own domestic determinants, saving minus investment, and the external balance adjusts through changes in the relative price of exports and imports; but large economies also have a determining effect on the global system as a whole.

The distribution of current account balances across major regions of the world economy is shown in table 1-1. National current account balances are shown as a percentage of world GDP for the period of 1980 through 2013. Before the 1970s, current account imbalances were strictly limited, as most national financial markets operated as closed systems. With the emergence of large-scale cross-border capital flows, countries have become capable of financing larger imbalances on a sustained basis. The major feature of the table is the dominant role of the United States as the source of the deficits over the past thirty years. At the same time, many of the other economies have a relatively small influence, since their deficits or surpluses have averaged small shares of world GDP. Japan

Table 1-1. *Current Account as a Share of World GDP, Selected Regions and Years*[a]

Percent

Economies	1980–89	1990–99	2000–05	2006–08	2009	2010	2011	2012	2013
United States	-0.53	-0.42	-1.38	-1.32	-0.65	-0.70	-0.65	-0.61	-0.51
Japan	0.28	0.36	0.35	0.33	0.25	0.32	0.17	0.08	0.05
European Union	-0.11	-0.03	-0.02	-0.15	0.01	0.03	0.12	0.24	0.44
PRC	-0.01	0.04	0.13	0.59	0.41	0.37	0.19	0.27	0.26
Emerging Asia (excluding the PRC)	-0.03	0.02	0.24	0.24	0.27	0.22	0.15	0.09	0.20
Latin America and the Caribbean	-0.14	-0.15	-0.04	0.01	-0.05	-0.10	-0.11	-0.15	-0.21
Middle East and North Africa	0.11	-0.04	0.22	0.53	0.08	0.28	0.59	0.59	0.44
Other countries	-0.70	-0.49	-1.15	-1.15	-0.65	-0.65	-0.58	-0.65	-0.63
Discrepancy	0.60	0.30	0.26	-0.40	-0.33	-0.48	-0.52	-0.47	-0.55

Source: International Monetary Fund, *World Economic Outlook* database (April 2014).

a. Emerging Asia comprises Hong Kong, China; Republic of Korea; Singapore; and Taipei,China.

used to provide a consistent offset to the U.S. deficits, but the magnitude of its surplus has declined since 2011. The offsets to the increased U.S. deficit appear to be large surpluses in the emerging economies of Asia, including the PRC, and the oil-producing economies of the Middle East and North Africa. Given the rise of oil prices, the surge of saving within the oil-producing economies is not a surprise, but the sudden emergence of a large current account surplus in emerging Asia is less expected. There is also a substantial current account discrepancy at the global level.[1] Historically, the discrepancy was thought to arise primarily from the underreporting of investment income and transportation services, but in the past decade it has changed sign as countries are reporting more receipts than payments, largely in the area of business services (International Monetary Fund 2009, p. 35).

The dominant roles of the United States, Japan, and emerging Asia are highlighted further in figure 1-1. Their imbalances are marked by a large bilateral trade deficit-surplus between the United States and Japan until around 2000 and between the United States and the PRC since then. But a focus on recent bilateral trade flows can easily mischaracterize the nature of the imbalance because the PRC is part of a broader production network within Asia. It is often the terminal or assembly point for product components that are made throughout the countries of East and Southeast Asia. However, apart from the oil-producing countries of the Middle East and North Africa, the global trade imbalance is largely a product of economic developments in the United States and emerging Asia. As discussed above, there have been substantial declines in the magnitude of the two regions' trade imbalances since the global financial crisis. Major questions arise with respect to the durability of those changes.

Some insight into the domestic determinants of changes in imbalances is provided in figure 1-2, which reports rates of gross domestic saving and investment for four economic centers: the United States, Japan, the PRC, and emerging Asia excluding the PRC and India. The narrowing of the imbalance for the United States, which started in 2007, can be traced to the severity of that country's economic disequilibrium since it is the result of a collapse of both domestic saving and investment. The increase in the budget deficit far exceeded the rise in private saving, and national saving fell to near zero on a net basis, after adjustment for capital depreciation (not shown in the figure). The current account has improved only because of an even larger reduction in investment. Similarly, Japan suffered large declines in both saving and investment. In contrast, the PRC shows a moderation in domestic saving and a strong surge in investment. The investment to

---

1. The International Monetary Fund reports the discrepancy as the sum of the current accounts across all reporting countries. In the table, the sign is reversed so that the current accounts will sum to zero.

Figure 1-1. *Current Account as a Share of World GDP, United States, Japan, and Emerging Asia, 1980–2013*[a]

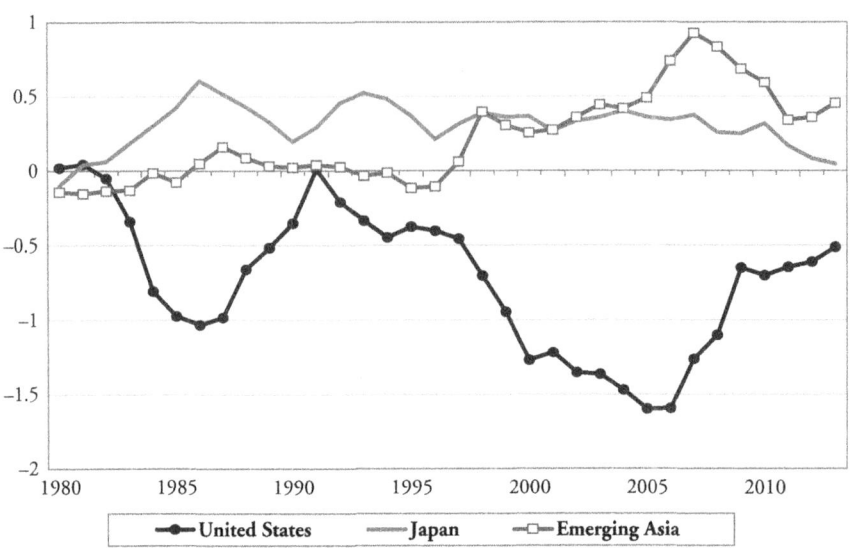

Source: International Monetary Fund, *World Economic Outlook* database (April 2014).
a. Emerging Asia comprises all Asian developing and emerging economies, particularly Hong Kong, China; Republic of Korea; Singapore; and Taipei,China.

GDP ratio rose from 42 percent in 2007 to 48 percent in 2012, while the saving to GDP ratio declined slightly from 52 percent to 51 percent over the same period. Essentially, the PRC's current account surplus shrank mainly due to the sharp rise of domestic investment, which started with a 4-trillion-yuan fiscal stimulus package adopted in response to the global financial crisis (Kawai 2010). But this high investment ratio has created overcapacity and financial vulnerabilities, particularly in the shadow-banking sector, and is likely to be unsustainable. The separate treatment of the PRC also highlights a different pattern in the rest of East Asia, where saving has remained high since the late 1990s and investment collapsed as a result of the 1997–98 financial crisis without recovering much since then. India was little affected by the past crises, and it has maintained a very large, but balanced, increase in both saving and investment.

On the external side, changes in the balance of exports and imports are driven by differences in relative rates of domestic and foreign income growth, the relative prices of domestic and foreign production, and underlying structural factors that determine nations' propensities to export and import specific products. The concept of the real exchange rate provides a simple measure of relative prices, and it is defined as the nominal exchange rate (e), defined as the foreign currency

Figure 1-2. *Saving and Investment, Various Countries, 1980–2013*[a]

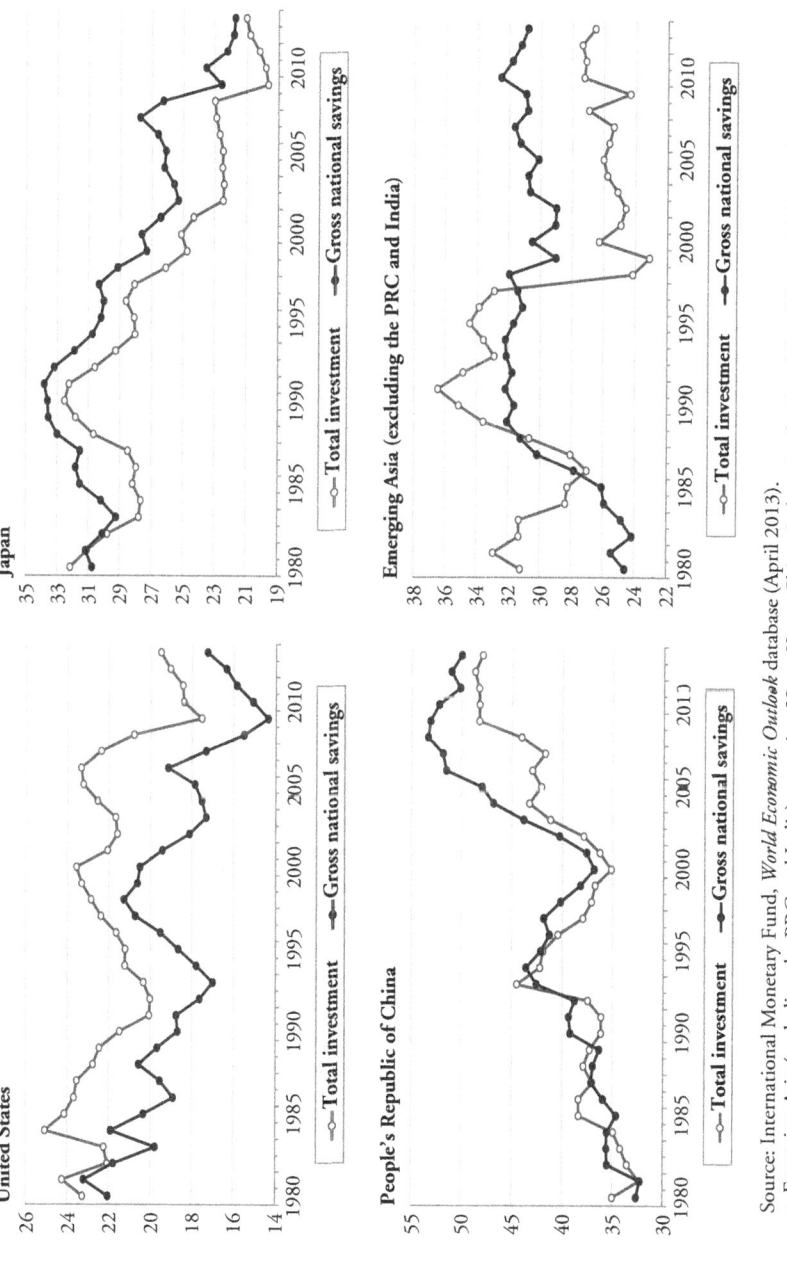

Source: International Monetary Fund, *World Economic Outlook* database (April 2013).

a. Emerging Asia (excluding the PRC and India) comprises Hong Kong, China; Indonesia, the Republic of Korea; Malaysia; the Philippines; Singapore; Taipei,China; Thailand; and Viet Nam.

price of domestic currency, multiplied by the ratio of foreign and domestic prices (P_d/P_f):[2]

$$q = e \times (P_d/P_f).$$

Figure 1-3 displays trade-weighted indexes of the real exchange rates, or real effective exchange rates (REERs), of the major countries and economies. The first panel contrasts the real effective exchange rates for the PRC and the United States to highlight the extent of departure in recent years. The United States has experienced a substantial depreciation of the real effective exchange rate relative to its peak in 2002, interrupted by a sharp but brief appreciation at the beginning of the financial crisis. Meanwhile, the PRC has had a substantial real effective appreciation since 2005, largely because of persistent nominal appreciation of the renminbi (RMB) against the U.S. dollar. The real effective appreciation of the RMB was also a result from substantial depreciations by some of the PRC's other major trading partners (such as Hong Kong, China; the Republic of Korea; and Taipei,China). The divergent trend changes between the U.S. dollar and the RMB are consistent with declines in U.S. deficits and Chinese surpluses.

Indexes of real effective exchange rates of the eurozone and Japan are shown in the middle panel, and they indicate a range of variation as wide as that for the PRC and the United States. Indexes for India and a composite of the emerging East Asian economies (excluding the PRC and India) are shown in the third panel. Except for the obvious effects of the 1997–98 Asian financial crisis, their exchange-rate changes have been small and largely free of a notable trend.

A Look Ahead

The objective of the following chapters is to examine factors that would achieve balanced, sustainable growth in the two regions, the United States and Asia, and the policy implications of these adjustments in both regions. The chapters that focus on individual countries address several specific issues, including the appropriate levels of domestic saving-investment (S-I) balances, the scope for policy changes to alter these balances, and the magnitude of exchange-rate changes required to switch the composition of demand between domestic and foreign sources and reallocate supply between tradables and nontradables sectors. There are also a series of major questions that we hope to address, and in some cases resolve. For example, why is saving so low in the United States, and what will be

---

2. The exchange rate is shown as the foreign price of domestic currency so that an appreciation of the currency is recorded as an increase in the exchange-rate index.

Figure 1-3. *Real Effective Exchange Rate, Various Economies, 1990–2014*[a]

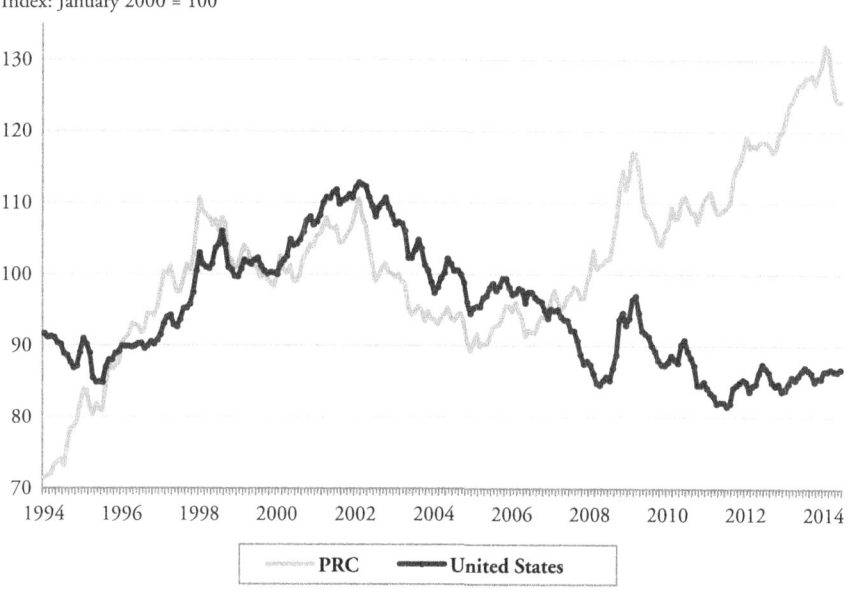

People's Republic of China and the United States

Index: January 2000 = 100

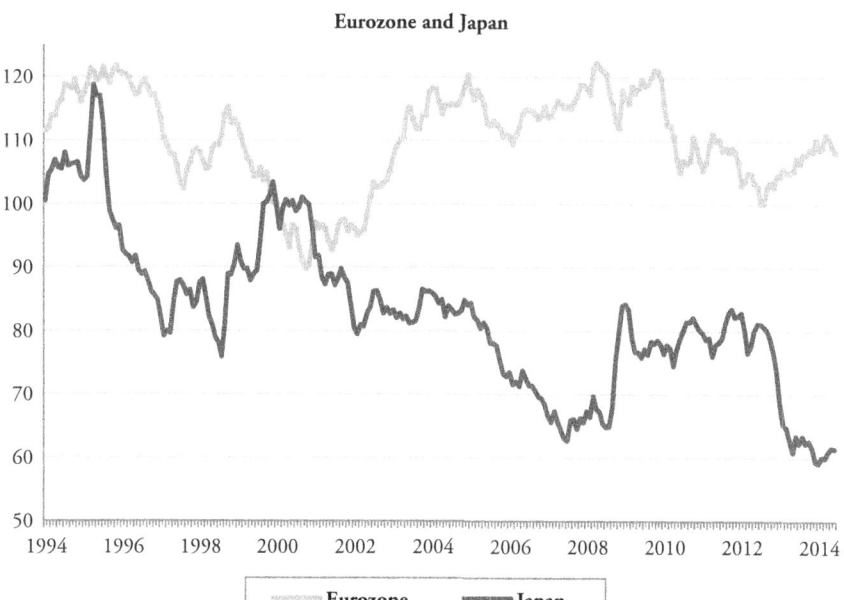

Eurozone and Japan

Figure 1-3. *(Continued)*

India and East and Southeast Asia

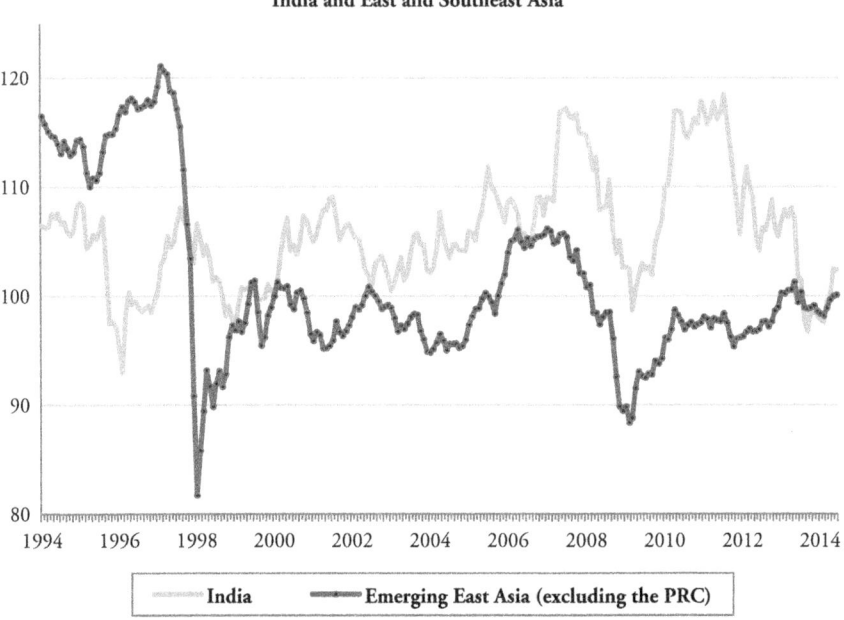

Source: BIS, Broad Real Effective Exchange Rate.

a. Emerging East Asia (excluding the PRC) comprises Hong Kong, China; Indonesia; Republic of Korea; Malaysia; the Philippines; Singapore; Taipei,China; and Thailand. Average regional exchange rate is calculated by using weights based on PPP GDP in 2000 from International Monetary Fund, *World Economic Outlook* database (April 2014).

the effect on consumption of the recent wealth losses and of debt decumulation? Can the government budget deficit be brought back under control? What would be the required change in the real exchange rate to bring about the realignment of resources? On the Asian side, why is saving so high? How is the high saving distributed among the household, business, and government sectors? What needs to be done to promote domestic growth without creating or exacerbating external imbalances? Can growth be sustained at a high rate without a large stimulus of exports to the U.S. market? Finally, is it necessary to establish a transpacific mechanism to facilitate needed adjustments?

Transpacific Payments Imbalances: An Overview

Barry Eichengreen and Gisela Rua (chapter 2) provide an initial overview by surveying the existing literature on the causes of transpacific payments imbalances, analyzing past and current trends of these imbalances and drawing some implications for macroeconomic stability in both the United States and Asia.

They argue for a comprehensive approach to rebalancing that takes into account two key points:

—adjustments of current account balances must occur simultaneously in both deficit and surplus countries; and

—adjustments in the composition of final demand will be accompanied by endogenous shifts in foreign exchange rates, export prices, and import prices to support the new current account balance equilibrium.

Thus they stress the interrelated nature of the interactions that determine the composition of global trade imbalances and suggest that the debate over trade balances has gone awry by focusing on exchange rates as a primary issue rather than perceiving it as an endogenously determined price that adjusts to clear markets in response to changes in policy and other exogenous shocks.

The authors describe three sets of explanations for the development of large current account imbalances: a "new-conomy" argument; a more standard argument about the development of saving-investment imbalances; and aspects of the international monetary system, specifically the characteristics of international financial assets and liabilities. The new-economy view highlights the development of high rates of productivity growth in the United States, especially in the high-technology sector, that attracted inflows of foreign capital in search of higher returns. However, following the collapse of the information technology bubble in 2000, this theory seems less plausible.

The second explanation emphasizes the development of excess demand in the United States or excess saving in Asia (or both) as a result of structural factors. One version suggests that the imbalance can be attributed to a global "savings glut," the source of which was Asia (Bernanke 2005). The alternative version argues that the imbalance was driven by excess demand, both private and government, in the United States in the years before the financial crisis.

The third explanation focuses on the arguments about the relative returns on U.S. assets and liabilities in the international monetary order, where the U.S. dollar functions as the key reserve currency. This includes the argument that foreign investors were drawn to the United States in search of low-risk debt securities (Caballero 2010): larger and more rapidly growing emerging markets sought to import safe assets from the United States to build up their foreign exchange reserves and other pools of savings.

Eichengreen and Rua analyze the required adjustments in exchange rates needed to eliminate imbalances between the United States and the rest of the world. They use the two-region model of Maurice Obstfeld and Kenneth Rogoff (2007), which they regard as perhaps the simplest model for analyzing the general equilibrium effects of such an adjustment on prices, output, and the composition of final demand. They find that, based on various assumptions, the U.S. dollar would need to fall by about one-third in real terms to balance trade with the rest of the world. Not surprisingly, if certain countries do not allow their currencies to rise against the U.S. dollar, the required fall of the dollar against other currencies would be correspondingly larger. Therefore, the size of the rest of the world participating in the adjustment process is a crucial determinant of the required fall in the U.S. dollar.

They also examine the nature of the adjustment in surplus countries, as opposed to the more standard research that has been undertaken for deficit countries. They conclude that large current account surpluses do tend to come to an end, but sometimes only when they have been allowed to rise to exceptionally high levels, and they find that a moderation of the surpluses was associated with slower rates of economic growth.

Exchange Rates and Rebalancing

One key issue in the adjustment process is the sensitivity of exports and imports to exchange-rate changes, which determines the degree to which exchange rates must adjust to yield a significant alteration in the trade balance. Willem Thorbecke and Ginalyn Komoto (chapter 3) estimate export and import elasticities for the United States, the People's Republic of China, and other major transpacific economies. Their estimates of price elasticity for PRC exports to the United States range from 0.2 to 1.58, with an average level of about unity, suggesting that renminbi (RMB) appreciation would have a significant negative impact on PRC exports. On the other hand, the coefficient on the ASEAN (Association of Southeast Asian Nations) exchange-rate index in the PRC export equation is negative and significant, suggesting that PRC exports would rise in response to the appreciation of ASEAN currencies. Using a consistent methodology across countries, they also estimate income and exchange-rate elasticities for exports and imports of the United States; Japan; the PRC; the Republic of Korea; Taipei,China; Malaysia; the Philippines; and Thailand. All of the income elasticity estimates are large and positive, but the results confirm earlier findings of asymmetry, that is, the United States has a higher income elasticity of imports than exports, while the opposite holds for most Asian economies, which imparts a bias toward U.S. current account deficits.

The export and import price elasticities have the right signs for the United States, but many of those for Asian economies have the wrong signs, which may reflect econometric difficulties associated with the presence of production networks, aggregation biases, and other issues. They cite extensive reviews of earlier work by Menzie Chinn (2004, 2005a, 2005b) that suggest that U.S. export and import price elasticities barely satisfy the Lerner condition (sum greater than unity); and the U.S. income elasticity of imports is about 2.4 versus a range of 1.7–2.0 for exports, pointing to continued, albeit smaller, asymmetry. These results suggest that U.S. dollar depreciation per se may have only a small impact on the U.S. trade imbalance.

The authors also point to the desirability of a general rise in Asian currencies vis-à-vis the U.S. dollar to maximize the impact on trade adjustment. Such a joint appreciation would be beneficial to the region as it would help maintain exchange-rate stability within the region, facilitating the flow of capital goods and parts and components among the Asian supply chain economies. They suggest that one way for this joint appreciation to occur would be "for the PRC to adopt a regime characterized by a multiple-currency, basket-based reference rate based on a multiple-currency with a reasonably wide band."

Thorbecke and Komoto also look at exports, imports, and trade balances before and after the 2008 crisis. They show that while exports from most Asian countries and the rest of the world decreased and led to a lower trade balance with the United States, PRC exports to the United States were a major outlier in the global economy before the crisis and have remained so since the crisis began, so that the US-PRC bilateral trade imbalance has continued to be extremely large. This suggests that a decrease of income in the United States does not substantially reduce the PRC's exports to the United States, owing to the nature of the products exported—primarily basic goods, as compared with the high-end luxury products exported by Japan and the newly industrialized economies. Therefore, an appreciation of the RMB would be necessary to reduce exports from the PRC to the United States as part of the reduction of the overall imbalances of the United States and the PRC. Their estimates imply that a 10 percent appreciation of the RMB would reduce the PRC's exports to the United States by about 15 percent.

U.S. Payments Deficits and Adjustment

The global financial and economic crisis has brought about changes in aggregate demand as well as aggregate supply in both Asia and the United States. On the U.S. side, domestic consumption and private saving decisions have already adjusted substantially to reduce the S-I imbalance, even as early as 2009. The question is whether these adjustments are sustainable or whether U.S. consumers will revert to their precrisis pattern of low saving once the economy recovers. A related question is the expected trend growth rate of the U.S. economy going forward. Moreover, it is important to identify the effectiveness, sustainability, and consequences of the massive expansion of fiscal policy to cope with the painful adjustment processes in both the United States and Asia. These issues are addressed by Barry Bosworth and Susan Collins (chapter 4).

The widening of the U.S. current account deficit since 1990 was accompanied by a substantial fall in the U.S. household saving rate from an average of 7 percent of national income in the early 1980s to approximately 2 percent in the middle of the last decade. Bosworth and Collins argue that this was surprising in light of demographic trends and suggest that the decline was linked to increases in household wealth from capital gains in equities and housing during the period that reduced the perceived need to save. They find that, since 1995, more than 100 percent of the increase in wealth relative to disposable income is attributable to valuation changes, even after taking into consideration the crash in asset prices following the Lehman bankruptcy in 2008. Looking forward, the wealth losses and increased uncertainty associated with the financial crisis and the recession have raised the private saving rate, but this may be partially offset in future years by more negative demographic factors. They conclude that any further recovery of the private saving rate is likely to be modest.

The larger domestic problem is the surge in the public sector budget deficit and collapse of domestic investment. Despite the recovery of private saving, the net national saving rate turned negative in the aftermath of the crisis, and the rate of domestic investment fell to historic lows. Furthermore, the difficulties in the housing market, which triggered the financial crisis, are likely to continue to depress the investment outlook for many years. The policy challenge is in finding a path back to fiscal balance while continuing to promote economic recovery. Managing that process will be politically difficult. At the same time monetary policy has largely been exhausted as a tool of economic recovery since interest rates are at the zero bound.

Given the large collapse of domestic demand, attention has turned increasingly to the importance of generating an expansion of exports and a reduction in the trade deficit as the critical requirement for economic recovery. The authors note the new National Export Initiative announced by U.S. President Obama in January 2010, which sets the goal of doubling exports in the next five years. However, in light of the administration's lack of the Trade Promotion Authority needed to effectively negotiate new trade agreements, the means to implement this objective are limited. Perhaps the most promising policy change would be a cut in the U.S. corporate income tax, which would improve international competitiveness. A recent study found that the United States had the second highest statutory corporate tax rate among member countries of the Organization for Economic Cooperation and Development in 2006, owing to significant tax reforms abroad (U.S. Department of the Treasury, Office of Tax Policy 2007).

Using gravity-type models to relate levels of exports and imports to GDP and other factors for a large sample of countries, Bosworth and Collins argue that U.S. exports underperform significantly, while the level of imports seems quite comparable to other high-income economies. Therefore, weak exports seem to be the main factor behind the large U.S. trade deficit, and it is important to understand what structural factors may account for the country's poor performance. Unfortunately, there is little clear evidence in this area. Bosworth and Collins suggest a partial explanation based on a greater tendency of U.S. manufacturing firms to locate production activity overseas. They argue that restrictions on U.S. defense-related high-technology exports cover only a small component of potential trade. They conclude that a substantial expansion of the export market will require further reductions in the price of American goods in world markets—that is, substantial exchange-rate depreciation.

Bosworth and Collins express a more optimistic interpretation of the potential response of U.S. trade to changes in both incomes and relative prices than is reported by Thorbecke and Komoto (chapter 3). They cite some studies that argue that the previous asymmetry in income elasticities for U.S. exports and imports has disappeared. As a result, a 1-percentage-point reduction in the aggregate trade deficit as a percentage of GDP may now be associated with a smaller real dollar depreciation, perhaps in the range of 8–15 percent, and there may not be a secular bias toward deterioration in the trade balance (see International Monetary Fund 2007; Crane, Crowley, and Quayyum 2007).

Japan's Current Account Rebalancing

Masahiro Kawai and Shinji Takagi (chapter 5) note that, for more than three decades, Japan's current account balance had been in surplus in the range of 1.5 to 4 percent of GDP until the outbreak of the global financial crisis in 2008. Japan's earlier surplus and the U.S. persistent deficit were at the core of global imbalances in the 1980s and 1990s. However, Japan's surplus was overtaken by the PRC's surplus in size in 2006 and began to shrink in the aftermath of the crisis as a result of both temporary and long-term structural factors.

Temporary factors include the reduction in global demand due to the global financial crisis, rapid yen appreciation reflecting the yen's safe-haven role during the crisis, and rising mineral fuel imports to secure electrical power supply following the triple disaster of March 2011. Mineral fuels had to be imported as virtually all nuclear power plants were shut down in Japan and no other source of energy was available domestically. Longer-term structural factors include the change in industrial structure of the Japanese economy (relocation of manufacturing production bases abroad and a trend shift of productive resources away from the tradable toward the nontradable goods sector) as well as population aging. It is the structural factors that will define the course of current account rebalancing for Japan over the medium to long term.

Kawai and Takagi raise two issues: whether the ongoing rebalancing of Japan's current account is transitory or permanent; and whether Japan's current account will turn into a deficit in the near future. There are two offsetting trends that will affect Japan's current account balance over the medium to long term. On one hand, the trade balance, which turned into a deficit in 2011, will continue to be adversely affected by the deindustrialization trend, large imports of mineral fuels, and the rapid aging of the Japanese population. On the other hand, Japan's transformation into a mature net-creditor country, which generates growing investment income from abroad, can exert favorable influences on the current account balance. Kawai and Takagi argue that when all factors are taken into consideration, Japan's current account balance is likely to shrink or may even turn into a deficit. This implies that, given net investment income at more than 3 percent of GDP, Japan will begin to run a sizable trade deficit. This trade balance adjustment would likely contribute significantly to supporting global economic growth.

Policymakers seem to be concerned about the shrinking current account surplus and the possible emergence of a current account deficit. The shrinking current account balance is often viewed as a sign of declining competitiveness of Japanese manufacturing. However, the issue of manufacturing competitiveness should be addressed from the perspectives of how employment could be created in non-manufacturing sectors and how stable energy supply can be secured, not from a current account perspective. A more serious concern would be the potential impact of any future current account deficit on the already precarious state of the public finances—as demonstrated by the high level of sovereign debt amounting to 220 percent of GDP. Once the current account balance turns to a deficit, more of fiscal deficit financing must come from foreign savings, which could affect market sentiments, pushing up long-term interest rates and making fiscal consolidation more difficult. In the absence of serous fiscal consolidation, the Japanese economy could be forced into a sovereign debt crisis.

Kawai and Takagi argue that Abenomics, adopted by Prime Minister Shinzo Abe in December 2012 (which has three arrows of monetary policy expansion, flexible fiscal policy, and structural reforms), has the potential to address these issues. First, heading off deflationary expectations and achieving a stable level of inflation of 2 percent would set a conducive macroeconomic environment for sustained economic growth. Second, structural reform policies can support Japanese manufacturing activity in leading-edge, knowledge- and high-tech-intensive products through R&D activities and innovation. Third, as in the United States, a high corporate tax rate could be reduced to a level common to Japan's global competitors. Fourth, a program of deregulation in services sectors (particularly health and other sectors) and a reduction of entry barriers can stimulate investment, raise productivity, and expand employment opportunities in services. Fifth, enhancement of social expenditures in the areas of child care, health and education, greater support for increased labor participation by women and the aged, and liberalizing immigration of foreign talents can augment labor supply. Sixth, concluding the Regional Comprehensive Economic Partnership (RCEP), the Trans-Pacific Partnership (TPP), and the Japan–European Union Economic Partnership Agreement would help in further opening the economy, leading to greater inflows of foreign direct investment. Finally, fiscal consolidation to ensure sovereign debt sustainability is also critical to avoiding a sovereign debt crisis even when the current account balance turns into a deficit. An increase in the consumption tax rate, from 5 percent to 8 percent in April 2014 and the subsequent

planned hike from 8 percent to 10 percent in October 2015 would be an important step for this objective.

Thus Japan's current account rebalancing is likely to persist in the medium to
long term. Public policy should not try to reverse this trend, but should focus on
achieving a stable level of inflation, improving productivity particularly in services
sectors, opening the economy, and consolidating the country's fiscal situations.

New Development Paradigm for the PRC

In 2008 the PRC had the world's largest current account surplus (US$468 bil-
lion, or nearly three times the size of Japan's), which was by far the single largest
counterpart to the current account deficit of the United States. The PRC also had
by far the largest bilateral surplus with the United States. Therefore, any discussion of transpacific rebalancing must focus heavily on the U.S.-PRC relationship.
Yiping Huang and Kunyu Tao (chapter 6) review a number of traditional explanations for the PRC's large trade surplus, including measurement error, factors
relating to the S-I balance, demographic transition, the shift of industry from
other Asian economies to the PRC as a result of the development of production
networks, strong growth policies, and exchange-rate distortions.

While they acknowledge the contribution from these factors, Huang and Tao
offer a provocative thesis, namely that asymmetric market liberalization and factor
market distortions are the main factors behind the imbalance. Specifically, markets
for export goods have largely been liberalized, but those for factor markets have
not. These cost distortions are equivalent to production and investment subsidies
and have generally tended to lower production costs of Chinese firms, encourage production, and improve international competitiveness. They also tend to
depress household income, leading to the abnormally low share of consumption
in GDP of only about 35 percent, far lower than in other Asian economies.

Huang and Tao identify major distortions in the markets for labor, capital,
land, energy, and the environment. In the labor market, the main distortion is
that Chinese firms do not pay social security costs for migrant workers, which
is estimated to reduce their payroll costs by 35–40 percent. Producers' capital
costs are reduced by financial repression, which keeps loan rates low, and restrictions on capital outflows, which limit alternative investment opportunities. Land
prices for industry are kept low, and electricity and other fuel prices are subsi-
dized. The degradation of the environment as a result of pro-growth policies is
well known, and it is not reflected in the costs to firms. Huang and Tao argue that
these effective subsidies probably contributed to the substantial rise of corporate
saving over the past decade, which reached almost 23 percent of GDP by 2007.

In earlier work, Huang (2010) developed a methodology for measuring the
magnitude of these distortions, what he refers to as producer subsidy equivalents,
as a percentage of GDP. In this chapter he and Tao extend his earlier analysis to

cover the period 2000–09. There are two major findings. First, capital market distortions are the largest, accounting for about 40 percent of the total measured distortions, followed by labor market and environmental distortions. Second, the aggregate estimates of cost distortions or producer subsidy equivalents match the trend of the current account imbalance data surprisingly well, tending to lead it by about one year. The cumulative distortion effect peaked in 2006, and its decline thereafter may have reflected both steps to liberalize factor markets as well as cyclical factors.

Huang and Tao's thesis also suggests a policy prescription, namely, to liberalize factor markets to reduce the distortions that have favored producers and damaged households. Reducing implicit and explicit subsidies for production should help reduce retained earnings of firms, or corporate saving, and increase household incomes. On the demand side, the main challenge for the PRC is to find ways to expand the share of household income and consumption in GDP and obtain a greater contribution to growth from this segment.

There are two broad approaches to boosting household income and consumption. The first is to design measures to encourage the corporate sector to distribute a large portion of the corporate surplus to labor. A direct way would be to have state-owned enterprises pay larger dividends to the state, which could indirectly support the household sector by channeling the increased revenue to households in various ways. For example, government can improve income distribution by providing greater income transfers to rural areas and inland provinces, where income levels lag behind. This includes improved inland transportation infrastructure and improvements in financial infrastructure to make financing more available to rural and inland households and small- and medium-size enterprises (SMEs). The second approach would be to craft policy measures to expand the social safety net, including health care and pensions, especially for migrant workers, and to increase government spending on education. This should reduce the need for precautionary savings in these areas.

Huang and Tao argue that the RMB is probably still undervalued and that further appreciation is necessary as part of the adjustment process. However, though they state that greater exchange-rate flexibility and gradual currency appreciation are important, they also believe that those measures need to be part of a comprehensive package that aims at removing factor market distortions. This should include making efforts to remove or reduce distortions in resource prices, reforming the household registration system and thereby reducing discrimination against rural workers, and continuing with capital market liberalization.

Asian Tigers' Choices

The abrupt shrinking of external demand in Asia during the global financial crisis has raised questions about the export-dependent growth strategies in emerging

Asia. The Asian tigers—or newly industrialized economies, including Hong Kong, China; the Republic of Korea; Singapore; and Taipei,China—suffered most since their dependencies on exports in GDP are higher than many other emerging Asian economies. They are also deeply involved in regional production networks for sectors such as autos and electronics. If export-led growth is hampered, what are their choices for economic growth? How much can be expected from policies to promote domestic demand and improve productivity in the services sector? Hwee Kwan Chow (chapter 7) suggests that the general approach should be to shift toward a new growth model that puts more emphasis on domestic demand as the source of growth. However, they acknowledge that this is not feasible for small and very open entrepôt economies, such as Singapore and Hong Kong, China, in which domestic demand is dwarfed by the external sector. Any demand stimulus would be undercut by large import leakages. In any case, their surpluses, although large relative to GDP, are modest in absolute terms, accounting for only about 3 and 5.4 percent, respectively, of the total Asian current account surplus in 2009.

Chow sees greater potential for a rebalancing of growth in the Republic of Korea and Taipei,China. The Republic of Korea's current account surplus was only 3.9 percent in 2009, and it averaged only 1.8 percent of GDP in the previous decade. Although the Republic of Korea's surplus cannot be regarded as a significant contributor to the global imbalances, the country would still benefit from a rebalancing of its growth to reduce its exposure to fluctuations in global trade. In contrast, Taipei,China had a large current account surplus of 11.4 percent of GDP (equivalent to 7 percent of the Asian total) in 2009.

Chow's recommendations are generally close to those of Kawai and Takagi for Japan. One is to encourage consumption spending by enhancing the social safety net, thereby lowering the need for precautionary savings. In the tiger economies, savings rates are likely to decline anyway because of the rapid aging of all of these populations. Second is to improve productivity growth of the services sector, such as education, business supporting services, and traditional services. Service sector productivity has generally lagged that of manufacturing, partly owing to its role as an absorber of excess employment from the manufacturing sector following the Asian financial crisis. Deregulation of the services sector could raise its growth potential and its contribution to overall growth. In addition, higher productivity and growth of services sectors can improve income distribution and thus tend to stimulate consumption growth.

The third recommendation calls for promoting investment in education and R&D activities, which can respectively help workers upgrade skills and productivity and help companies to move up the production value chain. There is also a need to raise productivity of SMEs, which account for a large share of total employment, and to take other steps to encourage the overall business climate to promote investment. Chow's final recommendation is to support establishment of a common market within the region to raise intra-Asian demand and invest-ment, and the author argues that Asian tiger economies should alter their pro-duction structure to maximize the favorable impact of demand growth in rapidly growing Asian economies such as the PRC and India.

ASEAN's Strategy

As a group, ASEAN has an economy slightly larger than India's and is there-fore considered a potential economic powerhouse in Asia. It aims to establish an ASEAN economic community by 2015 and to transform ASEAN into a region with free movement of goods, services, investment, and skilled labor and freer flows of capital. At present it has several free trade agreements with countries within and outside Asia. Its economy is powered by foreign direct investment and exports and has benefited much from joining Asia's production networks and supply chains. Like the rest of the export-reliant economies, ASEAN also suf-fered from shrinking external demand during the global financial crisis. Unlike most of the Asian tigers, some ASEAN members have large potential domestic demand. Any change in their development strategy must be consistent with the aim of establishing an ASEAN economic community.

Iwan Azis and Mario Lamberte (chapter 8) analyze developments in the ASEAN5 countries—Indonesia, Malaysia, Philippines, Singapore, and Thailand. They note that the first four of these saw a sharp drop in the ratio of investment to GDP following the Asian financial crisis of 1997–98, which led to a general shift from current account deficits to surpluses. Since then, consumption growth has generally been robust, but that of investment has not. Many ASEAN econo-mies became even more dependent on exports after the crisis, as a result of weaker domestic demand. Along with this, corporate saving rose significantly, reflecting an increased dependence on retained earnings and, in some cases, higher prof-its resulting from restrictions on market access that led to the development of oligopolistic markets. Second, they argue that growth in the period following the Asian financial crisis was accompanied by some undesirable trends, such as worsening income inequality and less rapid growth of employment. Third, they note that a large proportion of the economy, both households and SMEs, has inadequate access to financial services. Therefore, they take the view that, even though these countries do not have large current account surpluses, they could benefit from policies aimed at encouraging investment growth.

These views shape their policy recommendations. First, they favor procompe-tition policies to allow greater market entry to reduce oligopolistic profits and to encourage the expansion of banking services, thereby reducing the need for cor-porations to rely on retained earnings. Deregulation of the services sector to spur growth can have a large potential in view of its sizable share of total employment.

In forging the ASEAN Economic Community, in addition to cutting tariffs, further steps are needed to reduce "behind-the-border" obstacles to trade, such as harmonizing technical regulations and standards with international standards. Barriers to investment must also be reduced. Second, they suggest that expanding access to SMEs and household financial services could contribute to growth and employment by expanding investment opportunities. Third, they recommend increasing public investment in basic infrastructure, which has been neglected since the 1997–98 financial crisis, to improve the country's competitiveness, encouraging investment to raise worker skills and increase research and development, and supporting expansion of the social safety net. Fourth, given that domestic demand in ASEAN members—with the exception of Indonesia— is too small for it to become an effective driver of growth, steps should be taken to enlarge the potential market beyond ASEAN by further liberalizing trade and investment. In particular, each ASEAN economy needs to increase its capability to take advantage of the larger, expanding domestic markets in the PRC and India and the mature markets of Japan and other developed economies in Asia. Finally, they advocate more cooperative currency management in the region to allow a general rise of Asian currencies against the U.S. dollar as part of the process of adjusting global imbalances.

India's Emergence

At first blush, India seems not relevant to the issues on transpacific rebalancing because it does not have the trade surpluses found in other Asian economies. However, Rajiv Kumar and Pankaj Vashisht (chapter 9) argue that India, given its large and rapidly growing domestic market, could help other East Asian economies in their efforts to achieve greater export diversification and rebalancing of growth. Regarding India's role as a potential market for Asian exports, Kumar and Vashisht note that various trade initiatives would contribute to a sharp increase in India's bilateral trade with the PRC, ASEAN economies, and Japan. Somewhat paradoxically, India's trade has increased most rapidly with the PRC, which does not have any trade agreement with India. Although India has become more integrated with Asia, the gap between actual and potential trade remains high, ranging from 53 percent to 93 percent with the Philippines, Brunei Darussalam, Cambodia, the Lao People's Democratic Republic, Bangladesh, and Pakistan.

India can also provide a model for other Asian economies aiming to rebalance growth since it has a relatively low ratio of exports to GDP and a high contribution to growth from services. The rapid growth of Indian domestic demand since 1991 has largely been attributed to the spectacular performance of the services sector, especially the software and information technology–enabled services sector. This was also reflected in the services sector's success in attracting foreign direct investment, which ensured a wholesale movement in technological upgrading. However, the employment impacts have been disappointing. For example, Asheref Illiyan (2008) estimates that the software sector and information technology–enabled services sector have generated only 1.63 million employment opportunities.

Despite the potential of India's huge internal market, it is still hobbled by lack of development of its transportation and distribution infrastructure, interstate barriers to trade such as taxes, onerous regulations, and barriers to entry. Kumar and Vashisht argue in favor of policies to encourage more rapid expansion of the manufacturing sector, including having the government review all policies that have an impact on doing business in India with the objective of initiating another round of structural reforms to improve the investment climate. They also call for a general review of the regulatory and financial barriers that hinder the development of SMEs and recommend that the potential for further development of finance to SMEs and microfinance be assessed.

The authors identify several other sectors ripe for structural reforms. The education sector is characterized by massive capacity constraints, an acute shortage of adequately trained teachers, and poor curriculum quality. The agriculture sector, which employs nearly 50 percent of the working population but contributes less than a fifth of GDP, is lagging behind the rest of the economy in productivity. Finally, they call for reform of the delivery of public services, starting with law and order and including primary health, urban facilities, and better connectivity in the rural sector.

Conclusion

The potential for adjustment of the transpacific current account imbalances can be seen from two complementary perspectives—the needed structural changes and the required real exchange-rate changes. Neither can be considered without the other, although structural changes usually induce the required exchange-rate changes (see Kawai and Zhai 2009). For those economies with large imbalances, a combination of both will be required. For those Asian countries with modest surpluses or deficits, adjustment per se is less a priority, but they can still benefit from policies that reorient growth toward domestic and regional demand. This will be particularly the case if U.S. trend growth has slowed, making it a less attractive export market than earlier.

Evidence is mixed on the size of transpacific export and import price elasticities and hence on the estimates of the size of real exchange-rate adjustments needed to reduce the current account imbalances. On the positive side, taking into account recent developments and aggregation biases, price elasticity estimates have tended to be revised up. Furthermore, the asymmetry between the U.S. income elasticity of demand for exports and imports also has diminished, if not disappeared. However, the mystery of the underperformance of U.S. exports still appears unsolved, and the trend continues to worsen. The reasons for this need to be understood better, particularly if the United States has any hope of achieving its goal of doubling exports by 2015.

The United States needs an increase in domestic savings relative to domestic investment as well as a shift in production from nontradables to tradables. With private saving rates having already risen significantly after the global financial crisis, the large fiscal deficit, though gradually declining, is the main factor that sustains the current account deficit. For both this reason and the spiraling level of government debt, a tightening of fiscal policy will be the key policy priority over the longer term, and this will tend to weaken the dollar because of its impact on interest rates. However, the prospective normalization of monetary policy will also lead to an increase in interest rates and will thereby strengthen the U.S. dollar.[3] Although the United States appears to have limited scope for structural policy changes, apart from fiscal consolidation, to affect its current account balance, the most obvious policy changes could be an increase in fuel taxes, a limit of tax exemption of mortgage interest payment only to the first house, and the easing of the restrictions on U.S. high technology exports.

On the Asian side of the adjustment process, the PRC looms largest in view of its rapid growth of exports, huge current account surplus, and massive accumulation of foreign exchange reserves, and it needs to see the opposite changes, that is, a decrease in domestic savings relative to domestic investment and a shift of productive resources away from tradables to nontradables. Given that domestic investment is already high as a share of GDP, it needs to come down, implying that the even higher saving rate must be reduced by a much wider margin. The good news is that there appears to be plenty of scope for doing so. The PRC looks to be rich in opportunities for structural reforms that could tilt the balance in the direction of domestic demand. The high level of corporate saving appears to be biased upward by distortions that reduce the costs of labor, capital, energy, and the environment. These factors have also tended to depress the share of labor income in the economy, leading to the abnormally small share of consumption in GDP of only 35 percent. Undoing these distortions could help raise the share of labor income and contribute to improving the distribution of income. In addition, the PRC government has already recognized the importance of raising social expenditures, which will tend to reduce the need for precautionary savings.

3. So although the net results of unwinding lax monetary and fiscal policies on the real effective exchange rate of the U.S. dollar are uncertain, the most likely scenario would be a stronger dollar in the short-term owing to the earlier normalization of monetary policy, followed by a weaker dollar owing to fiscal consolidation, which takes a longer time to implement.

Finally, RMB appreciation would most likely lead to some reduction of the PRC's trade surplus. This impact would be larger if other supply chain currencies also appreciate vis-à-vis the U.S. dollar.

For other Asian economies, the prescriptions are broadly similar, although they differ in emphasis. Aside from India, services sectors in all countries lag in terms of productivity and can benefit substantially from liberalization, including easier foreign entry. Social expenditures can be increased to support consumer spending, while increased access to financial services can benefit both house-holds and SMEs, leading to higher employment, investment, and consumption and improved distribution of income. For larger economies with bigger domes-tic markets, steps to promote domestic demand can have large payoffs. In Japan, where current account surpluses are expected to shrink because of rapid aging, challenges are to reinvigorate economic activity through timely reconstruction from the triple disasters, improvement of productivity and competitiveness, reform of social security systems, and consolidation of public finance and debt. In the Republic of Korea and Taipei,China, policies to support consumer spend-ing are vital, while in middle-income ASEAN economies, the main priorities are to improve the investment climate, especially for SMEs, and to increase infra-structure spending. Asia's regional trade integration can increase the size of the potential market and increase access to expanding markets provided by rapidly growing middle classes, especially in the PRC and India.

References

Bernanke, Ben S. 2005. "The Global Savings Glut and the U.S. Current Account Deficit." Speech to the Virginia Association of Economics, Richmond, Va. March 10.

Caballero, Richard J. 2010. "The 'Other' Imbalance and the Financial Crisis." Working Paper 15636. Cambridge, Mass.: National Bureau of Economic Research.

Chinn, Menzie D. 2004. "Incomes, Exchange Rates, and the U.S. Trade Deficit, Once Again." *International Finance* 7, no. 3: 451–69.

———. 2005a. "Doomed to Deficits? Aggregate U.S. Trade Flows Reexamined." *Review of World Economics* [Weltwirtschaftliches Archiv] 141, no. 3: 460–85.

———. 2005b. "Still Doomed to Deficits: An Update on U.S. Trade Elasticities." Working Paper. University of Wisconsin.

Crane, Leland, Meredith A. Crowley, and Saad Quayyum. 2007. "Understanding the Evo-lution of Trade Deficits: Trade Elasticities of Industrial Countries." *Economic Perspectives* [Federal Reserve Bank of Chicago] 31, no. 4: pp. 2–17.

Huang, Yiping. 2010. "China's Great Ascendancy and Structural Risks: Consequences of Asymmetric Market Liberalization." *Asian-Pacific Economic Literature* 24, no. 1: 65–85.

Illiyan, Asheref. 2008. "Performance Challenges and Opportunities of India Software Export." *Journal of Theoretical and Applied Information Technology* 4, no. 11: 1088–106.

International Monetary Fund. 2007. "Exchange Rates and the Adjustment of External Imbal-ances." *World Economic Outlook* (September): 81–120.

Kawai, Masahiro. 2010. "Global Rebalancing: An Asian Perspective." In *Rebalancing the Global Economy: Four Perspectives on the Future of the International Monetary System; Europe in Dialogue 2010–11,* edited by Stefan Collignon and others, pp. 79–102. Gutersloh, Germany: Bertelsmann Stiftung.

Kawai, Masahiro, and Fan Zhai. 2009. "China-Japan–United States Integration amid Global Rebalancing: A Computable General Equilibrium Analysis." *Journal of Asian Economics* 20, no. 6: 688–99.

Obstfeld, Maurice, and Kenneth Rogoff. 2007. "The Unsustainable U.S. Current Account Position Revisited." In *G7 Current Account Imbalances: Sustainability and Adjustment,* edited by Richard H. Clarida, 339–76. University of Chicago Press.

U.S. Department of the Treasury, Office of Tax Policy. 2007. "Approaches to Improve the Competitiveness of the U.S. Business Tax System for the 21st Century."

2

Exchange Rates and Global Rebalancing

BARRY EICHENGREEN AND GISELA RUA

W e all agree that global rebalancing is needed. We just do not agree on what it entails. American commentators talk about the need for increases in consumption spending in Asia without equal emphasis on the need for more saving in the United States. Asian commentators emphasize the need to raise savings in the United States without acknowledging that increased saving in one region needs to be accompanied by increased spending in other regions to avoid a shortfall in global demand. Some point to the need for the United States to produce additional traded goods but neglect the need for other regions to produce less of the same, absent a significant change in relative prices. Some commentators insist that exchange-rate changes are central to the adjustment process, while others insist that they are peripheral. This inability to agree does not enhance the regard with which practitioners of the dismal science are held in the policy community.

Confusion and disagreement frequently arise because the problem is inadequately specified. In some cases the question is framed in terms of the impact on global imbalances of an exchange-rate increase by the People's Republic of China (PRC), without specifying what other variables are to be taken as endogenous if the exchange rate is treated as exogenously set. In other cases the question posed is, how would the exchange rate have to adjust to accommodate a change in the level of spending? In still other cases the formulation distinguishes inadequately

The views in this chapter are those of the authors and do not necessarily represent the views or policies of the Board of Governors of the Federal Reserve System or its staff.

between spending on Chinese- and U.S.-produced goods. Some cases fail to distinguish between changes in spending on traded and nontraded goods. The substitutability of U.S.-produced and foreign-produced traded goods and of traded and nontraded goods produced within the United States is not specified. With the question underspecified, the answer is underspecified: it fails to distinguish between equilibrating changes in the real exchange rate (relative overall price levels in the PRC, the United States, and the rest of the world) and the single factoral terms of trade (the relative price—exchange-rate adjusted—of traded goods produced in the two countries).

Disagreement also stems from confusion over which countries and regions are involved in this rebalancing process. Are we talking about the PRC and the United States? The PRC economy is only 30 percent the size of the U.S. economy, a fact that may have important implications for the changes in relative prices that would have to accompany, say, an exogenously specified increase in U.S. savings rates.[1] Are we talking about a process of rebalancing wherein the United States is on one side and all of Asia is on the other—in which case the size imbalance is considerably less? Or are we talking about rebalancing between the United States and the rest of the world, in which case the United States is the smaller economy by a considerable margin?

Finally, there is confusion over the circumstances in which different categories of countries can contribute to the process of global rebalancing. The empirical literature has focused on adjustment by deficit countries, asking, under what circumstances have such economies been able to eliminate large and persistent current account deficits? This literature has identified a useful set of stylized facts about the circumstances under which adjustment has occurred. But such emphasis fails to acknowledge that the coin has two sides. It is equally important to ask, under what circumstances have economies with large and persistent current account surpluses been able to eliminate these successfully? With large surpluses heavily concentrated in emerging markets and in oil-producing countries, it is important to ask, are the circumstances in which these economies have succeeded in eliminating large current account surpluses different from those of advanced countries and nonoil exporters that find themselves in this position? It may be unwarranted to assume that findings about the characteristics of economies that have succeeded in eliminating large deficits carry over, up to a sign change, to economies that have eliminated large surpluses. It may be similarly reckless to simply assume that findings that apply to advanced countries and nonoil exporters mechanically carry over to emerging markets and oil exporters.

In this chapter we use the simplest model capable of shedding light on the exchange rate and terms-of-trade implications of various rebalancing scenarios:

---

1. The comparison is at market exchange rates, presumably what is relevant for an experiment in which relative price adjustments eliminate initial imbalances in markets for traded goods.

the Obstfeld-Rogoff two-country endowment model (Obstfeld and Rogoff 2007). In this model, each of two countries possesses an endowment (produces a fixed quantity) of traded and nontraded goods that are imperfect substitutes in consumption.[2] Given an assumption about the level of spending in both countries, it is possible to solve for the relative prices (the real exchange rate and terms of trade) that clear markets. This makes it possible, in turn, to solve for the changes in relative prices (the exchange rate and terms of trade changes) needed to clear markets when levels of spending change.

This is the question, in our view, that is most central to global rebalancing and to the role of the exchange rate in that process. Starting from a situation in which the United States is in current account deficit and the rest of the world is in surplus, what is the effect on the real exchange rate and other relative prices of, among other things, an increase in U.S. savings owing to a financial crisis that wipes out households' retirement accounts? What is the effect of an increase in PRC spending owing to financial reforms that eliminate households' credit constraints and to the development in the PRC of a social safety net that reduces the need for precautionary saving?

This initial analysis simply replicates the findings of the Obstfeld-Rogoff (2007) study. But we then apply the same model to additional questions. How dramatically do relative price effects differ when it is only the PRC, or all of Asia, or the entire rest of the world minus the PRC, on the other side of the U.S. rebalancing process? What difference does it make when the increase in spending in the PRC falls mainly on traded or nontraded goods? How is the relative price and adjustment impact affected when the increase in spending in the PRC takes the form of investment in infrastructure and capacity that can then be used to produce traded or nontraded goods?

Under what circumstances have economies eliminated persistent current account surpluses? To explore this question, we review the literature on elimination of large deficits and then apply similar methods to constructing a sample of cases in which large surpluses were eliminated. We compare the results with those in the mirror-image (large-deficit) cases and then contrast findings for advanced countries with those for emerging markets and oil exporters.

This is an important extension of earlier literature focusing on circumstances under which large deficits were eliminated. When the deficit economy was small, the circumstances under which its external imbalance was eliminated could reasonably be considered in isolation. But when that economy was large, there also had to be significant adjustment on the surplus side. In this case, analyzing the circumstances in which large deficits were eliminated makes little sense without also analyzing the circumstances under which large surpluses were eliminated. The earlier literature having addressed the first question, we

---

2. We add more precision to this statement below.

add evidence on the second. Putting the pieces together, we are then able to say something about the likelihood that we will now see a sustained reduction in global imbalances.

Overview of Global Imbalances

The debate over global imbalances is of long standing, reflecting the persistence of those imbalances. Figure 1-1 (in chap. 1) summarizes the developments in the United States and emerging East Asia. There are two important facts. First, the United States accounted for the largest share of global current account deficits; any explanation for imbalances and their evolution will have to account for U.S. behavior. The year 2009 was the first time in years that the United States did not account for the greater part of the world's deficits. The question now, of course, is whether its share of deficits is likely to expand again as the U.S. and global economies recover.

Second, though the PRC is prominent on the surplus side, it is not alone. In most years the contribution of oil exporters and surplus European countries (such as Germany) was even greater. In some years (early in the period), the PRC contribution was matched by those of other emerging Asian countries (emerging East Asia excluding the PRC) and Japan. Only in 2009 was the global surplus heavily a PRC surplus. Although any explanation for global imbalances clearly will have to reckon with the behavior of the PRC, an analysis limited to the bilateral U.S.-PRC imbalance will not adequately capture the problem.

Some years ago, one of us (Eichengreen 2006) published an article distinguishing several classes of explanations for global imbalances. The first of these is the new economy or relative profitability interpretation emphasizing the contrast between the rapid productivity growth associated with the rollout of new information and communications technologies in the United States and slower growth and lower profitability in other crisis-ridden emerging East Asia countries and Japan. This plausibly accounts for some widening of global imbalances in the late 1990s, but less so after the tech bubble burst and other emerging East Asia countries recovered from its crisis.

The second explanation, the standard analysis, focuses on declining U.S. savings and corresponding increases in saving in Asia (U.S. Federal Reserve chairman Ben Bernanke's 2005 "global savings glut"). The initial decline in U.S. savings was ascribed mainly to growing government dissaving following the Bush tax cut of 2001 (figure 2-1). After 2004 the focus shifted to household dissaving associated with the boom in asset prices (figure 2-2), home prices in particular. On the surplus side, different explanations applied to different economies. The oil exporters ran large net surpluses in the period of strong global growth and high energy prices between 2004 and 2008. High internal and external savings in European countries with trade surpluses reflected policies of restraint aimed at

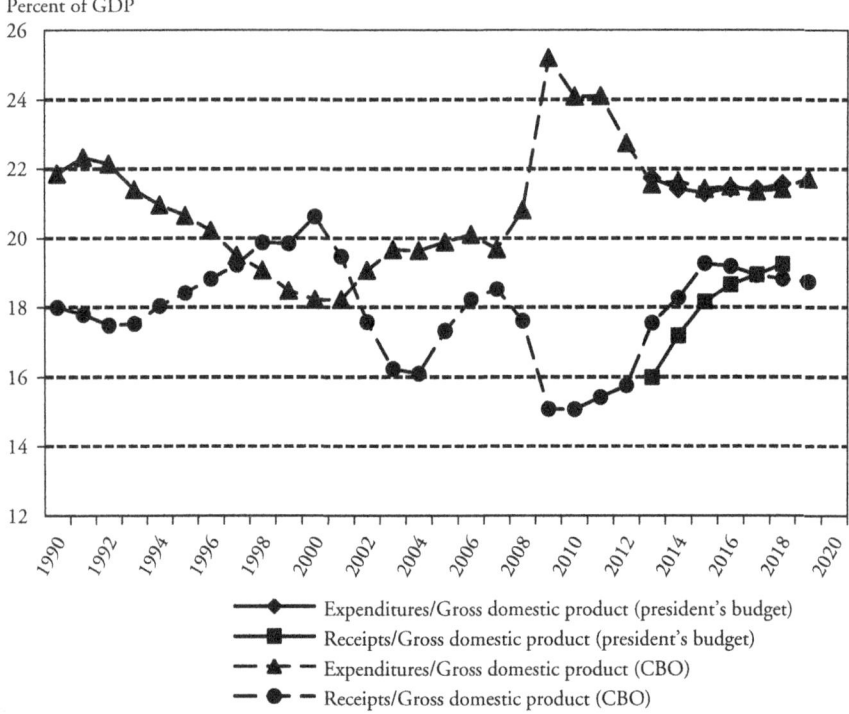

Figure 2-1. *U.S. Federal Expenditures and Revenues as Share of GDP, 1990–2020*

Percent of GDP

Expenditures/Gross domestic product (president's budget)
Receipts/Gross domestic product (president's budget)
Expenditures/Gross domestic product (CBO)
Receipts/Gross domestic product (CBO)

Sources: White House (2009) and Congressional Budget Office (2009a and 2009b).

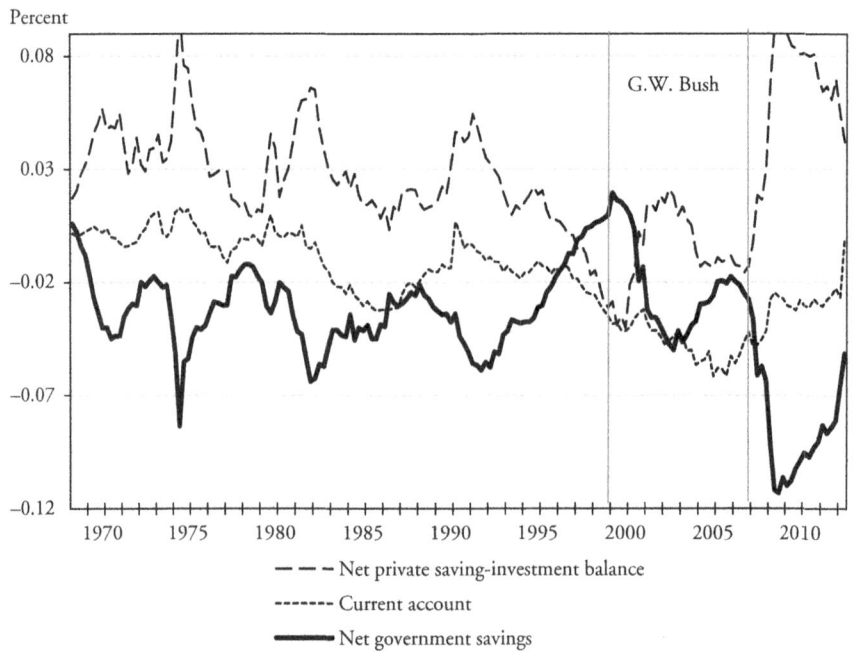

Figure 2-2. *United States Savings and Investment, Normalized by Nominal GDP*

Percent

G.W. Bush

Net private saving-investment balance
Current account
Net government savings

Source: Bureau of Economic Analysis (2009).

containing wages and consumption.[3] In other emerging Asian countries (that is, emerging Asia excluding the PRC), net external savings reflected stagnant investment more than a surge in savings.[4] High savings in the PRC was a function of high growth,[5] strong demand for precautionary saving in the presence of capital market imperfections and the absence of a well-developed social safety net, and lack of pressure on profitable state-owned enterprises to pay out dividends.

The third class of explanation focuses on the characteristics of international assets and liabilities. The dark-matter or exorbitant-privilege view emphasizes the tendency for the United States to earn a higher return on its external assets than it pays on its liabilities, enabling it to run current account deficits without increasing its net indebtedness to the rest of the world. One interpretation of this differential is that U.S. investors are savvier. A more plausible variant is that U.S. investors have greater risk tolerance: they are willing to hold relatively risky foreign direct investments, while other investors prefer relatively safe U.S. debt securities. Pierre-Olivier Gourinchas and Hélène Rey (2007) document the existence of this rate-of-return differential and establish the link with the composition of external assets and liabilities. Richard Caballero (2010) makes an influential statement of the view that the demand in emerging markets for relatively safe debt securities—which the United States has a comparative advantage in producing—could rationalize the existence of not just rate-of-return differentials but also growing imbalances as larger and more rapidly growing emerging markets seek to import additional safe assets from the United States.

Although these three interpretations are different, they are not necessarily incompatible, insofar as they apply to different periods, and, particularly, different economies. Each class of explanation can shed some light on what is likely to happen next. The new-economy view does not predict the rapid reemergence of global imbalances, given that the postcrisis U.S. economy is unlikely to be characterized by high levels of investment.[6] The standard analysis points to the importance of higher U.S. savings rates, which, recent research suggests, will continue to run in the mid-single digits.[7] It points, similarly, to the likelihood

3. This can be understood as reflecting the absence of a housing boom in countries like Germany and that only a small fraction of the population holds a significant share of its savings in the form of stocks. The effects of the asset boom were thus less.

4. A thorough analysis is in Asian Development Bank (2009).

5. This is understood in terms of the predictions of the life-cycle model: with younger generations saving out of higher incomes and older generations dissaving out of lower incomes, national savings will be high in fast-growing economies. See Modigliani and Cao (2004).

6. Rapid productivity growth there has been, of course, in recent quarters, but there is reason to think this was a one-off event, as firms laid off workers and closed plants that were least efficient. The difficulty of structural change, the likelihood of a creditless recovery, and the growing debt overhang are all reasons to worry that U.S. investment rates will lag (Goldman Sachs 2010).

7. This according to Carroll and Slacalek (2009); Lee, Rabanal, and Sandri (2010); and Mody and Ohnsorge (2010).

that household savings in the PRC will begin to decline with better public provision of health care and a more effective social safety net.[8] But it also suggests that adjustment in the PRC will remain slow insofar as household savings are inertial and there is still little pressure on PRC enterprises to reduce their retained earnings.[9] Finally, to the extent that the United States is no longer viewed as a reliable supplier of safe assets, emerging markets wishing to accumulate them may now turn to other sources. This will mean less foreign financing of U.S. current account deficits.

Note that this analysis has been presented entirely without reference to the exchange rate. Indeed, how exchange rates fit into this story is not entirely clear. It is to this issue that we now turn.

Implications of Various Rebalancing Scenarios

The model used here is Obstfeld-Rogoff's two-country model with exogenous endowments. Prices were assumed to be flexible, and the law of one price was assumed to hold for individual tradable goods. Home consumption bias within tradable goods was assumed, which could differ among countries. This is captured by the parameters α and α^*. Countries may also assign different preference weights to tradable goods relative to nontradable goods. This is captured by the two parameters γ and γ^*. The values of θ and η correspond to (constant) elasticities of substitution between tradable and nontradable goods and domestically produced and imported tradables, respectively.

The Home consumption index is expressed in the nested form

$$(2\text{-}1) \qquad C = \left[\gamma^{\frac{1}{\theta}} C_T^{\frac{\theta-1}{\theta}} + (1-\gamma)^{\frac{1}{\theta}} C_N^{\frac{\theta-1}{\theta}} \right]^{\frac{\theta}{\theta-1}},$$

and the Home consumer price index corresponding to the preceding Home consumption index C is

$$(2\text{-}2) \qquad P = [\gamma P_T^{1-\theta} + (1-\gamma) P_N^{1-\theta}]^{\frac{1}{1-\theta}},$$

---

8. Barnett and Brooks (2010) found that one additional yuan of government spending on health care produced a two-yuan increase in consumption spending. In contrast, they found little impact on consumption of increases in education spending.

9. It is on these grounds that the International Monetary Fund projects the reemergence of large surpluses in the PRC by 2012 (Blanchard and Milesi-Ferretti 2009). The decline in household savings rates in the PRC will presumably accelerate after 2015 with the rapid rise in old-age dependency ratios, but this is still far in the future from the perspective of policy analysis.

with tradables and nontradables consumption given by

(2-3)
$$C_T = \left(\frac{P}{P_T}\right)^{\theta} \gamma C$$

and

(2-4)
$$C_N = \left(\frac{P}{P_N}\right)^{\theta} (1-\gamma)C,$$

respectively.

Similarly, the tradables consumption index C_T is expressed as

$$C_T = \left[\alpha^{\frac{1}{\eta}} C_H^{\frac{\eta-1}{\eta}} + (1-\alpha)^{\frac{1}{\eta}} C_F^{\frac{\eta-1}{\eta}}\right]^{\frac{\eta}{\eta-1}},$$

and the price index for tradables is given by

$$P_T = [\alpha P_H^{1-\eta} + (1-\alpha) P_F^{1-\eta}]^{\frac{1}{1-\eta}},$$

with Home and Foreign tradables consumption

$$C_H = \left(\frac{P_T}{P_H}\right)^{\eta} \alpha C_T$$

and

$$C_F = \left(\frac{P_T}{P_F}\right)^{\eta} (1-\alpha) C_T,$$

respectively. In Foreign tradables there are isomorphic indexes, but with the parameters α^* and γ^*.

The terms of trade, τ, and the real exchange rate, q, are

$$\tau = \frac{P_F}{P_H} = \frac{P_F^*}{P_H^*}$$

and

$$q = \frac{\varepsilon P^*}{P},$$

respectively.[10] Even though the law of one price holds for individual tradable goods, purchasing power parity does not hold for the differing preferred baskets of tradable goods in each country. This means that $P_T \neq \varepsilon P_T^*$, where ε is the nominal exchange rate.

Given this structure, market clearing conditions for the Home produced good H, the Foreign tradable good F, Home nontradables N, and Foreign nontradables N^* are

$$Y_H = C_H + C_H^* \Leftrightarrow$$

$$Y_H = \alpha \left(\frac{P_H}{P_T} \right)^{-\eta} \gamma \left(\frac{P_T}{P} \right)^{-\theta} \underbrace{C}_{C_T} + \left(1 - \alpha^* \right) \left(\frac{P_H/\varepsilon}{P_T^*} \right)^{-\eta} \gamma^* \left(\frac{P_T^*}{P^*} \right)^{-\theta} \underbrace{C^*}_{C_T^*},$$

$$Y_F = C_F + C_F^* \Leftrightarrow$$

$$Y_F = (1 - \alpha) \gamma \left(\frac{P_F}{P_T} \right)^{-\eta} \left(\frac{P_T}{P} \right)^{-\theta} C + \alpha^* \gamma^* \left(\frac{P_F/\varepsilon}{P_T^*} \right)^{-\eta} \left(\frac{P_T^*}{P^*} \right)^{-\theta} C^*,$$

$$Y_N = C_N \Leftrightarrow Y_N = (1 - \gamma) \left(\frac{P_N}{P} \right)^{-\theta} C,$$

and
$$Y_N^* = C_N^* \Leftrightarrow Y_N^* = \left(1 - \gamma^* \right) \left(\frac{P_N^*}{P^*} \right)^{-\theta} C^*.$$

Finally, the current account is

$$\text{Home: } CA = P_H Y_H + iF - P_T C_T$$

and
$$\text{Foreign: } \varepsilon CA^* = P_F Y_F - iF - P_T C_T^* = -CA,$$

where F is Home net foreign assets and i is the interest rate, in Home currency units, and the real exchange rate is

$$(2\text{-}5) \qquad q = \frac{\left[\alpha^* \tau^{1-\eta} + \left(1 - \alpha^* \right) \right]^{\frac{1}{1-\eta}}}{\underbrace{\left[\alpha + (1 - \alpha) \tau^{1-\eta} \right]^{\frac{1}{1-\eta}}}_{\frac{\varepsilon P_T^*}{P_T}}} \times \frac{\left[\gamma^* + (1 - \gamma^*)(P_N^*/P_T^*)^{1-\theta} \right]^{\frac{1}{1-\theta}}}{\left[\gamma + (1 - \gamma)(P_N/P_T)^{1-\theta} \right]^{\frac{1}{1-\theta}}}.$$

10. Discussion here is in terms of the real exchange rate, this being a real rather than a monetary model. Readers who prefer to think in terms of the nominal rate can assume that central banks in each country target a stable price level.

In our calibration we initially adopted Maurice Obstfeld and Kenneth Rogoff's (2007) parameter values. We set the dollar value of tradable goods output to GDP at

$$\frac{P_H Y_H}{P_H Y_H + P_N Y_N} \approx 0.25.$$

Assuming that the U.S. current external deficit was about 5 percent of GDP, this implied a current account deficit-to-tradables ratio of

$$ca = \frac{CA}{P_H Y_H} = -0.05/0.25 = -0.2.$$

We set net U.S. foreign assets over the dollar value of traded goods output at

$$f = \frac{F}{P_H Y_H} = 0.8,$$

and the nominal interest rate at $i = 0.05$ per year. We also set

$$Y_N / Y_H = Y_{N*} / Y_F = 1,$$

$$\eta = 2, \theta = 1, \gamma = \gamma^* = 0.25, \alpha = 0.7,$$

and $\alpha^* = 0.925$. Under the assumption that $\sigma_T = Y_H / Y_F = 0.22$, the United States would account for 21 percent of the world economy.

We assumed a decline in U.S. spending and an increase abroad sufficient to eliminate the U.S. deficit. Suppose, for example, that a financial crisis depressed the value of U.S. households' retirement accounts and that financial reforms eliminated credit constraints in the PRC. Eliminating the imbalance would cause the dollar to depreciate by 32.3 percent. On one hand, there would be a shift in global demand away from the United States, which would cause a relative drop in demand for U.S.-produced tradable goods. This is because U.S. citizens were assumed to have a relatively strong preference for U.S.-produced tradables. The U.S. terms of trade would fall by 15.76 percent. On the other hand, because eliminating the U.S. current account deficit implied a 20 percent fall in demand for traded goods, a fall in the relative price of nontraded goods in the United States would be needed. In parallel with effects in the United States, a rise in the price of nontraded goods abroad would also occur. Given the large share of nontradables in the consumer price index, the overall real exchange-rate response would be magnified beyond terms of trade changes.

Changing the two elasticity parameters θ and η would have important effects. Higher elasticities of substitution between tradable and nontradable goods and domestically produced and imported tradables would lead to a smaller impact on the terms of trade and the real exchange rate.

Participation in Global Rebalancing

Our benchmark assumption was that all countries participated in the process of global rebalancing—the United States (which was 21 percent of the world economy) and the rest of the world. Here we ask how much difference it would make if the PRC (placed at 7 percent of the world economy) did not participate— that is, if it prevented its imports and exports from moving. When the PRC is removed from the picture, the rest of the world is smaller relative to the United States, and the United States becomes approximately 23 percent of the world economy. Accordingly, it was assumed that $\sigma_T = Y_H/Y_F = 0.2579$ instead of 0.22.[11] For different combinations of the two elasticity parameters, table 2-1 shows how the impact on exchange rates (the terms of trade and the real exchange rate) of eliminating the imbalance between the United States and the rest of the world varied according to participating countries and the relative size of the U.S. economy. Since U.S. citizens were assumed to have a relatively strong preference for home-produced goods, the fall in the terms of trade increased with the size of the United States relative to the world economy. Furthermore, the larger the relative size of the U.S. share of the world economy, the larger the initial current account surplus in the rest of the world. For example, a U.S. current account deficit of 5 percent of GDP corresponded to a current account surplus in the rest of the world of

$$\frac{CA^*}{GDP^*} = -\frac{CA}{GDP} \times \frac{P_H Y_H}{P_F Y_F} = -(-0.05 * 0.2579/0.8843) = 1.46\%,$$

when the United States was 23 percent of the world economy, and of

$$\frac{CA^*}{GDP^*} = -(-0.05 * 6.71/2.2357) = 15\%,$$

when the United States was 75 percent of the world economy. Adjustment abroad caused the relative price of foreign nontraded goods to rise in parallel to the fall in the relative price of domestic nontraded goods, which magnified the effect on the real exchange rate. Therefore, if the PRC does not participate in eliminating the imbalances, there will have to be a larger dollar depreciation.

11. See appendix 2A for details.

Table 2-1. *Rebalancing Scenarios with Different Participating Countries*[a]

Country	U.S. share of world economy (percent)	θ	η	Fall in terms of trade Δτ	Real depreciation Δq
United States and the rest of the world	0.21	1	2	15.76	32.30
		1	3	9.44	26.37
		2	2	15.76	19.09
		2	3	9.44	14.37
		0.5	2	15.76	64.36
United States and the rest of the world minus the PRC	0.23	1	2	16.65	33.58
		1	3	10.09	27.47
		2	2	16.65	20.06
		2	3	10.09	15.14
		0.5	2	16.65	66.41
United States and all Asia	0.5	1	2	30.87	57.83
		1	3	20.91	52.26
		2	2	30.87	36.69
		2	3	20.91	30.45
		0.5	2	30.87	108.97
United States and the PRC	0.75	1	2	51.34	115.66
		1	3	37.57	143.47
		2	2	51.34	69.96
		2	3	37.57	78.27
		0.5	2	51.34	225.18

Source: Authors' simulations.

a. θ = elasticity of substitution between tradable and nontradable goods, η = elasticity of substitution between domestically produced and imported tradables, τ = terms of trade, q = real exchange rate.

Alternatively, the cases in which the United States was on one side of the rebalancing process and either all of Asia or only the PRC was on the other were explored. In the first case, it was assumed that all non-Asian countries prevented any movement in their imports and exports, whereas in the second case all of Asia except the PRC joined the non-Asian group by excluding itself from the process of rebalancing. Since the economic size of the United States, on its own, was one-and-a-half times that of Asia and three times that of the PRC, its share in collective output was 0.50 and 0.75, respectively.

It followed that the impact on the terms of trade and the real exchange rate would be much bigger. For example, when only the PRC and the United States participated in the rebalancing, the dollar depreciation was above 69 percent for any reasonable combination of the two elasticity parameters.

The conclusion is that it matters greatly how many countries are on the other side of the U.S. current account adjustment. If there is only one (the PRC), the real exchange effects will be extremely large. If all of Asia is on the other side

Table 2-2. *Exchange-Rate Responses to Productivity Shocks*[a]

	20 percent increase in foreign production of tradables	20 percent increase in foreign production of nontradables
σ_T	0.2	0.22
σ_N	1	1
σ_N^*	5/6	1.2
CA	−0.2	−0.2
f	−0.8	−0.8
$\Delta\%\tau$	−3.22	0
$\Delta\%q$	10.97	−13.68

Source: Authors' simulations.

a. σ_T is the ratio between Home and Foreign tradable goods output, σ_N is the ratio between Home nontradable and tradable goods output, σ_N^* is the ratio between Foreign nontradable and tradable goods output, and f is net U.S. foreign assets over the dollar value of traded goods output.

of the U.S. current account adjustment, the real exchange effects will be smaller. If the rest of the world excluding the PRC is on the other side, the effects will be even smaller. The effects would be smaller yet if the entire rest of the world including the PRC were on the other side of the U.S. current account adjustment.

Sectoral Productivity Shocks

Returning to our benchmark model, in which the United States accounts for 21 percent of the world economy, we now explore the effects of productivity shocks in the rest of the world. First, we look at an increase in foreign production of tradable goods (think of this as infrastructure investment undertaken by the PRC in 2008–09 that increased the supply of exportable goods). We also explore the effect of assuming an increase in foreign capacity to produce nontradable goods. The real exchange-rate changes needed to accommodate these different patterns of increased output would be, not surprisingly, very different.

The real exchange-rate response is determined by changes in both the terms of trade and the relative prices of domestic and foreign nontradable goods (see equation 2-5 below). Given the large share of nontradable goods in the consumer price index, changes in the relative prices of nontradable goods had a higher weight in the determination of the overall exchange-rate response than did changes in the terms of trade.

An increase in foreign production of tradable goods caused the relative prices of both domestic tradable goods and foreign nontradable goods to rise. The former relative price change corresponded to an improvement in the U.S. terms of trade, and the combination of both caused the dollar to depreciate. When the increase in foreign production was concentrated in the nontradable goods sector, there was no change in the terms of trade. Nevertheless, the drop in the relative price of foreign nontradable goods caused the dollar to appreciate. Table 2-2 reports parameter values and exchange rate changes (the terms of trade and the real exchange rate) for 20 percent variations in foreign production.

It thus matters tremendously whether surplus countries like the PRC, as they continue to grow, concentrate their investment in productive capacity in traded or nontraded goods. In the first case, the U.S. terms of trade would have to increase and the dollar would depreciate in real terms. In the second case, in contrast, there would be no change in the terms of trade and the dollar would appreciate in real terms.

Preference Shocks

In this simulation, structural reforms (for example, social safety net or financial market reforms) that changed spending patterns were assumed. First, we assumed an increase in the foreign preference for U.S. exports. This was, in effect, an increase in the foreign preference weight on U.S. tradable goods, $1 - \alpha^*$, or, equivalently, a reduction in foreign home bias in tradables. Raising $1 - \alpha^*$ from 0.075 to 0.200 caused the U.S. terms of trade to rise by about 35 percent and the dollar exchange rate to appreciate by 31 percent.[12] This reflects the shift in global demand toward U.S. exports. If foreign home bias were to increase to the level of the United States, $\alpha = \alpha^* = 0.7$, the rise in the terms of trade would be larger than 50 percent and the dollar real exchange rate would appreciate by 45 percent.

Next, we assumed a reduction in U.S. home bias in tradables from 0.7 to 0.4. This caused the terms of trade to fall by 37 percent and the dollar to depreciate 33 percent in real terms. This transpired because lower U.S. home bias caused global demand for U.S. tradable goods to fall.

Finally we looked at changes in foreign preferences for tradables. This corresponds to the foreign preference weight on tradable goods, γ^*. Because this parameter affects only relative consumption of tradable and nontradable goods (see equations 2-1 to 2-4), it had no effect on the terms of trade. However, because it had an impact on the price of foreign nontradable goods (relative to tradable goods), the real exchange rate changed. This may be seen from equation 2-5: the dollar depreciated in real terms when γ^* fell and appreciated when γ^* increased. Lowering γ^* from 0.25 to 0.19 caused the dollar real exchange rate to depreciate by about 35 percent, whereas a real appreciation of the same magnitude could be generated by raising γ^* from 0.25 to 0.33. The effect of raising the U.S. preference for tradables, γ, is similar to lowering the foreign preference for tradables, γ^*. An increase in γ from 0.25 to 0.32 will cause the real exchange rate to depreciate by 33 percent.

This shows that changes in spending patterns can result in significant changes in the real exchange rate and terms of trade. Stronger foreign taste for U.S. exports

12. We assumed the size of the United States to be 21 percent of the world economy and the elasticity parameters θ and η to equal 1 and 2, respectively.

or for tradable goods caused the dollar to appreciate. On the other hand, declines in U.S. home bias in tradables, declines in foreign preference for tradable goods, or increases in U.S. preference for tradable goods caused the dollar to depreciate. As expected, changes in domestic or foreign preferences for tradable goods had no effect on the terms of trade, while changes in home bias in tradables did. A decline in U.S. home bias caused U.S. terms of trade to fall, while a decline in foreign home bias (or, equivalently, an increase in foreign preference for U.S. tradable goods) caused U.S. terms of trade to rise.

Current Account Surplus Reductions

Available literature examining how large current account surpluses end, especially in emerging markets, is limited. In contrast, available literature about the elimination of large current account deficits ("current account reversals") is considerable. Most studies identified reversals following the criteria proposed by Gian Milesi-Ferretti and Assaf Razin (1998).[13] These criteria identified, among other things, the initial current account ratio, the size of the adjustment (in percent of GDP and as a fraction of the initial deficit), and its duration. Bernardina Algieri and Thierry Bracke (2007) relaxed earlier criteria using sensitivity analysis to maximize the number of episodes. The International Monetary Fund (IMF) (2007) shifted the emphasis of previous studies toward both deficit and surplus reversals and proposed a set of criteria applicable to both. Additionally, the duration of the episodes was estimated instead of setting a fixed adjustment period.

Most papers focused on Organization for Economic Cooperation and Development (OECD) countries.[14] A few papers considered current account reversals in low- and middle-income economies (Milesi-Ferretti and Razin 1998) or in both industrial and emerging economies (Adalet and Eichengreen 2007; Algieri and Bracke 2007; and IMF 2007).

Although some dispute the main determinants of reversals, there is nonetheless some agreement regarding what variables to consider. Most studies included the current account ratio; macroeconomic variables such as domestic growth, GDP per capita, and the fiscal balance; external sector variables such as the trade balance, trade openness, the real exchange rate, the terms of trade, and the exchange regime; and world variables such as world growth, OECD growth, or U.S. real interest rates. Although these papers focused on current account deficit

---

13. Algieri and Bracke (2007) and IMF (2007) are exceptions; see below.

14. Freund (2005); Croke, Kamin, and Leduc (2005); Freund and Warnock (2007); Debelle and Galati (2007); and de Haan, Schokker, and Tcherneva (2008). This is evidence of the recent interest in the U.S. situation, as a few papers used analysis of OECD experience to draw inferences for the United States.

reversals,[15] which may differ beyond a sign change from reductions in current account surpluses, they are nonetheless a logical starting point for this discussion.

Data and Variable Definitions

Our analysis used data for forty-six emerging economies and twenty-six advanced economies over the period 1980–2008.[16] The main sources of data were the World Economic Outlook database (IMF 2009) and the World Bank's (2009) *World Development Indicators*. We started by identifying persistent reductions in current account surpluses. Because the defining criteria have important implications for episode selection and thereby for the results, we considered three different sets of criteria inspired by the above-mentioned literature on deficit reversals.

Our first definition, EP1, is a variant of the measure proposed by Algieri and Bracke (2007). For an economy to have an episode that qualified as a persistent reduction in the current account surplus, it must have met the following five criteria:

—The current account was in surplus before the reduction.

—Adjustment took place within four years.

—Within four years the current account decreased by at least one standard deviation of the economy's current account ratio.

—The current account reduction was sustained over five years—that is, the maximum current account ratio in the five years after the adjustment should have remained below the minimum current account ratio in the three years before the adjustment.

—There was not another reduction in the following four years.

Alternatively, EP2 was constructed following (with necessary modifications) Milesi-Ferretti and Razin (1998) and subsequent studies that adopted their criteria:[17]

—The current account surplus exceeded 2 percent of GDP before the reduction.

—The average surplus was reduced by at least 2 percent of GDP over three years (from the maximum to the three-year average).

15. Except IMF (2007).

16. The emerging economies: Argentina; Bahrain; Bangladesh; Botswana; Brazil; Bulgaria; Chile; PRC; Colombia; Côte d'Ivoire; Croatia; Cyprus; Czech Republic; Egypt; Estonia; Hungary; India; Indonesia; Jordan; Kenya; Lithuania; Macedonia; Malaysia; Mauritius; Mexico; Morocco; Nigeria; Oman; Pakistan; Peru; Philippines; Poland; Qatar; Romania; Russian Federation; Serbia; Slovak Republic; Slovenia; South Africa; Sri Lanka; Taipei,China; Thailand, Tunisia; Turkey; United Arab Emirates; and Viet Nam. The advanced economies: Australia; Austria; Belgium; Canada; Denmark; Finland; France; Germany; Greece; Hong Kong, China; Ireland; Israel; Italy; Japan; Republic of Korea; Luxembourg; Netherlands; New Zealand; Norway; Portugal; Singapore; Spain; Sweden; Switzerland; United Kingdom; and United States.

17. Freund (2005); Croke, Kamin, and Leduc (2005); Freund and Warnock (2007); Adalet and Eichengreen (2007); Debelle and Galati (2007); and de Haan, Schokker, and Tcherneva (2008).

—The maximum current account ratio in the five years after the reduction was not larger than the minimum current account ratio in the three years before the reduction.

—The current account ratio decreased by at least one-third of the initial surplus value.

—There was not another reduction in the following three years.

Finally, we constructed EP3 using the four criteria adopted by the IMF (2007), to which we added a fifth:

—At the beginning of the reduction (year 0), the average reduction in the imbalance over the next three years must have been at least 0.5 percentage point of GDP.

—At the end of the reduction (year T), the episode finished when a local minimum was reached—that is, when the current account ratio ca_t remained above ca_T for three consecutive years, and 0.5 percent or more of the reduction was overturned:

$$\left|ca_T - ca_{T-1}\right|/\left|ca_0 - ca_{T-1}\right| \geq 0.005.$$

—Compared with the initial year, the current account ratio in T must have fallen by at least 2.5 percentage points of GDP and by at least one-half of the initial level.

—In each of the five years after the beginning of the episode, the current account ratio must have been smaller than the initial level.

—There was not another reduction while one was still ongoing, where the duration of each reduction was determined in the second criterion listed above.

Unlike the first two measures, which looked at adjustments over a fixed period of three to four years, EP3 allowed for longer-lived reductions in current account surpluses and estimated the duration of each episode. EP3 was less restrictive than EP1 and EP2 as it required only a 0.5 percent of GDP reduction as opposed to one standard deviation for EP1 and 2 percent of GDP for EP2. EP1 and EP2 are thus referred to as capturing substantial surplus reductions, and EP3 is referred to as identifying both substantial and moderate surplus reductions. EP3 generated many more episodes (sixty-nine in emerging economies and twenty-six in advanced economies) than EP1 (twenty-eight episodes in emerging economies and thirteen in advanced economies) and EP2 (thirty-four episodes in emerging economies and thirteen in advanced economies).[18]

18. After this paper was drafted, the IMF (2010) studied the consequences (as opposed to the causes, our concern here) of ending sustained current account surpluses. The methodology used was similar to our definition of EP2. Of the 20 episodes listed after 1980, 7 were also included in our measure EP1, 9 in our measure EP2, and 14 in our measure EP3. The IMF publication thus provides something of an independent check on our methodology. See Eichengreen and Rua (2011) for the full list of episodes.

Table 2-3. *Data Description and Sources*

Variables	Description of variables	Sources
CA/GDP	Current account as percent of GDP	IMF (2009)
Real growth	Growth in real GDP per capita	World Bank (2009)
Openness	Trade openness = (imports + exports)/ GDP	World Bank (2009)
Trade balance	Trade balance/GDP	World Bank (2009)
REER appreciation	Growth in the real effective exchange-rate index [2000 = 100]; an increase means appreciation	World Bank (2009); IMF (various years)
Government deficit	Government deficit/GDP	IMF (2009)
World growth	World GDP growth	World Bank (2009)
Oil exporter	Dummy variable that equals 1 if the share of oil exports on total exports is higher than 20 percent	World Bank (2009)
Real oil price	Nominal oil price adjusted by U.S. consumer price index	IMF (2009)
Emerging/advanced	FTSE Global Equity Index Series Country Classification	FTSE (2009)

Source: Authors' calculations.

If we compare episodes picked up by EP1 and EP2, we notice some cases in which the same episode was captured by both but with a divergence of several years, and others in which episodes were captured by only one definition. One way of choosing between these definitions would be to select the one that has the highest proportion of episodes also picked up by the other two—allowing for three years of divergence with regard to the starting year. Of the forty-seven episodes identified by EP1, twenty-eight were also picked up by EP2 and 39 by EP3. On average, 71.3 percent of episodes identified by EP1 were also identified by the other two definitions. Since the comparable fraction for EP2 was 70.7 percent, EP1 did the best job in identifying a consistent set of episodes in this sense.

Univariate Patterns

We now turn to the choice of explanatory variables, guided by the literature on current account deficit reversals. These variables and their sources are listed and described in table 2-3. Table 2-4 shows their means, differences in means, and significance in a two-tailed *t* test, with the sample divided into emerging economies and advanced economies to allow for different determinants of reductions in these economies.[19]

19. Germany was excluded from the advanced economy subsample because the current account reduction identified after reunification in 1989 had its own historical determinants.

Table 2-4. Summary Statistics: Means and Difference in Means[a]

	Obs.	EP1			EP2			EP3		
		0	1	Diff.	0	1	Diff.	0	1	Diff.
Emerging economies										
CA/GDP$_{t-1,t-3}$	1,183	(1.20)	11.31	12.51***	(1.15)	12.03	13.17***	(1.19)	3.32	4.51***
Real growth$_{t-1,t-3}$	1,160	2.40	0.63	(1.77)**	2.39	0.90	(1.49)	2.43	1.17	(1.26)***
Openness$_{t-1}$	1,174	76.25	84.99	8.74	76.32	84.62	8.3	76.43	77.23	0.8
ΔTradeBal$_{t-1,t-3}$	999	0.12	(1.81)	(1.92)***	0.10	(1.30)	(1.4)**	0.13	(0.81)	(0.95)***
REER appreciation$_{t-1,t}$	550	0.11	7.96	7.85***	0.29	1.63	1.34	0.15	2.96	2.81
Fiscal balance$_t$	138	(2.98)	1.50	4.48**	(2.92)	(1.27)	1.65	(2.97)	(1.03)	1.94
World growth$_t$	1,380	2.63	2.66	0.02	2.63	2.62	(0.01)	2.62	2.88	0.27
Real oil price$_t$	1,380	35.68	38.08	2.4	35.57	43.98	8.42**	36.00	30.73	(5.27)**
Oil exporter	977	0.17	0.19	0.02	0.16	0.33	0.17	0.16	0.22	0.05
Advanced economies										
CA/GDP$_{t-1,t-3}$	710	0.69	4.82	4.13***	0.64	7.42	6.78***	0.71	2.33	1.63
Real growth$_{t-1,t-3}$	780	2.41	2.17	(0.25)	2.38	4.00	1.62***	2.40	2.69	0.29
Openness$_{t-1}$	731	84.90	97.37	12.47	83.87	160.42	76.56***	85.44	76.55	(8.89)
ΔTradeBal$_{t-1,t-3}$	710	0.24	1.23	0.89	0.24	(0.49)	(0.73)**	0.25	(0.42)	(0.67)***
REER appreciation$_{t-1,t}$	695	0.34	1.23	0.89	0.34	1.62	1.29	0.35	0.36	0
Fiscal balance$_t$	777	(1.86)	(1.10)	0.76	(1.90)	1.03	2.93**	(1.86)	(1.48)	0.38
World growth$_t$	780	2.63	2.84	0.21	2.62	3.61	1*	2.62	3.06	0.45
Real oil price$_t$	780	35.72	36.63	0.91	35.74	35.44	(0.3)	35.84	32.80	(3.04)
Oil exporter	707	0.04	0.00	(0.04)	0.04	0.00	(0.04)	0.04	0.00	(0.04)

Source: Authors' calculations. See table 2-3 for data sources.

a. TradeBal = trade balance. Two-tailed t-test.

***Significant at less than 1 percent. **Significant at less than 5 percent. *Significant at less than 10 percent.

For emerging markets, the univariate comparisons suggested that reductions occurred in economies with higher initial current account surpluses and with slower domestic growth. Reductions in surpluses also appeared to be associated with earlier decreases in trade balances, higher real appreciation, and higher public savings. Substantial reductions occurred when oil prices were higher, while substantial and moderate reductions transpired when they were lower. Similarly, in advanced economies, reductions seemed to occur in those with higher current account ratios and higher public savings. They were also associated with faster growth, higher openness to trade, earlier decreases in trade balances, and higher world growth.

Figures 2-3 and 2-4 provide a graphical depiction using our first definition, EP1, of the behavior of the current account ratio and various correlates during episodes of surplus reductions in emerging economies (figure 2-3) and advanced economies (figure 2-4), where the reduction started in year zero. The first graph in each eight-graph figure reports the median and average current account ratio over all economies five years before and five years after reductions. The other seven graphs in each figure compare averages for domestic growth, trade openness, trade balance, the real exchange rate, fiscal balance, world growth, and the real oil price in economies that experienced reductions and those that did not in the five years before and after they occurred. These variables behaved very differently in emerging economies as compared with advanced economies. In emerging economies, reductions happened after increases in the current account ratio. This contrasts with advanced economies, where this ratio did not show much variation before reductions. Domestic growth in emerging economies accelerated in the years preceding reductions—perhaps reflecting demand-driven growth that translated into increased domestic absorption—while it decelerated slightly in advanced economies.

In both emerging and advanced economies, reductions seemed to occur after a deceleration in the rate of growth of the trade balance. Openness to trade moved in tandem with the trade balance in its improving phase but did not follow its deceleration in subsequent years. This behavior may have been caused by the rise in imports owing to exchange-rate appreciation.

The real exchange rate was defined such that an increase represents an appreciation. In line with the theoretical model sketched in the previous section, reductions seemed to be preceded by two years of significant real appreciation in emerging economies and one year of mild appreciation in advanced economies. The fiscal balance was very volatile before reductions in emerging economies but more stable in advanced economies. Public savings fell in advanced economies in the year immediately preceding reductions following two to three years of growth. In both emerging and advanced economies, fiscal savings deteriorated markedly in the year of the reduction.

Figure 2-3. *Dynamics of Key Variables before and after Substantial Reductions in Current Account Surpluses (EP1), Emerging Economies*

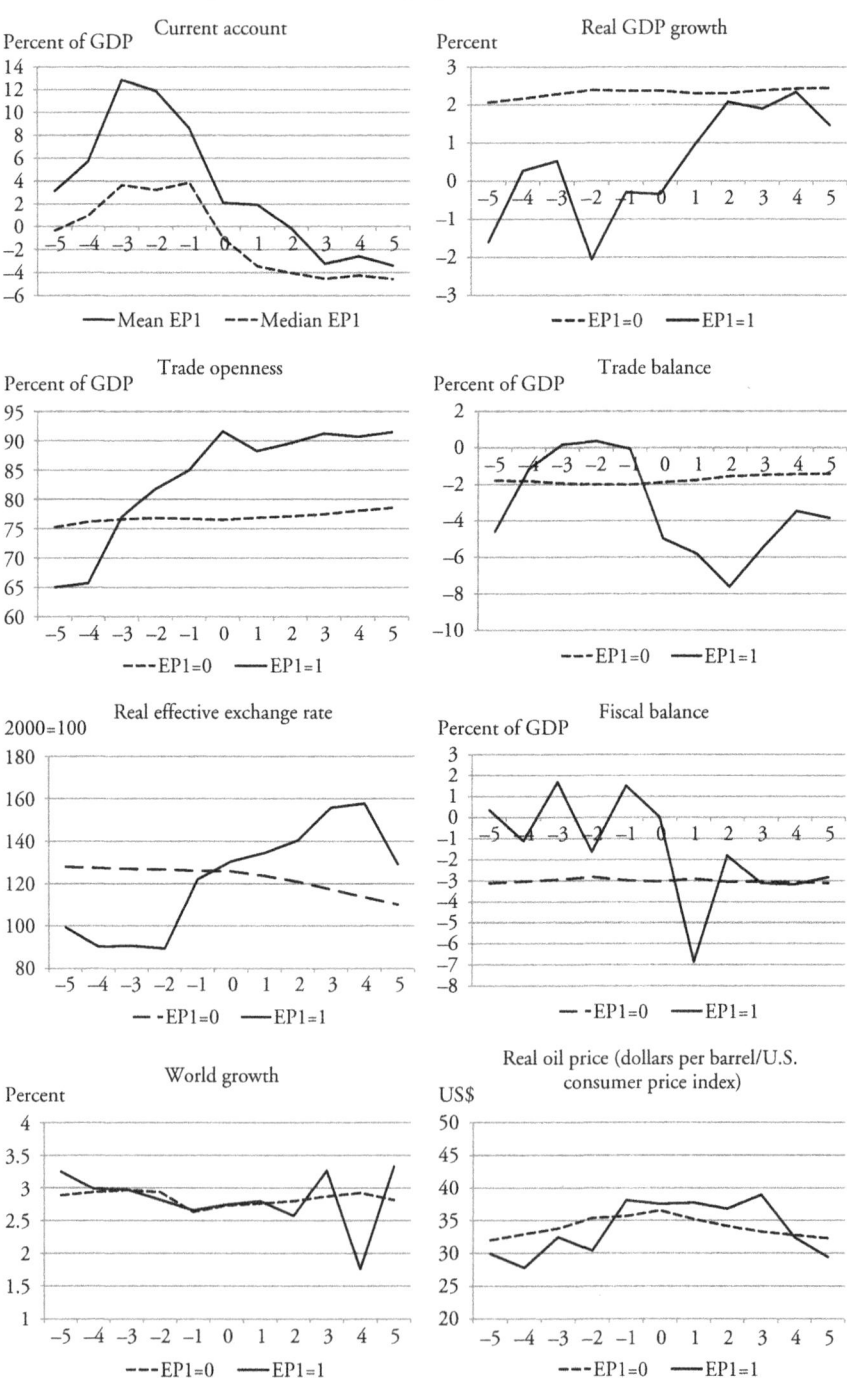

Source: Authors' calculations.

Figure 2-4. *Dynamics of Key Variables before and after Substantial Reductions in Current Account Surpluses (EP1), Advanced Economies*

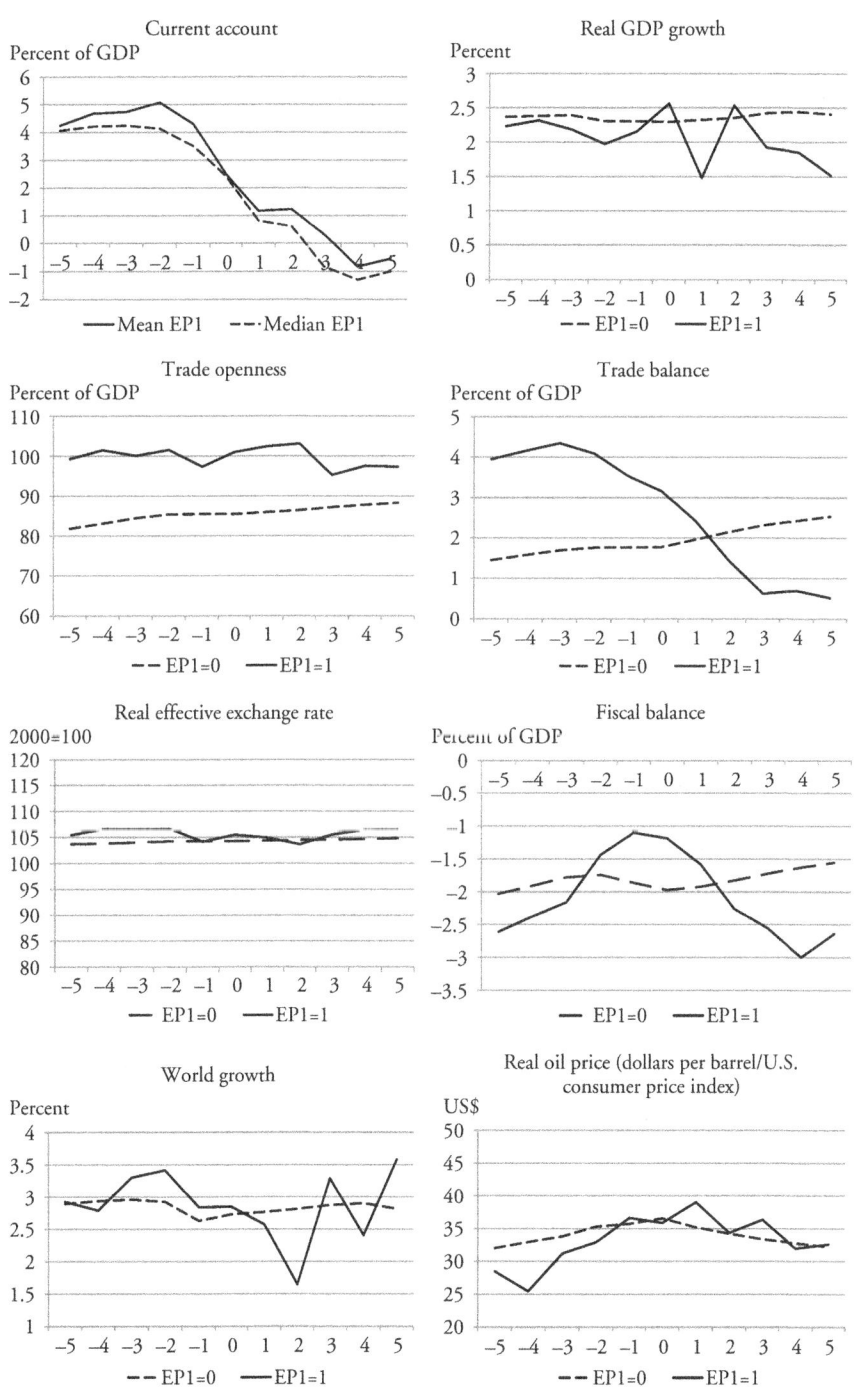

Source: Authors' calculations.

Reductions occurred after one to three years of decelerating world growth in both emerging and advanced economies. Substantial reductions tended to be preceded by two to three years of improving oil prices, whose subsequent fall seemed to trigger these reductions. This may reflect the impact of falling oil prices on oil producers' export receipts. Substantial and moderate reductions in advanced economies occurred after smaller increases in oil prices without a subsequent fall, while in emerging economies they seemed to be preceded by two years of falling oil prices. The distinct behavior exhibited by several variables before substantial reductions and before substantial and moderate reductions showed that how current account reductions are defined matters greatly.[20]

The one clear conclusion from this univariate analysis was that the behavior of macroeconomic variables around the time of reductions in large current account surpluses was very different in emerging economies compared with advanced economies. Consequently, the two types of economies are disaggregated in the multivariate analysis that follows.

Multivariate Analysis

Logit analysis was used to determine which variables helped predict whether an economy experienced a substantial reduction or a substantial and moderate reduction in its current account surplus. Our dependent variable took a value of 1 if there was a current account reduction and 0 otherwise. Given the similarities between logit and probit models with binary dependent variables, the two models would deliver qualitatively similar conclusions. However, fixed-effects probit analysis introduces what Jeffrey Wooldridge (2002) calls an incidental-parameters problem. Because the fixed-effects logit maximum-likelihood estimator does not treat the fixed effects as parameters to be estimated along with the betas, it produces consistent estimators.

To avoid problems of endogeneity, and for consistency with prior studies, three-year-lagged averages were used for the current account ratio, domestic growth, and the change in the trade balance.[21] Since observations for the same economy in different years were not independent, standard errors were clustered by economy. However, this did not control for unobserved economy-specific characteristics, for which economy fixed effects were used. Year fixed effects were also added to control for unobserved factors that affected all economies in each given year. The inclusion of year fixed effects permitted comparison of the effects

20. For the case of current account deficit reversals, Algieri and Bracke (2007) showed, similarly, that small modifications of the criteria used in the literature can change considerably the selection of reversals and significantly affect the results.

21. Other explanatory variables were trade openness, real appreciation, fiscal balance, world growth, the real oil price, and a dummy for oil exporters. World growth and the real oil price were meant to capture the effect of external (and exogenous) factors on the probability of a current account reduction.

of various factors across economies. When economy fixed effects were instead included—effectively dummying out cross-economy differences—we focused on the effects of changes in an explanatory variable within an economy over time on the probability of a surplus reduction.

Results are shown in tables 2-5 and 2-6. Although we would have liked to have had a consistent set of explanatory variables in the two subsamples, the fiscal balance had to be excluded from the emerging economy subsample, and the dummy for oil exporters had to be excluded from the advanced economy subsample. Fiscal balance data were available for most advanced economies but not for many emerging economies—especially in earlier years—causing a large number of missing observations in the regressions that used the emerging economy subsample. The dummy for oil exporters was dropped from the advanced economy subsample because there was only one economy classified as an oil exporter (Norway).

The first regression in each group considered several domestic determinants of reductions and two external variables.[22] The second regression controlled for unobservable economy-specific characteristics, and the third for year-specific factors. In discussing the results, we focus on substantial surplus reductions identified by EP1—which for the reasons presented above dominates EP2—and on substantial and moderate surplus reductions identified by EP3.

Not surprisingly, both groups of reductions were more likely to occur in economies with higher current account surpluses (columns 3, 6, and 9 in tables 2-5 and 2-6). Substantial and moderate reductions were also more likely after periods of increase in the current account ratio (column 8 in tables 2-5 and 2-6). Fast-growing emerging economies were less likely to experience both groups of reductions than slow-growing emerging economies, but differences in growth among advanced economies had no significant effect on the likelihood of reductions.

Reductions were less likely in more open emerging economies. More open economies produce more exportables, making policies designed to shift resources toward the production of nontradables more difficult politically. Comparable evidence for advanced economies was weaker, even though there was some evidence that increasing trade openness reduced the probability of current account reductions. In both emerging and advanced economies, substantial reductions were more likely after deceleration in the growth of the trade balance, which may be associated with slower export growth or acceleration in import growth. There was similar evidence for substantial and moderate reductions in advanced economies, but not in emerging economies.

Our discussion of Obstfeld and Rogoff's theoretical model shows that real appreciations accompanied reductions in the current account surplus. Figures 2-3

---

22. This corresponds to columns 1, 4, and 7 in tables 2-5 and 2-6.

Table 2-5. Determinants of Current Account Reductions in Emerging Economies[a]

Item	(1)	(2)	(3)	(4)	(5)	(6)	(7)	(8)	(9)
	Substantial reductions						Substantial and moderate reductions		
	EP1			EP2			EP3		
CA/GDP$_{t-1,t-3}$	0.485	3.013	0.431	0.304	0.898	0.304	0.204	0.314	0.248
	[0.16]***	[2.07]	[0.24]*	[0.06]***	[0.45]**	[0.16]*	[0.06]***	[0.06]***	[0.06]***
Real growth$_{t-1,t-3}$	0.127	0.753	0.280	0.174	0.654	0.457	0.109	0.0791	0.127
	(0.127)	(0.82)	(0.280)	(0.174)	(0.654)	(0.457)	(0.109)	(0.0791)	(0.127)
Openness$_{t-1}$	0.0402	0.166	0.0644	0.0228	0.0593	0.0217	0.00625	0.0209	0.00798
	[0.01]***	[0.11]	[0.03]**	[0.01]**	[0.14]	[0.01]**	[0.00]*	[0.02]	[0.00]*
ΔTradeBal$_{t-1,t-3}$	(0.516)	0.998	0.505	(0.464)	1.258	0.341	0.0647	0.0171	0.0383
	[0.16]***	[0.48]*	[0.28]*	[0.18]***	[0.56]**	[0.30]	[0.12]	[0.15]	[0.16]
REER appreciation$_{t-1,t}$	0.116	0.450	0.133	0.0644	0.0690	0.0337	0.0316	0.0429	0.0359
	[0.04]***	[0.19]**	[0.06]**	[0.03]**	[0.09]	[0.03]	[0.01]***	[0.02]***	[0.01]***
World growth$_{t-1}$	0.289	0.918		0.535	0.191		0.359	0.317	
	[0.52]	[2.65]		[0.68]	[0.83]		[0.26]	[0.29]	
Real oil price$_{t-1}$	-0.0584	-0.110		0.0654	0.163		0.0154	0.0154	
	[0.05]	[0.10]		[0.04]	[0.07]**		[0.0886]	[0.103]	
ROP$_{t-1}$ * Oil exporter	(0.153)			(0.0437)			0.0886	0.0154	
	[0.14]			[0.03]			[0.03]***	[0.04]**	
Constant	(1.410)	(27.10)	(0.893)	(6.841)	(13.10)	0.933	(0.964)	2.265	(3.078)
	[1.95]	[11.15]**	[1.49]	[3.24]**	[13.69]	[1.94]	[1.21]	[3.11]	[1.35]**
Observations	448	182	113	448	130	84	448	369	262
Fixed effects	No	Country	Year	No	Country	Year	No	Country	Year
Log-likelihood	(22.68)	(9.473)	(14.96)	(21.67)	(11.57)	(13.46)	(81.81)	(74.79)	(66.87)
McFadden pseudo-R^2	0.435	0.711	0.482	0.319	0.524	0.377	0.176	0.205	0.211
No. clusters	22	8	22	22	6	22	22	17	22

Source: Authors' calculations. See table 2-3 for data sources.

a. Robust standard errors in brackets, clustered by country. The current account ratio, domestic growth, and the change in trade balance are defined as averages over the three years preceding the event. ROP = real oil price.

***Significant at less than 1 percent. **Significant at less than 5 percent. *Significant at less than 10 percent.

Table 2-6. *Determinants of Current Account Reductions in Advanced Economies*[a]

Item	Substantial reductions						Substantial and moderate reductions		
	EP1			*EP2*			*EP3*		
	(1)	(2)	(3)	(4)	(5)	(6)	(7)	(8)	(9)
CA/GDP$_{t-1,t-3}$	0.263	1.490	0.334	0.336	1.576	0.442	0.148	0.208	0.181
	[0.07]***	[0.33]***	[0.09]***	[0.16]**	[0.53]***	[0.26]*	[0.05]***	[0.10]**	[0.06]***
Real growth$_{t-1,t-3}$	0.0499	0.626	0.626	0.440	2.316	0.707	0.119	0.0346	0.120
	[0.26]	[1.01]	[0.22]	[0.51]	[0.73]***	[0.63]	[0.21]	[0.27]	[0.27]
Openness$_{t-1}$	0.00141	0.00133	0.00107	0.00638	0.153	0.00680	0.00425	0.0203	0.00453
	[0.01]	[0.05]**	[0.01]	[0.01]	[0.08]**	[0.02]	[0.00]	[0.02]	[0.00]
ΔTradeBal$_{t-1,t-3}$	0.974	2.488	1.532	0.612	3.819	1.298	0.750	0.806	0.778
	[0.26]***	[1.36]*	[0.35]***	[0.53]	[1.63]**	[0.62]**	[0.32]**	[0.42]*	[0.34]**
REER appreciation$_{t-1,t}$	0.0129	0.0346	0.0332	0.0661	0.0372	0.0329	0.0151	0.00570	0.0311
	[0.06]	[0.10]	[0.06]	[0.09]	[0.24]	[0.09]	[0.03]	[0.04]	[0.03]
Fiscal balance$_{t-1}$	0.127	0.659	0.189	0.140	0.748	0.371	0.0664	0.0169	0.0474
	[0.07]*	[0.30]**	[0.10]*	[0.10]	[0.43]*	[0.17]**	[0.05]	[0.06]	[0.05]
World growth$_{t-1}$	0.413	1.214		0.899	2.757				
	[0.39]	[0.91]		[0.27]***	[1.37]**				
Real oil price$_{t-1}$	0.0269	0.0763		0.00686	0.0701		0.00602	0.00591	
	[0.03]	[0.07]		[0.02]	[0.10]		[0.02]	[0.02]	
Constant	4.316	2.530	3.005	9.542	25.88	6.153	3.683	2.542	2.907
	[1.33]***	[2.92]	[1.25]**	[1.81]***	[9.99]***	[1.70]***	[0.99]***	[1.07]**	[1.17]**
Observations	549	201	196	549	126	110	549	408	256
Fixed effects	No	Country	Country	No	Country	Year	No	Country	Year
Log-likelihood	(42.06)	(20.81)	(30.64)	(27.65)	(11.78)	(18.66)	(79.19)	(72.09)	(60.25)
McFadden pseudo-R^2	0.158	0.476	0.224	0.262	0.564	0.284	0.0779	0.0968	0.142
No. clusters	23	8	23	23	5	23	23	16	23

Source: Authors' calculations. See table 2-3 for data sources.

a. The current account ratio, domestic growth, and the change in trade balance are defined as averages over the three years preceding the event. REER appreciation is the lagged annual percentage change in the real effective exchange rate index. Robust standard errors in brackets, clustered by country.

***Significant at less than 1 percent. **Significant at less than 5 percent. *Significant at less than 10 percent.

and 2-4 show that this was mostly the case in emerging economies. In the multi-variate regression analysis we verified this evidence for emerging economies, finding positive coefficient estimates for one-period lagged real appreciations.[23]

Substantial reductions were more likely to occur in advanced economies with smaller fiscal surpluses. Because current account surpluses may be fed by increases in fiscal savings, these reductions were more likely after increases in the fiscal balance. This may be seen as a variant of the twin-deficits hypothesis. We did not find any effect of the fiscal balance on substantial and moderate reductions.[24]

In summary, we found that large current account surpluses do not last forever: the larger the surplus, the more likely it will eventually diminish. Such adjustment is more likely in less open economies, where political resistance is usually weaker. It also is more likely in emerging market economies when a period of exceptionally high growth has come to an end, and when expansion in the supply of exportables presumably has begun to slow and demand is rebalancing toward domestic goods. Such adjustment in these economies is also associated with real appreciation. In advanced economies, however, it is more likely after reductions in budget surpluses.

The robustness of our results was checked against outliers by removing current account reductions that may have had a significant impact on the results. All regressions were reestimated twice: after removing reductions with a very low initial current account ratio (smaller than 0.5 percent of GDP) from our list of episodes;[25] and after removing reductions with a very large initial current account ratio (two standard deviations higher than the period average for each economy).[26] All coefficient estimates kept their sign and magnitude. However, some coefficients that were previously significant at 10 percent became insignificant. This occurred because there were more economies and years in the sample with only zeroes (that is, no reductions), and these observations were therefore dropped from the estimates with fixed effects.

Given the nonlinearity of the empirical model, it is difficult to interpret the coefficient estimates in terms of discrete changes. The marginal effect of each regressor was calculated using all observations in the sample. Their average values

23. IMF (2010) also finds that the ending of sustained current account surpluses tended to be associated with real exchange-rate appreciation, although no explicit hypothesis tests were provided.

24. Additionally, we found no significant effect of the two external variables (world growth and real oil prices), even after controlling for the potentially different effect of oil prices on oil exporters, which does not validate our previous univariate analysis.

25. This corresponds to three episodes picked up by EP1 (one from the emerging economy subsample and two from the advanced economy subsample) and twelve episodes picked up by EP3 (four from the emerging economy subsample and eight from the advanced economy subsample).

26. This corresponds to four episodes picked up by EP1 (all from the emerging economy subsample), seven episodes picked up by EP2 (all from the emerging economy subsample), and seven episodes picked up by EP3 (six from the emerging economy subsample and one from the advanced economy subsample).

Table 2-7. *Average Marginal Effects*

Economy	EP1		EP2		EP3	
	reg.(2)	reg.(3)	reg.(5)	reg.(6)	reg.(8)	reg.(9)
Emerging economies						
$CA/GDP_{t-1, t-3}$	0.0486	0.0172	0.0244	0.0146	0.0178	0.0184
Real growth$_{t-1, t-3}$	0.0121	(0.0109)	(0.0178)	(0.0219)	(0.0047)	(0.0095)
Openness$_{t-1}$	0.0027	(0.0026)	(0.0016)	(0.0010)	(0.0012)	(0.0006)
$\Delta TradeBal_{t-1, t-3}$	(0.0162)	(0.0206)	(0.0342)	(0.0163)	0.0008	0.0028
REER appreciation$_{t-1, t}$	0.0072	0.0053	0.0019	0.0016	0.0024	0.0026
World growth$_{t-1}$	0.0147		0.0052		0.0181	
Real oil price$_{t-1}$	(0.0018)		0.0044		(0.0058)	
Advanced economies						
$CA/GDP_{t-1, t-3}$	0.0532	0.0109	0.0472	0.0122	0.0098	0.0109
Real growth$_{t-1, t-3}$	0.0086	(0.0205)	0.0618	0.0078	0.0036	0.0051
Openness$_{t-1}$	(0.0047)	0.0000	(0.0052)	(0.0002)	(0.0011)	(0.0003)
$\Delta TradeBal_{t-1, t-3}$	(0.0712)	(0.0504)	(0.1132)	(0.0294)	(0.0397)	(0.0476)
REER appreciation$_{t-1, t}$	0.0048	0.0015	0.0057	0.0001	(0.0014)	(0.0008)
Fiscal balance$_{t-1}$	0.0261		0.0273		0.0012	
World growth$_{t-1}$	(0.0306)		0.0891		(0.0042)	
Real oil price$_{t-1}$	0.0017		0.0017		0.0004	

Source: Authors' calculations. See table 2-3 for data sources.

are presented in table 2-7.[27] As seen before, economies with larger surpluses had a higher likelihood of experiencing a reduction. The second, fourth, and sixth columns show that, for each additional percentage-point increase in the current account ratio, the likelihood of a reduction increased by between 1.46 and 1.84 percentage points in emerging economies and between 1.10 and 1.20 percentage points in advanced economies. For example, the current account ratio in the PRC in 2007 was 10.9 percent of GDP. The likelihood of the PRC experiencing a reduction was, on average, 7.00 to 12.00 percentage points higher than that of Chile, Japan, the Philippines, or the Russian Federation in the same year.[28]

The fifth row of table 2-7 shows the magnitude of the real appreciations that accompanied reductions. Each percentage-point increase in the rate of real appreciation raised the likelihood of a reduction by 0.20 to 0.70 percentage points, on average. For example, the rates of appreciation of the Malaysian ringgit, the Philippine peso, and the PRC yuan in 2006 increased between 3 and 4 percentage points. This corresponded to a 1 to 3 percentage-point higher likelihood of a significant reduction in their current account surpluses.

27. Notice that this is different from looking at the marginal effects at the average of all regressors or at some other point in the space of regressors.
28. In 2007, the current account ratio in Chile was 4.4 percent; in the Philippines, 4.9 percent; in the Russian Federation, 6 percent; and in Japan, 4.8 percent.

Because the marginal effect of a specific regressor depends on the values of other regressors, in figure 2-5 we examine how this response varied with the level of other regressors, focusing on the emerging economy subsample. In the first four graphs it can be seen that faster currency appreciation increased the marginal effect of changes in the current account ratio and accelerations in appreciation itself. For substantial reductions, the marginal effect of changes in the current account was significantly different from zero when real appreciation was strong (between 10 percent and 28 percent). For substantial and moderate reductions, the marginal effect of changes in the current account was significantly different from zero even when appreciation was weak. For both groups of reductions, the marginal effect of accelerations in real appreciation was significantly different from zero for levels of currency appreciation below 15 percent.

The remaining four graphs in figure 2-5 show that output growth had a different impact on the marginal effect of these variables on the likelihood of substantial reductions and the likelihood of substantial and moderate reductions. For substantial reductions, the response to changes in the current account ratio was significantly different from zero when the growth of economies was between 5 percent and 10 percent and remained stable at around 0.05 in this interval. The response to faster real appreciation increased with the rate of growth and was significantly different from zero when growth was between zero and 5 percent. In contrast, the response to changes in the current account ratio and to accelerations in real appreciation increased with reductions in domestic growth. It was significantly different from zero when growth was between −5 and 7 percent.

In summary, higher rates of currency appreciation increased the impact of other determinants—such as the current account ratio and real appreciation itself—on the likelihood of reductions. Slower growth increased the impact of these determinants on the likelihood of substantial and moderate reductions but not on the likelihood of substantial reductions.

Conclusion

Economists disagree about the role of the exchange rate in the process of global rebalancing. Some argue that the imbalances problem is fundamentally an imbalance between saving and investment in the United States and a mirror-image imbalance in the PRC. Consequently, since there is no reason to think that a change in the exchange rate should have a significant impact on saving or investment, there is no reason to advocate a yuan revaluation–dollar devaluation as part of the rebalancing process.[29] Others insist that exchange-rate adjustments are indispensable to rebalancing. The resulting controversy has been a source of

29. Examples of this point of view include Laurenceson and Qin (2005) and McKinnon and Schnabl (2006).

Figure 2-5. *Evaluating Marginal Effects over the Response Surface*[a]

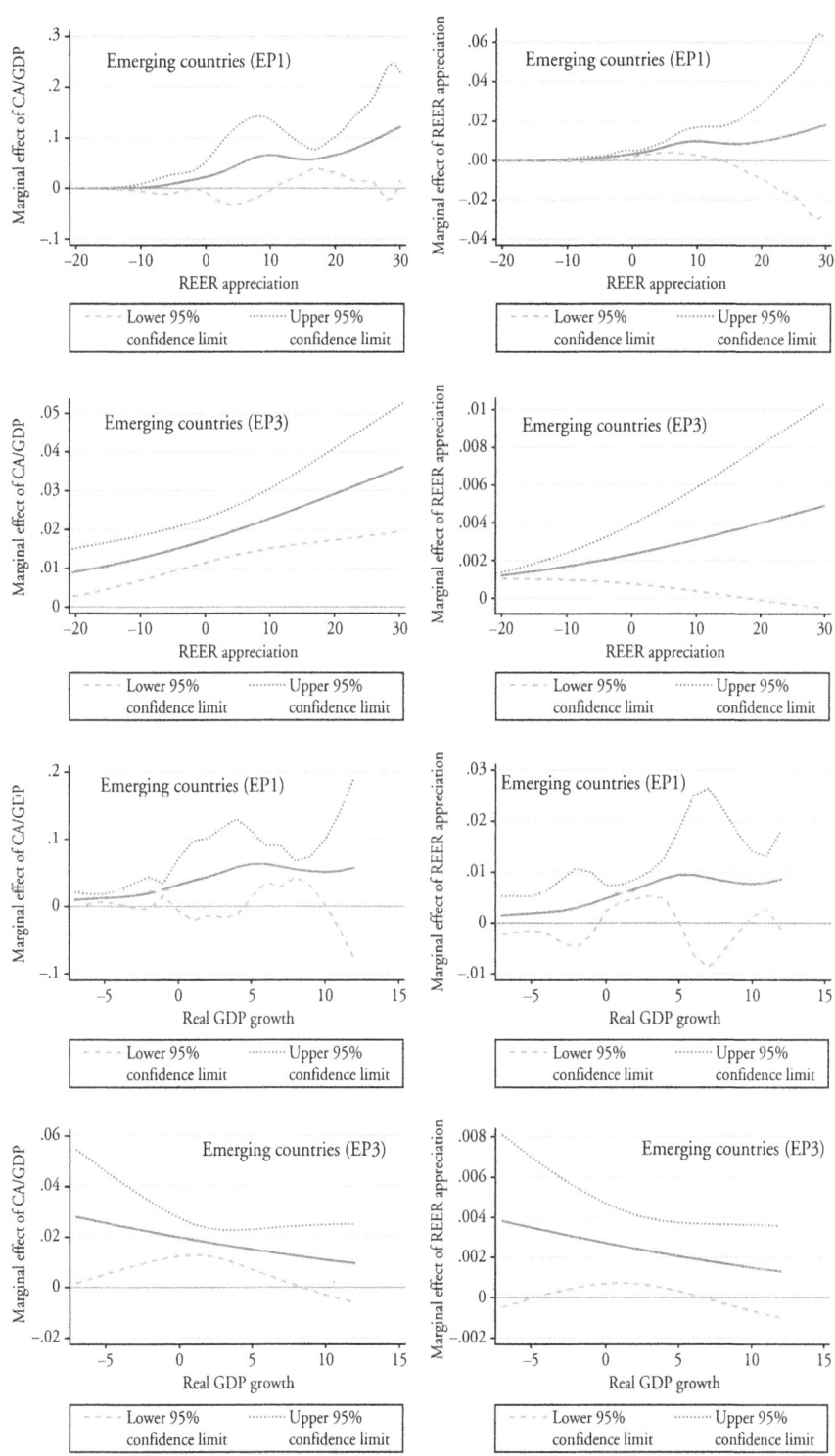

Source: Authors' calculations.
a. REER appreciation is the lagged annual percentage change in the real effective exchange rate index.

confusion that has not aided the adoption of policies conducive to rebalancing. The danger is that confusion may continue to disrupt efforts to put in place policies needed for a sustainable resolution of imbalances.

In this chapter we have attempted to reduce the confusion by making some simple points and exploring their implications. First, the exchange rate is not a primitive. The exchange rate is an endogenously determined relative price that adjusts to clear markets in response to shocks. When considering global rebalancing, it is more productive to think in terms of primitives: what is the shock in response to which rebalancing must occur—an increase in PRC spending? a reduction in U.S. spending? something else? What are the behavioral parameters that shape the impact of the shock on prices and quantities? Given assumptions about these primitives, it is then possible to ask whether and by how much the exchange rate must adjust. The debate over global imbalances has gone awry by focusing on the exchange rate. The exchange rate is better thought of as one of a number of endogenous relative prices that must adjust in response to policy initiatives or other events precipitating the rebalancing process. The simulation exercises undertaken in this chapter underscore this point.

The empirical literature tends to forget that not one but two or more countries will be involved in the rebalancing process. The literature on large current account deficits has asked, are circumstances in the United States such that we can now expect a persistent fall in the deficit? For a large economy like the United States, however, this question makes sense only if one also asks, are circumstances in other countries now such that we can expect a persistent fall in the surplus? Is this the case in a sufficient number of other countries to match the adjustment in the United States? In this chapter we have included an analysis of the second set of country participants in an effort to gain a better sense of the overall choreography of the rebalancing process.

We found that large current account surpluses tend to come to an end when they had been allowed to rise to exceptionally high levels. Less open economies (where political resistance to resource reallocation is weaker) were also found more likely to see large current account surpluses come to an end, as were economies where an earlier period of rapid growth had come to an end (presumably moderating the growth of capacity to produce tradables and rebalancing toward domestic goods). For oil-exporting emerging markets, large current account surpluses tended to come to an end when the price of oil was unusually low. Although limited, available data on government budgets suggested that smaller budget surpluses also helped end large current account surpluses.

Some of these patterns bode well for future reductions in the PRC's large current account surplus. That surplus has risen to extraordinarily high levels, but cross-country evidence suggests this is unlikely to continue without end. Both domestic and foreign pressures make some reduction of these extraordinarily large surpluses probable. The ongoing demographic transition and the likely deceleration of economic growth in the face of more spending on social programs should boost the likelihood of some reduction in the PRC current account surplus. The increases in government spending in general support this view. On the other hand, that the PRC economy is so open, making output and employment growth dependent on exports, is likely to create political resistance to adjustment.

These arguments underscore the fact that the requisite adjustments are not guaranteed and are not likely to occur automatically. Appropriate policy action would greatly increase the likelihood that countries on the surplus side of global imbalances contribute constructively to global rebalancing.

Appendix 2A: Derivation of σ_T for Different U.S. Sizes

Assuming that the share of tradable goods output to GDP is approximately 0.25 in the United States and in the rest of the world, the share of tradables to nontradables is approximately 1/3:

$$\frac{P_H Y_H}{P_H Y_H + P_N Y_N} \approx 0.25 \Rightarrow \frac{P_H Y_H}{P_N Y_N} \approx \frac{1}{3}$$

$$\frac{P_F^* Y_F}{P_F^* Y_F + P_N^* Y_{N^*}} \approx 0.25 \Rightarrow \frac{P_F^* Y_F}{P_N^* Y_{N^*}} = \frac{P_F Y_F}{\varepsilon P_N^* Y_{N^*}} \approx \frac{1}{3}.$$

With the relative size of the United States is given by

$$\frac{\text{U.S. GDP}}{\text{World GDP}} = \frac{P_H Y_H + P_N Y_N}{P_H Y_H + P_N Y_N + P_F Y_F + \varepsilon P_N^* Y_N^*} \approx \frac{4 P_H Y_H}{4 P_H Y_H + 4 P_F Y_F} = \frac{P_H Y_H}{P_H Y_H + P_F Y_F},$$

the value of $\sigma_T = Y_H / Y_F$ such that the United States is ω percent of the world solves the following nonlinear equation:

$$\frac{\sigma_T / \tau(\sigma_T)}{1 + \sigma_T / \tau(\sigma_T)} = \omega,$$

where $\tau(\sigma_T)$ is given by the equilibrium condition

$$1 = \alpha \frac{1}{[\alpha + (1-\alpha)\tau^{1-\eta}]}(1 + if - ca) + (1 - \alpha^*) \frac{1}{[\alpha^* \tau^{1-\eta} + (1-\alpha^*)]}\left(\frac{\tau}{\sigma_T} - if + ca\right).$$

In the benchmark model, the United States is approximately 21 percent of the world and σ_T equals 0.22. The initial value of the terms of trade is 0.8439. When

China does not participate in the rebalancing, the relative size of the United States is approximately 23 percent. In this case, $\sigma_T = 0.2579$ and the initial value of τ is 0.8843. In the case where the United States and Asia do the rebalancing, the relative size of the U.S. is 50 percent, and both σ_T and τ are equal to 1.5361. If only the United States and China participate, the relative size of the United States is 75 percent, $\sigma_T = 6.7068$, and $\tau = 2.2357$.

References

Adalet, Muge, and Barry Eichengreen. 2007. "Current Account Reversals: Always a Problem?" In *G7 Current Account Imbalances: Sustainability and Adjustment,* edited by Richard H. Clarida, pp. 205–46. University of Chicago Press.

Algieri, Bernardina, and Thierry Bracke. 2007. "Patterns of Current Account Adjustment: Insights from Past Experience." Working Paper. Munich Society for the Promotion of Economic Research. Munich Center for Economic Studies.

Asian Development Bank. 2009. *Asian Development Outlook 2009: Rebalancing Asia's Growth.* Manila.

Barnett, Steven, and Ray Brooks. 2010. "China: Does Government Health and Education Spending Boost Consumption?" Working Paper 10/16. Washington: International Monetary Fund.

Bernanke, Ben. 2005. "The Global Savings Glut and the U.S. Current Account Deficit." Speech to the Virginia Association of Economics. Richmond, Va.

Blanchard, Olivier, and Gian M. Milesi-Ferretti. 2009. "Global Imbalances: In Midstream?" Staff Position Note SPN/09/29. Washington: International Monetary Fund.

Bureau of Economic Analysis. 2009. "National Income and Product Accounts," tables 3.1, 4.1, and 5.1. United States Department of Commerce (www.bea.gov/iTable/iTableHtml.cfm?reqid=9&step=1&isuri=1).

Caballero, Richard J. 2010. "The 'Other' Imbalance and the Financial Crisis." Working Paper 15636. Cambridge, Mass.: National Bureau of Economic Research.

Carroll, Christopher D., and Jiri Slacalek. 2009. "The American Consumer: Reforming or Just Resting?" Johns Hopkins University and European Central Bank.

Congressional Budget Office. 2009a. "Budget Projections: 2009 to 2019" (www.cbo.gov/topics/budget/budget-projections/data-and-technical-information).

———. 2009b. "Historical Budget Data" (www.cbo.gov/topics/budget/historical-budget-data/data-and-technical-information).

Croke, Hilary, Steven B. Kamin, and Sylvain Leduc. 2005. "Financial Market Developments and Economic Activity during Current Account Adjustments in Industrial Economies." International Finance Discussion Paper 827. Washington: U.S. Federal Reserve System Board of Governors.

Debelle, Guy, and Gabriele Galati. 2007. "Current Account Adjustment and Capital Flows." *Review of International Economics* 15: 989–1013.

de Haan, Leo, Hubert Schokker, and Anastassia Tcherneva. 2008. "What Do Current Account Reversals in OECD Countries Tell Us about the U.S. Case?" *World Economy* 31: 286–311.

Eichengreen, Barry. 2006. "Global Imbalances: The New Economy, the Dark Matter, the Savvy Investor, and the Standard Analysis." *Journal of Policy Modeling* 28, no. 6: 645–52.

Eichengreen, Barry, and Gisela Rua. 2011. "Exchange Rates and Global Rebalancing." Working Paper 278. Tokyo: Asian Development Bank Institute (www.adbi.org/working-paper/2011/04/13/4509.exchange.rates.global.rebalancing).

Freund, Caroline. 2005. "Current Account Adjustment in Industrial Countries." *Journal of International Money and Finance* 24: 1278–1298.

Freund, Caroline, and Frank Warnock. 2007. "Current Account Deficits in Industrial Countries: The Bigger They Are, the Harder They Fall?" In *G7 Current Account Imbalances,* edited by Richard H. Clarida, pp. 133–68. University of Chicago Press.

FTSE. 2009. "FTSE Global Equity Index Series Country Classification" (www.ftse.com/products/indices/country-classification).

Goldman Sachs. 2010. "Recovery Unlikely to Reverse Global Rebalancing." *Global Economics Weekly.* New York and London.

Gourinchas, Pierre-Olivier, and Hélène Rey. 2007. "From World Banker to World Venture Capitalist: U.S. External Adjustment and the Exorbitant Privilege." In *G7 Current Account Imbalances,* edited by Richard H. Clarida, pp. 11–66.

International Monetary Fund (IMF). 2007. "Exchange Rates and the Adjustment of External Imbalances." In *World Economic Outlook,* April. Washington.

———. 2009. World Economic Outlook database. *World Economic Outlook,* October. Washington.

———. 2010. "Getting the Balance Right: Transitioning out of Sustained Current Account Surpluses." In *World Economic Outlook,* April. Washington.

———. Various years. *International Financial Statistics.* Washington.

Laurenceson, James, and Fengming Qin. 2005. "China's Exchange Rate Policy: The Case against Abandoning the Dollar Peg." Working Paper 2005-70. Tilburg, Neth.: Center for Economic Research.

Lee, Jaewoo, Pau Rabanal, and Damiano Sandri. 2010. "U.S. Consumption after the 2008 Crisis." Staff Position Note SPN/10/01. International Monetary Fund.

McKinnon, Ronald, and Gunther Schnabl. 2006. "China's Exchange Rate and International Adjustment in Wages, Prices, and Interest Rates: Japan Déjà Vu?" *CESifo Economic Studies* 52: 276–303.

Milesi-Ferretti, Gian M., and Assaf Razin. 1998. "Sharp Reductions in Current Account Deficits: An Empirical Analysis." *European Economic Review* 42: 897–908.

Modigliani, Franco, and Shi L. Cao. 2004. "The Chinese Saving Puzzle and the Life-Cycle Hypothesis." *Journal of Economic Literature* 42: 145–70.

Mody, Ashoka, and Franziska Ohnsorge. 2010. "After the Crisis: Lower Consumption Growth but Narrower Global Imbalances?" Working Paper 10/11. Washington: International Monetary Fund.

Obstfeld, Maurice, and Kenneth Rogoff. 2007. "The Unsustainable U.S. Current Account Position Revisited." In *G7 Current Account Imbalances,* edited by Richard H. Clarida, pp. 339–76.

White House, Office of Management and Budget. 2009. "Summary of Receipts, Outlays, and Surpluses or Deficits: 1930–2014," table 1.1. (www.whitehouse.gov/sites/default/files/omb/budget/fy2015/assets/hist01z1.xls).

Wooldridge, Jeffrey M. 2002. *Econometric Analysis of Cross Section and Panel Data.* Cambridge, Mass.: Massachusetts Institute of Technology Press.

World Bank. 2009. *World Development Indicators.* Washington.

3

The Effect of Exchange-Rate Changes on Transpacific Rebalancing

WILLEM THORBECKE AND GINALYN KOMOTO

The U.S. current account deficit as a share of GDP grew from 2 percent in 1997 to 4 percent in 2002 to 6 percent before the financial crisis that began in October 2008. The United States ran large trade deficits with East Asia, oil-producing countries, and the rest of the world. Since the crisis began, however, America's deficit with most regions has fallen while its deficit with the People's Republic of China (PRC) has remained intransigent.

Table 3-1 shows exports, imports, and the trade balance between the United States and the rest of the world before and after the Lehman Brothers shock in September 2008. Exports and imports both exhibited sharp drops beginning in October 2008. The sample is thus divided into the year before the crisis erupted (October 2007–September 2008), the first year after the Lehman shock (October 2008–September 2009), and forecasts for the second year after the Lehman shock (October 2009–September 2010). For non–East Asian countries, the deficit fell by 76 percent during the postcrisis period, equaling US$227 billion between October 2008 and September 2009. For the PRC, it fell by less than 12 percent and equaled $237 billion in the same period. The last three columns on the figure indicate that this pattern continued during the second year after the crisis. The U.S. trade deficit with the PRC since October 2008 roughly equals the US deficit with all non–East Asian countries combined.

The authors thank Muhamed Ariff, Barry Bosworth, Masahiro Kawai, Mario Lamberte, Jong-Wha Lee, Kui-Wai Li, Deunden Nikomborirak, Chalongphob Sussangkarn, Shujiro Urata, Yuqing Xing, and other participants at the Trans-Pacific Rebalancing Conference for their very helpful comments.

Table 3-1. *U.S. Exports, Imports, and Trade Balance before and after the Lehman Brothers Shock*[a]

Country or region	Year before Lehman Brothers shock			First year after Lehman Brothers shock			Second year after Lehman Brothers shock (forecast)		
	Exports to U.S.	Imports from U.S.	Bilateral trade balance with U.S.	Exports to U.S.	Imports from U.S.	Bilateral trade balance with U.S.	Exports to U.S.	Imports from U.S.	Bilateral trade balance with U.S.
East Asia									
People's Republic of China	337	71	266	300	63	237	317	87	230
Japan	146	66	80	99	52	47	109	56	53
Republic of Korea	49	37	12	40	27	13	39	34	6
Taipei,China	38	27	10	29	17	12	31	23	8
	99								
East Asia, total	569	201	368	468	160	308	496	200	297
Rest of the world (excluding East Asia)	1,581	1,097	484	1,126	899	227	1,198	953	245

Source: U.S. Census Bureau (2010).

a. The year before the Lehman Brothers shock is from October 2007 to September 2008. The first year after the Lehman Brothers shock is from October 2008 to September 2009. The second year after the Lehman Brothers shock is from October 2009 to September 2010. The forecast for the second year is derived by multiplying data for the five months for which data are available (that is, October 2009 to February 2010) by 2.4.

Figures 3-1 and 3-2 highlight the unusual nature of the PRC's exports to the United States. Figure 3-1 presents predicted and actual multilateral exports and imports for the thirty-one largest exporting countries in 2007, just before the crisis. The results were obtained from a gravity model described in appendix 3A. Figure 3-2 presents data from 2007 on predicted and actual exports from the PRC to the other thirty countries and predicted and actual imports to the United States from the other thirty countries. The figures indicate that PRC exports, U.S. imports, and especially PRC exports to the United States are clear outliers in the global economy.

Given the distinctness of these imbalances, we begin this chapter by examining the factors affecting PRC exports to the United States. The findings indicate that a 10 percent appreciation of the yuan would cause the PRC's exports to fall by 10 percent or maybe a little more. On the other hand, the results also indicate that a decrease in income in the United States would not cause a large drop in the PRC's exports. This evidence is supported by recent experience. During the 2008–2009 crisis, the yuan remained tightly pegged to the dollar. As table 3-1 shows, a once-in-a-generation crisis barely reduced the PRC's exports to the United States. If policymakers want to reduce imbalances between the PRC and the United States, a real appreciation of the yuan is thus probably necessary.[1]

We then present aggregate import and export elasticities for the United States and Asian countries that were estimated using a consistent methodology. Results from a dynamic ordinary least squares (DOLS) model indicate that trade elasticities for aggregate U.S. exports and imports are small. Thus exchange rate changes alone may not be sufficient to significantly reduce America's global trade deficit.

These estimates, though, are subject to the aggregation bias first discussed by Guy Orcutt (1950). They can also be distorted by the nature of Asian trade. For example, many of the imports into Asian countries are parts and components that are used to produce goods for reexport to the rest of the world. An exchange rate appreciation that reduces a country's exports can also reduce its demand for imported goods that are used to produce exports. This can cause the estimated exchange rate coefficient in import equations to be biased toward zero (see Kamada and Takagawa 2005).

We supplement the aggregate estimates of exchange-rate elasticities with a review of previously published results. The evidence indicates that a depreciation of the dollar alone may not be sufficient to substantially reduce America's global current account deficit; sophisticated exports produced within regional production networks depend on exchange rates throughout the region; labor-intensive

---

1. A real appreciation could be accomplished by either an appreciation of the nominal exchange rate or an increase in the price level.

Figure 3-1. *Predicted and Actual Exports and Imports, Thirty-One Largest Exporting Countries, 2007*

Exports

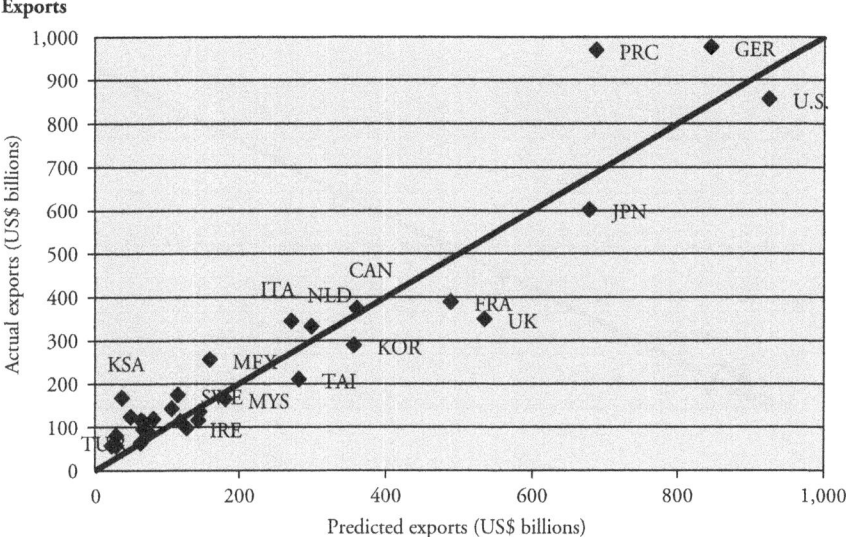

Imports

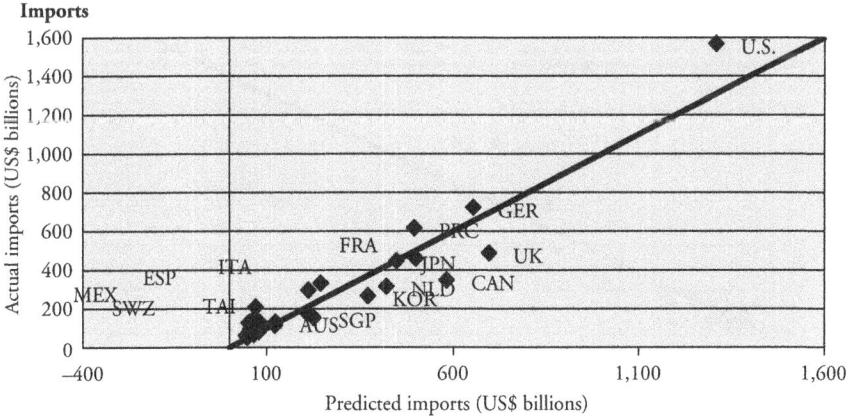

a. AUS = Australia; AUT = Austria; BRZ = Brazil; CAN = Canada; DNK = Denmark; ESP = Spain; FRA = France; FIN = Finland; GER = Germany; IDN = Indonesia; IND = India; IRL = Ireland; ITA = Italy; JPN = Japan; KOR = Republic of Korea; KSA = Kingdom of Saudi Arabia; MEX = Mexico; MYS = Malaysia; NLD = Netherlands; NOR = Norway; PHL = Philippines; POL = Poland; PRC = People's Republic of China; SGP = Singapore; SWE = Sweden; SWZ = Switzerland; TAI = Taipei,China; THA = Thailand; TUR = Turkey; UK = United Kingdom; US = United States.

Figure 3-2. *Predicted and Actual PRC Exports and U.S. Imports to and from Thirty-One Largest Exporting Countries, 2007*[a]

PRC exports

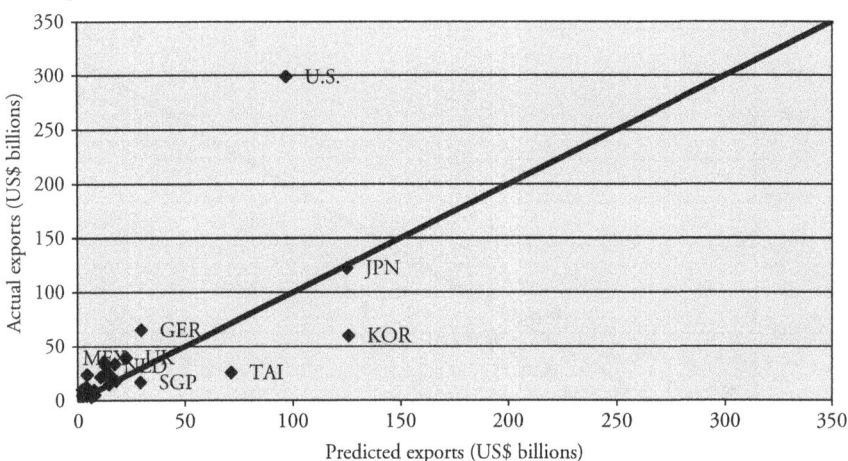

U.S. imports

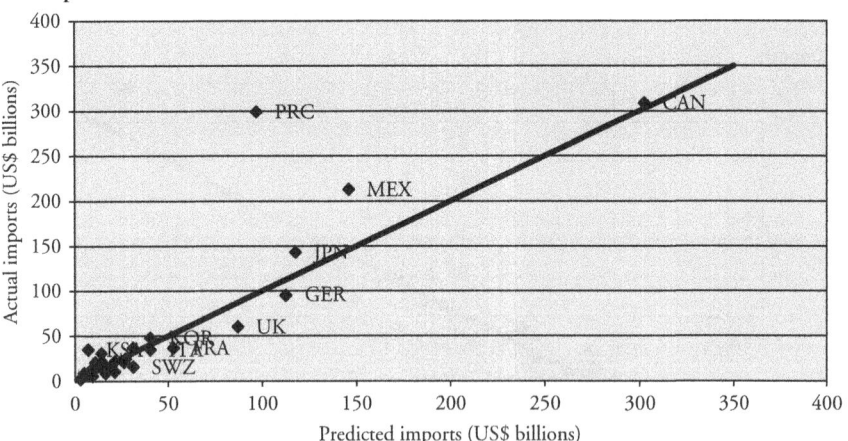

Source: Data from Centre d'Études Prospectives et d'Information Internationales Chelem database. Authors' calculations.

a. Predicted exports or imports represent the sum of predicted exports or predicted imports, respectively, from thirty-one countries based on a gravity model. The gravity model contains income in the exporting and importing countries, the real exchange rate, distance, a common language dummy, importer and exporter fixed effects, dummy variables for Mexico and Canada, and a time trend as explanatory variables. For identification of countries, see footnote to table 3-1.

exports from developing Asian countries are strongly influenced by each country's own exchange rate; developing Asian countries compete extensively with one another in exports to third markets; a currency appreciation in emerging Asia would increase capital and consumption goods imports; and exchange-rate volatility deters parts and components trade in Asia.

Two policy implications flow from these findings. First, if the U.S. current account deficit needs to be reduced in the future, absorption-reducing policies such as fiscal consolidation will probably be required. The expenditure-switching effect of a dollar depreciation may not be large enough to significantly reduce America's trade deficit. Second, a joint appreciation throughout East Asia would be beneficial for the region and the world. It would help maintain exchange-rate stability within the region, facilitating the flow of capital goods and parts and components among Asian countries. It would increase the purchasing power of consumers in the PRC and other countries. It also would help reduce Asia's overreliance on exports to the United States and Europe. Finally, it would help overcome prisoner's-dilemma problems that arise from the fear that losing competitiveness relative to Asian trading partners might prevent countries in the region from allowing their currencies to appreciate. One way for East Asian countries to appreciate together would be for the PRC to adopt a regime characterized by a multiple-currency, basket-based reference rate with a reasonably wide band. In this case, the huge surpluses generated within East Asian production networks would cause currencies in the region to appreciate together. Market forces could then allocate these appreciations across supply chain countries as a function of the size of their surpluses in processing trade.

New Evidence on the PRC's Exports to the United States

Table 3-1 shows that the PRC's exports to the United States exceed the PRC's imports from the United States by a five-to-one ratio. Figure 3-2 shows that the PRC's exports to the United States (but not U.S. exports to the PRC) represent a major outlier for both countries.

As Ryuhei Wakasugi (2009) has argued, there is a fundamental difference between exports from Japan to the United States and exports from the PRC to the United States. Exports from Japan tend to be high-end, knowledge-intensive goods. Exports from the PRC tend to be more labor-intensive, owing to the abundance of unskilled labor in the PRC. The Japanese Ministry of Economy, Trade, and Industry (METI 2009) similarly reports that Japan's exports to the United States are dominated by high-value-added consumer durables, whereas the PRC's exports are dominated by basic goods such as clothing. The Republic of Korea's and Taipei,China's exports to the United States are also dominated by high-value-added goods such as passenger cars, household appliances, semiconductors, and computers.

Figure 3-3. *Exports from Japan, Republic of Korea, and Taipei,China to the United States and U.S. GDP, 1990–2008*[a]

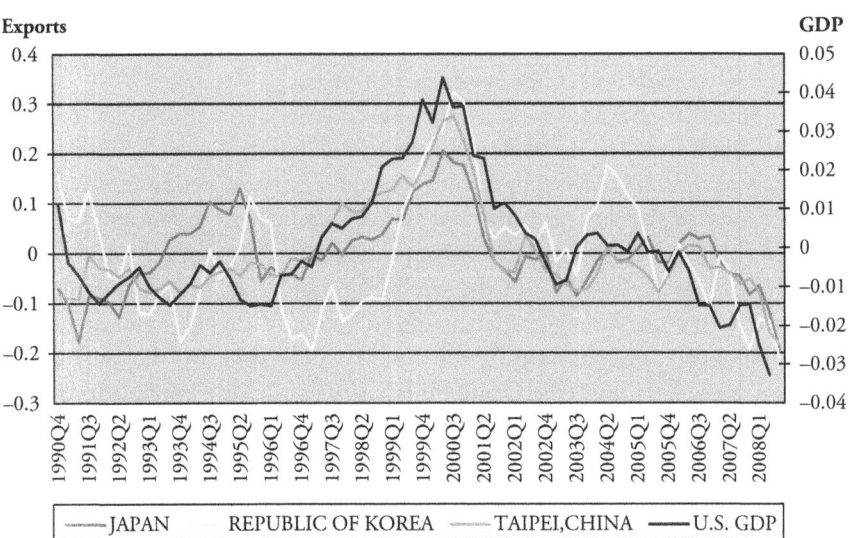

Source: Data from U.S. Census Bureau, Federal Reserve Bank of St. Louis, Federal Reserve Economic Data; calculations by the authors.

a. Exports detrended and deseasonalized; GDP detrended. For identification of countries, see footnote to table 3-1.

Wakasugi (2009) and METI (2009) note that since the PRC exports primarily basic goods to the United States and Japan and the newly industrialized economies export primarily high-end luxury products, the income elasticity of demand for exports from the PRC to the United States should be smaller than for exports from more advanced Asian economies to the United States. Peter Petri and Michael Plummer (2009, p. 705) similarly discuss how the product mix of PRC goods may lead to what they call the "Walmart effect." By this they mean that "if Chinese exports are at low price points within various product categories, they will benefit from a down-market shift in the composition of consumption even if demand for the category as a whole declines" (Petri and Plummer 2009, 705). In other words, the product composition and low price of the PRC's exports may sustain demand even when income in the United States falls.

Informal evidence from the data in figures 3-3 and 3-4 supports the hypothesis that the PRC's exports respond less to changes in U.S. income than exports from developed Asia do. Both figures show detrended quarterly output in the United States. Figure 3-3 also shows detrended, deseasonalized real exports from Japan, Korea, and Taipei,China to the United States, and figure 3-4 shows detrended, deseasonalized real exports from the PRC to the United States. The large increase

Figure 3-4. *Exports from the People's Republic of China to the United States and U.S. GDP, 1990–2008*[a]

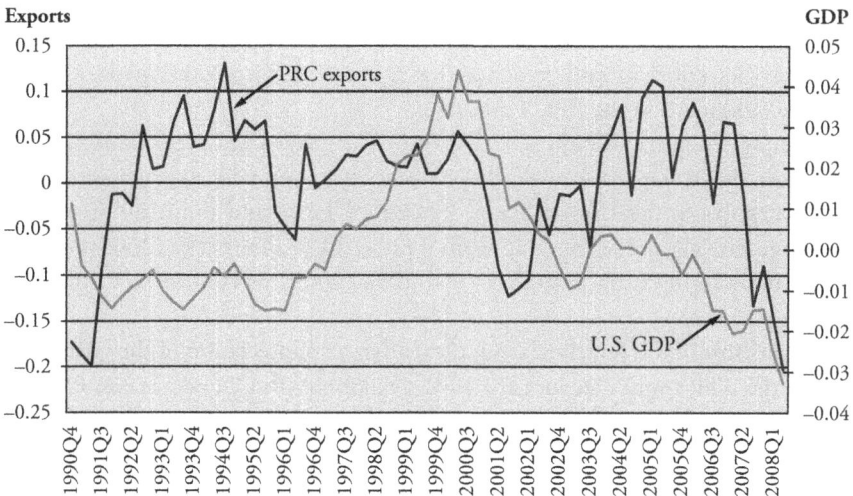

Source: U.S. Census Bureau, Federal Reserve Bank of St. Louis, Federal Reserve Economic Data; calculations by the authors.
a. Exports detrended and deseasonalized; GDP detrended.

in detrended output up until the second quarter of 2000 and its subsequent large fall are associated with the dot-com bubble in the United States and its bursting. Figure 3-3 shows that detrended, deseasonalized exports from developed Asia mirrored the pattern of U.S. output at this time. On the other hand, figure 3-4 shows a more tenuous relationship between U.S. income over this period and PRC exports to the United States.[2]

Several authors have presented formal evidence indicating that income elasticities are higher for exports from Japan, the Republic of Korea, and Taipei,China to the United States than for exports from the PRC to the United States. Willem Thorbecke (2008b), using a variety of cointegration estimators and quarterly data over the 1988–2005 period, reports that the income elasticity of demand for Japan's exports to the United States was approximately 3. Ae Cha Kim (2009), using a Johansen cointegration model and quarterly data over the 1981–98 period, reports that the income elasticity for Korea's exports to the United States was 3.5. Hui-Chuan Chen (2001), using ordinary least squares (OLS) techniques and quarterly data over the 1981–98 period, reports that income elasticity for

2. Figure 3-2 shows aggregate PRC exports. Some categories of PRC exports are more sensitive to income. Thorbecke and Smith (2010) report that sophisticated processed exports from the PRC to the rest of the world have higher income elasticity than less sophisticated ordinary exports.

Taipei,China's exports to the United States was 2.6. In contrast, both Yin-Wong Cheung, Menzie D. Chinn, and Eiji Fujii (2010), using DOLS methods and quarterly data over the 1993–2006 period, and Thorbecke (2006), using DOLS and Johansen maximum likelihood estimation and quarterly data over the 1988–2005 period, failed to find evidence that an increase in income in the United States would increase the PRC's exports.

Cheung, Chinn, and Fujii (2010), Thorbecke (2006), and Miaojie Yu (2009) all report that a depreciation of the yuan is associated with an increase in the PRC's exports to the United States. Cheung, Chinn, and Fujii (2010) report exchange-rate elasticities ranging from 0.80 to 2.03, Thorbecke (2006) reports elasticities ranging from 0.40 to 1.44, and Yu (2009) reports an exchange-rate elasticity of 1.23.

Results from DOLS estimation indicate that an appreciation of the yuan relative to the dollar would reduce the PRC's exports to the United States. On the other hand, the econometric results do not provide convincing evidence of a strong relationship between U.S. income and the PRC's aggregate exports.

Data and Methodology

The imperfect substitutes model of Morris Goldstein and Mohsin Khan (1985) implies that export functions can be written as $ex_t = \alpha_{10} + \alpha_{11}\,rer_t + \alpha_{12}\,rgdp_t^* + \varepsilon_t$, where ex_t represents the log of real exports, rer_t represents the log of the real exchange rate, and $rgdp^*$ represents the log of foreign real income.[3]

To deflate the PRC's exports to the United States, we used the U.S. Bureau of Labor Statistics' price deflator for manufactured imports from nonindustrial countries. Chinn (2006) finds that this series closely matches the Bureau of Labor Statistics' price deflator for imports from the PRC, which became available in 2003.[4]

The real exchange rate was calculated as the product of the yuan price of dollars and the ratio of the United States to the PRC price levels. An increase in the real exchange rate thus represents a depreciation of the yuan. In one specification, we followed Cheung, Chinn, and Fujii (2010) in using exchange rates before 1994 that are adjusted for the fact that some transactions took place at the official exchange rate and some took place at the "swap" rate.

Thorbecke (2006) argues that the PRC's exports to the United States compete with exports from emerging Asia. Alan Ahearne and others (2003) present evidence that economies in Asia follow a "flying geese" pattern, with the PRC and the Association of Southeast Asian Nations 4 (ASEAN4) moving into prod-

---

3. Monthly data on exports from the PRC to the United States are available from the U.S. Census Bureau. These data were summed to obtain quarterly values.

4. Data for quarterly real GDP for the United States were obtained from the Organization for Economic Cooperation and Development trade statistics. These data were seasonally adjusted.

uct categories relinquished by the Asian newly industrialized economies as they move up the value chain.[5] Similarly, Guillaume Gaulier, Françoise Lemoine, and Deniz Unal-Kesenci (2005) report, based on a detailed analysis of trade flow data, that there is essentially a complementary relationship between the PRC and the newly industrialized economies. On the other hand, they find that there is a competitive relationship between the PRC and ASEAN in the export of labor-intensive final goods to third countries. Thus, in empirical work, it is important to control for competition between exports from the PRC and exports from ASEAN.

A real exchange-rate index (I_t) between the United States and the ASEAN4 countries (Indonesia, Malaysia, Philippines, and Thailand) can be calculated using the following formula:

$$I_t = I_{t-1} \prod_{i=1}^{4} \left(r_{i,t} / r_{i,t-1} \right)^{w_{i,t}},$$

where $r_{i,t}$ is the real exchange rate between ASEAN country i and the United States in quarter t, and $w_{i,t}$ is the weight assigned to ASEAN country i in quarter t. $r_{i,t}$ equals the currency price of dollars times the ratio of the U.S. price level to the price level of country i. An increase in $r_{i,t}$ (and thus I_t) represents an appreciation of the dollar. $w_{i,t}$ is calculated as the ratio of exports from country i to the United States divided by exports from the ASEAN4 countries to the United States. The sum of the $w_{i,t}$ thus equals 1. I_t is set equal to 100 in the first quarter of 1985.

Following Cheung, Chinn, and Fujii (2010), we also included the capital stock to control for supply-side factors. For the PRC, Chong-En Bai, Chang-Tai Hsieh, and Yingyi Qian (2006) have constructed data on the capital stock. These data were converted to quarterly values using linear interpolation and updated over the last few years using data from the Economist Intelligence Unit database.

The model was estimated using DOLS, which involves regressing the left-side variable on a constant, the right-side variables, and lags and leads of the right-side variables. The equation has the form:

$$x_t = \beta_0 + \beta_1 rer_t + \beta_2 rgdp_t + \beta_3 K_t + \beta_4 eri_t + \beta_5 Time + \sum_{j=-p}^{p} \alpha_{rer,j} \Delta rer_{t-j}$$

$$+ \sum_{j=-p}^{p} \alpha_{rgdp,j} \Delta rgdp_{i,t-j} + \sum_{j=-p}^{p} \alpha_{K,j} \Delta K_{t-j} + \sum_{j=-p}^{p} \alpha_{eri,j} \Delta eri_{t-j} + u_t,$$

---

5. They define the newly industrialized economies as the Republic of Korea, Singapore, and Taipei,China and ASEAN4 as Indonesia, Malaysia, Philippines, and Thailand.

where x_t represents exports from the Asian country to the United States, rer_t represents the bilateral real exchange-rate index, $rgdp_t$ equals real income in the United States, K_t denotes the capital stock in the Asian country, eri represents the exchange-rate index for other Asian countries, and *Time* is a time trend. Seasonal dummy variables are also included. The values for x_t, rer_t, $rgdp_t$, K_t, and eri_t are measured in natural logs.

Data on the import price indexes are available beginning in 1990Q4, and data on the consumer price index are available until 2008Q4. We estimated equation 3-1 (below) using a DOLS (2, 2) model.[6] Because this involves using two leads and lags of the first differences of the right-side variables, the actual sample period for the estimation is 1990Q4–2008Q2.

Results

Tables 3-2 and 3-3 present the results. Table 3-2 contains the findings for the bilateral exchange rate adjusted for swap transactions, and table 3-3 contains the findings for the unadjusted bilateral exchange rate.

Willem Thorbecke and Gordon Smith (2010) argue that the preferred specification for the PRC should include the capital stock and exclude the time trend. In this specification the coefficient on the yuan exchange rate in tables 3-2 and 3-3 is statistically significant and equals about 1.5. These results imply that a 10 percent appreciation of the yuan would reduce the PRC's exports to the United States by about 15 percent. The coefficients on U.S. income and the PRC capital stock are positive, but in one case only the coefficient on U.S. income is statistically significant and in the other case only the coefficient on the capital stock is statistically significant. These conflicting results probably occur because both the PRC capital stock and U.S. income resemble deterministic trends. Finally, the coefficient on the ASEAN exchange-rate index is negative and significant. The results indicate that a 10 percent appreciation of ASEAN countries would increase the PRC's exports by 4 to 5 percent.

Across the sixteen different specifications in tables 3-2 and 3-3, the coefficient on the yuan exchange rate is positive in every case and statistically significant in fifteen of the sixteen cases. These results provide robust evidence that an appreciation of the yuan would reduce PRC exports to the United States. The average value across all of the specifications is approximately unity. For income and the PRC capital stock, the coefficient values are sensitive to the econometric specification.

The evidence of a tenuous relationship between aggregate PRC exports and U.S. income is supported by experience during 2008–09. The yuan remained tightly pegged to the dollar, and a once-in-a-generation crisis barely reduced the

---

6. A DOLS (2, 2) model employs two leads and two lags of the first differences of the right-side variables.

Table 3-2. *Adjusted Exchange Rate on the PRC's Exports to the United States, 1990–2008, DOLS Estimates*[a]

Independent variable	(1)	(2)	(3)	(4)	(5)	(6)	(7)	(8)
U.S. GDP	0.36	0.80	-0.16	-1.00	1.24*	6.00***	0.65	5.42***
	(0.85)	(0.96)	(0.76)	(0.79)	(0.73)	(0.12)	(0.48)	(0.07)
PRC-weighted RER relative to the dollar	0.95***	1.58***	0.50**	1.52***	0.66***	0.82***	0.52***	0.78***
	(0.33)	(0.14)	(0.23)	(0.13)	(0.11)	(0.14)	(0.09)	(0.15)
PRC capital stock	0.43	1.42***	-0.07	1.82***				
	(0.52)	(0.25)	(0.41)	(0.22)				
Indonesia, Malaysia, Philippines, Thailand RER indexes	-0.19	-0.39***			-0.13	-0.61***		
	(0.14)	(0.11)			(0.11)	(0.11)		
Time	0.03**		0.05***		0.04***		-0.04***	
	(0.01)		(0.01)		(0.00)		(0.00)	
Adjusted R^2	0.99	0.99	0.99	0.99	0.99	0.99	0.99	0.99
N	68	68	68	68	68	68	68	68

Source: Data from U.S. Bureau of the Census; U.S. Bureau of Labor Statistics; Organization for Economic Cooperation and Development; Bai, Hsieh, and Qian (2006). Authors' estimates.

a. DOLS (2, 2) estimates. Heteroskedasticity-consistent standard errors are in parentheses. DOLS = dynamic ordinary least squares; RER = real exchange rate.

***Significant at 1 percent level.

**Significant at 5 percent level.

*Significant at 10 percent level.

Table 3-3. Unadjusted Exchange Rate on the PRC's Exports to the United States, 1990–2008, DOLS Estimate[a]

Independent variable	(1)	(2)	(3)	(4)	(5)	(6)	(7)	(8)
U.S. GDP	0.76	2.48*	0.68	0.18	0.41	5.85***	−0.24	5.39***
	(0.82)	(1.45)	(0.61)	(1.36)	(0.71)	(0.11)	(0.36)	(0.08)
PRC RER relative to the dollar	0.52**	1.45***	0.20	1.20***	0.71***	0.78***	0.57***	0.55***
	(0.25)	(0.28)	(0.15)	(0.27)	(0.12)	(0.16)	(0.08)	(0.21)
PRC capital stock	−0.44	0.92	−0.68**	1.45***				
	(0.29)	(0.38)	(0.26)	(0.39)				
Indonesia, Malaysia, Philippines, Thailand RER indexes	−0.10	−0.48**			−0.08	−0.61***		
	(0.16)	(0.20)			(0.10)	(0.10)		
Time	0.05***		0.06***		0.04***		−0.04***	
	(0.01)		(0.01)		(0.00)		(0.00)	
Adjusted R^2	0.99	0.99	0.99	0.99	0.99	0.99	0.99	0.98
N	68	68	74	74	68	68	74	74

Source: Authors' estimates.

a. DOLS (2, 2) estimates. Heteroskedasticity-consistent standard errors are in parentheses. DOLS = dynamic ordinary least squares; RER = real exchange rate.

***Significant at the 1 percent level. **Significant at the 5 percent level. *Significant at the 10 percent level.

PRC's exports to the United States and its trade surplus. If policymakers want to reduce imbalances between the United States and the PRC, an appreciation of the yuan is probably necessary.

Estimating Elasticities of Exports and Imports for Transpacific Countries

This section presents estimates of aggregate trade elasticities estimated using a consistent methodology. Estimates are presented for the United States and for the PRC, Japan, Malaysia, Philippines, Thailand, and Taipei,China. For India and Indonesia, data were not available over a long enough time period to estimate the model using the same methodology.

Data and Methodology

Equation 3-1 presents export functions based on the imperfect substitutes model. Import functions based on the imperfect substitutes model can be written as

$$(3\text{-}1) \qquad im_t = \alpha_{10} + \alpha_{11}\,rer_t + \alpha_{12}rgdp_t + \varepsilon_t,$$

where im_t represents the log of real imports, rer_t represents the log of the real exchange rate, and $rgdp_t$ represents the log of domestic real income.

Quarterly data on aggregate exports and imports are available from the International Monetary Fund's *International Financial Statistics* (IFS). For most countries these data are measured in dollars and were deflated using the U.S. producer price index from the IFS. For Japan they are measured in yen and are deflated using Japanese export and import prices from the IFS. For the United States they are measured in dollars and are deflated using U.S. export and import prices from the IFS.

To calculate rest-of-the-world income for each exporting country we constructed a weighted index of income changes in the top ten export destinations. The index was calculated using the following formula:

$$rgdp_t^* = rgdp_{t-1}^* \prod_{i=1}^{10} \left(rgdp_{i,t} / rgdp_{i,t-1} \right)^{w_{i,t}},$$

where $rgdp_t^*$ is rest-of-the-world income for an exporting country, the subscript i indexes the ten largest export markets, $rgdp_i$ is income in country i, and w_i is the share of exports going to country i relative to exports going to the ten largest export markets. The weights were calculated using annual data from the CEPII-Chelem (Centre d'Études Prospectives et d'Information Internationales) database and converted to quarterly data using linear interpolation. The index was set equal to 100 in 1981Q1.

Data on real income and the real effective exchange rate were obtained from various sources. These are discussed in appendix 3B.

Export and import functions are estimated using DOLS:

$$(3\text{-}2) \quad x_t = \beta_0 + \beta_1 rer_t + \beta_2 rgdp_t^* + \sum_{j=-p}^{p} \alpha_{rer,j} \Delta rer_{t-j} + \sum_{j=-p}^{p} \alpha_{rgdp,j} \Delta rgdp_{i,t-j}^* + u_t,$$

$$im_t = \beta_0 + \beta_1 rer_t + \beta_2 rgdp_t + \sum_{j=-p}^{p} \alpha_{rer,j} \Delta rer_{t-j} + \sum_{j=-p}^{p} \alpha_{rgdp,j} \Delta rgdp_{i,t-j} + v_t,$$

where the variables are defined above.

For most countries we used data from 1981Q1 to 2008Q3. We estimated equation 3-2 using a DOLS (2, 2) model. Because this involves using two leads and lags of the first differences of the right-side variables, the actual sample period for the estimation is 1981Q4–2008Q1. In the case of the PRC, the Philippines, and Thailand, we could only obtain consistent data over the 1990Q1–2008Q3 period, and the actual sample period for the estimation is thus 1990Q4–2008Q1.

Results and Discussion

Table 3-4 presents the results. Income coefficients for every country are positive and statistically significant. These results indicate that for each country an increase in domestic income would increase imports and an increase in rest-of-the-world income would increase exports.

There is evidence of an asymmetry between the income elasticities for imports and exports. For the United States, the income elasticity of imports is greater than the income elasticity of exports. On the other hand, for all the East Asian countries except Japan, the income elasticity of imports is less than the income elasticity of exports.

The exchange rate elasticities take on unexpected signs in many cases for Asian countries but take on the expected signs and are statistically significant for the United States. For Asian countries, the exchange-rate estimates may be distorted because of the nature of East Asian production networks (see, for example, Kamada and Takagawa 2005). For the United States, the results indicate that a 10 percent appreciation of the dollar would reduce exports by about 4 percent and increase imports by about 3 percent.

There are a few problems with the aggregate estimates reported in table 3-4. One, already mentioned, is that these estimates can be distorted by the nature of the processing trade within Asia. For example, many of the imports into Asian countries are parts and components that are used to assemble goods for re-export to the rest of the world. An exchange rate appreciation in the assembly country that reduces exports will also reduce the demand for imported goods that are used to produce the exports. This can cause estimated exchange-rate coefficients

Table 3-4. *Transpacific Export and Import Elasticities, DOLS Estimates*[a]

Explanatory variable	United States		Japan		Republic of Korea		Taipei,China	
	Exports	Imports	Exports	Imports	Exports	Imports	Exports	Imports
Income of trade partners	1.76***	2.14***	1.11***	2.31***	1.94***	1.32***	1.75***	1.45***
	(0.02)	(0.01)	(0.01)	(0.06)	(0.04)	(0.02)	(0.07)	(0.03)
Real exchange rate	−0.35***	0.28***	−0.32***	−0.34***	−0.21*	1.08***	1.12***	0.92***
	(0.05)	(0.03)	(0.02)	(0.04)	(0.11)	(0.08)	(0.20)	(0.12)
Adjusted R^2	0.99	0.99	0.99	0.96	0.97	0.98	0.95	0.97
Period	1981Q4–2008Q1	1981Q4–2008Q1	1981Q4–2008Q1	1981Q4–2008Q1	1981Q4–2008Q1	1981Q4–2008Q1	1981Q4–2008Q1	1981Q4–2008Q1
N	106	106	106	106	106	106	106	106

Explanatory variable	PRC		Malaysia		Philippines		Thailand	
	Exports	Imports	Exports	Imports	Exports	Imports	Exports	Imports
Income of trade partners	5.51***	1.74***	2.20***	1.57***	2.64***	1.62***	1.98***	1.54***
	(0.14)	(0.04)	(0.08)	(0.07)	(0.17)	(0.14)	(0.03)	(0.08)
Real exchange rate	−1.20***	−1.09***	0.59***	0.45**	0.44**	1.11***	0.78***	0.52***
	(0.25)	(0.26)	(0.14)	(0.18)	(0.19)	(0.16)	(0.12)	(0.14)
Adjusted R^2	0.96	0.97	0.98	0.96	0.86	0.85	0.98	0.87
Period	1990Q4–2008Q1	1990Q4–2008Q1	1981Q4–2008Q1	1981Q4–2008Q1	1990Q4–2008Q1	1990Q4–2008Q1	1990Q4–2008Q1	1990Q4–2008Q1
N	73	70	106	106	70	70	70	70

Source: Data from International Monetary Fund; *International Financial Statistics*; Centre d'Études Prospectives et d'Information Internationales Chelem database; Abeysinghe and Gulasekaran (2004). Authors' estimates.

a. DOLS (2, 2) estimates. Heteroskedasticity-consistent standard errors are in parentheses. DOLS = dynamic ordinary least squares; RER = real exchange rate.

***Significant at the 1 percent level. **Significant at the 5 percent level. *Significant at the 10 percent level.

in import equations to be biased toward zero. A second problem, noted long ago by Orcutt (1950), is that estimates of aggregate trade elasticities may be biased if elasticities differ by sector. A third problem, emphasized by Peter Kenen (2007), is that it may be necessary to disaggregate trade flows by country or by group of countries to avoid biased results. A fourth problem is that employing the same specification for all countries does not take into account country-specific characteristics.

It is thus useful to review other evidence concerning how exchange-rate changes affect exports and imports. Chinn and others (2004, 2005a, 2005b), in a series of valuable studies using cointegration techniques, uncovered several stylized facts concerning U.S. trade elasticities:

—Exchange-rate elasticities for U.S. exports in real terms are precisely estimated and range from 0.68 to 0.84.

—Exchange-rate elasticities for U.S. imports in real terms are not statistically significant unless computers and oil are excluded. These amount to 15 percent of total imports. If they are excluded, price elasticities for the remaining 85 percent of imports are statistically significant but low. They range from 0.29 to 0.49.

—The sum of the export and import elasticities just barely exceeds one (1.15 if we use the midpoints), implying that the Marshall-Lerner condition for a depreciation to improve the trade balance in nominal terms is just barely met.

—The income elasticity of demand for U.S. exports is between 1.7 and 2.0.

—The income elasticity of demand for U.S. imports is 2.4.

—The Houthakker-Magee (1969) effect (that is, the finding that income elasticities for U.S. imports substantially exceed income elasticities for U.S. exports) is still present in the estimates. The difference in the income elasticities, however, appears to have fallen since Houthakker and Magee's original work in 1969.[7]

Chinn concludes, based on these estimates, that a depreciation of the dollar, if not accompanied by a decrease in expenditures in the United States or an increase in expenditures in the rest of the world, would be unlikely to substantially reduce the U.S. trade deficit.

For Asian countries it has been useful to disaggregate imports and exports by category. Some of the key import categories are parts and components, capital goods, and consumption goods. Some of the key export categories are labor-intensive manufacturing goods and technologically sophisticated goods.

Parts and components trade within East Asia has exploded along with the growth of regional production and distribution networks. The IMF (2005) notes that the flow of imports for processing is driven by the demand for final exports

---

7. Bosworth and Collins (2010), on the other hand, find that the Houthakker-Magee asymmetry has disappeared, with income elasticity of demand for U.S. exports of 2.7 and income elasticity of demand for U.S. imports of 2.4. They also found larger exchange-rate coefficients than those reported by Chinn (2005a, 2005b).

in the rest of the world. It estimated that the exchange-rate elasticity for imports for processing in Asian processor economies is small (about 0.1).

Although the level of the exchange rate may not matter much for parts and components trade within East Asian production networks, both theoretical and empirical evidence indicates that exchange-rate volatility matters a lot. Theoretically, this effect arises because the service-link cost for production blocks separated by national borders is an increasing function of risk and uncertainty, and exchange-rate volatility increases risk and uncertainty. Empirically, using panel DOLS techniques over the 1985–2005 period, Thorbecke (2008a) reports that a one standard deviation increase in the coefficient of variation of the exchange rate between two Asian countries would reduce electronic components imports on average by US$300 million a year. Similarly, estimating a gravity model over the 1992–2005 period, Kazunobu Hayakawa and Fukunari Kimura (2009) find that exchange-rate volatility as measured by the standard deviation of the rate of change of the exchange rate decreased parts and components trade in Asia more than tariff barriers did. Takatoshi Ito and others (2008), surveying Japanese multinational corporations, report that exchange-rate stability between Asian countries is essential for the uninterrupted flow of parts and components within regional production networks.

In capital goods trade, there is essentially a complementary relationship between firms in Japan, the Republic of Korea, and Taipei,China and firms in developing Asia. Sophisticated capital goods are produced in developed Asia and exported to developing Asia, and many of these goods are difficult to procure elsewhere. Thorbecke (2008b, 2009d), using a gravity model and annual data over the 1982–2003 period, finds that an appreciation in developed Asia relative to developing Asia would cause a large drop in capital goods trade. This would harm firms in developed Asia by reducing their exports and also harm firms in developing Asia by making it harder to purchase vital inputs that are difficult to procure elsewhere.

Consumption imports also have the potential to play an important role in Asia. In the PRC, for instance, the lion's share of imports represents inputs into the production process, and consumption imports accounted for only 8 percent of the total in 2007.[8] An increase in consumption goods exports would benefit PRC consumers. Thorbecke (2009a), using a panel DOLS model and annual data over the 1985–2006 period, reports that a 10 percent appreciation of the yuan would increase the PRC's consumption imports from the rest of the world by 13 percent.

Two key export categories within Asia are final electronics goods, such as consumer electronics goods and computer equipment, and labor-intensive

8. In the United States, by contrast, consumption goods imports were 25 percent of total imports in 2007. The source of these statistics is the CEPII-Chelem database.

manufactures, such as clothing, furniture, and footwear. Final electronics goods are produced largely within East Asian production and distribution networks. Japan, the Republic of Korea, and Taipei,China produce sophisticated technology-intensive intermediate goods and ship them to the PRC and ASEAN countries for assembly and re-export. Value added in the assembly countries is typically small.[9] Labor-intensive manufactures, on the other hand, are typically produced in developing Asia largely using domestic inputs.[10]

For final electronics goods, the evidence indicates that exchange rates in the countries producing parts and components are an important determinant of exports from developing Asia. For instance, Shaghil Ahmed (2009) and Thorbecke and Smith (2010) find that an appreciation in East Asian supply chain countries would cause a large drop in processed exports. Thorbecke (2009c) reports similar results for the East Asian computer industry.[11]

For labor-intensive manufacturing goods, Thorbecke (2009b) and Thorbecke and Hanjiang Zhang (2009) find that an appreciation in the developing Asian country exporting the goods would cause a large drop in exports. The results indicate that there is also substantial competition between different countries in Asia that export labor-intensive goods to third markets. Similar results, reported above, indicate that a depreciation in ASEAN countries would cause a large drop in the PRC's exports to the United States.

Conclusion

This chapter documents that PRC exports to the United States were a major outlier in the global economy before the financial crisis that began in October 2008 and that imbalances between the PRC and the United States have barely fallen since the crisis began. Evidence presented here indicates that an appreciation of the yuan relative to the dollar would be necessary to reduce these imbalances.

At the global level, however, a depreciation of the dollar may not rebalance America's trade. Multilateral trade elasticities reported here and also those reported by Chinn (2005a, 2005b) indicate that a depreciation of the dollar would not substantially reduce the aggregate U.S. trade deficit. Thus if the current account deficit remains a problem for the United States going forward, absorption-reducing policies such as fiscal consolidation would probably be required.

9. According to Koopman, Wang, and Wei (2008), PRC value added in these sectors is small relative to the costs of the intermediate goods imported from abroad. For instance, they reported that PRC value added in electronic computers was less than 5 percent in 2002 and that PRC value added in telecommunications equipment was less than 15 percent.

10. Koopman, Wang, and Wei (2008) reported that PRC value added in these industries is approximately 70 percent.

11. In recent years more of the assembly operations have migrated to the PRC. As more of the value added is produced in the PRC, an appreciation of the yuan should have a larger effect on processed exports.

Concerning how exchange rates affect Asian exports and imports, the evidence indicates the following:

—Sophisticated exports produced within regional production networks depend on exchange rates throughout the region.

—Labor-intensive exports from developing Asian countries are strongly influenced by each country's own exchange rate.

—Developing Asian countries compete extensively with one another other in exports to third markets.

—An appreciation in developing Asia would increase capital and consumption goods imports.

—Exchange-rate volatility deters parts and components trade in Asia.

These findings imply that Asia and the rest of the world would benefit if East Asian currencies could appreciate together against external currencies while maintaining relative currency stability within the region. Since ordinary exports tend to be simple, labor-intensive goods whereas processed exports are sophisticated, capital-intensive goods, a generalized appreciation in East Asia would generate more expenditure switching toward goods produced outside the region and contribute more to resolving global imbalances than an appreciation of the yuan or of other Asian currencies alone. In addition, exchange rate stability in Asia would facilitate the flow of parts and components and provide a stable backdrop for regional production and distribution networks. Furthermore, it would prevent unpleasant outcomes such as beggar-thy-neighbor policies that arise because Asian economies not only cooperate within production networks but also compete in third markets.

One way for Asian countries involved in the processing trade to appreciate together would be for the PRC to adopt a regime characterized by a multiple-currency, basket-based reference rate with a reasonably wide band. In this case, the huge surpluses generated within East Asian production networks would cause currencies in the region to appreciate together. Market forces could then allocate these appreciations across supply chain countries as a function of the size of their surpluses in the processing trade.

Concerted appreciations in East Asia would give firms in the region an incentive to redirect production away from export markets toward domestic markets. This would not only lead to a more sustainable long-term equilibrium by reducing Asia's dependence on Western consumers but would also allow workers in the region to enjoy more of the fruits of their own labor.

Appendix 3A: Gravity Model Used to Construct Figures 3-1 and 3-2

Predicted exports and imports in figures 3-1 and 3-2 were derived from a gravity model. Gravity models posit that bilateral trade between two countries is directly proportional to gross domestic product in the two countries and inversely proportional to the distance between them. In addition to GDP and distance, these models typically include other factors that affect bilateral trade such as whether trading partners share a common language.[1] Edward Leamer and James Levinsohn (1995, p. 1384) state that gravity models yield "some of the clearest and most robust findings in economics."

The baseline model has the form

$$lnEx_{ijt} = \beta_0 + \beta_1 lnY_{it} + \beta_2 lnY_{jt} + \beta_3 lnDIST_{ij} + \beta_4 Lang + \beta_5 lnRER_{ijt}$$
$$+ \beta_6 USCAN + \beta_6 USMEX + \beta_7 TIME + \partial_i + \Omega_j + \pi_t + \varepsilon_{ijt},$$

where Ex_{ijt} represents exports from country i to country j, t represents time, Y_{it} and Y_{jt} represent real GDP in countries i and j, $DIST_{ij}$ represents the geodesic distance between countries i and j, $LANG_{ij}$ is a dummy variable equaling 1 if countries i and j share a common language and 0 otherwise, RER_{ijt} is the bilateral real exchange rate between country i and country j, $USCAN$ and $USMEX$ are dummy variables equaling 1 for trade between the United States and Canada or between the United States and Mexico and zero otherwise, and ∂_i and Ω_j are country i and country j fixed effects. The gravity model was estimated as a panel using annual data for thirty-one countries over the 1988–2007 sample period. The model performs well. All of the variables are of the theoretically expected sign and are highly statistically significant.[2]

Appendix 3B: Data Sources

The data were obtained from various sources:

Gravity Model for Thirty-One Leading Countries in 2007

Trade data for the thirty-one countries were obtained from the CEPII-Chelem (Centre d'Études Prospectives et d'Information Internationales) database (www.cepii.fr).

Real exchange rates also came from the CEPII-Chelem database.

Data on the consumer price index came from the International Monetary Fund's *International Financial Statistics* (IFS).

Data on real GDP, geodesic distance, and common language were obtained from the CEPII website.

---

1. Data sources are presented in appendix 3B.
2. Detailed results are available on request.

PRC's Exports to the United States

Data on exports of the People's Republic of China (PRC) and the Association of Southeast Asian Nations (ASEAN) to the United States were obtained from the U.S. Census Bureau.

Quarterly data on import price indexes from 1990Q4 to 2008Q4 were obtained from the U.S. Bureau of Labor Statistics. U.S. producer price index and U.S. consumer price index were obtained from the CEIC database.

Data on quarterly real GDP for the United States were obtained from the Organization for Economic Cooperation and Development trade statistics.

Data on nominal exchange rates and the consumer price index were obtained from the IFS.

Capital stock data were obtained from the University of Pennsylvania Center for International Comparison, Economist Intelligence Unit, and Cheung, Chinn, and Fujii (2010).

Export and Import Elasticities for Asian Countries and the United States

Quarterly export and import data were obtained from the IFS.

Data on nominal exchange rates, the consumer price index, the producer price index, import prices, and export prices were obtained from the IFS.

Quarterly GDP data for the PRC, Indonesia, Malaysia, the Philippines, and Thailand were obtained from Abeysinghe and Gulasekaran (2004);[3] quarterly GDP data for Australia, Belgium, Canada, France, Germany, Italy, Japan, the Republic of Korea, Mexico, Netherlands, the United Kingdom, and the United States were obtained from the Organization for Economic Cooperation and Development; and quarterly GDP data for India were obtained from the CEIC database.

Real effective exchange rates were obtained from different sources: for India, Indonesia, the Republic of Korea, and Taipei,China, data came from the Bank for International Settlements; for the PRC, Japan, Malaysia, the Philippines, and the United States, data came from the IFS; and for Thailand, data came from the Central Bank of Thailand.

Data on the top ten export destinations for countries in the sample were obtained from the CEPII-Chelem database.

---

3. Updated data are available from the National University of Singapore (http://courses.nus.edu.sg/course/ecstabey/gdpdata.xls). Following the authors' recommendation, these data were seasonally adjusted before being included in the model and were extended for the last couple of years using real GDP growth rates available from the Economist Intelligence Unit country data.

References

Abeysinghe, Tilak, and Rajaguru Gulasekaran. 2004. "Quarterly Real GDP Estimates for China and ASEAN4 with a Forecast Evaluation." *Journal of Forecasting* 23, no. 6: 431–47.

Ahearne, Alan G., and others. 2003. "China and Emerging Asia: Comrades or Competitors?" Federal Reserve Board International Finance Discussion Paper 789. Chicago: Federal Reserve Bank of Chicago.

Ahmed, Shaghil. 2009. "Are Chinese Exports Sensitive to Changes in the Exchange Rate?" International Finance Discussion Paper 987. Washington: Board of Governors of the Federal Reserve System.

Bai, Chong-En, Chang-Tai Hsieh, and Yingyi Qian. 2006. "Returns to Capital in China." *Brookings Papers on Economic Activity* 2: 61–88.

Bosworth, Barry, and Susan Collins. 2010. "Rebalancing the U.S. Economy in a Post-Crisis World." Paper presented at the Trans-Pacific Rebalancing Conference, Asian Development Bank Institute, Tokyo, March 3–4.

Chen, Hui-Chuan. 2001. *Applied Economics* 33, no. 10: 1283–87.

Cheung, Yin-Wong, Menzie D. Chinn, and Eiji Fujii. 2010. "China's Current Account and Exchange Rate." In *China's Growing Role in World Trade,* edited by Robert C. Feenstra, and Shang-Jin Wei, pp. 231–71. University of Chicago Press.

Chinn, Menzie. 2004. "Incomes, Exchange Rates, and the U.S. Trade Deficit, Once Again." *International Finance* 7, no. 3: 451–69.

———. 2005a. "Doomed to Deficits? Aggregate U.S. Trade Flows Re-examined." *Review of World Economics* [Weltwirtschaftliches Archiv] 141, no. 3: 460–85.

———. 2005b. "Still Doomed to Deficits: An Update on U.S. Trade Elasticities." Working Paper. University of Wisconsin–Madison.

———. 2006. "Estimating U.S.-China Trade Elasticities: Some Very Preliminary Results." *Econbrowser,* November 2 (http://econbrowser.com/archives/2006/11/estimating_usch).

Goldstein, Morris, and Mohsin Khan. 1985. "Income and Price Effects in Foreign Trade." In *Handbook of International Economics,* vol. 2, edited by Ronald W. Jones and Peter B. Kenen, pp. 1041–105. Amsterdam: North-Holland.

Government of Japan, Ministry of Economy, Trade, and Industry (METI). 2009. "White Paper on International Economy and Trade." Tokyo.

Hayakawa, Kazunobu, and Fukunari Kimura. 2009. "The Effect of Exchange Rate Volatility on International Trade in East Asia." *Journal of the Japanese and International Economies* 23, no. 4: 395–406.

Houthakker, Hendrik S., and Stephen P. Magee. 1969. "Income and Price Elasticities in World Trade." *Review of Economics and Statistics* 51, no. 2: 111–25.

International Monetary Fund (IMF). 2005. *Asia-Pacific Economic Outlook.* Washington.

Ito, Takatoshi, and others. 2008. "Currency Invoicing and Foreign Exchange Risk Management: A Case Study of Japanese Firms." Discussion Paper 08-J-009. Tokyo: Research Institute of Economy, Trade, and Industry.

Kamada, Koichiro, and Izumi Takagawa. 2005. "Policy Coordination in East Asia and across the Pacific." Working Paper 05-E-4. Tokyo: Bank of Japan.

Kenen, Peter. 2007. Comment on "Understanding the U.S. Trade Deficit: A Disaggregated Perspective." In *G7 Current Account Imbalances: Sustainability and Adjustment,* edited by Richard H. Clarida, pp. 279–83. University of Chicago Press.

Kim, Ae Cha. 2009. "An Empirical Analysis of Korea's Trade Imbalances with the U.S. and Japan." *Journal of the Asia Pacific Economy* 14, no. 3: 211–26.

Koopman, Robert, Zhi Wang, and Shang-Jin Wei. 2008. "How Much of Chinese Exports Is Really Made in China? Assessing Domestic Value-Added When Processing Trade Is Pervasive." Working Paper 14109. Cambridge, Mass.: National Bureau of Economic Research.

Orcutt, Guy H. 1950. "Measurement of Price Elasticities in International Trade." *Review of Economics and Statistics* 32, no. 2: 117–32.

Petri, Peter A., and Michael G. Plummer. 2009. "The Triad in Crisis: What We Learned and How It Will Change Global Cooperation." *Journal of Asian Economics* 20, no. 6: 700–13.

Thorbecke, Willem. 2006. "How Would an Appreciation of the Renminbi Affect the U.S. Trade Deficit with China?" *B.E. Journal of Macroeconomics* 6, no. 3: 1–15.

———. 2008a. "The Effect of Exchange Rate Volatility on Fragmentation in East Asia: Evidence from the Electronics Industry." *Journal of the Japanese and International Economies* 22, no. 4: 535–44.

———. 2008b. "Global Imbalances, Triangular Trading Patterns, and the Yen/Dollar Exchange Rate." *Journal of the Japanese and International Economies* 22, no. 4: 503–17.

———. 2009a. "Can East Asia Be an Engine of Growth for the World Economy?" Discussion Paper 09-E-006. Tokyo: Research Institute of Economy, Trade, and Industry.

———. 2009b. "An Empirical Analysis of ASEAN's Labor-Intensive Exports." Working Paper 166. Tokyo: Asian Development Bank Institute.

———. 2009c. "An Empirical Analysis of East Asian Computer Exports." Working Paper 160. Tokyo: Asian Development Bank Institute.

———. 2009d. "Trade Interdependence and Exchange Rate Coordination in Asia." In *Exchange Rate, Monetary and Financial Issues and Policies in Asia,* edited by Ramkishen S. Rajan, pp. 205–28. Singapore: World Scientific.

Thorbecke, Willem, and Gordon Smith. 2010. "How Would an Appreciation of the RMB and Other East Asian Currencies Affect China's Exports?" *Review of International Economics* 18, no. 1: 95–108.

Thorbecke, Willem, and Hanjiang Zhang. 2009. "The Effect of Exchange Rate Changes on China's Labor-Intensive Exports." *Pacific Economic Review* 14, no. 3: 398–409.

U.S. Bureau of the Census. 2010. "U.S. Trade in Goods, by Country" (www.census.gov/).

Wakasugi, Ryuhei. 2009. "Why Was Japan's Trade Hit So Much Harder?" In *The Great Trade Collapse: Causes, Consequences and Prospects,* edited by Richard Baldwin, chap. 27. London: VoxEU.

Yu, Miaojie. 2009. "Revaluation of the Chinese Yuan and Triad Trade: A Gravity Assessment." *Journal of Asian Economics* 20, no. 6: 655–68.

4

Rebalancing the U.S. Economy in a Postcrisis World

BARRY P. BOSWORTH AND SUSAN M. COLLINS

The United States has had a substantial current account deficit since the mid-1990s. For most of that period, the deficit increased steadily, reaching a peak of $800 billion, or 6.7 percent of national income, in 2006. There has been widespread agreement that deficits of that magnitude cannot be sustained. Before the financial crisis the deficit was associated with a pervasive fear that the economy might be heading toward a hard landing, with an abrupt collapse of the dollar and severe economic disruptions both domestically and globally.

For a brief period, it appeared that a relatively benign adjustment might be under way. A real depreciation of the U.S. dollar improved the competitiveness of American products, and the current account deficit gradually began to recede during 2007 and the first three quarters of 2008. The improvement would have been even more marked were it not for the sharp increase in the price of petroleum imports. Export volumes grew by 20 percent between the second quarter of 2006 and the second quarter of 2008, while import volumes were flat. The U.S. seemed to have begun a soft landing. There was, however, little evidence of adjustment on the domestic side. The national saving rate continued to fall, owing largely to sharply higher federal budget deficits. It was falling rates of investment, not increases in saving, that freed up domestic resources.

This chapter was revised in 2011, and some tables were updated in 2013. Rosanna Smart and Joshua Montes assisted with the research. Daniil Manaenkov provided the simulations of the Research Seminar in Quantitative Economics model of the University of Michigan. Financial support was provided by the Tokyo Club Foundation for Global Studies.

All of this changed in the fall of 2008 with the onset of a global financial crisis centered on the United States. Amid a severe contraction of domestic demand and employment, concerns about the composition of aggregate demand largely vanished in the wake of extreme countercyclical policies aimed at stabilizing the economy. The external economy experienced an even larger collapse as global trade declined 25 percent below trend in the first half of 2009. U.S. exports fell 19 percent below levels of a year earlier, with imports falling an even larger 28 percent. In 2009 the U.S. current account deficit was only 3.1 percent of national income—less than half its value in the peak year of 2006. Perversely, the U.S. real exchange rate also soared at the onset of the crisis, temporarily reversing about half of the prior decline from its peak as investors sought a safe haven in U.S. Treasury securities. By the end of 2009, the dollar had reversed about half of the prior rise, and the real exchange rate had returned to its average of the early 1990s.

What will be the future of external rebalancing, and should it still be a major policy concern? Officially, the recession has ended, but most forecasts for the United States suggest a weak recovery with high levels of unemployment continuing for several years. Furthermore, distortions in the domestic saving and investment balance are far worse than before the crisis: the fiscal deficit has pushed the national saving rate highly negative, and the rate of net investment is a third that of the precrisis years. In the financial crises of other countries, recovery was largely driven by improvements in the trade balance (export-led growth). However, such a scenario may be difficult in a global recession in which most countries will see increased exports as a solution to their problems. Will the recovery of trade flows leave the United States with an imbalance comparable to that of the precrisis years?

The objective of this paper is to explore how the U.S. economy and its external balance might progress in future years. In the following section, we review the evolution of the external imbalance over the past quarter century—both from the domestic perspective of the saving and investment balance and from the external side as reflected in the U.S. current account imbalance and international investment position. The bulk of the paper then focuses on future challenges to external rebalancing from both the domestic and external perspectives. We first examine the causes of low saving in the United States and how it might evolve in the future. Second, we highlight the challenges faced by the public sector owing to population aging and continued rapid growth of health care costs. On the external side, we summarize recent research on the determinants of trade flows and other elements of the current account. We focus particularly on the sensitivity of trade to variations in the real exchange rate and on concerns related to U.S. export performance. Finally, we pull these strands together to consider the risks to a resumption of the soft landing that the crisis has arrested.

Retrospect

Much of the debate and confusion surrounding the sources and consequences of the U.S. imbalance in its economic relations with the rest of the world result from the different perspectives from which the external imbalance can be analyzed. For example, the current account is defined as the difference between the income earned on exports and other transactions with the rest of the world and the payments to foreigners for imports and other services.[1] The dominant roles of exports and imports lead to a natural focus on the determinants of trade with other countries, such as exchange rates and the relative openness of markets. This focus also often leads to claims of unfair trade practices. From a domestic perspective, however, the current account is the difference between a nation's total income and its total expenditures: thus, a current account deficit is the counterpart to a nation's spending more than it earns, living beyond its means, and thereby borrowing from the rest of the world. The two perspectives are largely different sides of the same phenomenon, varying perhaps in the initiating source of any change. It is useful to review the imbalance from both of these perspectives, recognizing the interactions and the importance of both sets of factors. Moreover, the issues are inherently global because of a third requirement that national imbalances must be offset on a global basis, so that the deficits of some countries are matched by surpluses of others.

External Balance

Figure 4-1 shows the evolution of the U.S. external balance over the past quarter century. The balance of net resource flows as measured by the current account is shown in the top panel, and the cumulative net international investment (stock) position of the United States is shown in the lower panel. As the top panel makes clear, there have been two episodes of large current account deficits: the mid-1980s and the current episode, which emerged in the aftermath of the Asian financial crisis and has resulted in much larger and longer-lasting deficits. The top panel also shows the recent beginning of a correction in 2006–08 before the economic crisis precipitated a collapse in international trade that dramatically shrank the imbalance. The result of a quarter century of current account deficits is the buildup of a highly negative international investment position that plummeted from a net creditor position of 15 percent of national income in 1980 to a net indebtedness of 19 percent at the end of 2010.

It is noteworthy, however, that the balance sheet has not deteriorated as much as would be expected on the basis of the large current account imbalances of the

---

1. The current account is the sum of three main kinds of external transactions: trade in goods and services, net factor income receipts, and net transfer receipts. Most discussions of external economic relations focus on trade flows because they are the largest component.

Figure 4-1. *Stock and Flow Measures of the External Balance, as Share of National Income, United States, 1980–2012*

Percent of national income

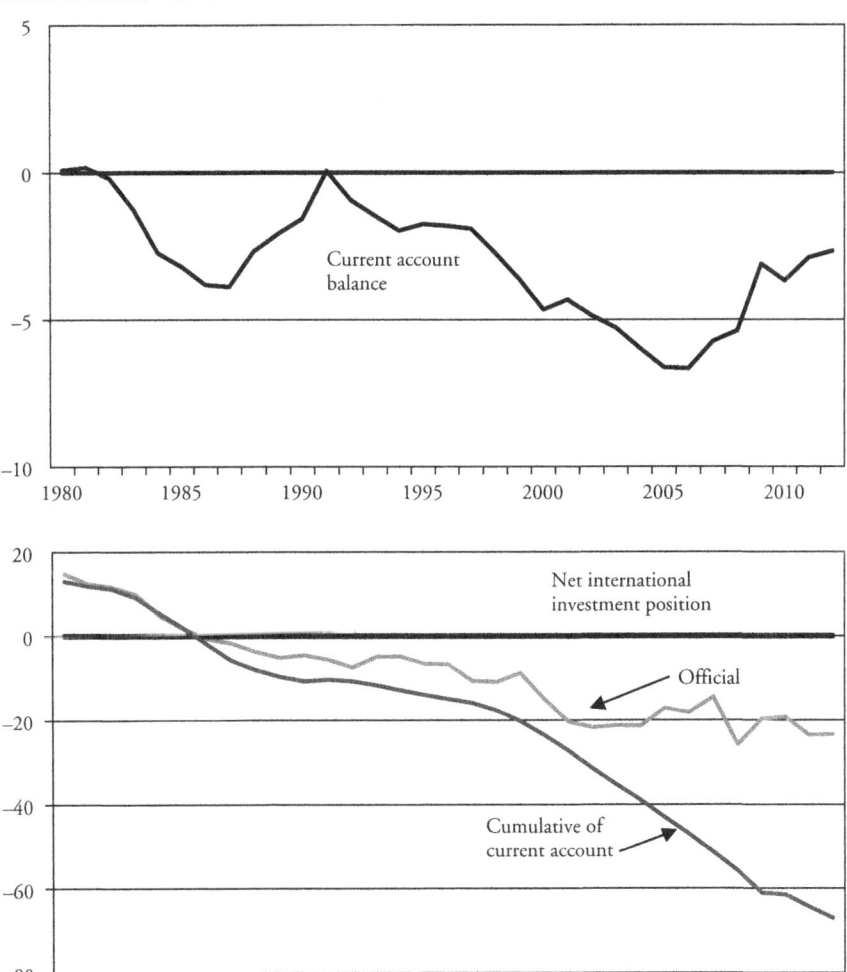

past decade. This is shown in the lower panel of figure 4-1 by cumulating the current account deficits since 1980 and expressing the result as a share of national income. This indicator suggests that the U.S. debt position would have been expected to exceed 60 percent of national income by 2010. The large difference between the two measures reflects the greater valuation gains on U.S. investments abroad relative to those on foreign investments in the United States.[2] Although capital gains and losses are excluded in the official balance of payments accounts, they are included in the balance sheet measures. A larger portion of U.S. foreign assets is invested in equity investments with a greater capital gain component. For example, foreign governments are large holders of U.S. Treasury securities without the potential for capital gain, whereas the foreign holdings of the U.S. government are trivial.

The U.S. imbalances are placed in a broader global context in table 1-1 (chap. 1), which provides a simple summary of the distribution of current account balances across major regions of the world for the period 1980 to 2010. Absent errors and omissions, the sum of current accounts across all economies should equal zero, with the deficits of some countries offset by surpluses of others.[3] The table highlights the sharp dichotomy between the external position of the United States and everyone else. The United States consistently reports large deficits, which are matched by surpluses in most other regions of the globe. Europe's surplus has declined, however, since the mid-1990s; and Japan's surplus has remained basically unchanged for nearly a quarter of a century. Similarly, little has changed in Latin America. Instead, offsets to the increased U.S. deficit are concentrated in the emerging economies of Asia and the oil-producing states of the Middle East. Given the rise of oil prices, the surge of saving within the oil-producing regions is no surprise, but the emergence of a large excess of saving over investment in Asia was less expected. Finally, a large change in the statistical discrepancy over the past decade compounds the difficulty of relating the U.S. deficit to surpluses in other specific regions.

Trade in goods and services constitutes the largest component of the current account. Its balance is driven by rates of growth in foreign incomes (Y_f)

---

2. For example, half of U.S. investments abroad are allocated to direct investment and corporate equities, compared with only a quarter of foreign investments in the United States. The role of capital gains is highlighted in Gourinchas and Rey (2007), updated in their later paper with Govillot (Gourinchas, Rey, and Govillot 2010). In a previous paper, we also argue that some of the discrepancy can be traced to the shifting of reported income by multinational companies to avoid U.S. taxation (Bosworth, Collins, and Reich 2007).

3. Before the 1970s, current account imbalances were strictly limited, as most national financial markets operated as closed systems. With the emergence of large-scale cross-border capital flows, countries have become capable of financing increasingly large imbalances on a sustained basis.

Figure 4-2. *Alternative Measures of the Real Exchange Rate, United States, 1975–2012*

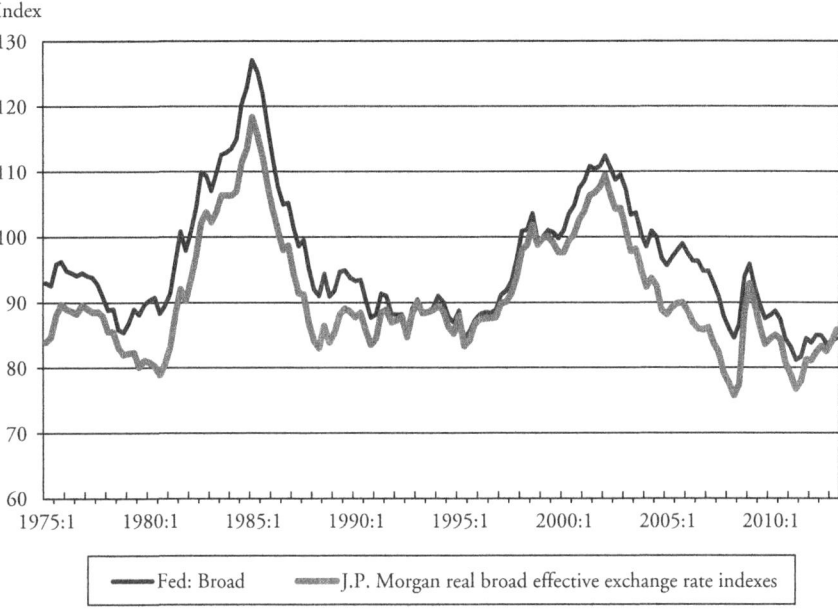

and domestic incomes (Y_d) and the relative price of domestic- versus foreign-produced goods (q):

$$NX = f\left(Y_f, Y_d, q\right).$$

The concept of the real exchange rate provides a simple measure of relative prices, defined as the nominal exchange rate (e) multiplied by the ratio of foreign and domestic prices (P_d/P_f):[4]

$$q = e \times \left(P_d / P_f\right).$$

Two alternative measures of the U.S. real exchange rate are shown in figure 4-2. Each is a weighted average of bilateral exchange rates with major trading partners, where weights are based on bilateral trade flows and a dollar appreciation

4. We measure the exchange rate as the foreign price of domestic currency so that an appreciation of the currency is recorded as an increase in the exchange-rate index.

is shown as a rise in the index.[5] The Federal Reserve measure uses consumer price indexes to adjust for differential rates of inflation, while J. P. Morgan publishes an index based on producer price indexes for manufacturing goods excluding food and fuels. The long-term movements in the two indexes are very similar, but the J. P. Morgan index indicates a slightly larger depreciation before the 2008 crisis and a sharper initial rise. Both indexes suggest that an adjustment was under way well before the crisis.

The real exchange rate also shows a strong negative correlation with the current account balance reported in figure 4-1, indicating that currency appreciation is associated with current account deterioration. However, the exchange rate only affects trade flows with a substantial lag because it takes time for exporters and importers to adjust to their competitive positions. A simple way to summarize the relationship is provided in figure 4-3, which graphs the nonoil trade balance against a three-year weighted average of the exchange rate.[6] While trade is affected by other factors, it seems evident that, after accounting for lags, the exchange rate plays a fundamental role. There is also evidence that the relationship has been shifting down over time. We explore these issues more fully later in this chapter.

The deteriorating U.S. international investment position generated frequent hard-landing forecasts based on the view that foreign investors would ultimately become unwilling to accumulate steadily rising shares of U.S. assets in their portfolios. Many of those scenarios envisioned a "sudden stop" of capital inflows to the United States, leading to an uncontrolled fall in the value of the dollar and sharply higher U.S. interest rates.[7] Paradoxically, the crisis that emerged in 2008 triggered a surplus of capital inflows, as investors fled to the safety of U.S. Treasury securities, rather than any shortage, and the dollar surged in value with the onset of the crisis. Some of these observers now perceive the crisis to have been the result of an excessive willingness of foreigners to allocate funds to the United States, which in turn contributed to a series of speculative bubbles in U.S. asset markets.

Internal Balance

For most of the past three decades, a growing trade deficit was associated with a buoyant domestic economy, rapid job growth, and a decline of unemployment to unprecedented levels. This domestic strength suggests that the trade deficit

5. Market shares of U.S. goods in foreign markets and foreign goods in U.S. and third-country markets are used to construct the currency weights. The weights are updated on an annual basis in the Federal Reserve Bank index, whereas those of J. P. Morgan change about once a decade. An advantage of the J. P. Morgan index is that comparable measures are provided for all of the major trading economies.

6. The nonoil trade balance is measured as a percentage of GDP, and the exchange rate is a weighted average of the Federal Reserve Board index with weights of .25, .5, and .25 on the rates lagged one, two, and three years. The figure is based on an earlier presentation in Baily and Lawrence (2006).

7. Obstfeld and Rogoff (2007); Bergsten (2009).

Figure 4-3. *Nonoil Trade Balance and Real Exchange Rate as Share of GDP, United States, 1980–2009*

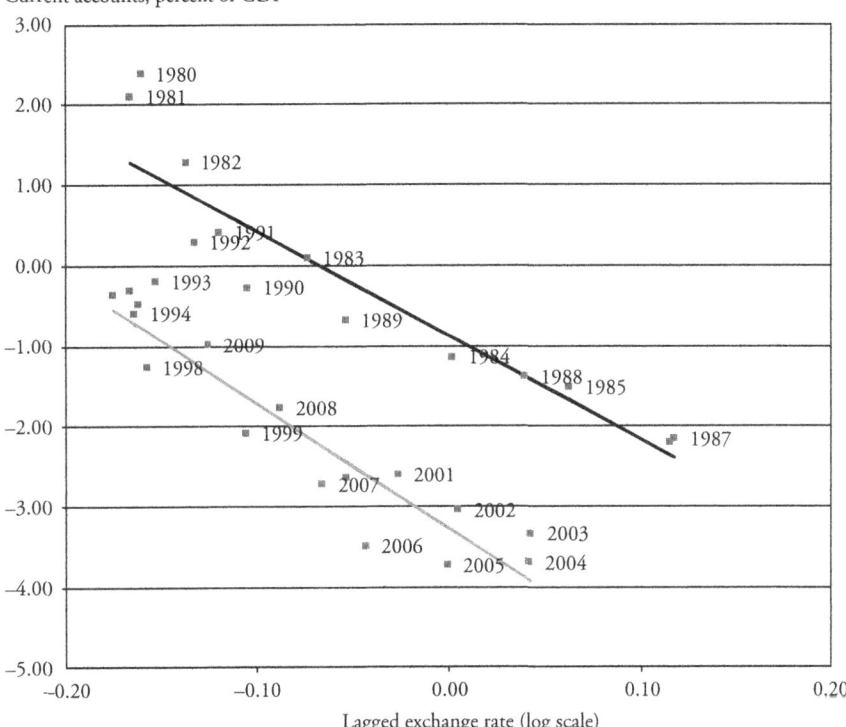

Current accounts, percent of GDP

Source: Data from U.S. Bureau of Economic Analysis and Board of Governors of the Federal Reserve. Authors' calculations.

was not something forced on the U.S. economy by outside pressures but rather was a response to changing domestic economic conditions that pushed aggregate demand beyond the nation's productive capacity.[8] The excess demand was satisfied in a noninflationary way by exporting less and importing more. This was reflected in turn by an increase in foreign financial investments in the United States, which came from a rise of saving relative to investment in other countries, a large growth of supply capacity in countries that export to the United States, and a stable or rising value of the dollar.

The changing composition of U.S. aggregate demand, shown in table 4-1, highlights the growing emphasis on private consumption as the secular counterpart

8. If the deficit had been the result of foreign production being unfairly dumped into the U.S. economy, we would expect ongoing problems of excess unemployment and job shortages, something that was not evident before the financial crisis.

Table 4-1. *Composition of Aggregate Demand, United States, 1980–2012*
Percent

Category	1980–84	1985–89	1990–94	1995–99	2000–07	2008	2009	2010	2011	2012
Consumption	80.4	82.2	83.1	82.0	85.0	86.9	88.1	87.7	85.2	84.3
Private	63.4	65.2	66.7	67.3	69.6	70.2	70.8	70.5	69.0	68.6
Government	17.0	16.9	16.4	14.7	15.4	16.7	17.3	17.2	16.3	15.7
Investment	20.7	20.3	17.8	19.6	19.7	18.1	14.7	15.8	18.4	19.0
Private	17.2	16.6	14.3	16.5	16.6	14.6	11.1	12.4	14.4	15.2
Government	3.5	3.8	3.4	3.1	3.2	3.5	3.6	3.5	4.1	3.8
Net exports	-1.1	-2.5	-0.9	-1.7	-4.7	-5.0	-2.8	-3.6	-3.7	-3.4
Total	100.0	100.0	100.0	100.0	100.0	100.0	100.0	100.0	100.0	100.0

Source: Data from U.S. Department of Commerce, Bureau of Economic Analysis, National Income and Product Accounts, 1980–2012. Authors' calculations.

to the growing trade deficit. Between 1980–84 and 2000–06, the share of GDP devoted to consumption rose by 5 percentage points, investment declined by 0.5 percent, and the net trade deficit increased to 4.5 percent of GDP. Furthermore, the two episodes of marked reduction in the trade deficit—the late 1980s and the current period—are both notable for sharp cyclical reductions in domestic investment, not a scaling back of consumption.

A domestic perspective also emphasizes the relationship between the nation's current account and its balance of domestic saving and investment. This follows directly from the basic national accounts identity that total domestic output (GDP) equals the sum of public and private consumption expenditures (C), investment (I), and exports (X), minus imports (M):

$$GDP = C + I + X - M,$$

which can be rewritten as

$$X - M = GDP - C - I$$
$$= S - I.$$

That is to say, the trade balance is equal to saving minus investment.

The situation is slightly more complex in practice because the residents of a country can earn income from overseas activity as well as from domestic production. Thus the national accounts distinguish between GDP and gross national income (GNI), where GNI includes net earnings from abroad. In addition, net transfers are added to both sides of the identity. The result is a small redefinition of national saving:

$$CA = (GNI - C) + NTR - I$$

or

$$CA = S - I.$$

Thus the current account (external) imbalance is precisely matched by an (internal) imbalance between national saving and investment.[9]

A summary of the U.S. saving and investment balance is shown in table 4-2 for the period 1960–2012. For several decades before the mid-1980s, variations in net national saving were largely driven by changes in government saving, as the private

9. It is also worth noting that the U.S. national accounts are structured to measure income, saving, and investment net of the depreciation of physical capital. The emphasis on net measures of saving and investment is common among advanced economies, but many developing economies do not undertake detailed estimates of capital depreciation and instead present estimates of saving and investment on a gross basis. This is an important distinction in the international comparisons.

Table 4-2. *Net Saving and Investment as Share of National Income, by Sector, United States, 1960–2012*[a]
Percent

Sector	1960–79	1980–89	1990–99	2000–07	2008	2009	2010	2011	2012
Saving	10.9	6.5	5.4	3.7	0.4	-2.2	-0.4	0.1	0.8
Private	10.9	10.0	6.9	5.4	5.9	8.4	9.7	9.3	9.0
Household	7.0	7.2	4.6	2.4	4.7	4.5	4.6	4.2	4.2
Corporate	3.9	2.9	2.3	3.0	1.2	3.9	5.1	5.1	4.9
Government	0.0	-3.6	-2.4	-1.7	-5.4	-10.7	-10.1	-9.2	-8.2
Domestic investment	11.1	9.4	7.9	8.4	5.8	1.5	3.3	2.6	3.3
Private	9.0	7.8	6.7	7.1	4.3	0.0	2.0	1.6	2.6
Government	2.1	1.6	1.2	1.3	1.5	1.5	1.3	1.0	0.8
Net foreign investment	0.4	-1.8	-1.7	-5.4	-5.3	-3.1	-3.7	-2.9	-2.6
Statistical discrepancy	0.7	1.1	0.8	-0.7	0.0	0.6	0.0	-0.3	-0.1
Capital consumption	11.8	14.1	13.3	13.7	14.7	15.4	14.6	15.5	15.4

Source: Data from U.S. Department of Commerce, Bureau of Economic Analysis, National Income and Product Accounts, 1960–2012.

a. Net saving excludes capital consumption allowances.

saving rate was stable and largely free of trend. The simultaneous emergence of a large federal budget deficit and a current account deficit in the early 1980s gave rise to a discussion of twin deficits, in which the two were viewed as tightly linked through the financial pressures of financing a large budget deficit, leading to higher U.S. interest rates, exchange-rate appreciation, and a trade deficit. However, the reemergence of large current account deficits in the late 1990s, despite a rapidly improving fiscal situation, suggested that the notion of a special link between government budget deficits and the external balance was an overly simplistic interpretation. Instead, the gap between national saving and investment in later years can be traced to a large drop in the private saving rate—owing to sharply lower rates of household saving—and to strong investment demand. The boom in information technology during the 1990s made the United States a particularly attractive location for business investment, and a strong expansion of residential investment also contributed to the growing domestic imbalance. The magnitude of the decline in household saving remains something of a puzzle, despite extensive research; some of the possible reasons are discussed more fully below.

The economic crisis has brought on another major realignment, with household saving showing a modest increase while investment demand has collapsed. The household saving rate began to rise in early 2008, before the financial collapse. In the early quarters of 2009, it rose to over 5 percent of national income and then leveled out, remaining in the 4–5 percent range. The most dramatic change has been a surge in corporate saving—a phenomenon not limited to the United States. Moreover, government budget deficits have reemerged during the current decade as a significant contributor to the low national saving rate, and extraordinary fiscal actions in 2008–10 turned the national saving rate negative.

Why Don't Americans Save?

Correcting the U.S. external imbalance will now require increasing both private and government saving, but in the years preceding the financial crisis, it was the fall in private saving that was particularly dramatic. Although private saving consists of the saving of households plus corporate retained earnings, the entire secular decline was within the household sector. The household (personal) saving rate fell from an average of 7 percent of national income in the early 1980s to approximately 2 percent in the middle of the past decade.

The drop in household saving has been particularly puzzling because the movement of the baby-boom generation into the ages of peak retirement saving was expected to cause a rise in the total saving rate. A second surprise has been surging wealth-to-income ratios in the face of the declining rates of saving. In other words, if Americans save so little, why are they so rich? In consequence, focus has shifted away from demographic explanations for saving behavior to emphasize the role of wealth in influencing consumption decisions.

The conventional measure of saving excludes all forms of capital gains; yet many economists have argued that wealth changes are a far better measure of changes in economic well-being than rates of saving alone.[10] Indeed, at the individual level there is much to be said for focusing on wealth accumulation rather than saving. By enabling greater future consumption, wealth is an important element of economic well-being, and it matters little how the individual accumulated it. Thus at the level of individual households, economists often focus on wealth as the best indicator of preparedness for retirement.

At the aggregate level, however, the issues are more complex. The measure of saving is part of a system of national accounts aimed at reporting the level of current production and its allocation among alternative uses and recipients. Those flow accounts are embedded in a more complete framework of wealth accumulation that makes a sharp distinction between saving and valuation changes. That is, the change in wealth is equal to saving plus the revaluation of existing wealth:

$$W_t = W_{t-1} + \left(\Delta P_t \middle/ P_{t-1} \right) * W_{t-1} + S,$$

where W_t is equal to wealth at time t and $\Delta P_t / P_{t-1}$ is the average revaluation of the wealth components resulting from asset price changes. There are, however, limited advantages to introducing valuation changes directly into the national accounts. The inclusion of valuation changes would reduce the usefulness of the accounts in measuring changes in production; and though most economists would agree that wealth and income are both important determinants of consumption, few would go so far as to argue that the marginal propensity to spend out of wealth is anywhere near that for changes in income.[11] It seems preferable to maintain the existing framework but to recognize wealth and its changes as major determinants of saving.

From this perspective, the strong capital gains in corporate equities and home ownership over the past two decades may have played an important role in stimulating consumption. Figure 4-4 shows the pattern of change in the household wealth-to-income ratio since 1980, separating the contribution of saving to wealth accumulation from that of valuation changes. Before the mid-1990s, valuation changes were a minor source of wealth gain, as most asset prices simply rose in line with the overall rate of price inflation, and household wealth varied within a narrow range of 4–5 times disposable income. More recently, increases

10. Some of the most-cited references are Auerbach (1985), Hendershott and Peek (1989), Bradford (1991), Eisner (1991), Gale and Sabelhaus (1999), and Peach and Steindel (2000).

11. In addition, not all wealth changes will have the same aggregate effect. For example, increases in home values are seen as a gain to current homeowners, but in the aggregate they largely reflect an intergenerational transfer as younger families pay higher prices to older homeowners to purchase the same flow of housing services.

Figure 4-4. *Household Wealth and Disposable Income, United States, 1960–2010*[a]

Ratio of wealth to income

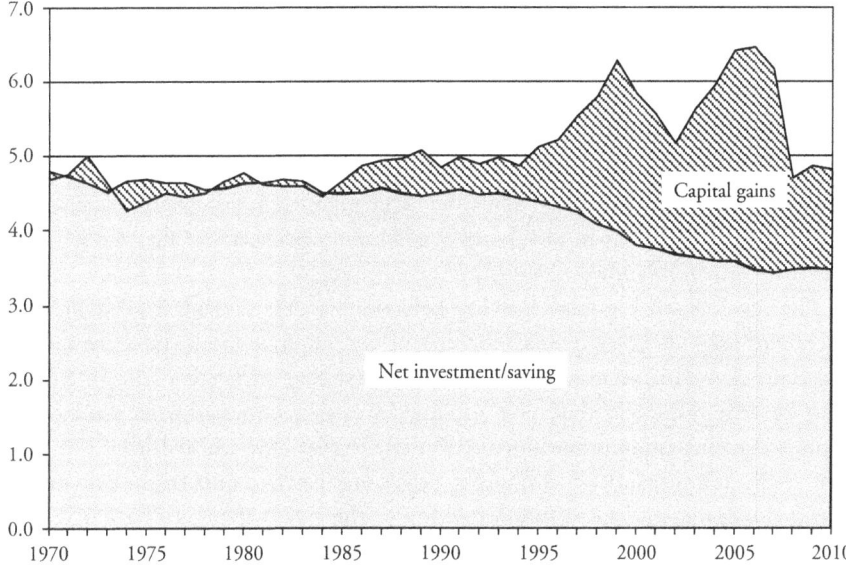

Source: Data from Flow of Funds Accounts, tables B100 and R100.
a. Net investment (tangible and financial) flows are converted to real values with the personal consumption deflator, cumulated, and converted back to nominal values. The measure of investment/ saving is taken from the flow of funds and includes consumer durables.

in the relative prices of housing and equities raised the wealth-to-income ratio to six in 1999 and 2004–07. In contrast, the contribution of saving began to decline in the 1990s; and by 2007, the wealth-to-income ratio exclusive of capital gains had fallen to 3.5 compared with a pre-1995 average of 4.5. Thus it is evident that reduced saving has slowed the rate of wealth accumulation, with valuation changes playing a much larger offsetting role.

In typical empirical formulations of the life-cycle model of consumption, researchers estimate that the long-run effect of a change in wealth on consumption is about 0.05.[12] That magnitude suggests that an increase in the wealth-to-income ratio from 4.75 in the 1980s to about 6 in 2000–07 contributed to a rise in the share of consumption in disposable income of 5–7 percentage points—a large proportion of the observed decline in the saving rate since the early 1980s. There is wide variation in the empirical estimates, however, and some studies maintain that the effects differ among the various categories of wealth, such as

12. Poterba (2000) provides a review of previous articles. More recent macroeconomic studies are those by Case, Quigley, and Shiller (2005) and Belsky and Prakken (2004).

equities and housing.[13] It is even more difficult to distinguish a causal relationship because consumption and asset valuations are influenced by many common factors. Finally, it is notable that a significant portion of the decline in saving preceded the surge in wealth valuations that began in the mid-1990s.

A variety of other factors have also been put forth to explain the collapse of saving. For example, some researchers would redefine saving to include consumer durables, make adjustments to offset the effects of inflation, or propose differing treatments of retirement accounts. However, as emphasized by Marshall Reinsdorf (2007), none of the adjustments change the fundamental conclusion of a large secular decline in the saving rate. More important, the alternatives provide little reason to anticipate a future turnaround.

The research on household saving behavior has left us with a great deal of uncertainty about future trends. The link in the life-cycle model between saving and desired wealth accumulation would suggest that saving will rise in future years because the forces that have sustained wealth accumulation in the face of depressed saving cannot continue indefinitely. As we have learned from the current crisis, neither equity nor housing prices are likely to outrun the growth of nominal incomes and substitute for saving to the extent that they have over the past two decades. The magnitude of the asset losses during the financial crisis should accelerate the process by which a slower rate of wealth accumulation leads to a rise in the saving rate.

However, other explanations that emphasize demographic factors, the growth of the public pension system as a substitute for private retirement saving, and behavioral factors would point to a more permanent shift toward a lower household saving rate. We conclude that any reversal of the private saving rate is likely to be modest in the near future and that a full recovery of national saving to its historical norm near 10 percent of national income will require a substantial change in the fiscal condition of the public sector.

Public Sector Fiscal Balance

As mentioned earlier, there is no longer much support for the twin-deficits notion of a direct one-for-one link between budget deficits and the current account. Government saving and investment, however, are still important components of the overall accounting identity linking national saving, investment, and the current account; rejection of the twin-deficits view does not imply that variations

13. The effect of variations in housing wealth on consumption is particularly controversial. Buiter (2008) and Sinai and Souleles (2005) have argued that home ownership is largely a hedge against future rent costs; and to the extent that the home value is equal to the present value of future consumption of housing services, fluctuations in home prices should imply no net aggregate wealth gain.

in the fiscal balance have no implications for the current account. Yet because the components are all endogenous with common determinants, it is difficult to measure the effect of an exogenous shift in the fiscal balance with any degree of precision.[14]

Slightly less than half of government spending (45 percent) is undertaken by state and local governments, and about 20 percent of their revenues are in the form of federal transfers. They are constrained to maintain relatively balanced budgets by constitutional requirements and fears of the migration of individuals and businesses to other tax jurisdictions. In the aggregate, the fiscal deficits of state and local governments have averaged less than 0.5 percent of national income, although their combined deficit was slightly above 1 percent in 2009–10. Thus nearly all discussions of U.S. fiscal policy focus on the federal government budget.

Some researchers have interpreted the finding of a limited link between fiscal and external balances to imply that deficit reduction cannot play a substantial role in reducing the external imbalance. Perhaps that was true a few years ago, when the projected fiscal deficit was a relatively modest percentage of GDP. However, as shown in figure 4-5, the financial crisis and the measures taken to reverse it have dramatically altered the fiscal outlook for the United States. The federal deficit was 10 percent of GDP in FY2009 and only slightly less in FY2010. Those deficits were sufficient to turn the net national saving rate negative for 2009 and 2010. As shown in the figure, they also represent an enormous shift in the budget outlook compared with the projections that accompanied the FY2008 budget. The baseline projections of the Congressional Budget Office (CBO) beyond FY2010 assume that all of the stimulus measures are allowed to expire and that the Bush administration tax reductions are reversed. They are a best-case scenario; yet the projected deficits still remain above 3 percent of GDP in future years. Even with the CBO baseline assumption, public debt will rise to 70 percent of GDP in 2011—double the level expected in the 2008 budget—and slowly rise thereafter.

Going forward, the United States faces a growing budget conflict as current policies call for an increase in government spending in excess of the growth in GDP, while there is strong political opposition to any tax increases. The basic challenge is illustrated in figure 4-6, which shows actual and projected levels of expenditures and taxes as shares of GDP. In prior decades, expenditures were a slowly falling share of GDP, as declining defense spending offset steadily rising outlays on medical and income transfers to the elderly. That pattern has been

---

14. Some recent empirical efforts to measure the net relationship between the two components suggest that 30–40 percent of a change in the fiscal balance will be reflected in the current account (Bartolini and Lahiri 2006). The remainder is absorbed by offsetting changes in the private saving–investment balance.

Figure 4-5. *Federal Budget Balance and the Public Debt as Share of GDP,*
1970–2020

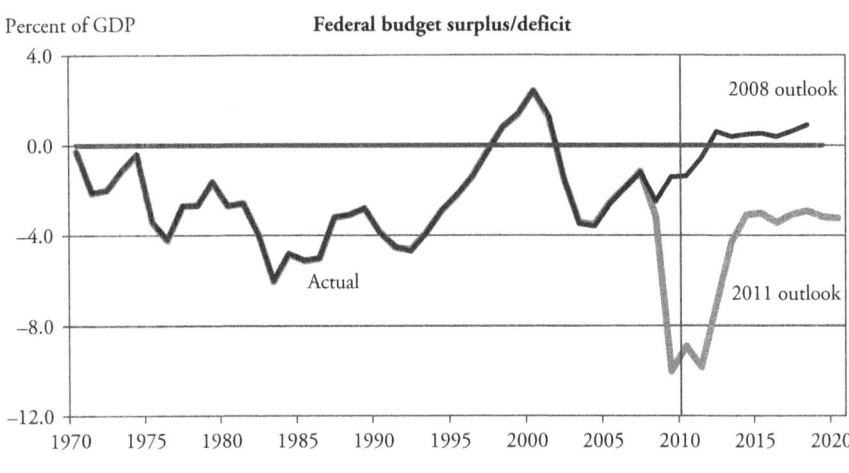

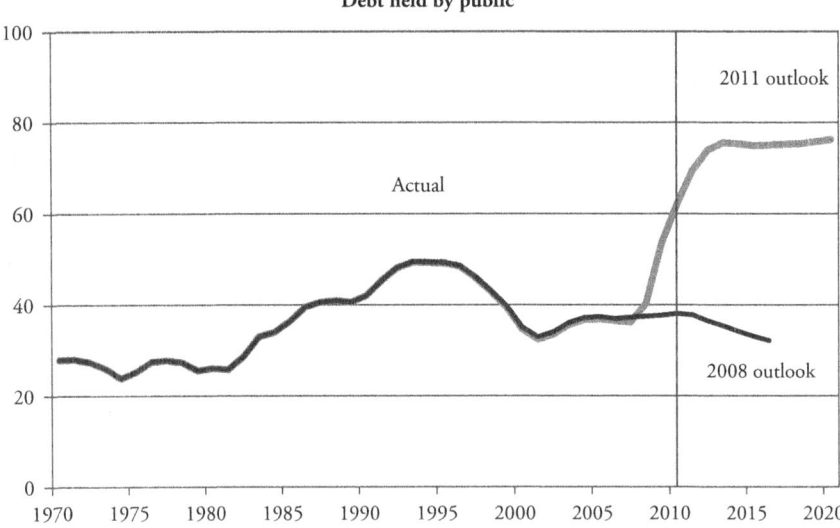

interrupted by the rising cost of wars in the Middle East and larger transfer payments to the unemployed. In future years, the total will rise further owing to
increased costs for a retiring baby-boom generation and to interest on the public
debt. Meanwhile, government revenues are well below their historical share of
GDP owing to temporary tax reductions that were enacted in 2000 and extended
as part of the 2009 fiscal stimulus.

Two alternative policy baselines are illustrated in figure 4-6. The first is the
standard CBO current-law baseline that assumes tax policy evolves in line with

Figure 4-6. *Federal Revenue and Expenditures as Share of GDP, 1970–2020*

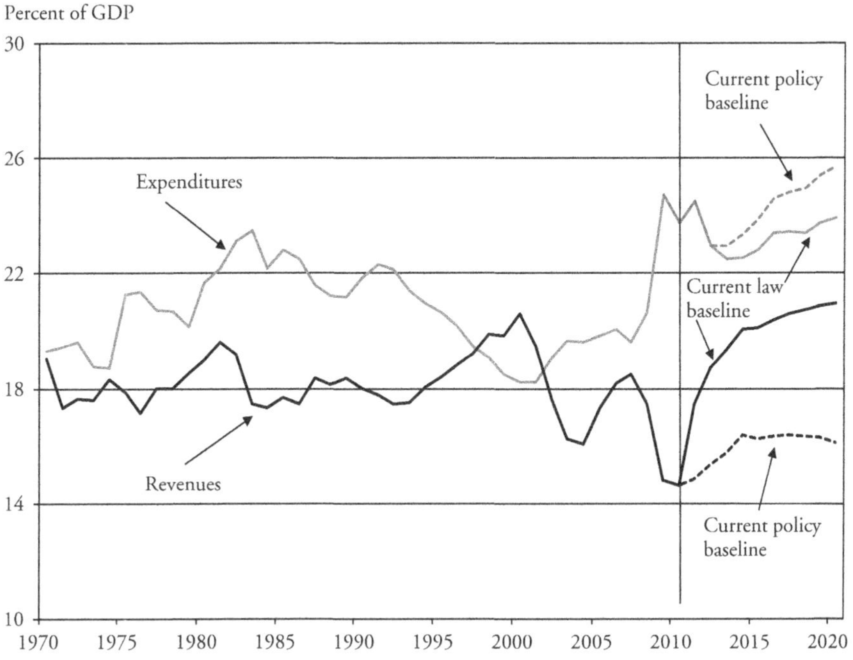

Percent of GDP

Source: Congressional Budget Office (2010).

existing legislation—that is, expiration of all of the temporary tax reductions. In addition, future increases in discretionary expenditures are limited to adjustments for price inflation. The alternative is a current-policy baseline that assumes continuation of the Bush-era tax cuts, inflation adjustments for the alternative minimum tax, and increases in discretionary spending in line with the growth of GDP.

If Congress and the administration simply adhered to the current law baseline budget of the CBO, much of the work of moving toward fiscal balance would be done and the deficit would be cut from 9 percent in fiscal year 2010 to less than 3 percent in 2015 and thereafter. That is, much of the fiscal problem could be resolved if the president and Congress agreed to do nothing. In that sense, a solution to the deficit does not require a grand bargain. However, neither the administration nor Congress is willing to advocate such a policy, particularly expiration of the tax cuts. The alternative of continuing present policies implies a budget deficit that remains in the range of 7–8 percent of GDP. Expenditures are well beyond their historical norm under both alternatives and would rise toward 26 percent of GDP if current policies continue. If the temporary tax cuts are allowed to expire, the effective tax rate would also be above its prior peak. On the other hand, continuation of the tax cuts would leave the effective tax rate at 17 percent, well below its historical average. Thus the range of options on the tax side is particularly wide. Under the current-law baseline, the public debt would stabilize at 75–80 percent of GDP; continuation of current policy would result in the debt-to-GDP ratio exceeding 100 by the end of the decade.

Why Is the U.S. Trade Deficit So Persistent?

We have already documented the persistently large U.S. external deficits over the past quarter century and in particular over the period from the early 1990s through the middle of the past decade, in which the deficit increased steadily to over 6 percent of GDP. We have also argued that a gradual tapering of this deficit began in 2006, associated with a substantial real depreciation of the U.S. dollar (and expenditure switching) but with little evidence of the internal rebalancing (expenditure reductions) also required for a sustainable transition to lower imbalances. Although the onset of the economic crisis, with its sharp dollar appreciation, arrested the fledgling "soft landing," the collapse in world trade cut the U.S. trade deficit in half in 2009 and 2010.

Figure 4-7 shows the evolution of exports and (total as well as nonoil) imports as a percentage of GDP since 1980. Although the United States did become somewhat more open during this quarter century, it is notable that most of this increase was associated with import growth in the second half of the period. In 2005 exports were about the same share of output as they had been in 1980. The figure also shows the two episodes of large imbalances. In the mid-1980s, the trade deficit was primarily a result of deterioration in exports generated by the expansive fiscal policy of the Reagan years, high interest rates, and a sharp appreciation of the U.S. exchange rate. In the more prolonged second episode, the issues have been steadily rising imports combined with weak export performance. The figure also shows the faster growth in exports over imports narrowing the deficit in 2006–07, as well as the sharp drop in exports and even more pronounced fall in imports in 2009. Exports recovered in 2010, but the import share remained well below its prior peak. It is evident that increased oil imports continue to constitute a major portion of the trade deficit.

Determinants of the U.S. External Balance

A large empirical literature studies the determinants of U.S. imports and exports, typically estimating the sensitivity of exports and imports to changes in (lagged) relative prices and incomes. During the past decade, there has been a focus on examining what it would take to achieve a sustained reversal of the U.S. current account deficits. However, there has been considerable variation in time period, specification, and measurement of key variables, resulting in a wide range of estimates.

Figure 4-7. *Exports and Imports as Share of GDP, United States, 1980–2012*

Percent of GDP

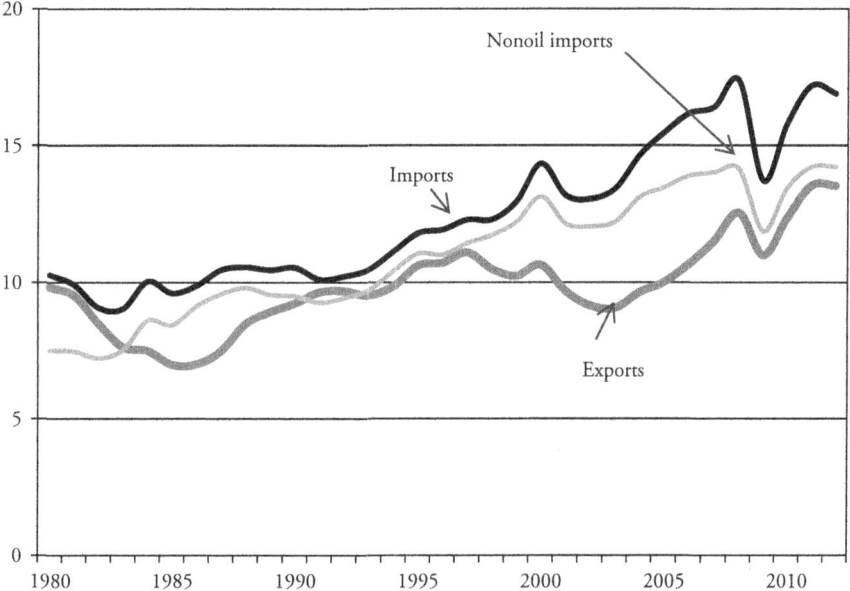

Source: U.S. Department of Commerce, Bureau of Economic Statistics, National Income and Product Accounts.

Until relatively recently, the empirical results tended to support what became known as "elasticity pessimism" for two reasons.[15] First, U.S. imports were found to be quite insensitive to changes in relative prices. Although exports seemed to be somewhat more price elastic, studies often found the overall price elasticities to be low enough that a depreciation of the dollar would only be associated with trade balance improvement because of the relatively low pass-through of nominal exchange rates into import prices. Conventional wisdom would suggest that to accomplish a 1 percentage point of GDP decline in the U.S. external deficit a relatively large real depreciation of the dollar would be required: by as much as 10 to 20 percent.

Second, the estimates tended to support a finding by Hendrik Houthakker and Stephen Magee (1969) that U.S. imports are considerably more sensitive

15. Examples include Hooper, Johnson, and Marquez (2000) and Chinn (2004). Unlike the earliest studies, these authors incorporate the more recent estimation techniques that allow for feedback among key variables and address nonstationarity in the trade data. The International Monetary Fund (2007) provides a summary of the literature, as well as new estimates of the relevant elasticities and an interesting review of forty-two episodes since 1960 in which advanced countries achieved reversals of large, sustained external deficits.

to increases in U.S. income than are U.S. exports to increases in the income of U.S. trading partners. Thus balanced growth in the United States and its trading partners would be associated with a deteriorating U.S. external balance.

More recent work benefits from improvements in specification and inclusion of data since 2000. In particular, researchers have explored issues related to vertical integration and trade in intermediates, as well as aggregation bias and the possibility that shifts in the composition of trade away from goods and toward services may have increased price and income responsiveness. There is no clear consensus on the magnitude of the relevant elasticities, but studies that use the same methodology to compare the past decade with prior periods tend to find that both exports and imports have indeed become more responsive to changes in both incomes and relative prices and, furthermore, that the Houthakker-Magee (1969) asymmetry in income elasticities has disappeared. Thus a 1-percentage-point reduction in the aggregate trade deficit may now be associated with less real dollar depreciation, perhaps in the range of 8 to 15 percent, and balanced growth need not imply trade balance deterioration.[16]

In table 4-3, we provide some empirical estimates of U.S. trade elasticities to illustrate the issues discussed above. The first panel reports a simple logarithmic regression that relates the real value of U.S. exports to global GDP, a four-year average of the real exchange rate, and a time trend. We also distinguish between exports of goods and services. In the middle panel we report similar equations for imports but use U.S. real GDP as the activity variable. The third panel focuses on the net trade balance, but because it is frequently negative, we measure the balance as the logarithm of the ratio of exports to imports. If trade is balanced, the ratio is unity. This specification constrains the coefficients on the two activity variables to be equal.[17]

We highlight three features of the regression results. First, we too find that the Houthakker-Magee (1969) asymmetry has disappeared, with the income elasticities of exports and imports both estimated to be about two. Since the U.S. and world economies grew at roughly equal rates over the past two decades while the world economy has grown significantly faster than the U.S. economy since 2000, income effects cannot account for the deterioration in the U.S. trade imbalance. Second, exports and imports have similar price elasticity magnitudes. Furthermore, their sum is well above one, implying that exchange rate depreciation will have a net positive effect on the trade balance.

Third, we find a significant negative trend in the equation for the total trade balance. As shown, this negative trend reflects a secular decline in exports relative

16. See International Monetary Fund (2007) and Crane, Crowley, and Quayyum (2007).

17. The trade data are from the U.S. national accounts. The contribution of the real exchange rate is maximized with a four-year lag, but we found no significant role for a lag of the activity variable.

Table 4-3. *Regression Equations for Exports and Imports, United States, 1976–2008*[a]

	Exports			Imports			Trade balance		
	Total	Goods	Services	Total	Goods (less oil)	Services	Total	Goods (less oil)	Services
Average FRB exchange rate	-.69***	0.76***	-.57***	0.65**	0.73***	0.43*	1.43***	-1.52***	-1.24***
	(0.15)	(0.19)	(0.16)	(0.19)	(0.26)	(0.17)	(0.20)	(0.29)	(0.14)
Time trend	-0.022	-0.035	0.007	0.006	0.007	0.002	-0.016**	-0.026***	0.006***
	(0.02)	(0.02)	(0.02)	(0.01)	(0.02)	(0.01)	(0.00)	(0.00)	(0.00)
Log(world GDP)	2.68***	3.17***	1.64**						
	(0.50)	(0.65)	(0.55)						
Log(U.S. GDP)				2.35***	2.65***	1.59***			
				(0.40)	(0.54)	(0.38)			
Log(world GDP/U.S. GDP)							2.00**	2.72**	0.22
							(0.59)	(0.86)	(0.52)
Constant	-7.02**	21.81**	-3.81	17.83***	21.32***	11.27**	4.70**	4.49*	5.46***
	(4.89)	(6.42)	(5.43)	(3.30)	(4.42)	(3.09)	(1.32)	(1.94)	(1.04)
N	33	33	33	33	33	33	33	33	33
Adjusted R^2	0.99	0.98	0.99	0.99	0.97	0.99	0.85	0.76	0.78
RootMSE	0.027	0.035	0.029	0.036	0.049	0.034	0.034	0.05	0.035
Rho	0.770	0.822	0.758	0.786	0.855	0.457	0.911	0.906	0.818

Source: Data from U.S. national accounts, the World Bank, and the Board of Governors of the Federal Reserve.

a. Standard errors are in parentheses. U.S. GDP, world GDP, exports, and imports are in real terms. Imports exclude petroleum. Average FRB exchange rate is the log of a four-year average of the Federal Reserve Board's broad real exchange rate index. The regressions have been corrected for autocorrelation using the Prais–Winsten methodology, and the autocorrelation transformation is indicated by the rho. FRB is Federal Reserve Bank; root MSE is root mean squared error.

*** Significant at less than 0.01 percent. ** Significant at less than 1.00 percent. * Significant at less than 5.00 percent.

to imports of goods. In contrast, the trend is positive for services trade, which accounts for a relatively small share of the total. We tested the hypothesis of a one-time shift in the constant term, as shown in figure 4-3, for a range of possible "shift dates." However, the gradual trend deterioration we report here was clearly preferred to a shift. We note that the trend is larger in the export than the import equations but not statistically significant. The finding of a gradual deterioration in U.S. exports relative to imports, when controlling for relative prices and incomes, is quite provocative. We discuss some aspects of the issue later in the chapter but a full exploration of the factors underlying this result is an interesting area for future work.

Can U.S. Exports Compete?

Martin Baily and Robert Lawrence (2006) identify weak U.S. export performance as the primary explanation for the secular decline in the trade balance. Similarly, our previous work argues that the United States underperforms as an exporter of goods relative to a peer group of high-income European countries and Japan.[18] Our analysis was based on a standard gravity-equation formulation that relates bilateral import and export flows to economy size, distance, and other measures believed to be associated with degree of trade resistance, such as common language and existence of colonial ties. We pooled the data for bilateral trade for each of three regions (the original fifteen members of the European Union, Japan, and the United States) with 162 other countries for the period of 1980 to 2005. We also included the real exchange rate for each of the three regions as a measure of relative price competitiveness. Those regressions are reproduced in table 4-4. A dummy variable for the United States in the combined export equation is consistently negative and significant. In contrast, we find no evidence that the United States performs differently from Japan or the European Union in terms of imports.

Why has U.S. export performance been so weak? This does not appear to be attributable to either a lack of growth in U.S. export markets or the commodity composition of trade. A partial explanation may relate to the willingness of American multinational firms to use the local production of foreign affiliates as an alternative to exporting. U.S. affiliates of foreign parent companies purchased 16.4 percent of their sales abroad in 2007, as reflected in U.S. imports for goods and services. In contrast, foreign affiliates of U.S. parents purchased just 6.2 percent of their total sales directly from the United States. If this share were increased to 16.4 percent, U.S. exports would rise by more than $600 billion, or more than one-third of their 2007 value.[19] Second, foreign observers often point

---

18. Bosworth and Collins (2008).

19. These data come from Lowe (2010). However, in our earlier work, we found little difference between U.S. and Japanese affiliates' activities in China. Thus we remain uncertain about the full implications of U.S. affiliates' behavior.

Table 4-4. Combined Gravity Model for the United States, Japan, and the EU15[a]

	Exports/GDP			Imports/GDP		
	(1)	(2)	(3)	(4)	(5)	(6)
Weighted distance	-1.102	-1.098	-1.123	-1.02	-1.02	-1.007
	(-61.2)	(-62.6)	(-63.4)	(-39.7)	(-39.7)	(-38.6)
Population	0.831	0.837	0.838	0.976	0.976	0.975
	(172.3)	(178.0)	(178.8)	(139.5)	(139.4)	(139.4)
GDP per capita	0.973	0.974	0.972	1.062	1.062	1.063
	(153.1)	(157.4)	(157.5)	(116.6)	(116.6)	(116.6)
Common language	0.258	0.529	0.544	0.562	0.562	0.554
	(10.9)	(20.7)	(21.3)	(16.7)	(15.0)	(14.7)
Colony	0.556	0.156	0.326	0.698	0.699	0.61
	(21.9)	(5.2)	(9.2)	(19.3)	(16.0)	(11.6)
East Asia region	0.4	0.407	0.414	0.755	0.755	0.751
	(15.1)	(15.8)	(16.1)	(19.9)	(19.9)	(19.8)
United States		-0.586	-0.609		0	0.012
		(-24.2)	(-25.1)		(0.0)	(0.3)
Log average exchange rate[b]		-1.119			0.586	
			(-8.7)			(3.1)
Constant	-34.325	-34.249	-28.94	-38.49	-38.49	-41.276
	(-170.8)	(-175.1)	(-45.1)	(-133.9)	(-133.8)	(-43.6)
Adjusted R^2	0.84	0.848	0.849	0.762	0.762	0.762
Observations	10,570	10,570	10,570	10,433	10,433	10,433

Source: Estimated by authors as described in text.

a. All of the regressions are estimated within a fixed-effects model allowing for shifts over years. All variables are measured as logarithms except for the categorical variables of common language, colony, the United States, and the East Asia region. EU15 comprises Austria, Belgium, Denmark, Finland, France, Germany, Greece, Ireland, Italy, Luxembourg, Netherlands, Portugal, Spain, Sweden, United Kingdom. t-statistics are shown in parentheses.

b. Computed as the trade-weighted real exchange rates of the United States, Japan, and the EU15, averaged over the prior five years. Data provided by J. P. Morgan.

to U.S. government restrictions on high-technology exports, but the magnitude of potential trade covered by those measures is relatively small.

Concern about export performance, though it is an area that would benefit from additional analysis, ought not to be exaggerated. Baily and Lawrence (2006) stress that only a quarter of the increased deficit between 1991 and 2005 can be attributed to the shift they uncover, with fully three-quarters associated with the much stronger value of the U.S. dollar.

Impact of the Crisis

Trade flows typically fall during global downturns, but the drop during the recent crisis was considerably more severe than historical evidence would have predicted. This has given rise to a growing empirical literature attempting to explain the magnitude of the trade collapse. Caroline Freund (2009) presents evidence that the sensitivity of world trade to global GDP has increased every decade since the 1960s and that the cumulated rise in this income elasticity is large and significant. Furthermore, the sensitivity tends to rise in the midst of a recession. The recession was heavily concentrated in the demand for durable goods, which make up a large share of global trade but are a declining share of GDP. Services, in contrast, are a rising share of GDP but display a lower elasticity with respect to short-run fluctuations in incomes. Thus the changes in aggregate GDP understated the magnitude of the decline in industrial output and the demand for imported materials and components.[20] Reduced demand also had a strong impact on commodity prices, whose fall accounted for a large portion of the drop in nominal trade values.

Researchers have explored a variety of additional factors that may have exacerbated the trade collapse. For instance, Freund (2009) also finds banking crises to be associated with somewhat larger import declines, supporting the hypothesis that the financial crisis may be partially to blame for the speed and extent of trade collapse. Similarly, Chor and Manova (2010) conclude that tighter trade finance conditions had a modest effect. However, Andrei Levchenko, Logan Lewis, and Linda Tesar (2009) argue that this factor played a minor role in the trade collapse. Instead, they emphasize compositional effects operating through the demand for durable goods. Jonathan Eaton and others (2011) find an even larger role for demand factors in a model that incorporates vertical linkages for trade and production. Studies have also looked at the role of international supply chains and the implications of increased specialization in the global supply chain (Bems, Johnson, and Yi 2009).

Unlike unemployment, trade flows tend to rebound quickly as output growth recovers in the aftermath of a crisis.[21] Freund (2009) has found that most of the

---

20. See also Crowley and Luo (2011).
21. Reinhart and Rogoff (2008, 2009); Freund (2009).

trade adjustment occurs within a year and the moderation of large imbalances seen in the midst of a downturn is typically short lived. Both global and U.S. trade did indeed rebound relatively quickly. As noted above, U.S. exports recovered unusually rapidly, while U.S. imports have rebounded somewhat more slowly (Crowley and Luo 2011). Thus in early 2011, U.S. external deficits remained below their precrisis levels.

Postcrisis Outlook

The financial crisis has had a major impact on the U.S. economy. The unemployment rate has been driven above 9 percent compared with 4.6 percent in 2006–07. The housing market collapse has left millions of homeowners with a negative equity position, and the market for corporate equities remains well below precrisis levels, creating severe problems for the private pension system. The financial system remains damaged, and difficulties in obtaining credit have slowed the pace of economic recovery. As discussed above, the crisis and the government's response have also left the United States with a severely distorted saving-investment balance. While the external deficit shrank to −3.1 percent in 2009 and rose partway back to −3.7 in 2010, the government budget deficit has exploded to over 10 percent of national income, and the net national saving rate has turned highly negative (see table 4-3). A smaller trade imbalance has only been possible because private investment has fallen to its lowest share of GDP since the depression of the 1930s.

Expectations are for a weak recovery of the U.S. economy relative to historical norms. Figure 4-8 shows the path of recovery to date and projections from the CBO. We contrast these with the average recovery from the eight prior U.S. business cycles. The initial few quarters after the recession trough in the second quarter of 2009 included sharp cyclical gains in inventory investment, but overall investment is projected to be weak for several years owing to excess capacity in residential and commercial real estate. The rise in the household saving rate has also moderated the growth of consumption. The CBO projects annual GDP growth at 3 percent or less through 2012, with the unemployment rate remaining above 8 percent. The International Monetary Fund (IMF 2007) projects a similarly weak recovery. In any case, these growth rates are far below the pace of recovery from prior recessions.

The sluggishness of the projected recovery arises from four sources. The first is the continuing and only gradually weakening effects of the financial crisis. Banks and other financial institutions have much deleveraging still to accomplish, partly to absorb additional large losses and partly to satisfy their own heightened risk aversion. The consequence could very well be the failure of private credit availability to expand sufficiently to sustain vigorous recovery. The second potential source of sluggishness is a weak investment recovery owing to the large excess

Figure 4-8. *Projected Level of Quarterly GDP, United States, 2004–11*

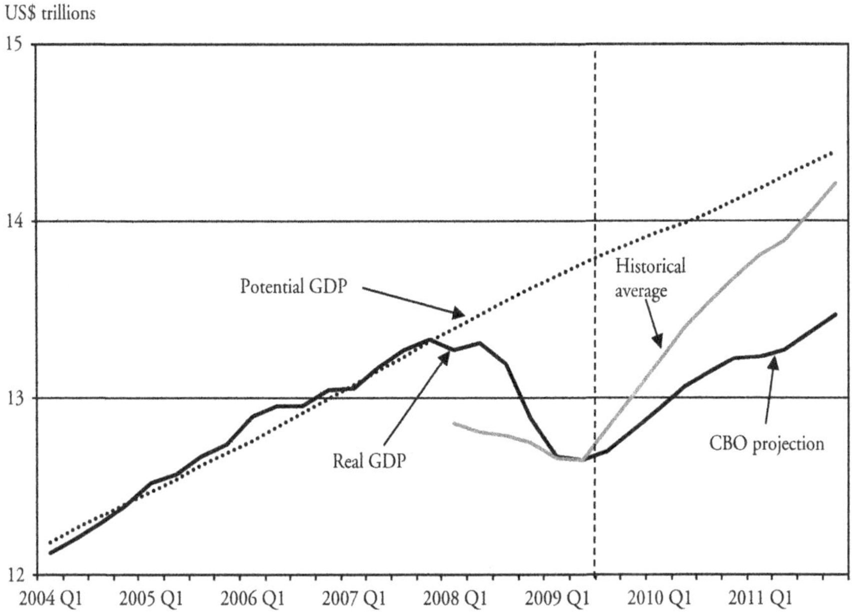

US$ trillions

Source: Data from Congressional Budget Office and Office of Management and Budget, 2010 economic reports. Authors' calculations.

supply in residential and commercial real estate. The third is an anticipated drag on consumption expansion from the huge losses in net worth suffered by households in recent years. And the fourth is a period of several years when budget policy will be tightening as the fiscal stimulus is phased out.

Adding to these challenges, if recovery is to be sustainable, the United States must prevent a return to the high-consumption, low-saving pattern of the pre-crisis era. Projections of weak income growth and a depreciated exchange rate are consistent with the current account remaining at a reduced level of about 3–4 percent of GDP; but in the short run, it is likely to be an external balance matched by low or even negative rates of national saving and continued low rates of domestic investment. This scenario is far from the soft landing that seemed achievable in mid-2008.

Fiscal Stimulus Scenarios

The slow pace of the U.S. recovery continues to generate pressures for additional fiscal stimulus. However, the magnitude of the existing budget deficit restricts the options. Many observers have already expressed concern about the ability to finance those deficits in future years. Model simulations provide valuable structure for looking more closely at possible implications of incremental fiscal stimulus. Here, we consider simulations using the University of Michigan's quarterly macroeconomic model of the research seminar in quantitative economics to illustrate the short- and long-run policy conflicts. This model is similar to others used to forecast future economic developments and to simulate the effects of policy options.

Table 4-5 reports the effects of two fiscal policy actions. The first is a permanent increase in the constant-dollar value of government purchases. The second assumes that the stimulus takes the form of an equal constant-dollar reduction in personal taxes.[22] To maximize their impact, we have also assumed that monetary policy accommodates the fiscal stimulus by maintaining a fixed level of nominal interest rates. Thus there is no monetary offset or fiscal crowding out. Both simulations are reported over a five-year horizon. The simple multipliers for the per dollar effect on real GDP are reported in the first column. As shown, the multiplier on expenditure is particularly large, peaking in the second year with a value of 2.5 owing to strong effects on private investment and gradually trailing off thereafter. The multiplier for a change in taxes or transfers is significantly smaller, owing to the partial and lagged response of consumption to the initial increase in disposable income. It peaks in the third year at 1.3. The effect on unemployment is correspondingly much larger for the purchases simulation than for the tax reduction. The change in the nominal measure of national income reflects both the increase in real output and its effect on inflation and the price level.

Our primary interest, however, is in how much the government budget balance changes and the means by which the change is financed. A portion of any government outlay is recovered owing to the feedback effects of higher GDP on tax revenues and transfer payments. Thus in the first year, a $75 billion increase in government purchases results in a budget deficit increase of $51 billion. This recovery rate of about one-third rises over time to about 50 percent. A large portion of the budget deficit is initially financed by an offsetting increase in private saving. However, the private saving-investment balance also turns negative as private consumption responds to the higher income and as private investment rises in response to the growth of GDP. Thus the fiscal stimulus has a large and growing impact on the trade deficit through increased imports that peaks in the third year of the simulation. Because the U.S. fiscal action is assumed not to be coordinated with its trading partners, there is no equivalent rise in foreign incomes, and the change in U.S. exports is small.[23]

22. The actual simulation assumed an increase in transfers to persons because it was easier to implement in the model. The simulations reflect sustained changes of $100 billion (2005 prices) a year beginning in the fourth quarter of 1998. In nominal terms, the initial expenditure stimulus was $73 billion, and the tax reduction was $82 billion.

23. In the Research Seminar in Quantitative Economics model, the nominal exchange rate depreciates, both to offset the higher domestic price level—effectively maintaining purchasing power parity—and in response to the larger current account deficit. As a result, there is little net change in the real exchange rate.

Table 4-5. *Simulation of Fiscal Stimulus and National Saving-Investment Balance*[a]
US$100 billion (2005$)

| Year | Multiplier | | National income | Government S–I balance | S–I balance | Private | | Current account |
	GDP	Unemployment rate				Net saving	Net investment	
Permanent increase in government purchases								
1	1.53	−0.5	88.2	−51.4	30.0	82.4	52.4	−21.5
2	2.49	−1.1	175.8	−32.5	−22.1	100.1	122.2	−54.6
3	2.42	−1.1	232.5	−35.6	−36.2	78.0	114.1	−71.8
4	1.87	−0.7	271.2	−48.7	−13.1	53.3	66.4	−61.7
5	1.52	−0.5	306.2	−58.7	18.8	46.1	27.3	−39.9
Permanent reduction in personal income tax								
1	0.61	−0.2	34.7	−74.7	65.8	91.3	25.4	−8.9
2	1.17	−0.5	78.1	−68.6	45.1	103.1	58.0	−23.5
3	1.33	−0.6	107.9	−69.7	34.9	96.9	62.0	−34.9
4	1.21	−0.5	124.7	−75.7	41.7	85.6	43.9	−34.0
5	1.13	−0.4	136.5	−82.6	57.2	82.1	24.9	−25.4

Source: Constructed by the authors from policy simulations of the Research Seminar in Quantitative Economics at the University of Michigan.
a. The two simulations incorporate permanent changes in government purchases and transfer payments in constant values.

The impact of the tax reduction is substantially smaller than that of the expenditure stimulus. This is because the early effect is largely limited to a transfer of funds between the government and households, and at least initially households save a large portion of the increment to their income. Without the expansion of tax revenues, there is a larger decline in the government budget, but much of it is offset by the increase in private saving. Again, the current account deteriorates, but by a smaller amount, in line with the smaller change in GDP.

The most striking aspect of the simulation is the large portion of the budget deficit that must be financed abroad. We conclude that additional fiscal stimulus (unaccompanied by any comparable fiscal actions by U.S. trading partners) would speed the recovery from the recession and promote job growth, but at the cost of an even larger budget deficit, a large deterioration in the trade deficit, and increased reliance on foreign financing. That result is financially unsustainable.

Tools to Achieve Rebalance

It seems obvious that restructuring the economy will require a much greater emphasis on tradable goods industries, but the available tools are limited. A sustainable economic recovery will require shifting the composition of GDP, consistent with maintaining the share of net exports at 3 percent of GDP or below. However, how to achieve this in the near term is not evident. In a fully employed economy, the standard approach would be to alter the mix of fiscal-monetary policy: a more restrictive fiscal policy aimed at raising domestic saving, offset by an easing of monetary policy to maintain total demand and encourage exchange rate depreciation. However, interest rates are already at historical lows, leaving little room to provide stimulus by conventional means. Furthermore, some countries have met the recent dollar depreciation with offsetting actions, ranging from direct intervention in exchange markets to capital controls, all aimed at preventing the realignment of trade flows.[24] Finally, direct restrictions on imports and promotion of exports are severely circumscribed by past treaties, with particularly (and deservedly) bad reputations for tariffs and quotas since politicians cannot avoid applying them in selective and distortionary ways. What is left?

The external balance has been a key economic policy target for many countries but has not generally been a focus of U.S. policy.[25] However, President Obama

24. Recent examples are new restrictions on inflows that have been introduced by Brazil and Taipei,China, while Thailand has relaxed restrictions on capital outflows. Given the required equivalence of the capital and current account balance it is striking that trade restrictions are universally condemned while proposals for capital controls are often embraced.

25. U.S. trade negotiators have not previously focused on export promotion beyond agriculture. Although other countries have used tax incentives, financing, and marketing assistance as export-promotion policies, the United States has eschewed the use of industrial policies, recognizing that they are distortionary and unlikely to be effective within the U.S. political system. For further discussion, see Schultze (1983) and Destler (2005).

announced a new National Export Initiative in his January 27, 2010, State of the Union Address to Congress, setting the goal of doubling exports in the next five years. In establishing the goal, the administration recognized the importance of stronger export performance—though it is notable that this initiative was explicitly motivated as a means of job creation, not external deficit reduction or sustainability. Furthermore, exports, like private saving, are difficult to influence through available policy instruments, especially in the short run.[26]

The administration currently lacks authority to negotiate trade agreements, and it seems unlikely that new authority will be granted by Congress anytime soon. Others have argued that there is little reason to believe that completing the Doha Round of World Trade Organization global trade negotiations would have a significant positive effect on the U.S. trade balance (Hufbauer and others 2010, box 2).[27] All the same, barriers to imports into the markets of many U.S. trading partners are higher than barriers into the U.S. market. Other countries are actively negotiating bilateral and regional trade agreements, and exclusion of the United States from those agreements may compound market access challenges for U.S. producers. The United States should develop a more active trade policy that focuses on the expansion of export opportunities. In past years, U.S. negotiators have emphasized access of American firms to foreign markets, but that is not the same as promoting exports.

There is also a concern that the U.S. corporate tax structure may reduce the competitiveness of U.S. businesses, with implications for location decisions and export performance. A recent study by the U.S. Treasury concludes that, although the United States had relatively low corporate tax rates in the 1980s, it had the second-highest statutory tax rate among OECD (Organization for Economic Cooperation and Development) countries in 2006, owing to significant tax reforms abroad (U.S. Department of the Treasury 2007). Specifically, the U.S. rate was 39 percent, including state corporate taxes, compared with an OECD average of just 31 percent—and a number of other advanced countries are continuing to reduce their tax rates. Relatively high domestic business taxes discourage investment by raising the cost of capital. The report also highlights concerns related to the distortionary impact of the unevenness of U.S. taxation across industries, sectors, and financing methods. This work strongly suggests that it is time for a comprehensive reform of the U.S. corporate tax system, expanding the base while lowering rates.

---

26. The main components of the National Export Initiative announced to date include creation of an export-promotion cabinet, with a private sector advisory group, additional trade finance through the Export-Import Bank (some targeted to small- and medium-size businesses), efforts to assist U.S. businesses to identify new markets abroad, and reforms to the U.S. export control system (to reduce processing time and harmonize standards).

27. However, completion of the Doha Round of World Trade Organization negotiations would have other positive benefits for the global trading system.

The United States should also carefully monitor the international discussion on the use of capital controls to limit variations in current account balances.[28] In contrast to its earlier advocacy of unfettered capital flows, the IMF recently advanced a more favorable view of capital controls as a legitimate element in a country's policy toolkit to help limit exchange rate appreciation and reduce the volume of capital inflows (Ostry and others 2010). In terms of effectiveness, the IMF concludes that the jury is still out, that the evidence does not point clearly to a preferred type of control, and that the efficacy of capital controls is likely to diminish over time.[29] It also stresses the need to consider multilateral implications of such measures and to ensure that such policies do not substitute for traditional macroeconomic policies and prudential regulation. But its conclusion is that such controls may be a valuable complement in situations in which traditional means are circumscribed. The IMF's analysis raises questions about the appropriate U.S. response, if capital controls were to become a widespread tool for the management of the external accounts of non-OECD countries.

Much of the recent domestic discussion has focused on the exchange rate of the People's Republic of China (PRC) and a belief that a revaluation of its exchange rate would solve U.S. export problems. However, the United States and the PRC produce quite different types of products. The PRC is a low-wage producer with a major role in an Asian production network as an assembler of products for transshipment to the United States. In contrast, the United States is a high-wage capital-goods producer whose competitors are largely in Japan and the European Union. The benefits of an appreciation of the renminbi would accrue mainly to other low-wage countries that compete with the PRC. It would benefit the United States by spreading the adjustment to a depreciated dollar more broadly, thereby reassuring countries that do allow their currencies to appreciate against the dollar that they will not suffer a competitive loss to the PRC. It is true that the PRC's policy of maintaining a large trade surplus at a time of weak global demand damages the global economy as a whole, but the associated costs are not borne primarily by the United States. A focus on the PRC does not obviate the need for the United States to address its own problems.

The absence of a clear path for the United States to escape the recession and emerge with a balanced economy is a cause for great concern. Without a stronger external account, any recovery is likely to be incomplete. As the focus of public

28. As a member of the Organization for Economic Cooperation and Development, the United States adheres to the codes of liberalization of capital movements, which generally prohibit the introduction of new restrictions on capital flows.

29. Magud, Reinhart, and Rogoff (2011) carefully review thirty prior studies, attempting to standardize assessment criteria for the effectiveness of capital controls. Their work supports the conclusion that controls on inflows can increase short-run monetary independence and can alter the composition of inflow. However, they seem to have no effect on total net inflows or on the current account balance. There is no systematic evidence that controls on outflows are effective.

attention on the trade imbalance increases, pressures for destructive trade actions are likely to grow, and with them the potential for trade conflicts. We are led to conclude that the exchange rate is the most important determinant for achieving adjustment of the U.S. trade balance. The level of the real exchange rates should be consistent with a gradual future reduction in the size of the external deficit. That may require some further decline. The challenge will be to prevent a real appreciation.

References

Auerbach, Alan. 1985. "Saving in the U.S.: Some Conceptual Issues." In *The Level and Composition of Household Saving,* edited by Patric H. Hendershott, pp. 15–38. Cambridge Mass.: Harper and Row, Ballinger.

Baily, Martin N., and Robert Z. Lawrence. 2006. "Competitiveness and the Assessment of Trade Performance." In *C. Fred Bergsten and the World Economy,* edited by Michael Mussa, pp. 215–42. Washington: Peterson Institute for International Economics.

Bartolini, Leonardo, and Amartya Lahiri. 2006. "Twin Deficits, Twenty Years Later." *Current Issues in Economics and Finance* 12, no. 7: 1–7.

Belsky, Eric, and Joel Prakken. 2004. *Housing Wealth Effects: Housing's Impact on Wealth Accumulation, Wealth Distribution, and Consumer Spending.* Report. Chicago: National Association of Realtors.

Bems, Rudolfs, Robert C. Johnson, and Kei-Mu Yi. 2009. "The Collapse of Global Trade: Update on the Role of Vertical Linkages." In *The Great Trade Collapse: Causes, Consequences, and Prospects,* edited by Richard Baldwin. A VoxEU.org report. Geneva: Graduate Institute, Centre for Trade and Economic Integration (November).

Bergsten, C. Fred. 2009. "The Dollar and the Deficits." *Foreign Affairs* 88, no. 6: 20–38.

Bosworth, Barry, and Susan M. Collins. 2008. "Determinants of U.S. Exports to China." *Asian Economic Papers* 7, no. 3: 1–26.

Bosworth, Barry, Susan M. Collins, and Gabriel Chodorow-Reich. 2007. "Returns on Foreign Direct Investment: Does the United States Really Do Better?" *Brookings Trade Forum, 2007,* edited by Susan Collins, pp. 177–210. Brookings.

Bradford, David. 1991. "Market Value and Financial Accounting Measures of National Saving." In *National Saving and Economic Performance,* edited by B. Douglas Bernheim and John B. Shoven, 15–48. University of Chicago Press.

Buiter, Wilhelm. 2008. "Housing Wealth Is Not Wealth." Working Paper 14204. Cambridge, Mass.: National Bureau of Economic Research.

Case, Karl E., John M. Quigley, and Robert J. Shiller. 2005. "Comparing Wealth Effects: The Stock Market versus the Housing Market." *Advances in Macroeconomics* 5, no. 1: 1–34.

Chinn, Menzie. 2004. "Incomes, Exchange Rates, and the U.S. Trade Deficit, Once Again." *International Finance* 7, no. 3: 451–69.

Chor, David, and Kalina Manova. 2012. "Off the Cliff and Back? Credit Conditions and International Trade during the Global Financial Crisis." *Journal of International Economics* 87: 117–33.

Congressional Budget Office. 2010. *The Budget and Economic Outlook: Fiscal Years 2011 to 2021* (January).

Crane, Leland, Meredith A. Crowley, and Saad Quayyum. 2007. "Understanding the Evolution of Trade Deficits: Trade Elasticities of Industrial Countries." *Economic Perspectives* 31, no. 4: 2–17.

Crowley, Meredith A., and Xi Luo. 2011. "Understanding the Great Trade Collapse of 2008–09 and the Subsequent Trade Recovery." *Economic Perspectives,* no. Q2: 44–70.

Destler, I. M. 2005. *American Trade Politics,* 4th edition. Washington: Peterson Institute of International Economics.

Eaton, Jonathan, and others. 2011. "Trade and the Global Recession." Working Paper 16666. Cambridge, Mass.: National Bureau of Economic Research (January).

Eisner, Robert. 1991. "The Real Rate of National Saving." *Review of Income and Wealth* 37, no. 1: 15–32.

Freund, Caroline. 2009. "The Trade Response to Global Downturns: Historical Evidence." Policy Research Working Paper 5015. Washington: World Bank (August).

Gale, William G., and John Sabelhaus. 1999. "Perspectives on the Household Saving Rate." *Brookings Papers on Economic Activity,* no. 1: 181–223.

Gourinchas, Pierre-Olivier, and Hélène Rey. 2007. "International Financial Adjustment." *Journal of Political Economy* 115, no. 4: 665–703.

Gourinchas, Pierre-Olivier, Hélène Rey, and Nicolas Govillot. 2010. "Exorbitant Privilege and Exorbitant Duty." Discussion Paper 10-E-20. Tokyo: Bank of Japan, Institute for Monetary and Economic Studies.

Hendershott, Patric H., and Joe Peek. 1989. "Aggregate U.S. Private Saving: Conceptual Measures." In *The Measurement of Saving, Investment, and Wealth.* Studies in Income and Wealth 52, edited by Robert E. Lipsey and Helen Stone Tice, pp. 185–223. University of Chicago Press.

Hooper, Peter, Karen Johnson, and Jaime Marquez. 2000. *Trade Elasticities for the G-7 Countries.* Princeton Studies in International Economics, no. 87. Princeton University, Department of Economics.

Houthakker, Hendrick S., and Stephen P. Magee. 1969. "Income and Price Elasticities in World Trade." *Review of Economics and Statistics* 51: 111–25.

Hufbauer, Gary, and others. 2010. "Figuring Out the Doha Round." Washington: Peterson Institute of International Economics.

International Monetary Fund (IMF). 2007. "Exchange Rates and the Adjustment of External Imbalances." In *World Economic Outlook,* September 2007, pp. 81–120. Washington.

Levchenko, Andrei A., Logan Lewis, and Linda L. Tesar. 2009. "The Collapse of International Trade during the 2008–2009 Crisis: In Search of the Smoking Gun." *IMF Economic Review* 58, no. 2: 214–53.

Lowe, Jeffrey H. 2010. "An Ownership-Based Framework of the U.S. Current Account, 1999–2008." *Survey of Current Business,* January: 44–46.

Magud, Nicolas E., Carmen M. Reinhart, and Kenneth S. Rogoff. 2011. "Capital Controls: Myth and Reality; A Portfolio Balance Approach." Working Paper 11-7. Washington: Peterson Institute of International Economics (February).

Obstfeld, Maurice, and Kenneth Rogoff. 2007. "The Unsustainable U.S. Current Account Position Revisited," in Richard Clarida (editor), *G7 Current Account Imbalances: Sustainability and Adjustment.*

Ostry, Jonathan D., and others. 2010. "Capital Inflows: The Role of Controls." Staff Position Note SPN/10/04. Washington: International Monetary Fund.

Peach, Richard, and Charles Steindel. 2000. "A Nation of Spendthrifts? An Analysis of Trends in Personal and Gross Saving." *Current Issues in Economics and Finance* 6, no. 2: 1–6.

Poterba, James M. 2000. "Stock Market Wealth and Consumption." *Journal of Economic Perspectives* 14, no. 2: 99–118.

Reinhart, Carmen, and Kenneth Rogoff. 2008. "This Time Is Different: A Panoramic View of Eight Centuries of Financial Crises." Working Paper 13882. Cambridge, Mass.: National Bureau of Economic Research (March).

————. 2009. "The Aftermath of Financial Crises." *American Economic Review* 99, no. 2: 466–72

Reinsdorf, Marshall. 2007. "Alternative Measures of Personal Saving." *Survey of Current Business* 87, no. 2: 7–13.

Schultze, Charles L. 1983. "Industrial Policy: A Dissent." *Brookings Review* 2, no. 1: 3–12.

Sinai, Todd, and Nicholas S. Souleles. 2005. "Owner-Occupied Housing as a Hedge against Risk." *Quarterly Journal of Economics* 120, no. 2: 763–89.

U.S. Department of the Treasury, Office of Tax Policy. 2007. "Approaches to Improve the Competitiveness of the U.S. Business Tax System for the 21st Century" (www.ustreas.gov/press/releases/reports/hp749_approachesstudy.pdf).

5

Japan's Current Account Rebalancing

MASAHIRO KAWAI AND SHINJI TAKAGI

For more than three decades, Japan's current account balance has been in surplus in the range of 1.5 to 4 percent of GDP, with a few exceptions. Before the People's Republic of China's current account surplus expanded remarkably in the 2000s, Japan's current account surplus was one of the largest in the world—particularly during 1984–88—and the United States had the largest current account deficit globally. Japan's surplus and the U.S. deficit were at the core of the global imbalances of the 1980s and 1990s. Even later—particularly between 2003 and 2008—Japan's current account surplus was above 3 percent of GDP because of a persistent surplus in the goods trade balance and a growing surplus in the investment income balance. However, the current account surplus shrank in the aftermath of the global financial crisis of 2007–09 as Japanese economic growth rapidly decelerated (Kawai and Takagi 2011) and in

This is a substantially revised and updated version of the paper presented at the conference Trans-Pacific Rebalancing, jointly organized by the Asian Development Bank Institute and the Brookings Institution, March 3–4, 2010, in Tokyo. The authors thank Peter Morgan for comments and Shigeru Akiyama and Atsuyuki Kato for excellent research assistance. The findings, interpretations, and conclusions expressed in the paper are entirely those of the authors and do not necessarily represent the views of the Asian Development Bank, its Institute, its executive directors, or the countries they represent.

connection with the triple disaster that began with the Great East Japan Earthquake of 2011.[1]

Japan's large current account surplus in the mid-1980s was a result of the high net savings of the household sector and an improved savings-investment (S-I) balance in the public sector, despite high levels of corporate investment. Clearly, the rapid appreciation of the yen, which was triggered by the Plaza Agreement of 1985,[2] contributed to a subsequent reduction in the current account surplus. During the 1990s the corporate sector improved its S-I balance significantly by raising savings and reducing investment, while the public sector S-I balance deteriorated quickly. The reemergence of a large current account surplus in the beginning of this century was a result of the massive improvement in the corporate sector S-I balance, which more than offset the deterioration in the household and public sector balances.

The global financial crisis, the subsequent yen appreciation, and the 2011 earthquake all contributed to recent current account rebalancing. This rebalancing has reflected a deterioration in the goods trade balance, the most important source of Japan's current account surplus for three decades, as exports of manufactured products declined and mineral fuel imports rose. Nonetheless, the current account balance remained in surplus because a large surplus in the investment income balance more than compensated for the trade deficit.

Two important issues are whether the ongoing rebalancing of Japan's current account is transitory or permanent and whether Japan's current account will turn into a deficit in the near future. Which of the following is ultimately more dominant, the persistent and widening trade deficit or the rising investment income surplus? There are two offsetting trends that will affect Japan's current account balance over the medium to long term. On one hand, the goods trade balance will continue to be adversely affected by such factors as a shift of manufacturing activity abroad and consequent deindustrialization (or "hollowing out" of the

---

1. The Great East Japan Earthquake on March 11, 2011, which registered 9.0 on the moment magnitude scale, was followed by an even more devastating tsunami that hit much of the coastline of three prefectures—Fukushima, Iwate and Miyagi. The tsunami, in turn, disabled the backup electricity-generating systems at the Fukushima Daiichi Nuclear Power Plant of the Tokyo Electric Power Company, resulting in the second most serious nuclear accident in world history. Following the nuclear failure, virtually all nuclear power plants were shut down throughout Japan, necessitating significant imports of mineral fuels, as the major sources of electricity shifted to thermal power.

2. The Plaza Agreement among the G-5 countries (France, Germany, Japan, the United Kingdom, and the United States) reached in September 1985 attempted to lower the value of the U.S. dollar vis-à-vis the Japanese yen and the deutsche mark and reduce trade deficits in the United States and trade surpluses in Japan and Germany. The agreement was a response to the rise of protectionist pressure in the U.S. Congress, owing to the large U.S. trade deficits partly reflecting a strong U.S. dollar. The United States, Japan, and Germany began currency market interventions and adjusted monetary policies to guide U.S. dollar depreciation against the yen and the mark.

manufacturing sector); a decline in manufacturing competitiveness relative to advanced emerging economies (such as the Republic of Korea and Taipei,China); large imports of mineral fuels for domestic power generation; and a deterioration in the terms of trade. In addition, the rapid aging of the Japanese population will reduce household savings, and sustained economic recovery will expand corporate investment. On the other hand, favorable influences on the current account balance will come from such factors as prospective fiscal consolidation, which will increase the government S-I balance, and Japan's transformation into a mature net-creditor country—particularly a major source of foreign direct investment (FDI)—which implies that it will earn growing investment income from abroad.

Another important issue is whether Japan's policymakers should be concerned about the shrinking current account surplus and the possible emergence of a current account deficit. Some may consider the shrinking current account balance to be a sign of deindustrialization. But a more serious concern would be the potential impact of any future current account deficit on the already precarious state of the public finances—as demonstrated by the high debt-to-GDP ratio, which is clearly unsustainable (see, for example, Doi, Hoshi, and Okimoto 2011; Hoshi and Ito 2012). Once the current account balance turns to deficit, more of fiscal deficit financing must come from foreign savings, which could affect market sentiments, pushing up long-term interest rates and making fiscal consolidation more difficult. This could eventually propel the Japanese economy into a sovereign debt crisis.

The current account balance can be analyzed either as a key item in the balance of payments or from the perspective of the savings-investment balance. We take the view that while the current account balance can be affected in the short run (one to three years) by relative incomes of home and foreign countries, real effective exchange rates, and terms of trade, the medium- to long-term determinants of the current account are structural changes in the savings-investment balance.

Japan's Current Account in the Balance of Payments

Japan has experienced persistent and often sizable current account surpluses annually since the 1980s, although in terms of the percentage of GDP these surpluses have been cyclical (see figure 5-1). Starting from a small deficit (1.1 percent of GDP) in 1980 associated with the second oil price shock, the current account balance sharply improved to a large surplus (4.2 percent of GDP) in 1986. The annual balance, continuously in surplus, has since fluctuated between a high of 4.8 percent (in 2007) and a low of 1.0 percent of GDP (in 2012). Although the surplus has declined sharply in recent years owing to the emergence in 2011 of a deficit in the goods trade balance—the surplus of 2012 was the smallest in nearly thirty years—the current account surplus has not disappeared because Japan continues to enjoy a sizable surplus in investment income.

Figure 5-1. *Current Account and Its Components as Share of GDP, Japan, 1980–2012*

Percent of GDP

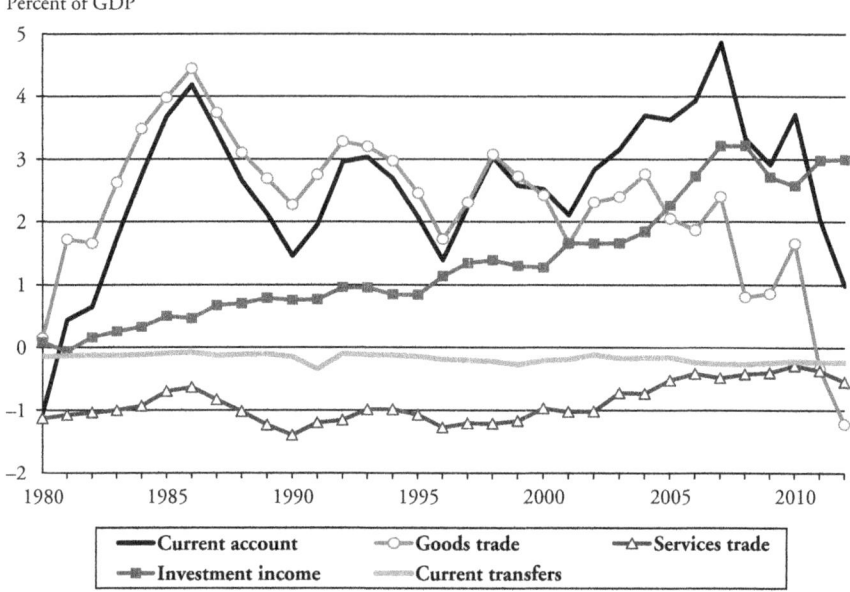

Source: Current account balance data from Bank of Japan, *Balance of Payments Statistics*; GDP data from Cabinet Office.

Japan has been undergoing a process of rebalancing its current account since 2008, with a significant shift in its composition. Whereas in the past the goods trade balance was the single most important contributor to the current account surplus, the major source of the surplus shifted to investment income, as the goods trade balance began to deteriorate in the mid-1980s along with a decline in manufacturing exports. The investment income surplus exceeded the goods trade balance surplus in 2005 for the first time and in 2007 reached more than 3 percent of GDP. As noted, in 2011–12, the current account balance remained in surplus only because the investment income surplus more than offset not only Japan's typical deficits in services trade and current transfers but also the newly emerged deficit in goods trade. Given Japan's international investment position, it is likely that net investment income from abroad will remain at 3 percent or more of GDP.

Goods, Services, and Investment Income

From the late 1980s to 2008, Japan saw a steady expansion of trade and persistent surpluses in the goods trade balance. During 2008–09, however, the surplus shrank sharply as global demand collapsed and the yen rose in real effective terms. During 2011–12, the balance even turned negative,[3] with the deficit on the order of 0.5 percent (2011) and 1.5 percent (2012) of GDP. The deficits stemmed from a decline in the export of machinery and electronic products and a rise in the import of mineral fuels. In particular, the triple disaster of March 2011 disrupted the supply chains in the Tohoku area, thereby cutting the export of parts and components. Later in the same year, large-scale flooding in Thailand halted manufacturing production there, further reducing demand for Japanese parts and components. On the import side, the failure of the Tokyo Electric Power Company's Fukushima Daiichi nuclear power plant led to the shutdown of virtually all nuclear power plants throughout Japan and required Japan to import large amounts of mineral fuels for thermal power generation.

Undoubtedly, the global financial crisis, the triple disaster, and the Thai flood were all significant determinants of Japan's recent balance of payments, but their impacts should be temporary. They certainly do not explain the sustained deterioration of Japan's goods trade balance, which had already been evident before 2008. In the longer run, structural factors will more likely determine Japan's trade balance. Important structural factors that have probably contributed to the sustained deterioration of Japan's trade balance in recent years include a shift of production facilities to emerging Asian economies, a relative decline in manufacturing competitiveness vis-à-vis the Republic of Korea and Taipei,China, among others, and a long-term deterioration in the terms of trade. The latest observed deficit in the goods trade balance may well be a sign that the ongoing deindustrialization of the Japanese economy has advanced considerably.

Exports and imports of services had expanded throughout the 1990s and the first decade of this century until the economy was hit by the global financial crisis (figure 5-2). Services trade has not recovered much since 2009. Japan's services trade has always been in deficit, but the deficit has narrowed recently from 1 percent or more of GDP to about 0.5 percent, reflecting a rise in the surplus in royalties and license fees, a decline in the deficit in travel services, and a shift in the balance on other business services from deficit to surplus.

The investment income balance, continuously in surplus since the 1980s, has increasingly been influenced by developments in receipts and payments of portfolio investment income (figure 5-3). On the income side, direct investment

---

3. The yen appreciated in real effective terms following the global financial crisis. Although the massive repatriation of dollar liquidity from abroad back to the United States caused the U.S. dollar to appreciate against most major currencies, the yen, regarded as one of the few safe-haven currencies (along with the Swiss franc), was an exception. More than two years later, in the immediate aftermath of the Great East Japan Earthquake, the yen renewed its sharp appreciation against the U.S. dollar, presumably reflecting the market's expectation that Japanese insurance companies would repatriate funds from abroad to make indemnity payments by the end of the fiscal year (March 31) and that some Japanese companies would need to raise yen funds in anticipation of higher expenditure requirements stemming from the disaster.

Figure 5-2. *Services Trade Balance as Share of GDP, by Category, Japan, 1990–2012*

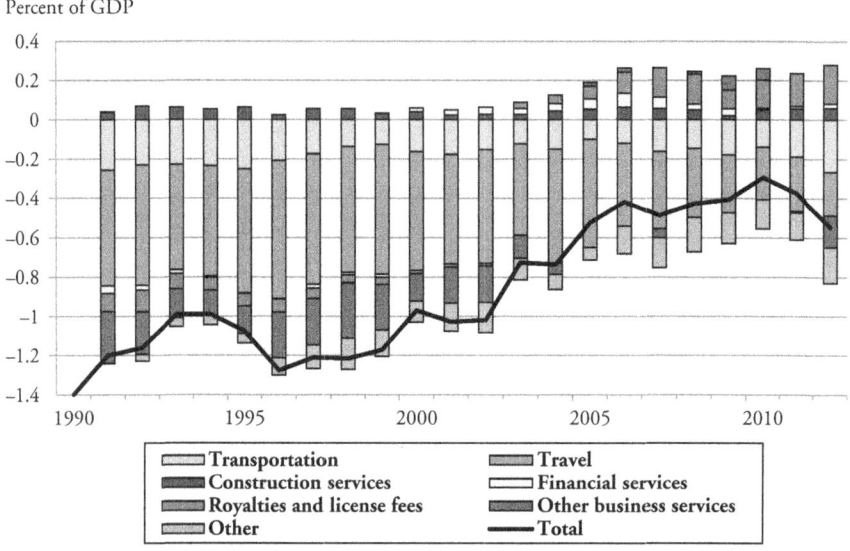

Source: Services trade data from Bank of Japan, *Balance of Payments Statistics*; GDP data from Cabinet Office.

Figure 5-3. *Investment Income Balance as Share of GDP, by Category, Japan, 1990–2012*

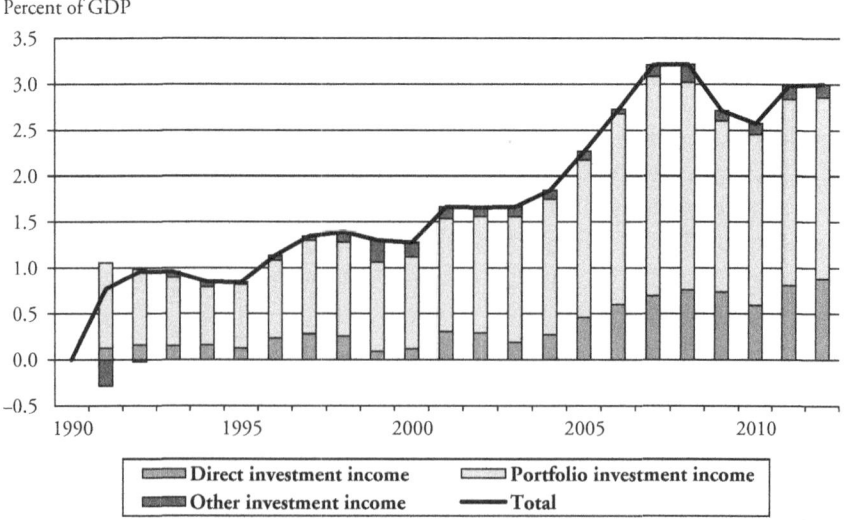

Source: Investment income data from Bank of Japan, *Balance of Payments Statistics*; GDP data from Cabinet Office.

Figure 5-4. *Components of the Financial Account Balance as Share of GDP, by Category, Japan, 1980–2012*

Percent of GDP

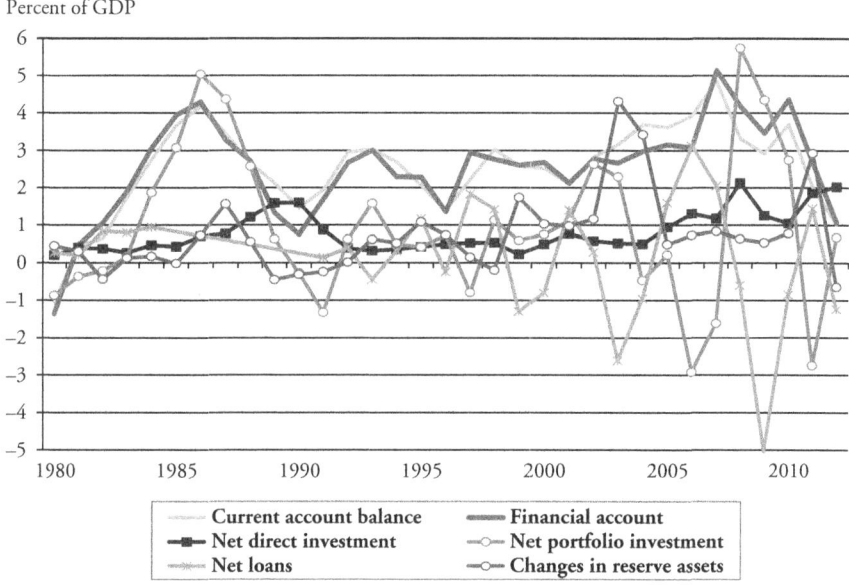

Source: Financial account balance data from Bank of Japan, *Balance of Payments Statistics* and International Monetary Fund, *International Financial Statistics*; GDP data from Cabinet Office.

income is also an important source, although smaller than portfolio investment income, reflecting the smaller share of FDI assets in Japan's net international investment position. The surplus in investment income has expanded over time, as income received from portfolio and direct investment has risen steadily. In 2012 Japan received about 4 percent of GDP in investment income and paid out about 1 percent of GDP. Net investment income earned from abroad rose from less than ¥4 trillion (less than 0.8 percent of GDP) in 1991 to over ¥14 trillion (3 percent of GDP) in 2012. A large portion—often more than half—of income from FDI, which amounts to nearly 1 percent of GDP currently, is reinvested abroad.

Financial Account and the Net International Investment Position

A current account surplus must be matched by net capital outflows. Figure 5-4 shows the components of Japan's financial account, where positive and negative values indicate net capital outflows and inflows, respectively. Except for net direct investment flows, individual components are quite volatile, although the financial account deficit (the counterpart of the current account surplus) has been relatively stable. Changes in reserve assets largely reflect official foreign-exchange market interventions, with the large positive values in 2003–04 and 2011 corresponding to the purchases of a substantial amount of U.S. dollars to stem yen appreciation. Of the capital flow components, FDI flows have been most stable and have seen a steady rise to the range of 2 percent of GDP in recent years.

As a persistent net exporter of capital, Japan's net international investment position has steadily increased over the past thirty years. Since the government effectively opened the capital account in the mid-1980s, Japan's external positions have expanded rapidly for both assets and liabilities. As the additions to the assets were larger, the net international investment position rose from ¥2.5 trillion (1 percent of GDP) in 1980 to ¥84 trillion (17 percent of GDP) in 1995 and further to ¥296 trillion (62 percent of GDP) in 2012. Of this ¥296 trillion, net private portfolio investment accounted for ¥125 trillion, net direct investment for ¥72 trillion, and official foreign exchange reserves for another ¥109 trillion.

Savings-Investment Balance

Structural changes in a country's savings-investment (S-I) balance are fundamental determinants of the current account. The S-I balance is also equivalent to the income-expenditure balance, so we briefly review the overall trend of income and expenditures.

National Income-Expenditure and Savings-Investment Balances

Among the major components of Japan's aggregate demand, with a long-term trend increase in private and government consumption, public capital formation has declined over time. The initial improvement in the current account balance, from a small deficit in 1980 to a surplus of 4 percent of GDP in 1985–87, reflected a decline in public capital formation (by as much as 2 percent of GDP) coupled with a modest decline in private consumption and capital formation. The current account surplus shrank through 1990 due to a steady pickup in private capital formation (by 4–5 percent of GDP). The surplus then remained relatively small, never exceeding 3 percent of GDP. The reemergence of a larger surplus during 2003–08 reflected a decline in private and public capital formation, even though private and government consumption increased.

Figure 5-5 depicts Japan's national savings and domestic investment, both gross and net, as a percentage of GDP. National savings include net factor income from abroad. Both savings and investment have declined over the past thirty years. The gap between national savings and domestic investment—the S-I balance—corresponds roughly to the country's current account balance, the difference being that the current account balance includes net current transfers.

Figure 5-5. *National Savings and Domestic Investment as Share of GDP, Japan, 1980–2011*[a]

Percent of GDP

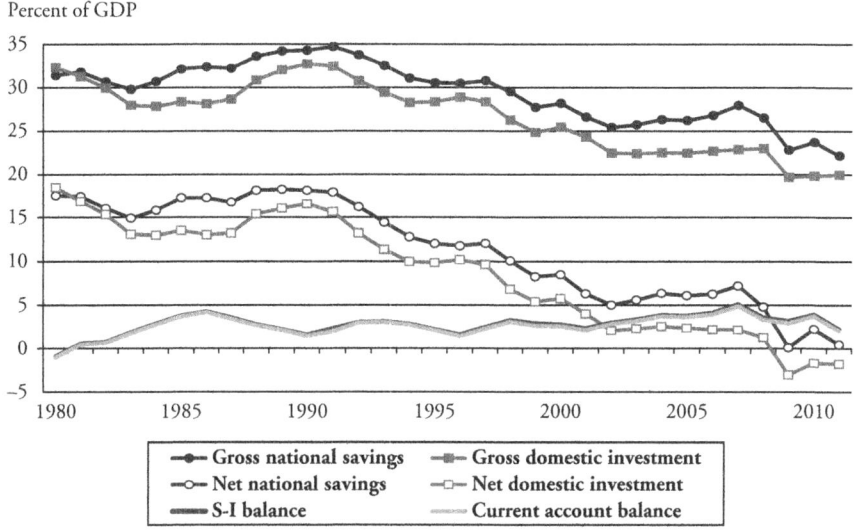

—•— Gross national savings   —■— Gross domestic investment
—○— Net national savings   —□— Net domestic investment
—— S-I balance   —— Current account balance

Source: Data from Cabinet Office, Government of Japan, *National Accounts*, 2009 and 2011.
a. Gross national savings is the sum of gross domestic savings (GDP less final consumption expenditures) and net factor income from abroad. Gross domestic investment is the sum of outlays on additions to fixed assets of the economy and net changes in the level of inventories. Net national savings and net domestic investment are gross savings and investment, respectively, minus the value of consumption of fixed capital.

Sectoral Savings and Investment Balances

Figure 5-6 plots the savings-investment (S-I) balance as a percentage of GDP for each of the corporate, household, government, and foreign sectors; the first two sectors constitute the private sector, and the foreign sector corresponds to the negative value of the current account balance. The figure shows that the S-I balance for each of the domestic sectors has exhibited large changes over time, although the balance for the foreign sector has been more stable.

Among the domestic sectors, the government S-I balance improved through the early 1990s (starting from an initial deficit) but, following the bursting of the asset price bubble, has recorded persistent deficits. The general government's net savings turned from positive to negative in the mid-1990s as tax revenue dropped and discretionary spending rose. This deterioration has continued into the present century owing to a continued drop in tax revenues and rising expenditures for aging-related social security and other welfare spending. The net savings declined to −5 percent of GDP in 2004 and, following a brief period of improvement, further to −8 percent of GDP in 2009–11. The general government's net investment, following a pickup associated with stimulus packages of

Figure 5-6. *Savings-Investment Balance as Share of GDP, by Sector, Japan, 1980–2011*[a]

Percent of GDP

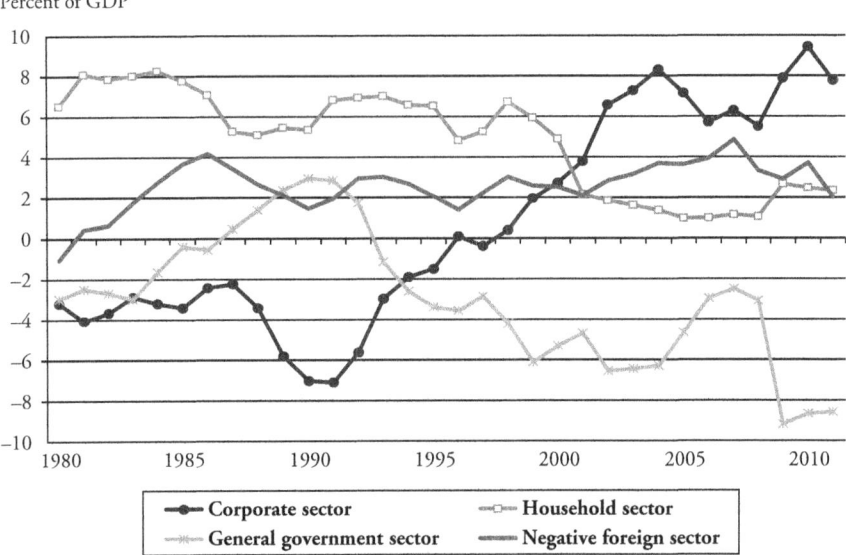

Source: Benchmark data for 2000 and 2005 from Cabinet Office, Government of Japan.

a. The household sector comprises private unincorporated enterprises and private nonprofit institutions serving households. The corporate sector comprises nonfinancial and financial corporations. The negative foreign sector figure is equivalent to the current account surplus.

the mid-1990s, similarly declined rapidly, but less markedly than net savings, during the past decade to a level below 0.3 percent of GDP in 2008–11. On balance, the general government's S-I balance deteriorated substantially from 3 percent of GDP in 1990 to around −6 percent in 1999–2004 and then to −9 percent in 2009–11.

The household sector's S-I balance, while remaining in surplus, has displayed a trend decline, from 8 percent of GDP in the early 1980s to the range of 1–2 percent in more recent years. The household sector's savings rate was high (at or above 8 percent of GDP) until the mid-1990s but declined afterward, especially in the past decade; the savings rate became as low as around 1.5 percent of GDP in 2009–11. Household net investment (mostly residential housing investment), which had been in the range of 2 percent or above, has since the mid-1980s declined to a negative range in recent years (around −1 percent of GDP in 2009–11). As the savings rate has fallen more rapidly than the investment rate, the S-I balance has declined over time. Charles Horioka (1992) notes that the trend pattern of Japan's household savings rate can be explained to a remarkable degree by demographic factors, namely, the low ratios of both the young and the aged to the working-age population. This suggests that rapid population aging has been the key factor explaining the recently observed decline in the household S-I balance.

In contrast, the corporate S-I balance has improved in the aftermath of the bursting of the bubble in the early 1990s. Although the balance was earlier in deficit (as much as 7 percent at the peak of the land price bubble in 1989–91), it recorded a surplus of 6–9 percent of GDP in 2002–11. The corporate sector's savings and investment moved in divergent directions before and after the bursting of the asset price bubble. That is, while its net savings averaged about 3 percent of GDP in much of the earlier period, they rose to more than 5 percent in the later period. In contrast, net investment exceeded 7 percent of GDP on average in the earlier period, while it declined to less than 2 percent of GDP or even to a negative range in the later period. These developments underlie the observed shift of the corporate S-I balance from a large deficit to a large surplus. The earlier deficit mainly reflected active corporate investment during an economic boom, while the subsequent narrowing of the deficit and the emergence of a surplus were a result of corporate restructuring, the resulting accumulation of corporate profits, lack of investment opportunities in an environment of low economic growth, and a shift of manufacturing production abroad.

The shrinking household S-I balance and the rising corporate S-I balance suggest that a substitution of savings may have been taking place between the corporate and household sectors. This may have occurred initially in the context of the 1997–98 banking crisis, which affected older working households disproportionately (Iwaisako and Okada 2009).[4] The crisis then led to corporate restructuring and caused a significant income shift from workers to shareholders, allowing firms to use the increased cashflows to write off nonperforming loans and to reduce the outstanding corporate debt. Even after the banking crisis receded, household income continued to stagnate while the corporate sector registered large net savings. The increasing use of nonregular workers by firms may also have been a factor contributing to the transfer of savings out of the household sector (Jones and Urasawa 2011).

Structural Changes in the Japanese Economy

The long-term deterioration of Japan's trade balance reflects structural changes in the supply side of the Japanese economy, such as the relocation of manufacturing activity abroad and the shift of productive resources away from the tradable to the nontradable sector. Another notable structural change is the transformation of the Japanese economy into a mature, international net-creditor nation,

---

4. In contrast, in the early 1990s the negative labor income shock associated with the beginning of the lost decade was borne mostly by younger generations.

Figure 5-7. *Production of Nontradable Goods Relative to Tradable Goods, Nominal and Real, Japan, 1980–2010*[a]

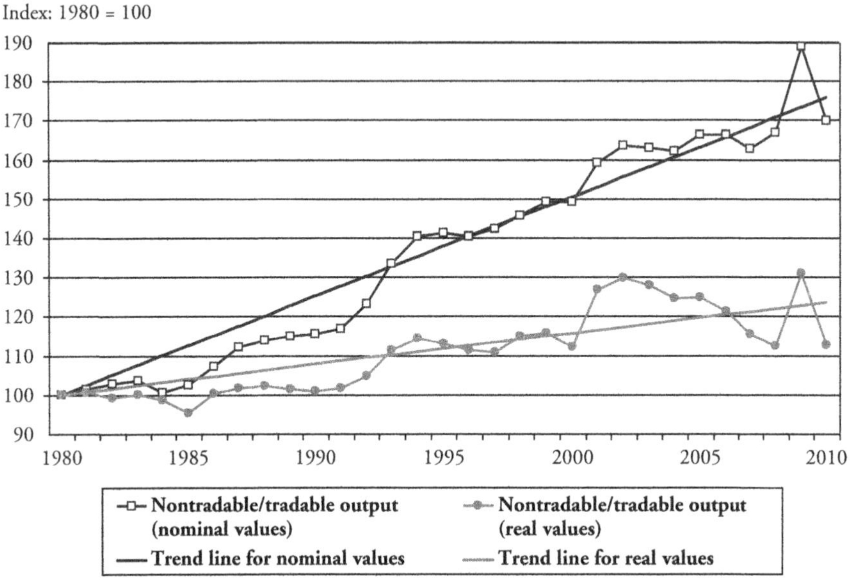

Index: 1980 = 100

-□- Nontradable/tradable output (nominal values)
-●- Nontradable/tradable output (real values)
—— Trend line for nominal values
—— Trend line for real values

Source: Constructed from GDP data from Cabinet Office, Government of Japan.
a. The tradable goods sector comprises agriculture, mining, and manufacturing industries, and the nontradable goods sector comprises construction, electricity, gas, water, wholesale and retail trade, banking and insurance, real estate, transportation, telecommunication, and services.

thereby generating sizable investment income abroad and contributing to its current account surplus.

Deindustrialization Trends

Deindustrialization is a common phenomenon in developed countries, and Japan is no exception. As have other developed countries, Japan has seen a trend decline both in the share of manufacturing value added in GDP and in the share of manufacturing employment in total employment. Although deindustrialization is not as extensive in Japan as in the United States, it has progressed faster than in Germany.

A good measure of deindustrialization is a shift in the economic structure away from the tradable to the nontradable goods industry. Figure 5-7 depicts the ratio of nontradable goods production to tradable goods production, using both nominal and real GDP data. The ratio exhibits an upward trend for both the nominal and real measures, implying a deindustrialization shift to the nontradables (or services) industry. The nominal measure exhibits a steeper trend than the real measure, mainly because nontradable goods prices rose more rapidly— owing to slower productivity growth—than tradable goods prices.

Other more direct measures of deindustrialization are the ratio of overseas to total output produced and sold by Japanese manufacturing firms and the ratio of overseas to total equipment investment made by Japanese manufacturing firms. Japan's overseas production ratio for all firms, including those not operating abroad, rose steadily from 3 percent in FY1985 to 18 percent in FY2011. The ratio for firms operating abroad is much higher and rose from 8 percent to 32 percent over the same period. The overseas equipment investment ratio for all firms rose from 5 percent in FY1986 to 22 percent in FY2011. Available data suggest that the transport machinery, information and communications machinery, and general machinery sectors exhibit particularly high ratios of overseas production.

The relocation of manufacturing activity away from the home to a foreign country is a rational response on the part of manufacturing firms to rising domestic costs. A shift of production abroad has mixed implications for Japan's external balance. First, Japanese parent firms, instead of importing materials and other resources for domestic production, may import final products manufactured by their overseas subsidiaries. These have offsetting influences on the trade balance, but the net impact is likely to be negative. Second, Japanese parent firms, in expanding supply chains abroad, can increase the export of capital goods and intermediate goods (parts and components) to overseas producers, subsidiaries or otherwise. This will have a positive impact on Japan's trade balance. Third, Japanese firms can expand the export of services in the form of intellectual property rights and earn royalties and license fees as they make foreign direct investments. Such services may also include various types of business support services for overseas Japanese subsidiaries, such as insurance, accounting, and legal and other services, which can be provided by Japanese services providers. These help to improve the services trade balance. Finally, Japanese FDI abroad can have a positive impact on the current account balance as it generates the repatriation of profits and investment income from abroad.

Yen Appreciation, Terms of Trade, and the Japanese Economy

In addition to the general trend of deindustrialization, the yen's real effective appreciation has had a significant negative impact on the profitability and overall economic activity of the Japanese manufacturing industry, while yen depreciation has had a positive impact. The global financial crisis and the subsequent eurozone crisis were associated with rapid yen appreciation, which aggravated the combined negative impact on the Japanese economy. Although the business sector was hit hard by the higher yen in recent years, the consumer price index (CPI)–based real effective exchange rate (REER) of the yen estimated by the Bank for International Settlements (BIS) shows that the yen's overall real effective value in 2011–12 was still about 35 percent and 25 percent lower than the previous peaks of 1995 and 2000, respectively. This raises the question, why was the manufacturing sector hit so hard by the higher yen?

Figure 5-8. *Real Effective Exchange Rates of the Yen, 1980–2012*

Index: 2005 = 100

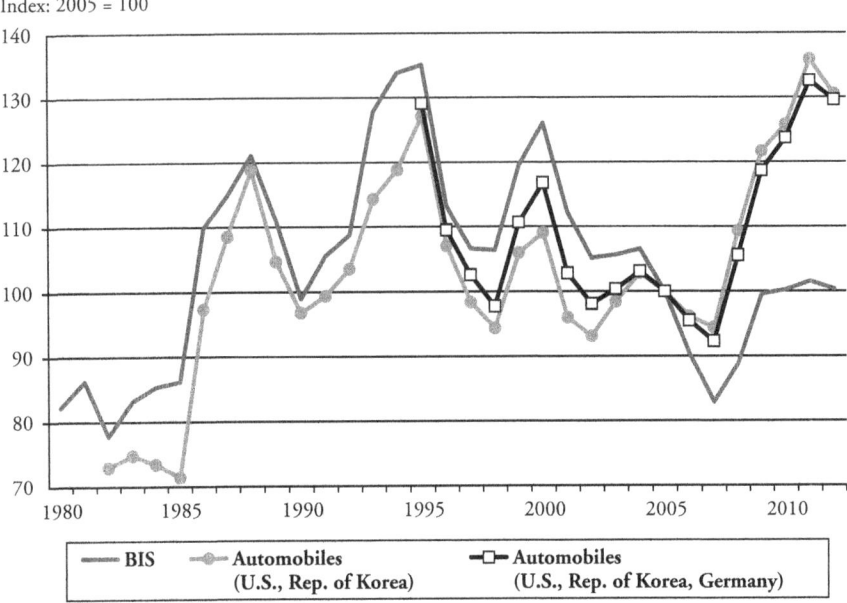

Source: Overall REER data from BIS; automobile REER data from U.S., German, and Korean national data on prices.

Part of the answer is that BIS's CPI-based overall REER index may not fully capture the difficulties of some key manufacturing sectors. First, manufacturing firms had grown accustomed to a lower yen during 2002–07 and may have found it difficult to adjust to the new, higher-yen environment. Second, the REER constructed for the automobile sector alone suggests that the yen's recent level was as high as the peak in 1995, in contrast to the indication given by the BIS overall REER index (figure 5-8). Many auto firms, including big and competitive ones like Toyota, Nissan, and Honda, were becoming unprofitable in domestic production for exports. Once the auto sector was severely hit, there were large negative spillover effects in the wider, auto-supporting sectors (steel, tires, sheet glass, electronics, and so on), dampening overall manufacturing activities.

A large part of the domestic manufacturing industry had lost cost competitiveness since the Plaza Agreement of 1985 and had relocated production bases from Japan to foreign countries, accelerating the deindustrialization process. Several sectors, such as electronics and electric appliances, had already exited from Japan and thus were not so much affected by the higher yen. However, the sectors that continued to operate in Japan, such as automobiles and the technology- and knowledge-intensive sectors, were severely affected by the waves of yen appreciation.

Figure 5-9. *Terms of Trade, Japan, 1980–2012*

Index: 2010 = 100

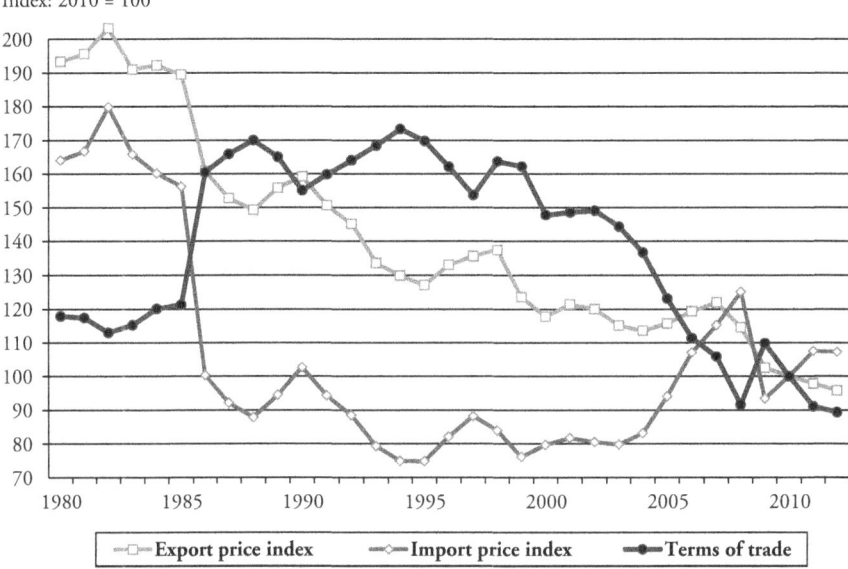

Source: Data from International Monetary Fund, *International Financial Statistics.*

Japan's terms of trade have worsened over the past twenty-five years. Figure 5-9 plots Japan's export price index, import price index, and terms of trade for the period 1980–2012. The terms of trade significantly improved in the mid-1980s, largely owing to the asymmetric impact of yen appreciation on export and import prices. The sharp yen appreciation that followed the Plaza Agreement of 1985 reduced import prices much more significantly than export prices and thereby improved the terms of trade by about 50 percent. But since then, the terms of trade have deteriorated persistently because export prices have declined while import prices have remained relatively stable (at least until about 2004). A rapid rise in import prices from 2005 to 2008, owing to global energy and commodity price hikes, has further worsened the terms of trade. The subsequent yen appreciation reduced import prices and improved the terms of trade, but the gradual recovery of import prices has again worsened the terms of trade as export prices have remained stagnant.

A deterioration of the terms of trade reduces gross national income, although GDP is not directly affected. Thus preventing an income loss resulting from a deterioration in the terms of trade becomes an important policy objective from a national welfare perspective. The fundamental reason behind the persistent deterioration in the terms of trade lies in the inability of Japanese manufacturing firms to avoid a global energy price increase or export price declines in the face of yen appreciation. Essentially, Japanese firms have not been able to adjust export prices in response to yen appreciation or an energy price rise because of tight price competition from domestic and foreign manufacturing firms. Japanese firms are known to have a tendency to maintain export volumes by cutting domestic costs and squeezing profit margins. A better strategy would be for them to focus on the production of goods and services for which quality competition rather than price competition matters and to pass higher costs to the yen price of final products and maintain profit margins. This would require fostering a competitive manufacturing industry backed by advanced technologies and high levels of human capital.

As figure 5-7 shows, the ratio of nontradable to tradable goods production has fluctuated around the long-term trend, but its short-term fluctuations appear to be associated with the yen's REER movements. Real appreciation tends to stimulate the production of nontradable goods relative to the production of tradable goods, while real depreciation tends to have an opposite impact. For example, when the yen's real effective exchange rate sharply appreciated above the historical average from 1985 to 1994, there was a shift of resources away from the tradable to the nontradable goods sector, with the ratio of nontradable goods production rising from an index of 95 to 115. A higher real value of the yen raised the relative price of nontradable goods for Japanese firms, thus encouraging their production away from tradable goods.

As the value of the yen began to revert back to a historical average after 1995, there was a moderate decline, from 1994 and 1997, of the relative share of non-tradable goods production, measured in real outputs. The share, if measured in nominal outputs, did not rise noticeably despite its upward trend. Again, as the real effective exchange rate depreciated by 34 percent from 2000 to 2007, the ratio of nontradable goods production declined by 14 percent between 2002 and 2008, measured in real outputs. The ratio measured in nominal outputs, however, remained relatively constant, coinciding with a recovery of the Japanese economy against the background of a falling yen.

Vector Autoregressive Model of Japanese Net Exports

Movements in the real exchange rate appear to have played a significant role in facilitating trade balance adjustment. To examine quantitatively the impact of exchange-rate changes on net exports, we consider a vector autoregressive model of Japanese net exports as a percentage of GDP (NEX), Japan's real GDP growth relative to world GDP growth (RY), and Japan's REER and analyze the impact of a REER shock on net exports.[5] We estimate the following equation:

$$y_t = \delta + \sum_{i=1}^{P} \Phi_i y_{t-i} + \sum_{i=0}^{\delta} \Theta_i x_{t-i} + \varepsilon_t,$$

5. A qualitatively similar result was obtained by using the current account balance instead of net exports. However, the estimated model fits considerably better when net exports are used.

where y is a column vector of endogenous variables, x is a column vector of exogenous variables; δ is a column vector of constants; Φ and Θ are matrices of coefficients, ε is a vector of random error terms, and t is a time subscript. For convenience, we consider three endogenous variables: *NEX, RY,* and *RER.* We also consider two exogenous variables: fiscal balance as a percentage of GDP (*GOV*) and Japan's terms of trade (*TT*). On the basis of standard information criteria, we include two lagged values of each endogenous variable and only the contemporary value of each exogenous variable. The sample period is 1981–2008, using annual data.[6] The sample period is truncated in 2008, to remove the possible impact of the global financial crisis that may have temporarily altered the long-run structural relationship between net exports and other variables of interest.

Because our primary interest lies in estimating how net exports respond to other endogenous and exogenous variables, we focus below on the response function of *NEX* only. The top panel of figure 5-10 shows the impulse response of *NEX* to one-standard-deviation shocks to *RY, RER,* and *NEX,* while the bottom panel shows the decomposition of the variance of *NEX* into those attributable to *RY, RER,* and *NEX.* All of the estimated coefficients of the lagged *RY* and *RER* terms have the expected (negative) signs, suggesting that Japan's faster growth relative to the rest of the world or the yen's real appreciation causes net exports to decline, although only the coefficient of lagged *RER* is statistically significant. Among the exogenous variables, the terms of trade (*TT*) have a significant positive impact on net exports, while the impact of *GOV* is not statistically significant. The estimated impulse response function suggests that a shock to the real effective exchange rate has a statistically significant negative effect on net exports for up to three years, while a shock to Japan's relative growth does not exert a strongly negative impact on net exports.

The variance decomposition reported in the bottom panel of figure 5-10 indicates that the variance of the real effective exchange rate explains about 20 percent of the variance of net exports during the current period, and its percentage increases to 50 percent in three years before declining to 40 percent. The variance of shocks to net exports can explain almost 80 percent of the variation of net exports in the current period, but this percentage declines over time toward 40 percent in three years. The variance of Japan's relative growth cannot explain much of the variance of net exports during the current period, but the percentage rises over time to about 20 percent in four years.

These findings indicate that changes in the real effective exchange rate have had a statistically significant and predictable impact on Japan's net exports, although the impact is temporary and lasts for only about three years. They suggest that Japan's external balance over the medium to long term depends largely

---

6. All data were obtained from IMF, *International Financial Statistics.* The hypothesis of a unit root was rejected by conventional unit root tests in all cases.

Figure 5-10. *Impulse Responses and Variance Decomposition for Net Exports, Japan, 1981–2008*

Responses to Cholsky One S. D. Innovations ± 2 S. E.

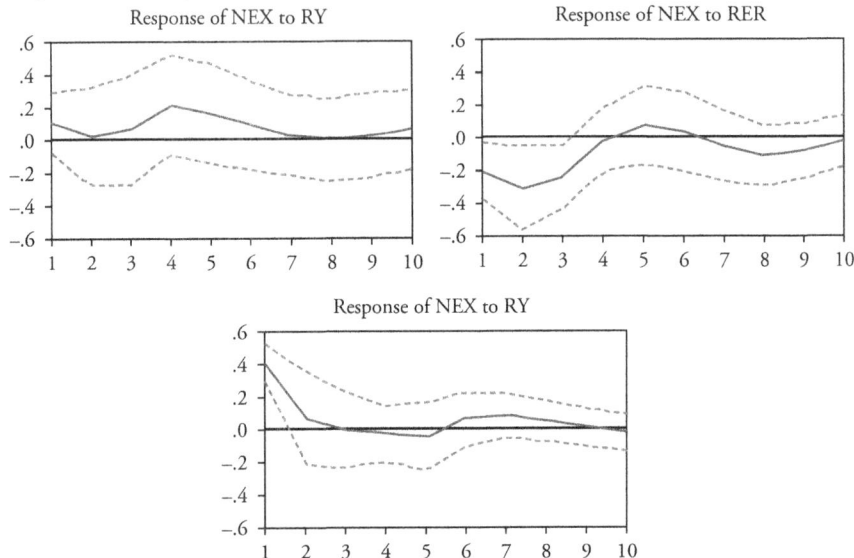

Variance Decomposition of Japan's Net Exports, 1981–2008

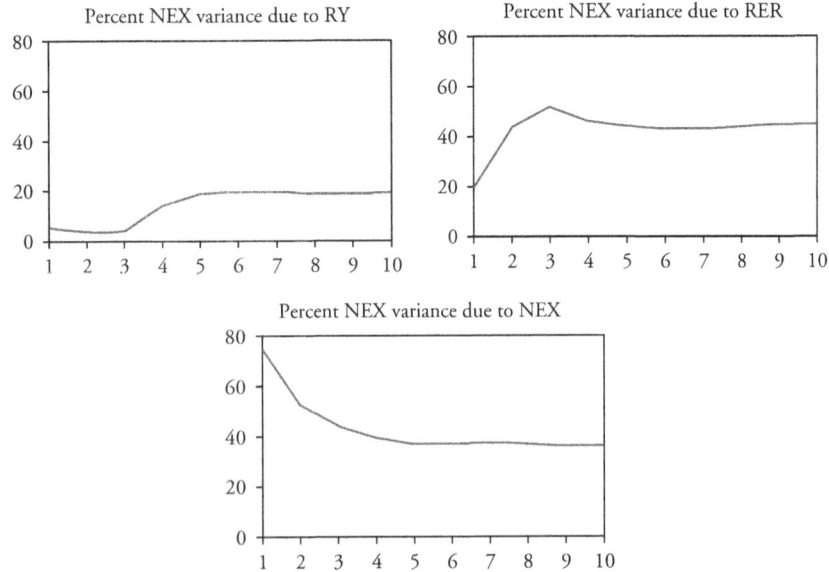

Source: Authors' computations.

Figure 5-11. *Rates of Return on External Assets and Liabilities, Japan, 1991–2012*[a]

Percent

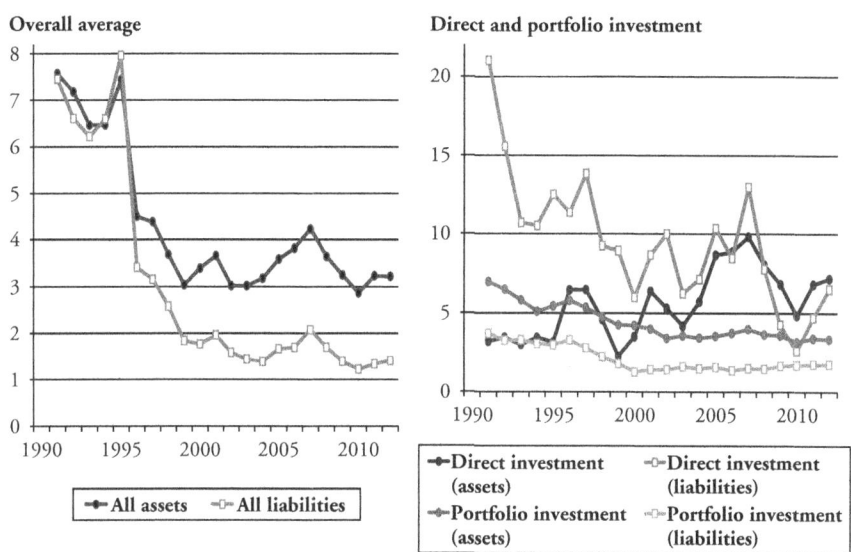

Overall average

Direct and portfolio investment

◆─ All assets   ○─ All liabilities

◆─Direct investment (assets)   ○─Direct investment (liabilities)
◆─Portfolio investment (assets)   ○─Portfolio investment (liabilities)

Source: International investment position data and investment income data from Bank of Japan, supplemented by International Monetary Fund, *Balance of Payments Statistics*.
a. The rate of return is computed as the ratio of investment income to the previous year's stock of assets or liabilities. Foreign exchange reserves are treated as portfolio investments.

on the fundamental determinants, that is, domestic savings and investment, independent of cyclical or transitory factors.

Japan as a Mature Creditor Country

As another important structural change, the Japanese economy has accumulated a sizable net international investment position and become a mature creditor country, earning net investment income from abroad to the tune of 3 percent of GDP. Thus the rise of Japan as a net creditor country can help sustain its current account surplus even if the trade balance turns into a deficit.

Figure 5-11 plots the computed rates of return on external assets and liabilities as well as those on direct investment and portfolio investment. The first panel shows that the overall rates of return on external assets and external liabilities were high, at 6–8 percent, in the early 1990s, but both declined in the mid-1990s. The decline was much smaller for external assets than for external liabilities and, as a result, the rate of return on external assets during the past decade was persistently higher, at 3–4 percent, than that on external liabilities, which was in the 1–2 percent range. Thus over the past fifteen years, the rate of return on external assets has been persistently higher, despite the fact that a significant proportion (an average of 17 percent during 2000–12) of them have been held as low-yield foreign exchange reserves.

The second panel of figure 5-11 shows that, until the mid-1990s, foreign firms earned a much higher rate of return (often exceeding 10 percent) on direct investment in Japan than Japanese firms did on their direct investment abroad. Since then, however, the rate of return on inward FDI in Japan has generally declined, while the rate of return on outward FDI abroad by Japanese firms has risen. The range of 5–10 percent observed for outward FDI abroad in the past decade, up from 3 percent in the early 1990s, was comparable to the rate of return on inward FDI in Japan. In contrast, Japanese portfolio investors have always earned a higher rate of return abroad than foreign portfolio investors earn in Japan, the average difference amounting to 2–3 percent. Japanese firms' outward FDI abroad has also earned a higher rate of return than the return on Japanese portfolio investment abroad since 2001, though this had not necessarily been the case earlier.

Thus the large investment income Japan receives from abroad comes from its large net international investment position, which amounted to almost ¥300 trillion at the end of 2012. Of this total, outward FDI abroad accounts for an increasing share: from 7 percent of total external assets in 1987 to 14 percent in 2012. Although both outward FDI abroad and inward FDI in Japan earn high rates of return, the size of inward FDI stock in Japan (only ¥19 trillion, or 4 percent of GDP in 2012) is small in comparison with the stock of outward FDI abroad (¥91 trillion, or 19 percent of GDP). As a result, in 2012, the stock of outward FDI abroad earned ¥5.4 trillion, while the stock of inward FDI in Japan earned a mere ¥1.2 trillion.

Japanese firms' outward FDI has in the past been concentrated in North America, particularly the United States, followed by Europe and emerging Asia. Japanese outward FDI in emerging Asia has risen rapidly over the last fifteen years, although the growth was adversely affected by the Asian financial crisis of 1997–98. The size of Japanese outward FDI stock in emerging Asia caught up with the FDI stock in the European Union in 2009 and the stock in the United States in 2012. By the end of 2012, Japan had invested US$289 billion (4.8 percent of GDP) in emerging Asia, US$287 billion (4.8 percent of GDP) in the United States, and US$238 billion (4 percent of GDP) in the European Union. Among emerging Asian economies, the major destinations of Japanese outward FDI are ASEAN economies (US$122 billion), the Asian newly industrialized economies (US$93 billion), and the People's Republic of China (US$93 billion).

The geographic shift of Japanese outward FDI to emerging Asia has significant implications for investment income earnings by Japanese firms. The rate of return on outward FDI in emerging Asia has been persistently higher than outward FDI returns in the United States and the European Union. Japanese outward FDI suffered during the Asian financial crisis, recording significantly negative returns in 1999 and 2000, but came back to the precrisis level in 2001. Japanese firms' outward FDI in emerging Asia is expected to expand further and to generate greater investment income, thereby having a positive impact on Japan's investment income balance and its current account balance.

Prospects for Japan's Current Account

The preceding vector autoregressive analysis of Japan's net exports has shown that, although the real effective exchange rate has a statistically significant impact on the trade balance, its impact is temporary, lasting only for up to three years. This finding suggests that Japan's current account balance over the medium to long term must depend largely on fundamental factors affecting domestic savings and investment. In considering the future prospects for Japan's current account balance, therefore, we need to examine the prospective determinants of domestic savings and investment, separately for the public, corporate, and household sectors.

Projection of the Current Account Balance

Given Japan's large public debt, amounting to more than 220 percent of GDP, it is only a matter of time before the public sector is forced to restore debt sustainability through significant fiscal consolidation. Unless the government takes measures to reduce the sovereign debt-to-GDP ratio, investors may lose confidence in the government's ability to pay and drive up long-term interest rates on Japanese government bonds sharply, thereby triggering a sovereign debt crisis. If this happens, it would also damage the banking sector, which holds a large amount of these government bonds. Fiscal consolidation—through revenue increases and spending cuts—is the only way to avoid the kind of sovereign debt and banking crisis that occurred in Greece and other eurozone countries in 2010–11. These considerations suggest that the public sector S-I balance will most likely improve in the near future, contributing to an increase in the national S-I balance.

When the public sector reduces its fiscal deficit and raises its S-I balance, however, the private sector is likely to reduce its S-I balance in an offsetting manner. This reflects the Barro-Ricardo view that consumers internalize the government's intertemporal budget constraint. Historical Japanese data show that, on average, a 1-percentage-point increase in the public sector S-I balance (in relation to GDP) tends to be associated with a 0.9-percentage-point decline in the private sector S-I balance. This means that a 1-percentage-point improvement in the general government fiscal position will most likely lead to a modest 0.1-percentage-point improvement in the current account balance.

Next, turning to the corporate sector S-I balance, its rise has more than offset the worsening of the negative government S-I balance. On one hand, low corporate investment has been primarily a response to stagnant domestic economic activity, a shift of manufacturing production abroad (deindustrialization), and the prospects of population decline. On the other hand, high corporate savings have resulted from the need to repay debt and accumulate retained earnings for contingency purposes. It is reasonable to assume that, once the Japanese economy fully recovers from the two "lost decades," corporate savings will decline to more normal levels and corporate investment, too, will recover to normal levels, although deindustrialization and aging trends may place a limit on the expansion of domestic investment. Nonetheless, the corporate S-I balance will quite likely decline over the medium to long term, with the resumption of sustained economic growth.

Finally, the household sector has experienced a decline in the S-I balance, particularly since the beginning of the past decade. The declining trend can largely be explained by demographic changes, that is, an increase in the population of older persons and a decline in the working-age population. The S-I balance has declined despite the working of such counterbalancing factors as greater future uncertainty associated with debt sustainability concerns and declining trust in the social security system owing to the deterioration in public finances. Once the offsetting effects of these concerns abate with fiscal consolidation, the household sector S-I balance can only decline further, as the negative impact of population aging is likely to dominate.

Putting all these pieces together, the expected improvement in the public S-I balance will be offset by a decline in the corporate and household S-I balances, with an ambiguous impact on the national S-I balance or the current account balance. Under the reasonable assumption that the negative impacts of demographic factors will eventually dominate the positive effect of fiscal consolidation, any surplus in the current account is likely to vanish, and a deficit may even emerge. Given that the net investment income balance will remain positive and continue to rise, even a small surplus in the current account would imply that the trade balance will be in substantial deficit over the medium to long term. This further implies that the Japanese economy no longer has the option of relying on external demand to propel growth. Japan must depend increasingly on the nontradable goods sector as an engine of growth and source of employment, while focusing on higher-value-added manufacturing activities in the tradable goods sector.

Several medium- to long-term projections have been made by private investors and organizations. The Japanese Cabinet Office has made the only official projection of the current account in the context of fiscal consolidation. It projects a continuation of current account surpluses until FY2023, when the current account would be a surplus of 1.5 percent of GDP under the cautious scenario and 1.6 percent under the growth strategy scenario (see table 5-1). The Ministry of Economy, Trade, and Industry (METI) has warned that the current account could turn into a deficit in the second half of the this decade. A dozen private institutions and think tanks have provided mixed projections. Some project the emergence of a current account deficit by 2015 and some a sustained surplus up until 2020 and beyond.

Table 5-1. *Official Projections of Current Account, Japan, FY2011–FY2023*[a]
Percent of GDP

| | Cautious scenario | | | Growth strategy scenario | | |
| | S-I balance | | | S-I balance | | |
	General government	Private	Current account	General government	Private	Current account
FY2011	−11.0	12.0	1.5	−11.0	12.0	1.5
FY2012	−10.1	11.6	1.5	−10.1	11.6	1.5
FY2013	−8.4	10.2	1.8	−8.4	10.2	1.8
FY2014	−6.8	9.0	2.2	−6.5	8.5	2.0
FY2015	−6.4	8.8	2.4	−5.8	7.8	2.0
FY2016	−6.2	8.5	2.4	−5.4	7.4	2.0
FY2020	−6.8	9.2	2.4	−5.3	7.4	2.1
FY2023	−7.6	9.1	1.5	−5.6	7.2	1.6

Source: Cabinet Office, *Medium to Long-Term Projections of the Economy and Finance,* August 2012.
a. The growth strategy scenario assumes higher real and nominal GDP growth rates than the cautious scenario. The S-I balance is the difference between savings and investment in each of the general government and private sectors.

We have made some simple projections based on preliminary estimates of the domestic savings and investment functions for Organization for Economic Cooperation and Development countries. The results suggest that a wide range of scenarios for Japan's current account are possible up to 2030 (see table 5-2). In the most optimistic scenario (in which the gross national savings rate remains high and the gross domestic investment rate low), the current account will continue to show a surplus. In the most pessimistic scenario (in which the gross domestic savings rate declines quickly and the gross domestic investment rate

Table 5-2. *Projections for Gross National Savings, Gross Domestic Investment, and the S-I Balance, Japan, 2011–30*[a]
Percent of GDP

| Period | Gross national savings/GDP | | | Gross domestic investment/GDP | | | S-I balance/GDP | | |
	SH	SM	SL	IH	IM	IL	SH–IL	SM–IM	SL–IH
2011–15	22.7	20.4	17.7	22.2	22.0	21.7	1.0	−1.6	−4.5
2016–20	21.5	18.3	14.7	19.9	19.5	19.1	2.4	−1.2	−5.2
2021–25	21.9	17.8	13.4	18.4	17.9	17.3	4.6	−0.1	−5.0
2026–30	23.0	17.9	12.7	17.4	16.7	16.1	6.9	1.2	−4.7

Source: Authors' preliminary estimates.
a. SH, SM, and SL refer to high, medium, and low savings rate, respectively, and IH, IM and IL refer to high, medium, and low investment rate.

stays relatively high), the current account will be in deficit. However, the optimistic scenario may not be good for the Japanese economy as this implies a stagnant economy with low corporate investment and low consumption. Similarly, the pessimistic scenario may not be bad for the economy as this implies a vibrant economy with high investment and consumption.

Policy Options for Supporting Rebalancing

Japanese policymakers often express two main policy concerns about the deteriorating current account balance. One is that a shrinking surplus could reflect Japan's loss of manufacturing competitiveness owing to a rise in the costs of domestic production, a shift of production activity abroad, and a declining ability to manufacture products that are attractive to consumers. A second concern is that the emergence of a current account deficit could jeopardize confidence in Japanese sovereign debt, as Japan will have to rely on external savings to finance the national S-I deficit, including more fiscal deficits.

The first concern is often expressed by METI officials, who argue that once deindustrialization proceeds to the extent of transferring entire supply chains—including high-value-added production of parts and components—abroad, they may never return to Japan, even if the real effective value of the yen depreciates significantly. In addition, rapid deindustrialization—for example, in the automobile sector—would make it difficult to maintain high employment, as the services sector would not be able sufficiently to absorb dislocated labor. These officials expect persistent trade deficits to continue and even grow larger if Japan experiences sustained deindustrialization and at the same time continues to import mineral fuels for electric power generation.

Although deterioration in manufacturing competitiveness is a valid concern, Japan should not be overly concerned with the deindustrialization issue and the shrinking current account surplus. Deindustrialization has significant positive aspects for the Japanese economy, as firms can improve their profitability by expanding their operations abroad, particularly in dynamically growing emerging Asian economies, and by penetrating these growing markets with an expanding middle class. An expansion of Japanese firms' operations abroad can be supported by domestic knowledge-intensive R&D activity and the production of high-value-added capital goods and intermediate goods. To secure domestic employment, policies will be needed to make the labor market more flexible and cross-sectoral labor migration easier (Jones and Urasawa 2011). To reduce reliance on imported mineral fuels, Japan needs to improve energy efficiency further and to reform the power market to encourage the entry of small power producers who rely on renewable sources of energy.

The second concern is held more widely by officials at the Ministry of Finance, the Cabinet Office, and, to a lesser extent, the METI. Once the current account turns to a deficit (or, equivalently, Japan's national S-I balance becomes negative), the deficit will have to be financed by foreign savings. This implies that more and more foreign investors would have to finance Japanese borrowing, including part of fiscal deficits, while the Japanese private investors—households and firms—have so far almost entirely financed the deficits. If foreign investors assess the riskiness of Japanese government bonds more critically, this could affect the sustainability of sovereign debt by driving up long-term interest rates. With higher debt-servicing costs for the government, fiscal consolidation would become more difficult and the risk of a sovereign debt (and banking) crisis significantly greater.

Several points need to be clarified on this concern. First of all, it is not correct to say that a current account surplus on its own would prevent a fiscal and sovereign debt crisis from occurring. If fiscal and debt sustainability is questioned by market participants—for example, because of a continuous rise in the debt-to-GDP ratio without any remedial action—confidence in Japanese government bonds could be lost regardless of whether the current account is in surplus or deficit. Or if market participants continue to have confidence in debt sustainability, the emergence of a current account deficit should not lead to a sovereign debt crisis.

Nonetheless, perceptions of market participants may involve a herd instinct, and the emergence of a current account deficit could trigger a sell-off of Japanese government bonds, thereby raising long-term interest rates. Thus the government needs to ensure that it does not watch passively while the current account turns into a deficit but rather accelerates fiscal consolidation efforts so that a sovereign debt crisis can be avoided, even if the current account turns into a deficit.[7]

While current account rebalancing is under way, Japan faces the enormous challenge of revitalizing its economy in an aged, and still aging, society with a significantly large government debt.[8] Prime Minister Shinzo Abe is attempting to address this challenge through the "three arrows" of Abenomics—aggressive monetary policy easing by the Bank of Japan, flexible fiscal policy, and a growth strategy to boost investment. The government expects these policies to end long-term deflation, stimulate aggregate demand, and improve productivity through structural reforms. Japan does have a growth challenge and must find new engines of growth and address the adverse impacts on growth posed by an aging and declining population and deindustrialization (Danninger and Steinberg 2012; Jones and Yoo 2011).

7. Guillemette and Strasky (2013) analyze the impact of Abenomics on the trajectory of public debt dynamics in Japan, showing that fiscal consolidation amounting to around 10 percentage points of GDP is necessary by 2020 to eliminate the primary deficit.

8. Katagiri (2012) provides an analysis of how Japan's population aging adversely affected growth, unemployment, and inflation from the early 1990s into the present century.

Although it is too early to assess the impact of Abenomics, the policies just described have the potential to restore sustained economic growth if the third arrow, the growth strategy, is carried out with determination and Japan's productivity grows quickly. Reforms need to focus on improving the quantity and quality of capital stock, labor, and the level of technology. First, given that net investment has been declining over the past twenty years (owing to low levels of gross investment and a rapid rise in capital depreciation), the focus should be on raising the capital stock through more aggressive gross investment and by improving its quality. A series of deregulation measures to remove business-unfriendly barriers to investment combined with a cut in the corporate tax rate would foster private sector investment. Second, encouraging women—particularly working mothers—and the healthy aged to return to, or stay in, the labor market is critical to maintaining, if not increasing, the labor supply (Steinberg and Nakane 2012). Investment in human capital, education, and skills training and a more liberal immigration policy toward skilled foreign labor can also improve the quality of labor. Third, providing the right environment for active R&D and innovations by the private sector is critical to improving technology and productivity.

The government is also focusing on manufacturing revitalization, strategic market creation (medical, old-age care, green), and electric power market reform. Although the capacity to absorb labor is high in the health-related services sector (medical, old-age care), low productivity has been a problem, and significant reforms are being considered to improve productivity. Agricultural sector reform is also on the agenda to improve productivity—through the concentration of farmland in the hands of entrepreneurial farmers or agricultural corporations—and to transform agriculture into a profitable industry (Jones and Kimura 2013). Electric power sector reform—through the separation of power generation and distribution and a more market-based pricing mechanism—can encourage greater generation of clean electricity and efficient allocation of electricity among consumers.

International partnerships—particularly through the Trans-Pacific Partnership, the Japan–European Union Economic Partnership Agreement, and the Regional Comprehensive Economic Partnership (RCEP)—could be valuable for Japan as they would open up the Japanese economy to the rest of the world. There would be significant synergies among the efforts to conclude these agreements. Given the relatively closed nature of the Japanese economy—as shown by its global ranking of 194 (out of 198 countries) in the stock of inward FDI and 167 (out of 172 countries) in imports, both in relation to GDP (see table 5-3)[9]—these trade agreements have the potential to further internationalize the Japanese economy

9. Japan has been a virtually closed economy in terms of the stock of inward FDI and imports relative to GDP. Countries behind Japan in terms of inward FDI include Burkina Faso, Burundi, Cuba, and Nepal; Japan's level is even lower than that for the Democratic People's Republic of Korea. Countries behind Japan in terms of imports include Brazil, Iran, Libya, Sudan, and Venezuela.

Table 5-3. *Indicators of Economic Openness, Japan, 2011*[a]

Openness indicators	Values (percent)	Global ranking	Advanced economy ranking
Exports/GDP	13.9	137 of 173	31 of 34
Imports/GDP	14.5	167 of 172	34 of 34
Stock of outward FDI/GDP	16.5	46 of 155	28 of 34
Stock of inward FDI/GDP	3.9	194 of 198	34 of 34

Source: Export, import and GDP data from International Monetary Fund, *International Financial Statistics;* stock of FDI data from United Nations Conference on Trade and Development.

a. Advanced economies include thirty-five countries as defined by the International Monetary Fund, but no data are available for the Republic of San Marino.

and contribute to growth through efficiency gains (Benz and Yalcin 2013).[10] To pursue the Trans-Pacific Partnership, agricultural sector reform is vital as Japan will have to expose its agricultural product market to greater international competition.

Forging the RCEP among the ASEAN+6 countries (the ten ASEAN countries plus Australia, the People's Republic of China, India, Japan, the Republic of Korea, and New Zealand) is key for Japan. Open access to the entire Asian region would significantly expand the opportunities for Japanese firms to produce and export more and for Japanese households to consume and import more. The successful conclusion of the RCEP would allow Japanese firms to consider emerging Asia as part of their own business area. An important step for successful RCEP negotiations is the completion of a trilateral agreement with the People's Republic of China and the Republic of Korea, which is an important missing link among the ASEAN+6 countries. To conclude these agreements, Japan must achieve a high level of external liberalization through domestic structural reforms—particularly in agriculture—and various types of behind-the-border deregulation, including standards, rules, and in some cases laws.

Conclusion

The process of current account rebalancing has been under way in Japan since the outbreak of the global financial crisis, as a result of both temporary factors (such as the reduction in global demand, rapid yen appreciation, and rising mineral fuel imports to secure the electrical power supply following the triple disaster) as well as longer-term structural factors (such as the change in industrial structure and population aging). It is the structural factors that will define the course of current account rebalancing for Japan over the medium to long term.

10. Benz and Yalcin (2013) show that the Japan–European Union Economic Partnership Agreement would raise Japanese GDP by 0.86 percent if non-tariff barriers are removed comprehensively, while the gains to the European Union (at 0.21 percent of GDP) are smaller.

The industrial structure of the Japanese economy has been shifting away from manufacturing to services mainly because of deindustrialization brought on by the rise of emerging Asia as a viable manufacturing base for Japanese multinational firms. This will most likely lead the trade balance toward persistent deficits while increasing net investment income from abroad in a mutually offsetting way. Population aging will probably reduce household savings and at least partially offset the government's fiscal consolidation efforts, which will improve the public sector S-I balance. Once the Japanese economy returns to normal economic growth, corporate investment is expected to rise and savings to decline, leading to a decline in the corporate sector S-I balance.

When all these prospective developments are taken together, the country's S-I balance is likely to shrink, and a surplus in the current account balance may vanish or the balance turn into a deficit. This implies that, given net investment income at more than 3 percent of GDP, Japan will probably run a sizable trade deficit. The envisaged trade balance adjustment would thus be likely to contribute significantly to supporting global economic growth.

However, rapid current account rebalancing concerns policymakers because it is taking place in the context of declining manufacturing competitiveness, deindustrialization's negative impact on employment, an uncertain energy policy, and rising mineral fuel imports. Policymakers worry that this may lead to a loss of confidence in Japanese government bonds. To address these concerns, Japan needs to implement a comprehensive growth strategy that raises the value added in manufacturing, improves the productivity of agriculture and such nontradable sectors as medical and old-age care, secures low-cost, clean energy, and supports manufacturing by concluding the RCEP, the Trans-Pacific Partnership, and the Japan–European Union Economic Partnership Agreement. Japan must also forge ahead with fiscal consolidation to ensure sovereign debt sustainability, but in a way that is consistent with nurturing sustained economic growth.

Thus Japan must increasingly rely on domestic and Asian demand to pursue sustainable growth as it recovers from two decades of stagnation and from the major economic dislocation caused by the global financial crisis. To do so, it needs not only to revitalize its economy through a comprehensive growth strategy but also, as argued by Kenichiro Kashiwase, Masahiro Nozaki, and Kiichi Tokuoka (2012), to reform the social security system effectively to support its rapidly aging population.

References

Benz, Sebastian, and Erdal Yalcin. 2013. "Quantifying the Economic Effects of an EU-Japan Free Trade Agreement." Working Paper 4319. Munich: Ludwig-Maximilians University Center for Economic Studies and Ifo Institute.

Danninger, Stephan, and Chad Steinberg. 2012. "Japan's Growth Challenge: What Needs to Be Done and What Can Be Achieved?" In *Japan: Selected Issues,* pp. 21–37. Country Report 12/209. Washington: International Monetary Fund.

Doi, Takero, Takeo Hoshi, and Tatsuyoshi Okimoto. 2011. "Japanese Government Debt and Sustainability of Fiscal Policy." Working Paper 17305. Cambridge, Mass.: National Bureau of Economic Research.

Guillemette, Yvan, and Jan Strasky. 2013. "Japan's Challenging Debt Dynamics." Working Paper 1085. Paris: Organization for Economic Cooperation and Development, Economics Department.

Horioka, Charles Yuji. 1992. "Future Trends in Japan's Saving Rate and the Implications Thereof for Japan's External Imbalances." *Japan and the World Economy* 3, no. 4 (April): 307–30.

Hoshi, Takeo, and Takatoshi Ito. 2012. "Defying Gravity: How Long Will Japanese Government Bond Prices Remain High?" Working Paper 18287. Cambridge, Mass.: National Bureau of Economic Research (www.nber.org/papers/w18287).

Iwaisako, Tokuo, and Keiko Okada. 2009. "Understanding the Decline in the Japanese Saving Rate in the New Millennium." Working Paper 34. Kunitachi: Hitotsubashi University, Research Center for Price Dynamics.

Jones, Randall S., and Shingo Kimura. 2013. "Reforming Agriculture and Promoting Japan's Integration in the World Economy." Working Paper 1053. Paris: Oragnization for Economic Cooperation and Development, Economics Department.

Jones, Randall S., and Satoshi Urasawa. 2011. "Labour Market Reforms in Japan to Improve Growth and Equity." Working Paper 889. Paris: Organization for Economic Cooperation and Development, Economics Department.

Jones, Randall S., and Byungseo Yoo. 2011. "Japan's New Growth Strategy to Create Demand and Jobs." Working Paper 890. Paris: Organization for Economic Cooperation and Development, Economics Department.

Kashiwase, Kenichiro, Masahiro Nozaki, and Kiichi Tokuoka. 2012. "Pension Reforms in Japan." Working Paper 12/285. Washington: International Monetary Fund.

Katagiri, Mitsuru. 2012. "Economic Consequences of Population Aging in Japan: Effects through Changes in Demand Structure." Discussion Paper 2012-E-3. Tokyo: Bank of Japan, Institute for Monetary and Economic Studies.

Kawai, Masahiro, and Shinji Takagi. 2011. "Why Was Japan Hit So Hard by the Global Financial Crisis?" In *The Impact of the Economic Crisis on East Asia: Policy Responses from Four Economies,* edited by Daigee Shaw and Bih Jane Liu, pp. 131–48. Cheltenham, U.K.: Edward Elgar.

Steinberg, Chad, and Masato Nakane. 2012. "Can Women Save Japan?" IMF Working Paper 12/248 (October). Washington: International Monetary Fund.

6

The Role of Factor Market Distortion in the People's Republic of China's External Imbalances

YIPING HUANG AND KUNYU TAO

The current account surplus of the People's Republic of China (PRC) and the high growth rate of its gross domestic product have been at the center of numerous international economic policy debates in recent years. Some Western politicians have blamed the PRC for its huge current account surpluses, which they claim have contributed to its undervalued currency. This external pressure has principally advocated for the appreciation of the yuan; this emphasis has worsened trade relations between the PRC and countries with large current account deficits, especially the United States, which has seen a widening of current account imbalances with the PRC in recent years.

The surge in the PRC's current account surplus in 2004 contributed a great deal to this global imbalance. Maurice Obstfeld and Kenneth Rogoff (2009) have demonstrated that this global imbalance was intimately connected with the financial crisis. They also note that the PRC's export success and dramatic current account surpluses fueled both a rapid growth rate and strong protectionist sentiment in destination markets.

We wish to thank our discussants Shin-ichi Fukada, Liqing Zhang, Bhnupong Nidhiprabha, and Yonghyup Oh for detailed comments on the paper. Barry Bosworth, Masahiro Kawai, Harry Wu, Wing Thye Woo, JoonKyuang Ha, Chalongphob Sussangkarn, Frederick Sjoholm, Ligang Liu, John Knight, Don Hanna, and Premchandra Athukorala also provided useful comments. We also wish to thank the Asian Development Bank Institute, the China Center for Economic Research at Peking University, and the China Economy and Business Program at the Australian National University for support at various stages of this research.

At the same time, both PRC economists and the PRC government were also uneasy about the rapidly expanding external sector imbalances. Yongding Yu (2007) identifies a number of reasons why the growing imbalances were not in the PRC's interest and points out that persistent current account surpluses indicated that the PRC as a low-income economy exported capital to rich countries. Rising external surpluses often worsened the PRC's trading relations with its major trading partners. Finally, rapid accumulation of foreign exchange reserves also made the PRC vulnerable in the face of U.S. dollar adjustments.

Since the current account surplus soared in 2004, the PRC economy has maintained a high growth rate. Its GDP growth rate has risen almost three times from 3.5 percent in 2004 to 10.8 percent in 2007. Owing to the global economic crisis, the rate dropped to 9.7 percent in 2008, but the amount of the current account surplus was twenty-five times higher in 2008 than in 2002 and reached US$421 billion in 2008.

The surge that occurred in 2004 and has lasted till now has raised numerous concerns and criticisms. The PRC government has tried numerous times to reduce the imbalances, by, among other things, appreciating the yuan, reducing the export tax rebate, and increasing government procurement from abroad. These policies failed when faced with the continuing discrepancies in the current account surplus. The implied message is that maybe the government has not been aggressive enough, or it has not yet identified the root cause of the problem.

We argue that asymmetric market liberalization and the related factor market distortion is the reason for the PRC's external imbalances. During the reform period, the government almost completely liberalized the goods markets. The factor markets, however, remain heavily distorted. These distortions have a general tendency to depress factor prices and lower production costs, which, taken together, artificially increase producer incentives, raise investment returns, and improve the international competitiveness of PRC products. All these boost the PRC's exports. In addition, they distort broad income distribution in favor of the government and the corporate sector but at the expense of household income. This weakens consumption and further boosts the external sector surplus (Huang 2010).

Evolution of the PRC's Current Account Imbalances

During more than thirty years of reform, the PRC incurred current account deficits in only five years: 1985, 1986, 1988, 1989, and 1993. It is, therefore, true that the PRC's economic system shows a tendency toward current account surpluses. Until recently, however, those surpluses remained small relative to GDP. From 2003 to 2008, the surplus rose from US$45.9 billion to US$426.1 billion, an increase of more than 800 percent (see figure 6-1).

Figure 6-1. *Current Account Balances as Share of GDP, People's Republic of China, 1985–2012*

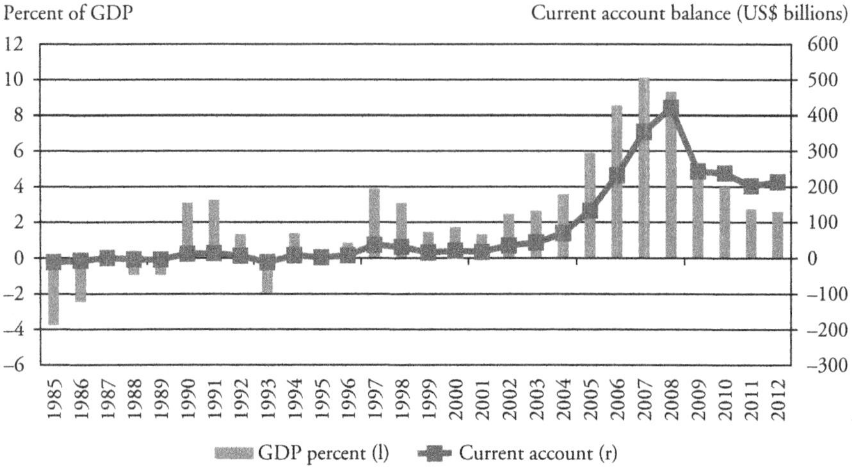

Percent of GDP   Current account balance (US$ billions)

Source: International Monetary Fund, *World Economic Outlook* database, April 2013.

Although it is true that the PRC's account surpluses in 2007 already amounted to more than 50 percent of the U.S. current account deficit (thus likely to require coordination with PRC efforts for any successful adjustment of U.S. external imbalances), historical data do not definitively suggest that the PRC's surplus was the original cause of the U.S. deficit. Current account deficits in the United States first surged from 1.7 percent of GDP in 1997 to 4.3 percent in 2000. During the same period, the PRC's current account surpluses narrowed from 3.8 percent to 1.7 percent. One possible implication is that, though the United States needs the PRC's cooperation in rebalancing its own economy, perhaps it should also focus on its own structural reforms to remove the distortions.

The PRC's current account surpluses have always been dominated by goods trade surpluses (see figure 6-2). Before 2003, merchandise trade surpluses were greater than the overall current account surpluses. The relationship reversed after that because the combination of the remaining current account items also turned positive. These suggest that any policies dealing with the external imbalance problem would have to address merchandise trade imbalances.

Current transfers stayed in surplus through 2012 and rose from US$5.1 billion in 1997 to a peak of US$45.8 billion in 2008 (see figure 6-2). Even in its peak year, however, it only accounted for slightly above 10 percent of overall current account surpluses. Service trade remained in deficit, widening from US$3.4 billion in 1997 to US$11.8 billion in 2008.

More interesting, regarding goods trade imbalance, is that processing trade constitutes almost 100 percent of the total surplus (see figure 6-3). General trade

Figure 6-2. *Current Account Balances, by Category, People's Republic of China, 1997–2012*

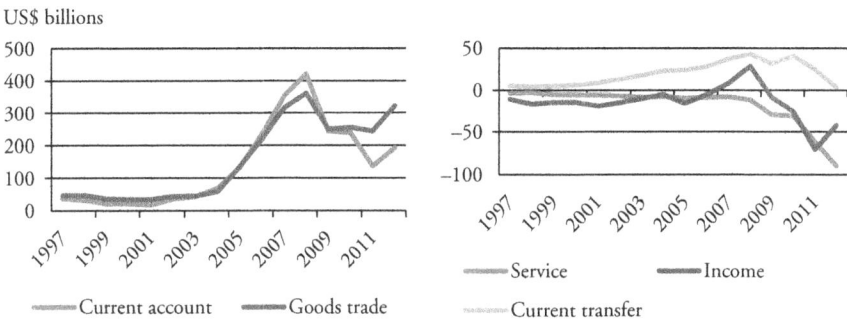

Source: Data from CEIC.

Figure 6-3. *Goods Trade Surplus, by Category, People's Republic of China, 1997–2012*

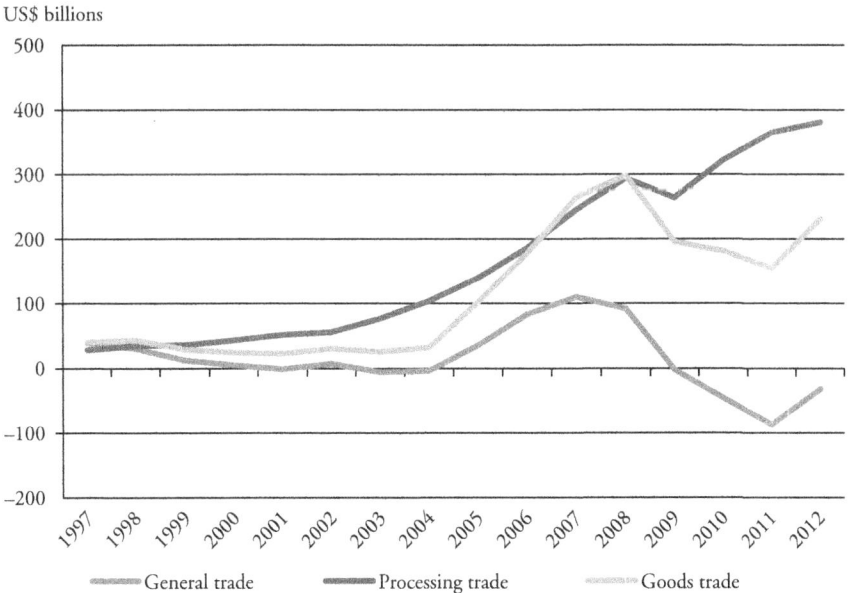

Source: Data from CEIC.

Figure 6-4. *Current Account Balances, by Sector, People's Republic of China, 1997–2012*

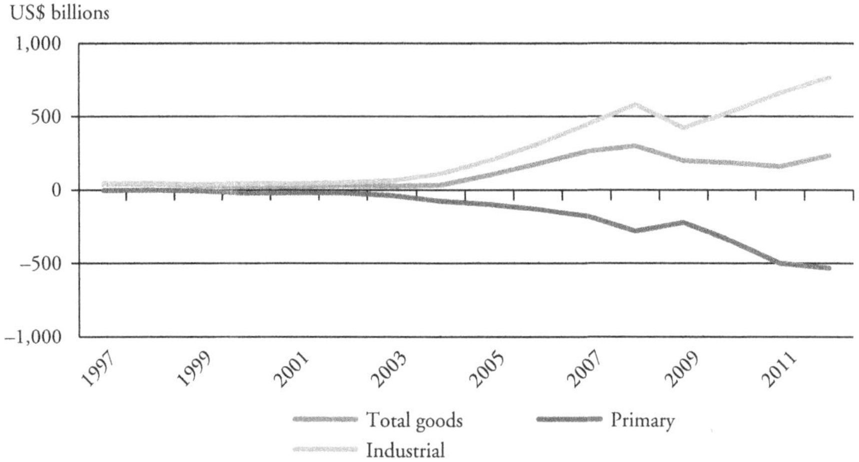

US$ billions

Source: Data from CEIC.

was relatively balanced during the past fifteen years. This sheds light on the sustainability of the PRC's external surpluses. Processing trade is mainly based on the PRC's cost advantages, particularly labor cost advantage. If such advantages disappear sometime in the future, then all the surpluses might also evaporate. This has important implications for what the government should do to deal with the current imbalance problems.

We can further delineate goods trade surpluses by sector. The first finding is that the PRC's goods trade surpluses came entirely from industrial products (see figure 6-4). Primary goods trade has been in deficit for at least the past decade, with aggregate deficits rising from US$4.7 billion in 1997 to US$284.9 billion in 2008. This was most clearly shown by the PRC's increasing imports of commodities and its growing influence in global commodity markets.

A further look at the disaggregated industrial product trade data suggests that the most dramatic increase in trade surpluses occurred in machinery and transport equipment (figure 6-4). Between 2003 and 2008, this sector's trade balance improved from a small deficit to a huge surplus of US$231 billion, which was about 80 percent of total merchandise trade surplus. Textiles, rubber, and associated products, taken together, have been a strong export sector, but its surplus also picked up recently. Chemical and associated products is the only major sector that saw its trade deficits widen in recent years.

Service trade deficits were only a small part of the current account picture. These deficits, however, were persistent and growing during the past ten years.

Disaggregation of service trade data, however, also reveals very different stories for different components. For instance, travel and other business services have always been in surplus, while transportation, insurance services, and royalties and licenses have been the major deficit items.

A Critical Review of the Literature

The PRC's external imbalances have been a popular topic for both economic analyses and policy debate (Yu 2007; Goldstein and Lardy 2009). The importance of this issue has been further underscored in the wake of the U.S. financial crisis, especially in discussions of global rebalancing (Kawai and Zhai 2009).

What are the fundamental factors contributing to the PRC's growing current account surpluses? Explanations for the huge current account surpluses in the PRC can be grouped into six broad categories: measurement error, savings and investment gap, demographic transition, industry relocation, policies promoting strong growth, and exchange-rate distortion.

It should be noted that these explanations are not necessarily mutually exclusive. For instance, the perceived exchange-rate distortion might be applied as a part of the general policy supporting growth, and the effect of demographic transition is blended with the saving and investment gap.

These explanations are helpful for understanding the PRC's growing external imbalance problem. The savings and investment gap hypothesis, however, is really an identity and does not offer proper insights into the problem. The hypotheses that point to policies promoting strong growth and industry relocation do not generate specific policy recommendations to remedy the problem. Finally, the exchange-rate hypothesis, while not controversial, could lead to superficial policy implications.

Before examining possible remedies, we need to understand the fundamental causes of the PRC's current account surplus. The literature has produced a long list of explanations, which may be broadly grouped into six categories: measurement error, savings and investment gap, demographic transition, industrial relocation, policies promoting strong economic growth, and exchange-rate distortion. We review these hypotheses in this section and then turn to an alternative hypothesis in the next section.

Measurement Error

The quality of PRC statistics has been a widely discussed issue among economists. In a recent paper, however, Zhiwei Zhang (2009) identifies another possible measurement error: overestimation of the PRC's current account surpluses in recent years. Zhang's key proposition is that there are capital inflows, which would otherwise be prohibited given capital account controls, disguised in the form of export revenues or income transfers.

Figure 6-5. *Current Account Surpluses, Official and Adjusted, as Share of GDP, People's Republic of China, 2003–08*

Percent of GDP

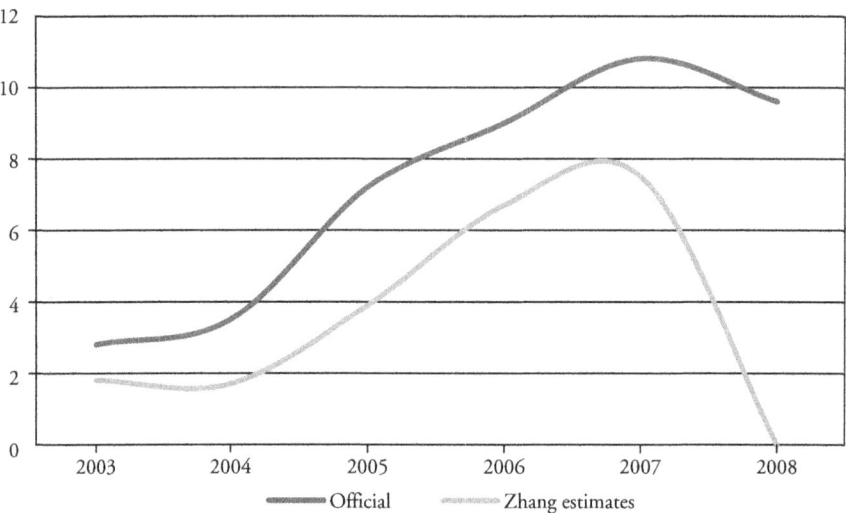

Source: Data from CEIC; Zhang (2009).

Indeed, the surge of current account surpluses after 2004 coincided with reform of the yuan exchange-rate policy in mid-2005. Data on nondeliverable forward markets confirmed that expectations for yuan appreciation increased from 2005. This probably led to increases in disguised capital inflows from then on.

By regressing current account surpluses on nondeliverable forward markets' expectation for yuan appreciation, Zhang computed a portion of current account surpluses that could be explained by currency expectation. By assuming this portion as disguised capital inflows, Zhang calculated the "actual" current account surpluses for the period 2003–2007, by stripping the disguised capital inflows from the official data (see figure 6-5).

Zhang's estimates suggest that the official data on current account surpluses have been overreported by 2 to 3 percentage points in recent years. For instance, according to the official data, the current account surplus was 10.8 percent of GDP in 2007. According to Zhang's (2009) estimation, however, the actual surplus was probably only around 7.5 percent.

Identification of possible measurement error in current account data was an important step in correctly assessing the problem. The techniques applied for stripping noncurrent account items, especially their reliability and accuracy, might be subject to criticism. The logic behind such exercises, however, is sound.

Figure 6-6. *Savings and Investment Rates as Share of GDP, People's Republic of China, 1982–2012*

Percent of GDP

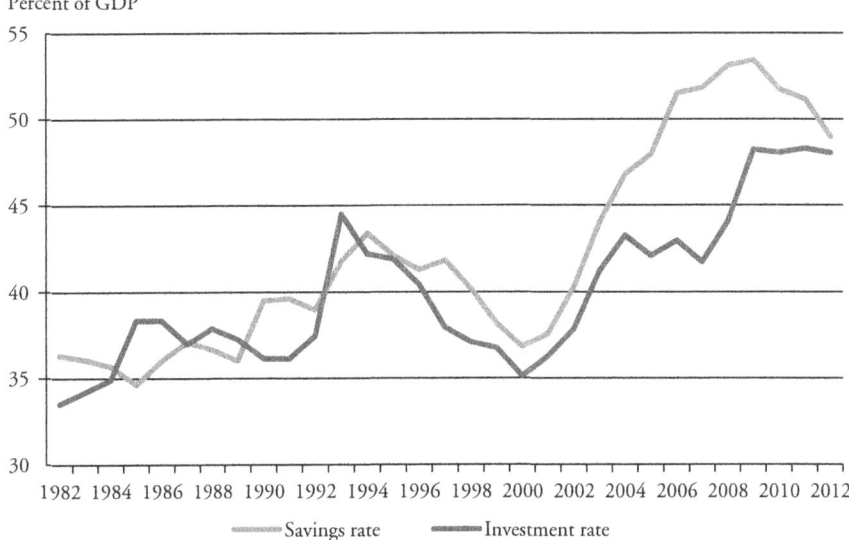

Savings rate   Investment rate

Source: World Bank, *World Development Indicators*, 1982–2012.

Given the PRC's capital account controls, "hot money" flows always existed and were, at times, large and volatile. Anecdotal evidence confirms that "disguised" capital inflows to the PRC accelerated after its exchange-rate policy reforms were enacted in mid-2005 and persisted until mid-2008, when the economy was badly hit by the global crisis.

However, data adjustments still do not change the fact that the PRC's "actual" current account surpluses are large compared with those of other large economies, nor do they change the trend of the growing imbalances. Therefore, we still need to find satisfactory explanations for this unusual phenomenon and, better yet, find effective policy solutions.

Savings and Investment Gap

The current account imbalance is, by definition, the difference between savings and investment. The PRC's investment share of GDP rose steadily from about 36 percent in 1999 to almost 48 percent in 2009 (see figure 6-6). However, savings rates increased even faster, from 38 percent to 54 percent during the same period. Clearly, savings played a very significant role in the recent surge of the PRC's current account surpluses, with some economists seeking to explain the PRC's large external imbalances by examining the structural factors behind its savings and investment behavior.

Robert Feenstra and others (1999) claim that the major cause of the PRC's current account surplus was its high household savings rate. They also argue that this was, in turn, generated by the PRC's demographic profile, the absence of social insurance for the bulk of the population, and the post-1978 appearance of investment-motivated savings in response to the scarcity of formal interme- diation to finance investment in the nonstate sector. They suggest that import liberalization would reduce the PRC's current account surplus.

Ben Bernanke (2007) attempts to explain U.S. current account deficits by focusing on the "savings glut" in emerging Asia and oil-producing countries. Specifically, he points out that while rates of both savings and investment in the PRC rose from 1996 to 2004, the savings rate increased faster, which led to an increase in the current account surplus of $60 billion. Bernanke's policy prescrip- tions refer to greater financial and institutional development in the long run.

Menzie Chinn and Hiro Ito (2007) tested this proposition by applying a com- puter model that controlled for institutional factors. According to their study, the PRC experienced a highly impressive 32.4 percent increase in private credit cre- ation (net change in the weighted world average) between 1996 and 2004. This development alone led to an increase in national savings of 1.7 percent but also an increase in investment of 2.4 percent. Therefore, financial development had a negative effect on net savings through a faster increase in investment, as opposed to a reduction in savings.

Xiaochuan Zhou (2009) explains that the PRC's high gross saving rate is related to its unique income distribution pattern. Household savings as a share of GDP were stable at around 20 percent over the period 1992–2007. Corporate savings, however, were about 22.9 percent of GDP in 2007, roughly double their share in 1992. Zhou suggests that, given the current income distribution pattern, the PRC should increase the investment rate, in addition to lowering the saving rate, to reduce its current account surplus. Justin Lin (2010) also stresses the decom- position of the PRC's savings rate (see figure 6-7) and concludes that the rapid growth in corporate savings was caused by the overconcentration of the financial system, the low taxation on national resources, and the monopoly power of state- led industry.

Warner Corden (2006) developed the so-called parking theory to explain large current account surpluses in high-savings developing economies. He argues that it is perfectly rational to invest some of the extra savings abroad, given the inef- ficiency of both the financial system and the public sector at home. These savings are "parked" overseas until domestic investment allocation improves.

The savings-investment gap explanation is really a restatement of an identity in economics textbooks and therefore is of little dispute. But the common belief that PRC households save too much is plainly wrong. The household savings rate has been stable for the past fifteen years, fluctuating slightly around 30 percent. This rate is certainly high compared with those in industrial economies, but it

Figure 6-7. *Components of National Savings as Share of GDP, People's Republic of China, 1992–2007*

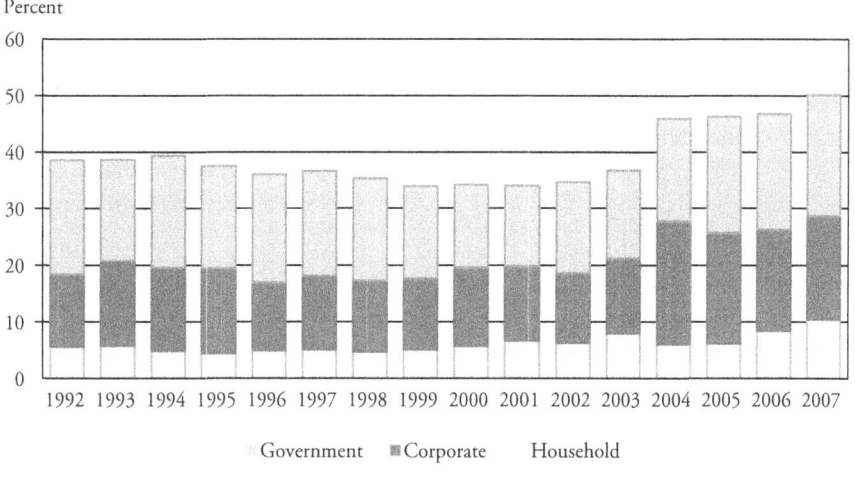

Percent

Government ▪Corporate Household

Source: Lin (2010).

is not unusual compared with the PRC's East Asian neighbors. That the savings rate has changed little in over a decade also suggests that household savings was probably not the key cause of growing current account surpluses in recent years.

Zhou (2009) is right in pointing out the unique corporate saving behavior and its importance to the macroeconomic picture. His policy prescription is to increase the investment rate, which can certainly be effective in reducing the current account imbalance. The only problem is that the PRC's investment share of GDP is already close to 45 percent, an unusually high level even in the East Asian context. The PRC probably has limited room now for a further increase in the investment rate.

Finally, applicability of the parking theory to the PRC is also questionable. Investment returns, on average, are much higher in the PRC than in the rest of the world. Otherwise it would be difficult to understand the massive inflows of foreign investment into the PRC during the past decades. The funds parked overseas are held by the central bank, not the private sector. Retaining higher returns was never a key priority for the central bank's management of funds parked overseas. Therefore, while the parking theory could apply to many developing economies, it does not appear to be relevant to the situation in the PRC.

Demographic Transition

The PRC has been implementing family-planning policies, which stipulate one child per family, since the 1970s. These policies, after more than thirty years, have generated important consequences for the economy. For instance, the male-to-female ratio is now an astonishing 1.26, and the ratio of the young, dependent population also dropped steadily, which most likely affects the savings behavior of the population.

Using panel data from twenty-five Organization for Economic Cooperation and Development countries between 1971 and 2002, Andreas Andersson and Par Osterholm (2006) confirm that the demographic structure in the PRC explains much about its exchange rate, which is consistent with the life-cycle hypothesis. They found that an active populace has a depreciative effect on the real exchange rate, whereas a retired population exerts appreciation pressures on the currency.

In an empirical study, Qing Zhu (2007) argues that the PRC's abundant labor supply is behind its labor cost advantage and huge current account surpluses. Guonan Ma and Zhou Haiwen (2009) examine causes of the PRC's increasing external wealth. They identify demographic conditions, especially having a labor force growing temporarily faster than the population, as one of the reasons behind the PRC's external imbalances.

During 1985–2007, the youth dependency ratio fell by half. During the same period, the dependency ratio of the elderly population rose slightly. The overall dependency ratio, however, dropped. Ma and Zhou (2009) found that the increase in the youth dependency ratio of nearly 20 percent contributed to the increase in the PRC's net foreign asset position of 90 percent of GDP.

The so-called population dividend may not last forever. A World Bank study (Commission on Growth and Development 2008) demonstrates how aging might affect savings and investment. Initially, anticipation of aging may increase a country's saving, which, again, could boost its current account positions. Once the society ages, however, the savings ratio could drop and the current account could deteriorate. Fang Cai and Meiyan Wang (2007) believe that the PRC's labor cost advantage is disappearing very rapidly.

Industry Relocation

A new economic trend emerging in Asia is the increased relocation of industries to the PRC. This process started in the textile and clothing industries in the 1980s, continued in the white-goods sectors in the 1990s, and is now occurring in information technology, pharmaceuticals, and other more sophisticated industries. Industry relocation accelerated after the PRC's accession to the World Trade Organization in late 2001. Many economists argue that industry relocation was one of the key factors behind the PRC's growing current account surpluses.

As early as 1994, Nicholas Lardy (1994) noted that increases in the PRC's trade surplus with the United States were, to a large extent, accompanied by decreases in other East Asian economies' trade surpluses. Later, he further argued that the U.S.-PRC trade deficits were a global issue (Lardy 2006). In the processing industries, usually 60–70 percent of the value of manufactured products was imported content. As an assembler, the PRC is the last stage of the international supply chain.

Alan Greenspan (2005) associates the U.S. current account deficits with a corresponding widening of external surpluses in some of its major trading partners. Because the last processing and export procedures are increasingly concentrated in the PRC, the U.S. deficits with the PRC replaced deficits with other Asian economies.

Daokui Li and Danning Li (2006) look at the industry relocation issue from a broader perspective, arguing that, over the years, the PRC's industries evolved from agriculture to manufacturing, in the process benefiting from cheap labor and an influx of foreign investment. Transfer of production facilities, alongside inflows of foreign direct investment, contributed to the PRC's growing current account surplus.

Relocation of industries and associated migration to trade surplus from other Asian economies to the PRC is, again, a reasonable explanation for the PRC's growing external sector imbalances. This hypothesis, however, fails to explain why the PRC became a global manufacturing center so quickly. Were there unique factors behind the PRC's unusual cost advantage and industrial competitiveness? The relocation hypothesis also does not yield practical policy recommendations for dealing with the imbalance problem.

Policies Promoting Strong Growth

The PRC government's policy bias in favor of strong economic growth is well known. Therefore, policymakers naturally pay closer attention to production than anything else. Some economists claim that the large external sector surplus was a by-product of the policies supporting growth.

Yanhui Fan and Huifeng Pan (2008) argue that a key challenge facing the government is employment pressure, since the PRC still has huge surplus labor in the countryside and at the same time does not have a well-developed social welfare system. Job creation is a top priority since it is the basis for social security. The widely accepted 8 percent growth target, for instance, was formulated based on needed job creation. Therefore, the government sometimes boosts production at whatever cost.

Corden (2009) argues that the PRC's current account surplus and especially its rise since 2005 is, in fact, a by-product of various developments, such as productivity improvements, and a variety of policies, such as the exchange-rate policy. He notes that there were two parts to PRC exchange-rate policy: protecting the exchange rate for the export sector by currency undervaluation and maintaining a stable exchange rate. Another policy orientation is to build up foreign-exchange reserves as a form of self-insurance, especially after the Asian financial crisis in 1997–98. These inevitably led to large current account surpluses as a by-product.

Yu (2007) identifies the government's export promotion policy, which includes the so-called self-balancing regulation, exchange-rate policy, and tax rebates, as a contributing factor to the current account surplus. For instance, for a long time, the government demanded that foreign investors guarantee the self-balancing of foreign exchange for important investment projects. Therefore, foreign direct investment must be export oriented. As a result, when foreign direct investment was introduced, corresponding deficits were minimized.

This hypothesis itself is probably not controversial. The government has room to narrow external surpluses by reducing policy measures that support exports and economic growth. The question is how realistic it is for the government to give up its policy emphasis on growth.

Exchange-Rate Policy

The exchange-rate policy has been most frequently referenced in public debates about the PRC's external imbalances. An undervalued currency is often associated with higher exports and lower imports, which then lead to a large trade surplus or current account surplus. This was probably the most obvious logic behind foreign politicians' criticisms about the PRC's exchange-rate policy.

Morris Goldstein and Nicholas Lardy (2006) use the underlying balance approach to evaluate the misalignment of the yuan. The essence of their approach was to calculate the needed adjustments in the yuan's real effective exchange rate to return to "normal" current account balance. They conclude that the PRC's undervalued currency contributed to growing trade surpluses and, at least in some years, to large portfolio capital inflows, which appeared motivated by an expectation of appreciation.

It must be noted that the methodology applied by Goldstein and Lardy does not reveal how the exchange-rate policy caused current account surpluses. Instead, they infer currency undervaluation from current account imbalances.

Xiangqian Lu and Guoqiang Dai (2005) partly fill this gap by examining the long-run relationship between the PRC's international trade and the yuan's real effective exchange rate, applying data for the period 1994–2003. Results of their cointegrated vector autoregression model suggest that the yuan's real effective exchange rate had significant impacts on the PRC's exports and imports. These confirm that the exchange rate was indeed an important determinant of the current account imbalances.

Findings of empirical studies, however, are not uniform. For instance, Li and Li (2006) found no statistically significant effect of either the nominal exchange rate of the yuan or its real exchange rate on the PRC's exports to and imports from the United States. Instead, they found that changes in foreign direct investment inflows had a significant effect on exports to the United States.

Exchange-rate policy is probably the most reasonable explanation for the PRC's current account surplus, at least on the surface. The policy recommendations derived from it, however, might not be as reasonable. A common policy prescription is that the PRC should let its currency rise by a certain margin to eliminate the external imbalances. It is unrealistic to expect that the PRC government will permit its currency to appreciate sharply in the near term. Many PRC officials are concerned about the negative consequences of sharp currency appreciation, given their own interpretation of Japanese economic stagnation following the Plaza Accord.

An alternative recommendation is for the PRC to increase exchange-rate flexibility. This is probably good advice by itself. But can a more flexible exchange-rate regime automatically eliminate current account imbalance? The answer may be no, at least according to international experiences.

In a study applying a data set covering 170 countries over the period 1971–2005, Menzie Chinn and Shang-Jin Wei (2009) found no strong, robust, or monotonic relationship between exchange-rate regime flexibility and the rate of current account reversion, even after controlling the degree of economic development and the degree of trade and capital account openness. This conclusion can in fact be observed by simply surveying the data: there is no systemic relationship between a country's current account position and its exchange-rate regime flexibility. While strongly recommending an increase in exchange rate flexibility, Yu (2007) also cautions against expectations of significant adjustments to the current account surplus as a result of the exchange-rate policy reform.

So the notion that greater flexibility in a de facto nominal exchange-rate regime implies speedier adjustment in the current account is just based on faith and cannot be supported by data. What mattered for current account adjustment was the real, as opposed to nominal, exchange rate. In theory, the government can artificially revalue the currency by a big margin to strengthen the real effective exchange rate substantially. But this is probably difficult for the government to adopt, given corresponding structural adjustments the economy has to go through.

Factor Market Distortions: An Alternative Hypothesis

We now present an alternative hypothesis that the PRC's asymmetric liberalization of its product and factor markets can explain its large current account surplus. We first formulated this theory when we attempted to explain the unique macroeconomic phenomenon during the PRC's reform period: the combination of both extraordinary economic growth and deteriorating structural risks (Huang 2010).

The purpose of this exercise is not to replace the existing hypotheses. In a way, our hypothesis and the hypotheses presented within the literature may be supplementary and even overlapping. But, as we elaborate later, the factor market distortion hypothesis not only offers a fundamental explanation about the external imbalance but also produces a systemic policy prescription for curing the problem.

Asymmetric Market Liberalization

During the reform period, the PRC government focused on actions to reform the product markets, including abandoning policy interventions in domestic markets and liberalizing trade of goods and services. Today, free markets determine the prices of more than 95 percent of products.

In contrast, factor markets, including markets for labor, capital, land, energy, and the environment, remain highly distorted. For instance, many employers of migrant workers still do not make social welfare contributions for their employees. Outside the property sector, land prices are artificially determined by the government. These distortions generally push factor prices, and as a result, production costs are below what they would otherwise be in a market environment.

Cost distortions in the PRC are equivalent to production and investment subsidies. They artificially increase production profits and raise investment returns. Both PRC citizens and foreigners invest massively in the PRC because of its cheap labor, cheap capital, cheap land, and cheap energy. Producers enjoy extraordinary profits that are not possible in other countries.

Without a doubt, the fundamental cause of the PRC's strong growth of exports, investment, and production is the reform and open-door policy. But cost distortion, or subsidy equivalent, further lifts producers' profitability, investors' returns, and the international competitiveness of PRC products to even higher levels. Perhaps this is why the PRC's investment and production have been unusually strong during the reform period, particularly during the past years.

Meanwhile, these cost distortions are also equivalent to taxes on owners of these factors, mainly households. They reduce households' income and depress consumer spending. The combination of boosted investment and depressed consumption leads to imbalances between domestic and external demand. Low factor prices also cause distorted industrial structures, such as outsized heavy industry as a result of the cheap cost of capital, in addition to waste and inefficiency.

It is thus easy to predict that factor market distortion will lead to unusually large external imbalances, especially large trade surpluses and current account surpluses. The cost distortion improves exporters' profitability and exports' competitiveness in the international markets. Depressed consumption also widens the savings and income gap and, therefore, further boosts external sector surpluses.

Some distortions in factor markets, such as the government's controls over energy prices and land use fees for manufacturing investors, are deliberate policy measures to support economic growth. Other distortions, such as the household registration system limiting labor mobility and regulation of interest rates, are phenomena found during economic transitions. But they are in one way or another related to the government policy preference favoring strong growth.

Indeed, this is not the first time that the PRC government has adopted measures distorting production costs to achieve rapid economic growth. In the prereform period, for instance, the authorities devised a set of institutions to ensure rapid development of urban industries. When the government embarked on urban industrialization, it lacked a reliable supply of funds. Agriculture was the largest economic sector at that time. The purpose of that set of policies was to deliver high profits in urban industries, which could be reinvested to accelerate urban industrialization.

This first step was to depress agricultural prices, which could reduce production costs in urban industries by lowering both input cost and labor cost. Therefore, the government introduced a unified purchase and marketing system for agricultural products. Under this system, the state purchased agricultural products from farmers at below-market prices. To ensure that farmers would sell their products to the state, the authorities took the second step by abolishing all free markets. To make sure that farmers would produce according to the central plans, the authorities took the third step of collectivizing agriculture, handing all agricultural decisionmaking power to production team leaders, who were selected by the government. Finally, to guarantee that farmers would participate in collective farming, the authorities took the fourth step of introducing the household registration system, effectively prohibiting farmers from leaving their villages.

This system of urban industrialization policy was, for a while, quite successful. But it failed in the end. Otherwise, the PRC would not have had to start economic reforms in the late 1970s. There were two main reasons for the failure of the prereform policy system. First, since there was no free market for products, resource allocation was inefficient. All factories produced according to the central plans. In the end, lots of heavy industry products were produced for which there was no demand. At the same time, there was a significant shortage of consumer goods. Second, since there was no autonomy or incentive at the firm or individual levels, production efficiency was quite low. Shirking was a common phenomenon in urban factories and rural collectives.

Both of these problems were resolved with the beginning of economic reform, which is why the new policy system has been much more successful in supporting economic growth. But the new system has also given rise to structural risks, such as imbalances between investment and consumption and between domestic and external demand.

It should be clear by now that the factor-market-distortion hypothesis is related to some of the existing hypotheses reviewed earlier. For instance, the depressing of domestic consumption also contributes to the savings and investment gap. Reduction of production costs accelerates relocation of industries to the PRC. The cost distortion, intentionally or accidentally, is driven by the government's growth-centered policy strategy. Finally, currency undervaluation is a form of underpriced capital.

Remaining Distortions in Factor Markets

Introduction of free markets has been the central theme of economic reforms during the past three decades. But prices of almost all factors, including labor, land, capital, energy, and the environment, remain highly distorted.

LABOR MARKET. The PRC is known for its abundant and cheap labor, which was a key factor behind its success in labor-intensive manufacturing exports. But PRC labor costs may be distorted for two interrelated reasons: segmentation of rural and urban labor markets and underdevelopment of social welfare systems.

Labor market segmentation was largely a result of the household registration system introduced in the prereform period. The policy requires that people, whether urban or rural, stay where they were born their entire lives. Migration is possible only if approved by the government. The effectiveness of this system has weakened in recent years, as evidenced by a large number of migrant workers roaming the cities. Local authorities in Shandong, Henan, and Hainan also experimented with doing away with the restrictions on rural-urban migration.

By and large, however, the household registration system still erects important barriers for labor mobility. The location of an individual's household registration makes a significant difference. Urban residents are entitled to social welfare benefits, such as medical insurance, pension, unemployment support, and education, although most of these systems are still underdeveloped. Migrant workers, however, cannot access any of them, even if they have been working in cities for years.

The most important area of underpayment is social welfare contributions. Were urban employers to make social welfare contributions for their migrant workers, their payrolls would rise by about 35–40 percent, which includes contributions to pensions (20 percent of payroll), medical insurance (6 percent), unemployment benefits (2 percent), work injury insurance (1 percent), maternity benefits (0.8 percent), and housing entitlements (5–10 percent).[1]

CAPITAL MARKET. Distortions in capital markets exist at two levels. Domestically, the financial system remains repressed, as evidenced by highly regulated interest rates and state influences on credit allocation. Externally, capital account controls are more restrictive on outflows than on inflows. The currency is generally undervalued; at least it has been during the past fifteen years.

The PRC's financial system, especially its banking sector, has gone through a major transformation. Financial intermediation, however, remains overly dependent on banks, especially the large state-owned commercial banks. The government influences lending decisions. Despite significant reforms during past years, including introduction of foreign-strategic investors and public listings, most large banks are still majority owned by the state, and their top executives are still appointed by the government.

---

1. These estimates for a typical year were provided to the author by Fan Zhai, who was an official of the PRC's Ministry of Finance in 2002.

The PRC still maintains interest-rate regulation. Despite numerous reforms giving banks more flexibility in determining the actual rates, the People's Bank of China still maintains floors for lending rates and ceilings for deposit rates, ensuring minimum interest spread to facilitate reforms of the commercial banks. In reality, however, the actual lending rates have always been close to the benchmark rates.

This financial repression most likely reduced capital efficiency and therefore capital costs. A World Bank study suggests that financial liberalization in emerging market economies often raises domestic interest rates by a couple of percentage points (Caprio, Atiyas, and Hanson 1994).

Changes in the exchange-rate policy offer another example of cost distortion. Today, most economists believe that the yuan is still undervalued, although they disagree on the degree of undervaluation (Goldstein and Lardy 2008).

The larger gap between nominal GDP growth potential and long-term government bond yields in the PRC, relative to the gaps in other Asian economies, also suggests that the PRC's capital is excessively cheap. At the end of 2008, the difference was 10 percentage points in the PRC, compared with 6.5 in India, 6.2 in Thailand, 5.7 in Malaysia, and 2.6 in the Republic of Korea.[2] Compared with other Asian economies, the PRC's nominal growth potential was the highest, but its treasury yield was among the lowest.

MARKETS FOR LAND, ENERGY, AND THE ENVIRONMENT. In the PRC, land is owned by the state in the cities and by collectives in the countryside. Recently, local governments began to sell land use rights to property developers through negotiations and auctions. However, there is no market mechanism for determining prices for industrial land use. They are often set by government departments through negotiation. To attract investment and promote growth, regional governments often offer land use rights to investors at discounted or even zero-cost rates. Local governments sometimes compete with one another in offering preferential policies to attract investment. In recent years, the average fees collected from negotiated granting of land use rights were only about 16 percent of those collected through auctions.

Prices of key energy products, such as oil, gas, and electricity, are also regulated by the state. Electricity tariffs are set by the National Development and Reform Commission (NDRC), although the authorities sometimes hold public hearings to improve decisionmaking quality. Tariffs are different for agricultural, industrial, and residential uses. Electricity prices have been under pressure for upward adjustment in recent years as costs of oil and coal rose significantly.

In 1998 in an important step of oil price liberalization, the PRC State Council announced a formula linking domestic prices to the weighted average of prices in New York, Singapore, and Rotterdam. The NDRC would adjust domestic prices,

2. The difference is calculated by subtracting the five-year government bond yield from the economy's nominal GDP growth potential forecast, which was estimated by Citigroup economists.

with a couple of months' delay, if the international weighted average moved by more than 8 percent. In 2000 the agency raised oil prices seven times to bring domestic prices closer to international levels.

However, when international prices moved violently, the NDRC was reluctant to follow for fear of disrupting economic growth. For instance, when international crude prices reached their recent peak at close to US$150 a barrel in 2008, the equivalent domestic prices were only around US$80 a barrel. But oil price distortions are highly volatile, given the State Council's formula and fluctuations in the international markets.

The PRC has introduced a series of environmental laws and regulations. Their enforcement, however, has been rather random, as the government emphasizes economic growth. Pollution of air, water, and land, the most visible negative by-product of the PRC's rapid economic growth, has not only affected productivity but also generated serious health consequences. Environmental degradation in the PRC has contributed to global climate change, as evidenced by the rapid melting of ice on the Himalayas. It also has led to regular drought in the north and frequent floods in the south.

According to a joint study by the National Bureau of Statistics and the State Agency for Environmental Protection, an incomplete count of the costs of environmental damage amounted to about 3.05 percent of GDP in 2004 (Huang 2007). Since producers do not always fully compensate for damage to the environment, short-term production costs are reduced at the expense of the long-term development of the whole economy and society.

Crude Estimations of Factor Market Distortions

A critical question here is whether cost distortions are a good explanatory variable for the recent surge in the current account surplus. Any review of policy changes would suggest that, despite slow progress, factor market controls have gradually become less strict. Therefore, it might appear to contradict the fact that current account surpluses widened sharply in recent years.

To gauge the significance of such factor market distortions, we made some crude quantitative estimations. Yiping Huang (2010) made one of the first attempts at measurement and found distortions totaling CNY2.1 trillion in 2008, or about 7 percent of GDP. His estimation, however, was made only for one year, which is of limited use since we are trying to explain changes in current account surpluses in recent years. We extended the estimation by both improving the methodologies and extending the period to include nine years, from 2000 to 2008. Based on obtained estimates and other available information, we also made preliminary attempts to estimate a number for 2009, which is subject to revision in the future.

The estimation results are summarized in table 6-1, with more detailed explanations of the estimation methods included in the appendix at the end of this

Table 6-1. *Estimated Producer Subsidy Equivalents of Factor Market Distortions as Share of GDP, People's Republic of China, 2000–09*[a]

Percent

	Labor	Capital	Land	Energy	Environment	Total	Current account balance
2000	0.1	4.1	0.5	0.0	3.8	8.5	1.7
2001	0.2	3.9	0.5	0.0	3.5	8.1	1.3
2002	0.8	3.9	0.4	0.0	3.3	8.4	2.4
2003	1.0	3.8	1.1	0.0	3.3	9.2	2.8
2004	2.0	3.1	0.9	0.6	3.0	9.5	3.5
2005	2.4	3.0	1.3	1.7	3.0	11.4	7.2
2006	2.7	3.1	2.0	1.6	2.8	12.2	9.0
2007	3.2	3.6	1.2	1.6	2.4	12.0	10.8
2008	3.6	3.4	1.0	0.7	1.9	10.6	9.6
2009[a]	2.7	3.5	0.9	0.7	1.8	9.6	5.8

Source: Authors' estimations. Please refer to appendix 6-A for detailed estimation methods.

a. Estimates for 2009 are very preliminary based on estimates for other years and available information for 2009 and are subject to major revision when new information is available.

chapter. These results reveal several important findings. First, of all the factor market distortions, capital market distortion was by far the most important single item. Capital producer subsidy equivalents (PSEs) would contribute, on average, about 40 percent of total PSEs. This explains the overinvestment problem persistent in the PRC and also the rapid development of capital-intensive industries despite continued job market pressures.

Second, labor market distortions actually picked up in recent years despite the loosening of household registration system controls and increasing rural-urban migration. This was a result of both the rising number of migrant workers and persistent, even widening, income gaps between migrant workers and urban workers. Indeed, statistics show that while labor demand increased in recent years, migrant workers' pay did not keep pace with that of urban workers, especially when social welfare benefit contributions are included.

Third, energy cost distortions fluctuated widely across years, reflecting volatilities in international oil prices. The PRC had already adopted a price mechanism that would closely track changes in international energy prices. Authorities, however, would hold down domestic prices when international prices surged rapidly. Therefore, the energy cost distortions measured in this study were not a major problem until several years ago.

Fourth, environmental cost distortions were the only item that showed consistent improvement. This might be a surprise to some, at least initially, but individual and aggregate pollution indicators confirm fewer emissions in recent years.

Finally, the aggregate estimates of cost distortions or PSEs match the current imbalance data surprisingly well (see figure 6-8). Given a limited number of

Figure 6-8. *Estimated Cost Distortion and Current Account Balance as Share of GDP, People's Republic of China, 2000–09*

Percent of GDP

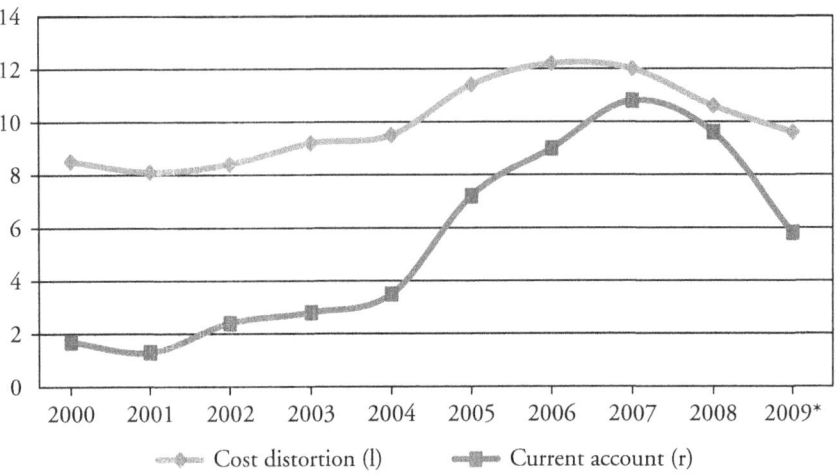

Source: Data from CEIC. Authors' estimation.

observations, we are not able to conduct any statistical analyses to test correlation or causality between the two sets of data. But these estimates at least provide partial evidence that factor market distortions were possibly an important element in the PRC's large current account surpluses.

The trends of both liberalization and recent increases in PSEs are not necessarily contradictory. For example, even if the factor market is gradually liberalized, cost distortions may rise dramatically as long as the distorted factor prices cannot keep pace with shadow market prices.

If PSEs provide any guide for the future development of the current account, then we may argue that the worst of the external imbalance is probably over. Factor market distortions as a share of GDP already peaked in 2006, followed by a peak of current account surplus as a share of GDP in 2007. Therefore, the narrowing of the current account surpluses in 2008 and 2009 was not entirely caused by weakening external demand. Unless cost distortions rebound again, current account surpluses may stay at relatively lower levels in the coming years.

Since labor cost distortion is the most challenged factor in policy debates, we also plot factor cost distortions by excluding labor from the calculation. Although both levels and curvature of the estimates changed somewhat, a significant increase in factor distortion from 2004 remains the case (see figure 6-9).

We should acknowledge that, owing to data limits, we did not conduct a causality test, and therefore we cannot claim statistically that these distortions

Figure 6-9. *Estimated Cost Distortion Excluding Labor Cost and Current Account Balance as Share of GDP, 2000–09*

Percent of GDP

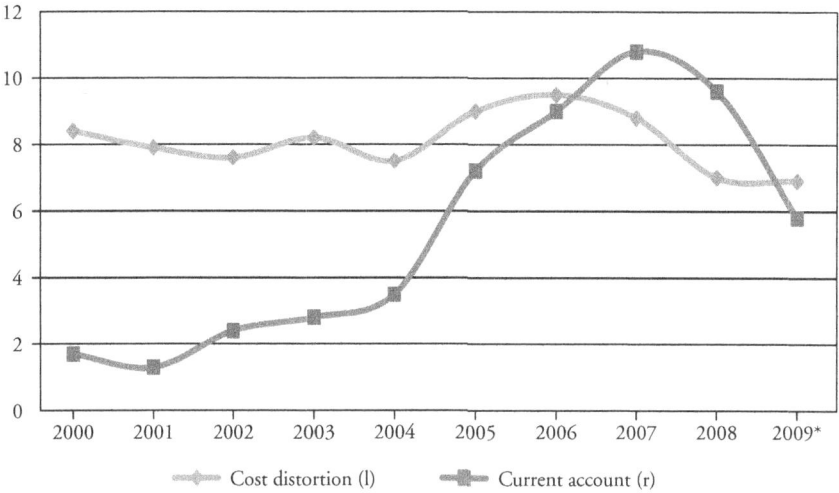

Source: Data from CEIC. Authors' estimation.

caused the PRC's current account surplus. We nonetheless try to offer an alternative but also supplementary explanation for the PRC's current account surpluses, especially for the recent surge. However, even if there is reverse causality between the cost distortion and the current account surpluses, or even if they are all the products of the PRC's promotion of growth policies, we may argue that the proper and feasible therapy is still to adopt a comprehensive package focused on removing the factor cost distortions.

First, these two problems are partially related. The possibility of reverse causality, that is, that the current account surpluses are the reason for the factor cost distortions, is closely related to the PRC's growth promotion strategy. Second, since the aim is to rebalance the economy rather than to stop growth, we cannot suggest that the PRC abandon its growth promotion strategy. We recommend that the PRC put more emphasis on factor market liberalization, adjusting the growth strategy to rebalance its external sector.

Policy Options for Rebalancing the External Sector

The findings of this study have important policy implications. If cost distortions (along with other factors such as industrial relocation and policies pursuing strong GDP growth) were a fundamental cause of the PRC's current account surplus, removal of these distortions should be a part of the solution. So far, however, this has not been a central strategy for rebalancing the PRC's economy.

Past Policies for Rebalancing the External Sector

When Wen Jiabao first took office in early 2003, the government immediately identified structural imbalances as a key threat to the PRC's growth model. The premier and other senior leaders repeatedly pointed out that the existing growth pattern was unstable and unsustainable.[3]

One of the imbalance problems was too much reliance on exports for economic growth. The export share of GDP rose from around 10 percent in the 1980s to above 20 percent in the early twenty-first century. Although such an export dependency ratio is not particularly high compared with other small, open Asian economies, it is extraordinary in comparison with other large economies such as the United States and Japan. The potential risk is that the PRC will probably face hurdles in sustaining export growth in normal years, let alone in those times when external demand weakens significantly.

More worrying are its growing trade and current account surpluses. Although the current account balances have always fluctuated, its surpluses rose quickly back to 3 percent of GDP in the years following the Asian financial crisis. Persistent and rising current account surpluses indicate the PRC's inefficient use of capital: as a low-income country, the PRC lends to the world market. More important, the large current account surplus every year adds further pressure on the economy, such as accumulation of foreign exchange reserves, excess liquidity in the domestic market, high inflation risks, and greater expectations for currency appreciation.

To reduce these and other structural risks, the Wen Jiabao government adopted several policy measures to rebalance the economy and improve growth quality. One type of policy attempts to directly address the surplus problem. This includes reduction of the export tax rebate and appreciation of the currency. Export-tax-rebate policy was introduced in 1994 to exempt exports from value-added taxes. The government, however, adjusts the rates from time to time either as an industrial policy or as a macroeconomic instrument. For instance, in June 2007, the Ministry of Finance and the State Administration of Taxation lowered the rebates for a list of exports to improve export structure and slow export growth.

The other type of measure attacks the imbalance problem indirectly. For instance, the government abolished agricultural taxes, increased spending on rural infrastructure, and strengthened social welfare systems. All these measures aimed at boosting domestic demand to reduce export growth and nar-

---

3. See, for instance, reports on Premier Wen Jiabao's press conference on March 16, 2007, following the annual National People's Congress meeting (Government of China 2007).

row the current account surplus. The authorities also raised interest rates and tightened controls over large investment projects to slow the expansion of export capacity.

All these efforts were probably useful and achieved some results, but as a whole they failed to contain external imbalances. In fact, between 2003 and 2007, the export share of GDP rose further, from 26.6 percent to 35.4 percent. And the current account surplus surged from 2.8 percent of GDP to 10.8 percent during the same period. An important reason why the government policies have not succeeded so far is that they did not deal with the root cause of the problem, that is, the distorted incentive structure. If capital is too cheap, then tighter controls by the NDRC on investment projects are not likely to be effective in alleviating the overinvestment problem.

Social Welfare Systems and the Currency

Economists also proposed some fundamental solutions to the PRC's current account imbalance problems. One is the development of a social welfare system, and another is an appreciation of the yuan.

The idea of developing a social welfare system is based on the belief that the savings and investment gap was caused by insufficient consumption. In the late 1990s, the PRC government dismantled the state-dominated social welfare systems and began to build market-based systems. Building new systems, however, is difficult, and the transition significantly increased uncertainty. Households probably increased their savings for their own future protection. Improved social welfare systems might be able to reduce savings and increase consumption, effectively narrowing the savings and investment gap.

This policy advice is reasonable. After all, social welfare systems are a critical part of a developed market system. It is unclear, however, whether improvement in the social welfare system alone is sufficient to reduce the external imbalances. First, as Zhou (2009) points out, household savings as a share of GDP have been relatively stable for the past twenty years, fluctuating slightly around 20 percent. What drove the significant increase in the national savings ratio, which is now well above 50 percent, was rising corporate savings, from 11.3 percent of GDP in 1992 to 22.9 percent in 2007. Therefore, improved social welfare systems may be able to reduce household savings, but their impact on overall national savings is likely to be limited.

More worrying trends during the past decade or so have been declining shares of labor compensation and household income in national income. According to Chong-En Bai and Zhenjie Qian (2009a, 2009b), the share of labor compensation in national income dropped from 51.4 percent in 1995 to 40.6 percent in 2006 (see figure 6-10). Similarly, the share of household income in national income declined from 66.8 percent in 1996 to 50.6 percent in 2007. We argue that the declining income shares of labor and households

Figure 6-10. *Labor Compensation, Household Income, and Household Consumption as Share of National Income, People's Republic of China, 1990–2009*

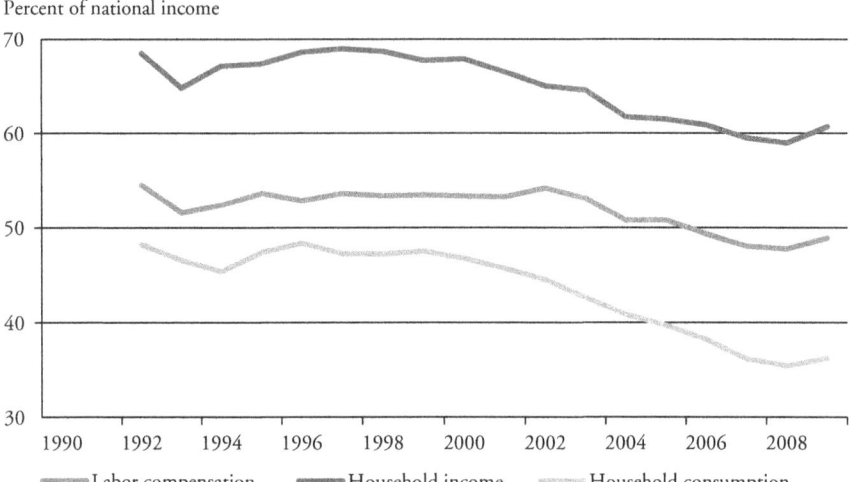

Percent of national income

Labor compensation   Household income   Household consumption

Source: Date from CEIC; Bai and Qian (2009a and 2009b).

are largely attributable to distortions in factor markets. Unless these macro trends are reversed, it would be unreasonable to expect consumption to pick up strongly.

The exchange-rate option is much more sensitive. For most economists and policymakers, there is little disagreement about the importance of a more flexible exchange-rate regime in the PRC. During the first fifteen years of the PRC's economic reforms, the yuan depreciated by 75 percent in real effective terms (see figure 6-11). Between January 1994 and June 2005, the real effective exchange rate of the yuan appreciated by 30 percent, and between June 2005 and December 2008, it appreciated by another 19 percent. Although the overall trend of appreciation is clear, the magnitudes of the changes were probably grossly insufficient, compared with the PRC's extraordinary productivity growth during the same period. Rising external imbalance is one important indication of an undervalued currency.

Exchange-rate policy reform should therefore be a part of the program dealing with the imbalance problem. In fact, the exit from the soft peg (allowing the exchange rate to fluctuate) and resumption of the track of gradual appreciation for the yuan began in mid-2010.

The risk now, however, is that often the exchange policy issue is singled out and sometimes even politicized. If this occurs, it will certainly prove counterproductive. Foreign pressures are sometimes useful for reformers to overcome domestic resistance. But as with U.S. policymakers, PRC leaders also have to

Figure 6-11. *Real Effective Exchange Rate Indexes of the Yuan and U.S. Dollar, 1990–2012*[a]

Index: 1990 = 1.0

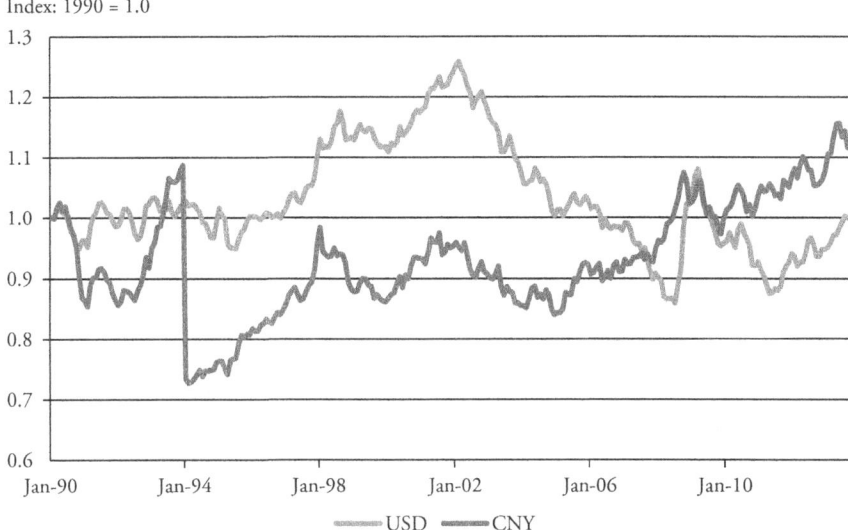

Source: Last price in each month from J.P. Morgan real broad effective exchange-rate indexes.
a. Indexes were set to 1.0 in January 1990.

entertain domestic politics. To be seen as giving in to foreign pressures on important issues like exchange-rate policy could significantly weaken the leader's political standing.

There is still significant disagreement on how much the currency is undervalued. For instance, Goldstein and Lardy (2009) suggest that, if half of 2008's current account surplus were to be eliminated, then by the end of that year, the yuan would probably be undervalued by only 12–16 percent. It is unlikely that such an adjustment, even if it took place, would satisfy demands by most foreign-country politicians. Politicians in the PRC would also be reluctant to introduce greater adjustment in the short term, given the likely consequences for PRC enterprises and financial institutions.

It might be worthwhile to point out the need for prudence regarding these estimations. For instance, a sharp rise in the yuan exchange rate may wipe out the PRC's current account surplus, but it might not reduce the U.S. current account deficits. The yuan accounts for only 15 percent of the U.S. Federal Reserve exchange-rate basket for the dollar. This implies that a 20 percent appreciation of the yuan would translate into appreciation of the dollar by only 3 percent. More important, the market vacuum left by PRC products might be quickly filled with products from other low-income countries, such as India, Indonesia, South Africa, and Viet Nam.

Even for the PRC, the exchange rate may not be the only, or even the most important, factor behind external imbalances. For instance, Wing Thye Woo (2006) argues that trade surpluses are better handled by establishment of an efficient financial intermediation mechanism than by appreciation of the currency. Similarly, Goldstein and Lardy (2009) argue that the exchange-rate policy alone is not likely to be effective. The PRC's recent experiences after the July 2005 reform provide a useful footnote to these arguments. Between mid-2005 and mid-2008, the real effective exchange rate of the yuan appreciated by 20 percent, but the PRC's current account surpluses surged during the same period.

Removing Factor Market Distortions

Given the structural nature of the PRC imbalance problem, a comprehensive package dealing with the problem is probably preferable to an exclusive focus on the exchange rate.[4] Greater exchange-rate flexibility and gradual currency appreciation should be part of that package. But the reality is that a sharp revaluation as demanded by some foreign politicians and experts is not only politically infeasible in the PRC but also probably economically undesirable, at least in the near term.

Following the findings in this study, we argue that extraordinary growth performance and growing structural imbalances are actually different sides of the same coin: asymmetric market liberalization. An effective solution to the imbalance problem, therefore, is to complete transition to the market economy by further liberalizing the factor markets and removing cost distortions. Reduction of producer subsidy equivalents associated with factor market distortions would correct the unusually high incentives for production, investment, and exports.

Introduction of market-based factor prices, however, cannot be done overnight. Some changes are relatively easy to make. The government is already looking at various ways of removing or reducing distortions in resource prices. In late 2009, the authorities began to make efforts in adjusting prices for fuel, gas, electricity, and water. In the past, the main hurdles for resource price liberalization were special interest groups such as agriculture, farmers, and low-income urban households. The government can deal with these special groups with fiscal instruments while pushing ahead with price liberalization.

Distortions to environmental costs are already falling, at least as shares of GDP. This reflects the government's increased efforts to protect the environment. Senior officials of the Ministry of Environmental Protection recently indicated that though the environmental turning point in developed economies normally

---

4. Goldstein and Lardy (2009) recommend a comprehensive package dealing with the PRC's imbalance problems focusing on four policy domains: fiscal, financial, pricing, and exchange-rate policies. Their policy recommendations share many similarities with suggestions in this study.

occurs when per capita income is US$8,000, in the PRC it could happen at US$3,000.[5] One official also mentioned that the Ministry of Finance, the State Administration of Taxation, and the Ministry of Environmental Protection were considering new environmental protection taxes.

Labor market liberalization is progressing rapidly, as demonstrated by the massive number of migrant workers. The government made a number of new breakthroughs in reform of the household registration system and promotion of urbanization in 2010, although bigger reforms were made in 2011 and 2014. But complete removal of this restriction and the discrimination against rural workers it implies will most likely take some time. One critical condition is the extension of social welfare systems to all rural residents. However, the earlier the Lewis turning point arrives—that is, the sooner the labor market transits from surplus to shortage—the faster the labor market liberalization will occur.

Capital market liberalization is already gaining momentum and, according to optimistic judgments, could see major breakthroughs in introducing market-based interest and exchange rates within the next five years. Of course, these changes are conditional on successful reforms of the state-owned enterprises and financial institutions and improvement in macroeconomic management skills.

Privatization of land might not happen any time soon. But clearly defined and well-protected leasing rights and the freedom to circulate according to market mechanisms could also reduce distortions to use rates for land.

Reduction or abolition of PSEs should also be supplemented by some related reforms. For instance, the government will need to give up overemphasis on growth performance, which in many cases has been the initial cause of persistent cost distortions. The government's role should be the provision of public services and maintenance of stable macroeconomic environment, not direct involvement in economic activities (Yao 2010).

The state sector, which is capturing an increasing portion of national income and causing the imbalance problem, needs further reforms to share more benefits with households. At a minimum, the state should collect more dividends and taxes from the state-owned enterprises for redistribution to the broader society. Ideally, the state sector should gradually give up monopoly power or be privatized.

Factor market liberalization is likely to help prevent a further slide of household income shares. But if this is insufficient to reverse the trend, the government may need to step in to redistribute more income and wealth to households. After all, enriching households, rather than keeping more wealth in the hands of the state-owned enterprises or the government, is the ultimate goal of economic reform and economic growth.

5. See, for instance, "Ministry of Environmental Protection: New Environmental Protection Taxes Are Under Consideration" (in Chinese), Xinhua News Agency, February 2, 2010. (http://news.xinhuanet.com/fortune/2010-02/10/content_12960850.htm).

Finally, rapid development of the service sector will be a critical benchmark for structural rebalancing. Factor market liberalization should realign incentives between manufacturing and service activities. But the government may need to help overcome some major obstacles for service sector development, especially with respect to insufficient financial services, high entry barriers, and lack of intellectual property rights.

Concluding Remarks

Structural rebalancing will quite likely remain a key policy challenge for both the global and the PRC economy in the years to come. Having a large current account surplus is a relatively recent phenomenon in the PRC and has occurred most clearly since 2004. A significant rise in the U.S. current account deficit happened a few years earlier. These suggest that the PRC should be a part of the solution to the global imbalance problem. It is not reasonable to blame the PRC for the large U.S. imbalance problem.

The six closely related hypotheses for the PRC's current account imbalances—measurement error, savings and investment gap, demographic transition, industrial relocation, policies pursuing strong growth, and exchange-rate policy—are important factors related to the PRC's imbalance problems. Unfortunately, they do not suggest actionable policy solutions for resolving such imbalance problems. Most critically, these factors generally fail to explain the sharp surge of current account surpluses in recent years.

We propose an alternative hypothesis: asymmetric market liberalization and the related factor market distortions during the reform period. This particular reform approach generally lowers production costs and provides producer subsidy equivalents. It artificially raises production profits, increases investment returns, and improves international competitiveness of PRC products. Continued factor market distortion is the cause for both extraordinary growth performance and growing structural imbalances during the reform period.

To offer some guidance, we made some crude estimations of cost distortions for the period 2000–09. The results suggest that capital cost distortion was by far the most important component of PSEs. Labor cost distortion jumped recently as the number of migrant workers increased. Surprisingly, distortions to environmental costs have already begun to decline in recent years, at least as shares of GDP.

Estimates of total PSEs provide an almost perfect fit for current account imbalances, rising steadily from 2000 and reaching their peak in 2006. Cost distortions increased despite gradual liberalization of factor markets, suggesting that the distorted factor prices did not keep pace with market prices. Total PSEs in 2009 were back to the levels of 2003–04, before the surge of current account surpluses. This may be an indication that though the surpluses may rebound somewhat as the global economy continues to recover, the worst of the PRC's external imbalances may be behind us.

The findings of this study have important policy implications for dealing with the current account imbalance problems. The PRC government has been trying hard to rebalance the economy since 2003 but has achieved limited results. In fact, most imbalance problems worsened in the following years. The reason for the lack of success was probably that the government addressed only the factors on the surface, not the root cause, that is, the distorted incentive structure for exporters, investors, and producers.

Recent popular policy advice includes development of social welfare systems and appreciation of the currency. Although these are probably useful steps to take, we do not think these measures alone would be effective in resolving the problem. As increasing portions of savings derive from the corporate sector and the household income share of the economy continues to decline, better social welfare systems would have limited impact on the national saving rate and consumption.

Greater exchange-rate flexibility and gradual currency appreciation should be important parts of the policy package, but exclusive focus on the issue may be counterproductive. Although the government began to reform the exchange-rate regime in mid-2010, it is politically infeasible and possibly economically undesirable for the PRC to implement large-scale appreciation in the short term. At minimum, yuan appreciation alone is not likely to resolve the U.S. imbalance problem. And the 2005–08 experiences suggest that currency appreciation should be combined with other policy measures in controlling current account surpluses.

We recommend a comprehensive policy package for dealing with the PRC's external imbalance problem. The core element of the package is to complete the transition to a market economy by further liberalizing the factor markets and removing all cost distortions. Exchange-rate adjustment serves as a part of this package. The liberalization may take years to accomplish, but some measures can be implemented relatively quickly. The government is already reforming resource prices. Environmental cost distortion is already on the decline. Both labor and capital market liberalization could gather momentum in the coming year or so. This core element also needs to be supplemented by other reforms, including reform of the government's overemphasis on GDP growth, liberalization of the state-owned enterprises and financial institutions, redistribution of income from the corporate sector to households, and removal of the barriers for service sector development.

If our analyses and prescription are correct, then we may conclude that the worst of the external imbalance problem is probably over, unless cost distortions rebound sharply. The current and future reform initiatives would also ensure further containment of external imbalances. Most of these reforms, however, cannot be implemented overnight. Rebalancing of the PRC's external sector may also take a few years to accomplish.

Appendix 6A: Estimation of Factor Market Distortions

This appendix explains how cost distortions are estimated. It should be noted that these estimates only provide rough guidance about cost distortions. In many cases, we do not have reliable benchmarks, and we often can only consider limited aspects of the distortions. However, if the methodologies are consistent, then the results should at least provide some good indications about changes over time.

Labor Market

The estimation of labor market distortion focuses on underpayment of migrant workers under the household registration system. Migrant workers' pay grew by an average of 7 percent between 2000 and 2008, which was only half the rate of increase of the national average of workers' pay. This is why the pay gap between migrant workers and urban workers widened significantly, from about 30 percent in 2000 to 50 percent in 2008. In estimating cost distortion, we assume that migrant workers should be paid 25 percent less than urban workers, given likely differences in human capital.

The total distortion is a product of the number of migrant workers multiplied by the pay gap. The distortion increased, partly because of the rapid rise in the number of migrant workers, from 88 million in 2000 to 140 million in 2008. As a result, labor cost distortion rose from 6 billion yuan (0.1 percent of GDP) in 2000 to 1.13 trillion yuan (3.6 percent of GDP) in 2008. In 2008 labor cost surpassed capital to become the largest cost distortion item.

Clearly, these figures probably still underestimate the actual labor cost distortion. At the very least they ignore underdeveloped social welfare systems. They may also, however, be biased in the opposite direction. Depressed wages for migrant workers would increase demand for labor and therefore create more jobs. Whether farmers' income would increase or decrease as a result depends on labor demand elasticity with respect to wages. Our simple exercise does not assume a change in labor demand behavior following changes in labor compensation.

Capital Market

Capital cost distortions show in at least two forms, the first being distorted interest rates and the second being distorted exchange rates. Instead of calculating cost distortions in these two forms, we compute aggregate cost of distortion owing to financial repression. The PRC still shows typical symptoms of a financially repressed economy: regulated interest rates, controlled exchange rates, managed credit allocation, and dominance of both state-owned commercial banks and state-owned enterprises.

Following Caprio, Atiyas, and Hanson (1994), Huang (2010) assumes that financial repression depressed the cost of capital by an average of 2 percentage points in 2008. To calculate variations of capital cost distortion, we borrow the financial repression index from Xun Wang (2010). By setting the index at 100 in 2008 and rebasing it to 2 percentage points, we can obtain the percentage-point distortions for other years covered in this study. The highest distortion was 3 percentage points, which occurred in 2000. Distortions then declined gradually.

The total cost distortions were calculated by multiplying the total bank deposits by cost distortions. The total amount of distortions increased steadily, mainly because total bank deposits grew rapidly during that period. One potential criticism is lack of explicit estimation of exchange-rate distortion. However, calculation of actual cost distortion owing to undervalued currency is difficult conceptually unless it directly involves imports or exports. The financial repression indicators should reflect, at least partly, cost distortion in both exchange rates and interest rates.

Land Market

In the PRC, there are different ways of setting land transfer fees. The first is essentially by negotiation between potential users and government entities. This is a nonmarket method and is normally applied to industrial activities. The actual fees set are often much lower than potential market rates as the government is inclined to attract investors. The other market forms include bidding and auctioning, which set market rates. The market rates are on average six times higher than the nonmarket rates.

To calculate distortions in nonmarket land transfers, we obtain the total area of land transferred under the nonmarket approach. Unfortunately we only obtained data from 2003 to 2007. The annual transferred land under the nonmarket approach fluctuated across years, from a low of 108,000 hectares in 2005 to 162,000 hectares in 2006.

In 2007 the nonmarket transfer rate was CNY637,888 per hectare, while the market rate was CNY3.23 million per hectare. This gap was somewhat narrower earlier, as the market rate was later pushed up by a property market boom. Total calculated land cost distortions increased from around CNY150 million in 2003–04 to CNY423 million in 2006. Since we do not have enough data to estimate cost distortion for 2000–02 and 2008–09, we simply assumed some numbers for these years, taking into account the trends during nearby years.

The main problem with land cost distortion estimates is that we do not have market rates for equivalent land uses. Obviously the market rates were substantially boosted by the housing boom. Such rates may not be applicable to industrial land. Also, we calculated cost differences only for land transferred. A better approach would be to look at the actual rental costs paid by industrial firms, compared with potential market rate.

Energy Market

Oil, coal, natural gas, and electricity constitute the majority energy use in the PRC. Although the PRC is the largest producer and consumer of coal, prices are more or less liberalized. Our calculation here focuses on oil products by looking at the equivalent price gaps for domestic and international oil prices and total oil consumption in the PRC. There is little difference in the prices of crude oil produced domestically or abroad. Price differences are mainly in finished goods.

The price gaps also fluctuate from year to year. The government has already adopted a mechanism that links domestic oil prices to international prices, with some time lags. Therefore, there would normally be no significant cost distortions. But when international prices rise sharply, the government is reluctant to let domestic prices follow for fear of disruptive effects on consumption and production. This happened in the years after 2005.

We chose the New York Harbor petroleum price as the benchmark for international petroleum prices. The PRC's petroleum prices are published by the National Development and Reform Commission. Then we took oil consumption into account to calculate the energy market distortion. It turned out that the calculated distortions were small negative numbers for the years 2000–03, which indicates effective taxes. We think these probably reflect more data noise rather than actual taxes, and we therefore set the numbers for those years to zero. Energy cost distortions reached their peak in 2007 at CNY400 million.

The Environment

Distortions in environmental costs mainly reflect polluters' undercompensation for their emissions. Following Huang (2010), we adopted the government estimate of environmental costs of 3 percent of GDP in 2004. We then looked at changes in emissions of SO_2 and CO_2 discharge, which are categorized by the State Environmental Protection Administration.

The aggregate emissions show peaking in 2005 and 2006. We then used these physical emission indexes to calculate the likely cleaning costs, benchmarking them at 3 percent of GDP in 2004 and applying a 5 percent inflation rate to obtain the nominal value of cost distortions. The total costs stagnated in 2006–09, but their shares of GDP declined steadily from 3 percent in 2005 to 1.9 percent in 2008.

References

Andersson, Andreas, and Par Osterholm. 2006. "Population Age Structure and Real Exchange Rates in the OECD." *International Economic Journal* 20: 1–18.

Bai, Chong-En, and Zhenjie Qian. 2009a. "Factor Income Share in China: Stories behind Statistics." *Economic Research Journal* (Jing Ji Yan Jiu) 3: 27–41.

————. 2009b. "Who Has Eroded Residents' Income? An Analysis of China's National Income Distribution Patterns." *Social Sciences in China* (Zhong Guo She Hui Ke Xue) 5: 99–115.

Bernanke, Ben. 2007. "Global Imbalances: Recent Developments and Prospects." Bundesbank Lecture, September 11, Berlin, Germany.

Cai, Fang, and Meiyan Wang. 2007. "How Will Population Aging Affect Economic Growth?" *China Economist* 1: 86–94.

Caprio, Gerald, Jr., Izak Atiyas, and James A. Hanson. 1994. *Financial Reform: Theory and Practice.* Cambridge University Press.

Chinn, Menzie D., and Hiro Ito. 2007. "Current Account Balances, Financial Development, and Institutions: Assaying the World 'Saving Glut.'" *Journal of International Money and Finance* 26: 546–69.

Chinn, Menzie D., and Shang-Jin Wei. 2009. "A Faith-Based Initiative: Does a Flexible Exchange Rate Regime Really Facilitate Current Account Adjustment?" Working Paper 12. Hong Kong Institute for Monetary Research. Hong Kong, China: Hong Kong Monetary Authority.

Commission on Growth and Development. 2008. *The Growth Report: Strategies for Sustained Growth and Inclusive Development.* Washington: World Bank (https://openknowledge.worldbank.org/handle/10986/6507 License: Creative Commons Attribution CC BY 3.0).

Corden, Warner M. 2006. "Those Current Account Imbalances: A Skeptical View." Working Paper 13/06. University of Melbourne, Melbourne Institute of Applied Economic and Social Research.

————. 2009. "China's Exchange Rate Policy, Its Current Account Surplus, and the Global Imbalances." In *China's New Place in a World in Crisis,* edited by Ross Garnaut, Ligang Song, and Wing Thye Woo. Canberra, Australia: ANU E-Press.

Fan, Yanhui, and Huifeng Pan. 2008. "RMB Appreciation Expectations and Trade Balance of China." *International Finance Research* 2: 52–59.

Feenstra, Robert C., and others. 1999. "Discrepancies in International Data: An Application to China–Hong Kong Entrepôt Trade." *American Economic Review Papers and Proceedings* 89: 338–43.

Goldstein, Morris, and Nicholas Lardy. 2006. "China's Exchange Rate Policy Dilemma." *American Economic Review* 96. no. 2: 422–26.

————. 2008. *Debating China's Exchange Rate Policy.* Washington: Peterson Institute for International Economics.

————. 2009. *The Future of China's Exchange Rate Policy.* Washington: Peterson Institute for International Economics.

Government of China. 2007. "Prime Minister Wen Jia Bao's Press Conference Questions and Answers" (in Chinese). March 16 (www.gov.cn/wszb/zhibo20070316b/wz.htm).

Greenspan, Alan. 2005. "Current Account." Speech delivered at the Advancing Enterprise Conference, London, U.K., February 4.

Huang, Yiping. 2007. "Environmental Costs of Economic Prosperity." June 20. Caijing.com.cn (www.caijing.com.cn/2007-06-20/100022693.html)

————. 2010. "China's Great Ascendancy and Structural Risks: Consequences of Asymmetric Market Liberalization." *Asian-Pacific Economic Literature* 24, no. 1: 65–85.

Kawai, Masahiro, and Zhai Fan. 2009. "China-Japan–United States Integration amid Global Rebalancing: A Computable General Equilibrium Analysis." *Journal of Asian Economics* 20, no. 6: 688–99.

Lardy, Nicholas R. 1994. *China in the World Economy.* Washington: Peterson Institute of International Economics.

————. 2006. "China: Toward a Consumption-Driven Growth Path." *Policy Briefs in International Economics* 6, no. 6 (www.petersoninstitute.org/publications/pb/pb06-6.pdf).

Li, Daokui, and Danning Li. 2006. "An Analysis of the Bilateral Trade Balance between China and U.S.: Exchange Rate, Savings, and World Trade Structure." Working Paper. Beijing: Tsinghua University, Center for China and World Economy.

Lin, Justin Y. 2010. "Dealing with Global Imbalances." Paper presented at the Conference on Reconstructing the World Economy. Seoul, Korea, Korean Development Institute/International Monetary Fund, February 25.

Lu, Xiangqian, and Guoqiang Dai. 2005. "The Influence of Fluctuation of Real RMB Exchange Rate to Chinese Import and Export: 1994–2003." *Economic Research* 5: 31–39 (www.oriprobe.com/journals/caod_3175/2005_5.html).

Ma, Guonan, and Haiwen Zhou. 2009. "China's Evolving External Wealth and Rising Creditor Position." Working Paper 286. Basel: Bank for International Settlements.

Obstfeld, Maurice, and Kenneth Rogoff. 2009. "Global Imbalances and the Financial Crisis: Products of Common Causes." Discussion Paper DP7606. Washington: Center for Economic and Policy Research.

Wang, Xun. 2010. "An Index of Financial Repression for China." Peking University, China Center for Economic Research.

Woo, Wing Thye. 2006. "The Structural Nature of Internal and External Imbalances in China." *Journal of Chinese Economic and Business Studies* 4, no. 1: 1–19.

Yao, Yang. 2010. "The End of Beijing Consensus." *Foreign Affairs,* February 2 (www.foreign affairs.com/articles/65947/the-end-of-the-beijing-consensus).

Yu, Yongding. 2007. "Global Imbalances and China." *Australian Economic Review* 40, no. 1, pp. 3–23.

Zhang, Zhiwei. 2009. "Dark Matters in China's Current Account." Paper presented at the Conference on Greater China Economic Integration. China Economist Society, Macau, March 30–31.

Zhou, Xiaochuan. 2009. "Thoughts on Saving Rate." Essay published on the official website of the People's Bank of China. March 24.

Zhu, Qing. 2007. "Analysis on Chinese Special International Income and Expenditure Structure: A Perspective of Population Age Structure." *World Economy Study,* no. 5: 36–56.

7

The Asian Tiger Economies' Choices

HWEE KWAN CHOW

The 2008–09 global economic crisis hit the Asian Tiger economies of Hong Kong, China; the Republic of Korea; Singapore; and Taipei,China hard, despite their strong macroeconomic fundamentals and sound financial systems. Following the 1997 Asian financial crisis, these economies had strengthened current accounts and had significant expansion in foreign reserves. Meanwhile, their financial systems had become more resilient, with the restructuring of balance sheets and the enhancement of surveillance. Nevertheless, each Tiger economy experienced a collapse in exports and an attendant sharp contraction of GDP in the second half of 2008 as global demand faltered. The GDP for Hong Kong, China; the Republic of Korea; Singapore; and Taipei,China contracted by −7.8 percent, −4.2 percent, −9.5 percent, and −10.1 percent, respectively, in the first quarter of 2009. Such developments reflect the small open nature of these economies and highlight their vulnerability to external shocks.[1] There were also signs of financial contagion in the case of the Republic of Korea, which at one juncture suffered from currency turmoil.[2]

Subsequently, toward the end of 2009, the Asian Tiger economies rapidly rebounded, with the support of swift domestic policy responses on both the fiscal

This chapter consolidates two ADBI working papers by Chow (2010) and Ha, Lee, and Sumulong (2010).

1. Merchandise exports as a percentage of GDP for Hong Kong, China; the Republic of Korea; Singapore; and Taipei,China are 169 percent, 45 percent, 185 percent, and 65 percent, respectively.

2. Hence, this chapter places special emphasis on the case of the Republic of Korea.

and monetary fronts. Fiscal stimulus measures amounted to around 2.6 percent of GDP for this group of countries, and by the first half of 2009, nearly 40 percent of the fiscal stimulus had been implemented (IMF 2009). Meanwhile, massive policy stimulation in the advanced countries led to the normalization of global trade, while public support of their financial sectors lifted financial market sentiment. The Asian Tiger economies on average grew 4.8 percent from 2010 to 2013 (IMF 2014). There has also been a resurgence of private capital flows into these economies in search of high-yielding investments, underscoring international investor optimism about the region's growth prospects. Consequently, stock prices and property prices have been trending up amid the flood of global liquidity inflows, and these developments have raised concerns about the emergence of asset-price bubbles in these economies.

By contrast, growth in the major advanced economies was modest at 3 percent in 2010. The recovery was weighed down by various factors such as high unemployment rates, large public debt, difficult financial conditions, and weak household balance sheets. In light of these challenges, the advanced economies experienced sluggish growth of 1.5 percent from 2011 to 2013 (see IMF 2014). Consequently, their demand for Asian exports will most likely remain subdued in comparison with the precrisis period. Hence to sustain the ongoing economic recovery, it is imperative for the Asian Tiger economies to rely on domestic and regional demand for growth. In other words, policymakers in these countries will need to work toward the rebalancing of demand from economies, such as the United States, that have large current account deficits in relation to the Asian countries that have large current account surpluses. Even though these imbalances did not directly cause the recent global turmoil, they still pose the risk of sparking another financial crisis, as the imbalances are deemed to be unsustainable and may unwind in a disorderly manner, involving a sharp fall in the U.S. dollar or a protracted economic downturn in the industrialized countries, either of which would have adverse consequences for the world economy, not least the Asian Tiger economies.

Addressing the issue of current account imbalances, however, requires a better understanding of the causes. Asia's current account surpluses grew rapidly after the 1997–98 Asian financial crisis, as a result of declining domestic demand. Investment rates fell sharply in the crisis-hit economies as well as in the region's newly industrialized economies (Lee and McKibbin 2007). External imbalances are not just an external problem and should not be judged solely by their size. In open economies, current account imbalances can naturally emerge from country-specific macroeconomic and financial factors; as long as the imbalances reflect economic fundamentals, these cannot be considered bad. However, current account imbalances can also result from internal microeconomic imbalances or from domestic distortions caused by market inefficiencies or public policies (Blanchard and Milesi-Ferretti 2009). The domestic saving-investment (S-I) imbalance, as well as policies on export orientation, exchange rates, and reserve management, can all have an impact on external imbalances. These internal factors suggest that exchange-rate adjustments alone will not bring about balanced growth.

Evolution of Saving and Investment

From 2000 to 2008 the overall gross national saving rate remained high, at an average rate of 31 percent of GDP. This high level of savings could be attributed to key factors that influence long-term development in private saving rates, such as economic growth, demography, precautionary savings by firms in the aftermath of the Asian financial crisis, and the level of financial uncertainty faced by households (see Loayza, Schmidt-Hebbel, and Servén 2000). Over the same period, overall gross investment hovered around a lower mean level of 26 percent of GDP. Possible explanations for the lower level of investment following the Asian crisis include the relocation of production facilities from the Asian Tiger economies to the People's Republic of China (PRC) and the shift in emphasis from capital-intensive production to an information technology– and knowledge-based economy (IMF 2005). In any case, both saving and investment rates fell in 2009 by about 3 and 5 percent, respectively, in the aftermath of the global economic crisis. The resulting S-I balance stayed positive throughout the period and widened by only 2 percent of GDP between 2000 and 2009. Concomitantly, the current account surplus shrank from more than 5 percent to around 4 percent in 2008 at the onset of the crisis, as the massive slowdown in exports was outweighed by an even sharper deceleration in imports. However, the dip proved temporary, as the current account surplus climbed to more than 6 percent of GDP in 2009.

Do these movements in overall rates mask variations across the countries? In what follows, we provide a series of charts that give an overview of the evolution of saving and investment in the individual countries. Figure 7-1 depicts trends in gross national saving and gross domestic investment, and figure 7-2 shows the current account balance, for each of the Asian Tigers.

The S-I balance in both the Republic of Korea and Singapore first increased and then narrowed over the past decade (figure 7-1). In the Republic of Korea, gross domestic investment overtook gross domestic saving, producing a negative current account balance in 2008 (figure 7-2).[3] In comparison, the S-I balance for Hong Kong, China and Taipei,China broadened between 2000 and 2008. In particular, Hong Kong, China's S-I gap widened considerably, from 4 percent to 14 percent of its GDP, over this period. From the external perspective, figure 7-2

3. The Economist Intelligence Unit revised its rating methodology in the second quarter of 2006, and until the third quarter of 2008 it classified the Republic of Korea as low risk, which may have contributed to the pickup in investment in 2008. This trend could very well have continued had the global financial crisis not erupted.

Figure 7-1. *Gross National Saving and Gross Domestic Investment,*
as Share of GDP, Asian Tigers, 2000–12

Percent of GDP

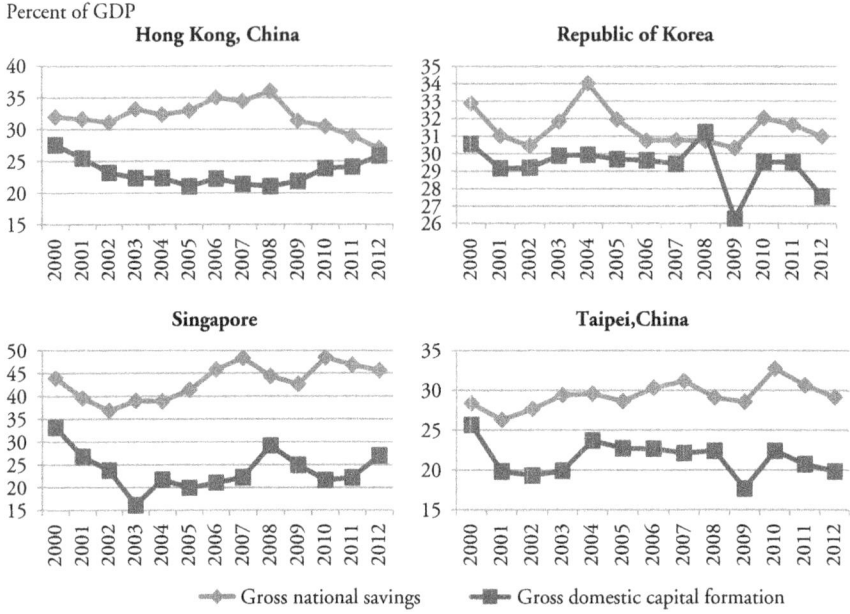

Source: International Monetary Fund, *World Economic Outlook* database, April 2013.

shows that the current account surplus in Hong Kong, China exhibited the most
persistent climb over the past decade. Between 2000 and 2008, the average
current account surplus amounted to 10.9 percent, 1.7 percent, 19.8 percent,
and 16.5 percent of GDP for Hong Kong, China; the Republic of Korea; Singapore; and Taipei,China, respectively, with the corresponding coefficient of variation at 0.3, 0.8, 0.3, and 0.2. Although the Republic of Korea has the lowest
mean current account surplus during this period, it has the highest volatility
among the four countries.

A better understanding of the determinants of the trends in gross saving and
investment would require a breakdown of the macroeconomic-level data into
sectoral-level data. Unfortunately, published data on the composition of saving
and investment in terms of government, corporate, and household sectors are
available only for the Republic of Korea. Although the dichotomy between public
and private domestic investment is available for the three other Asian Tiger economies, there are no official data on public and private saving. To gain a tentative
indication of the trends in public versus private saving rates, we compute public
saving as the difference between total government revenue and government consumption. Private saving is then estimated as the residual from gross saving. The
evolution of gross national saving and its various components for the individual

Figure 7-2. *Current Account Balance as Share of GDP, Asian Tigers, 2000–12*

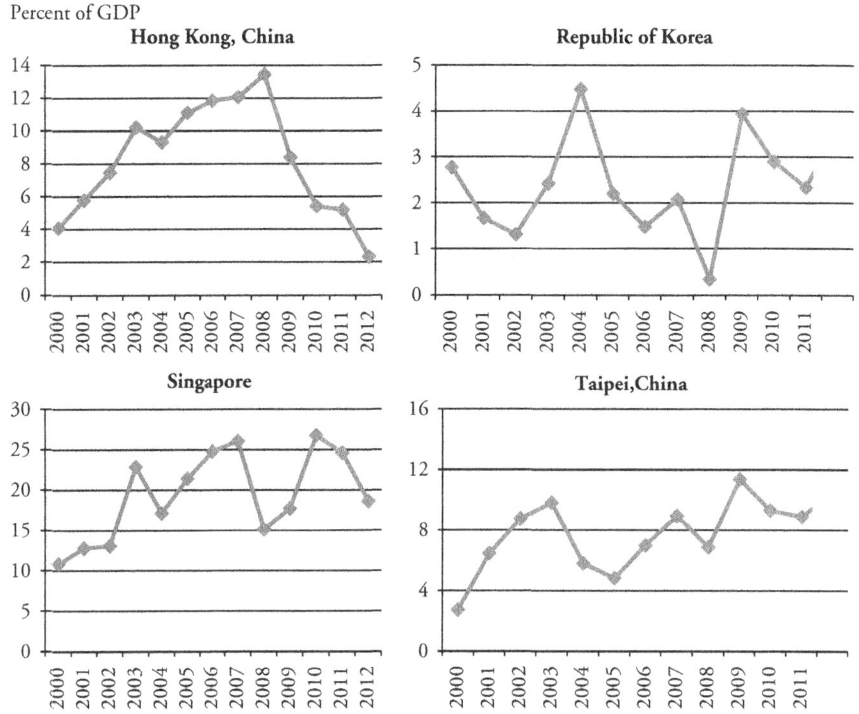

Percent of GDP

Source: International Monetary Fund, *International Financial Statistics* database.

economies are plotted in figure 7-3, and the corresponding data for investment are found in figure 7-4.

We observe from figure 7-3 that gross national saving in Hong Kong, China and Taipei,China rose by 3 and 4 percent of GDP, respectively, over the past decade. Although the increase in Hong Kong, China was largely driven by public saving, which went up by more than 2 percent of GDP, it was private saving, which rose by 8 percent of GDP, that led to higher gross saving in Taipei,China. By contrast, gross national saving in the Republic of Korea fell from 33 percent of GDP to 31 percent of GDP between 2000 and 2007 as household saving declined by more than half, from 9 percent to 4 percent. Government saving held steady at around 10 percent of GDP, while corporate saving increased by 3 percent of GDP over the same period.[4] As for Singapore, there was hardly any change in gross national

4. The leverage ratios of Korean firms declined dramatically after the Asian financial crisis. Total borrowings and bonds payable of manufacturing firms reached 50.1 percent of total assets in 1998; by 2008, this ratio had fallen to about 26.3 percent of total assets. Debt ratios (defined as the ratio of total liabilities to stockholders' equity) of manufacturing firms also declined substantially, from more than 300 percent to about 100 percent in the same period.

Figure 7-3. *Components of National Saving as Share of GDP, by Sector,
Asian Tigers, 2002–12*

Percent of GDP

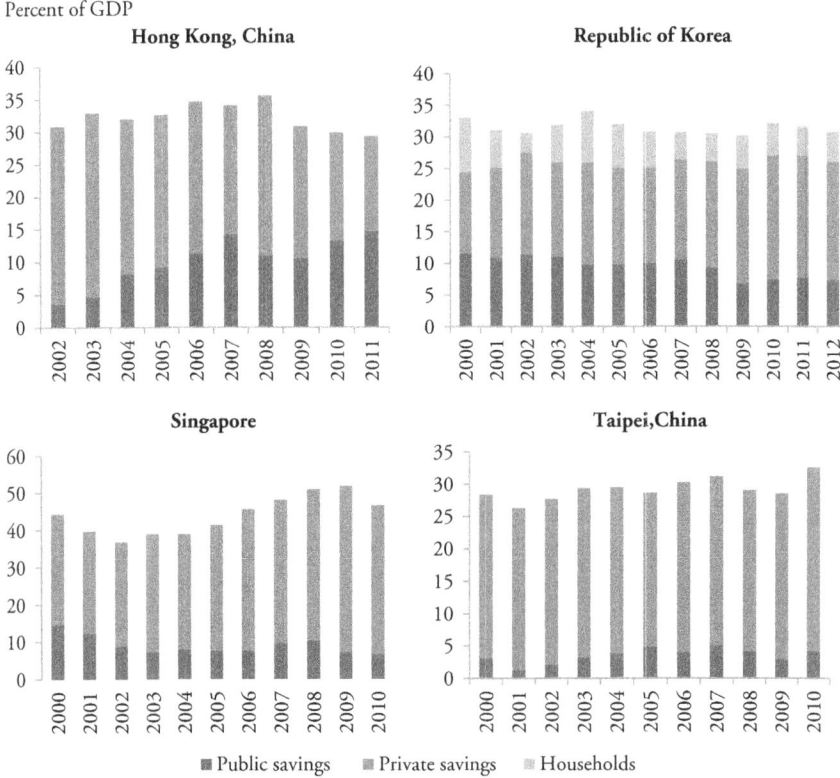

Source: Data from Census and Statistics Department, Hong Kong, China; Bank of Korea; Ministry of Trade and Industry, Singapore; and Directorate-General of Budget, Accounting, and Statistics, Taipei,China.

saving between 2000 and 2008. Public saving, which tended to be the driving force of the saving process in Singapore, fell by about 6 percent, but this was completely offset by an increase in private saving.

Fluctuations in investment from 2000 to 2008 also differed somewhat across the Asian Tiger economies (see figure 7-4). Gross domestic investment exhibited a downward trend over the past decade for Hong Kong, China and Taipei,China. The decline in both countries can be attributed to a drop in public investment and, in the case of Hong Kong, China, a slip in private investment, as well. By contrast, gross domestic investment in the Republic of Korea held steady over the period, and its composition remained broadly unchanged from 2000. As for Singapore, the gross domestic investment initially slowed and then picked up, despite a continuous decline in public investment. Singapore's high private investment rate is partly a result of its development strategy of attracting export-oriented foreign firms.

Figure 7-4. *Components of Domestic Investment as Share of GDP, by Sector, Asian Tigers, 2000–12*

Percent of GDP

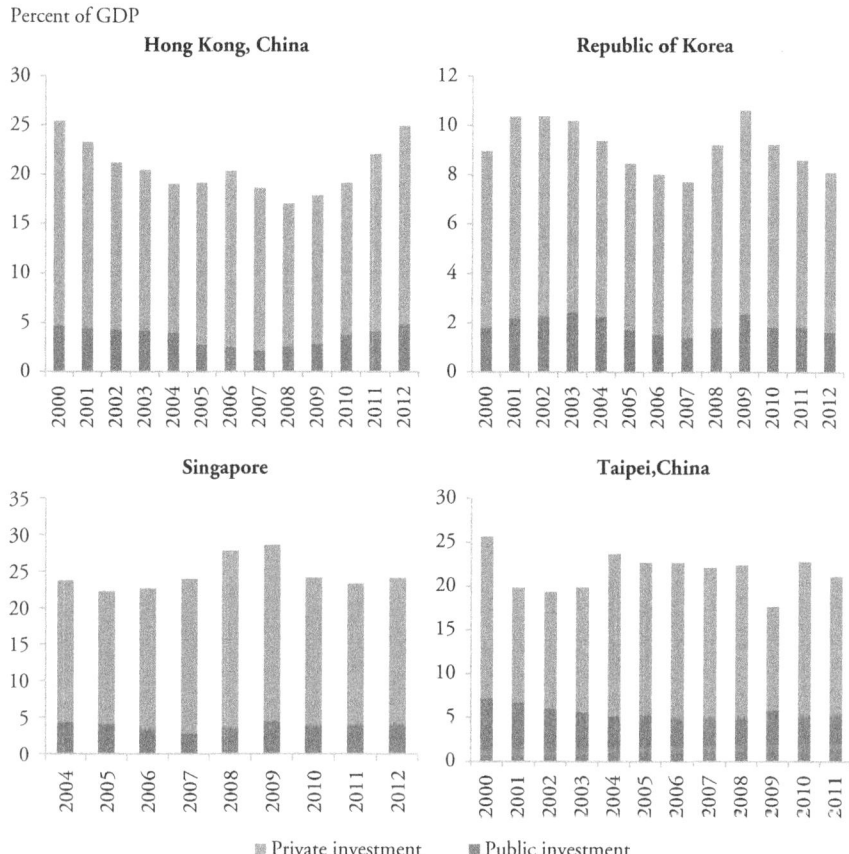

Source: Data from Census and Statistics Department, Hong Kong, China; Bank of Korea; Ministry of Trade and Industry, Singapore; and Directorate-General of Budget, Accounting, and Statistics, Taipei,China.

In summary, savings have generally been higher than investment in the past decade for the Asian Tiger economies. Over the longer term, however, the saving rates in these economies are likely to decline as household consumption increases along with the projected shifts in demographic profiles. With reference to the life-cycle hypothesis, an aging population tends to put downward pressure on the saving rate as there is a tendency for the elderly to consume out of savings on retirement. In addition, spending on social services for the elderly, coupled with a lower tax base owing to a smaller workforce, implies a reduction in public savings. The findings of an IMF (2005) study that uses panel regression analysis confirm that the old-age dependency ratio—the ratio of those aged sixty-five and

Figure 7-5. *Elderly Dependency as Share of Total Population, Asian Tigers, 1980–2050*

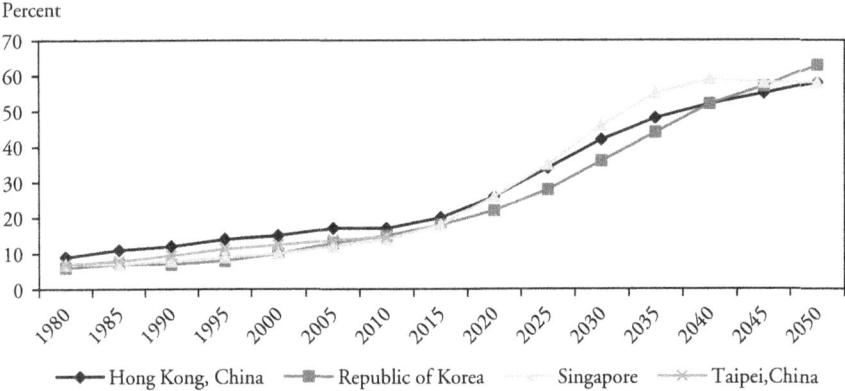

Source: Data for Hong Kong, China; Republic of Korea; and Singapore are sourced from United Nations (2008). Owing to unavailability of data for Taipei,China, we compute the old age dependency ratios from 1980 to 2009 based on data from CEIC.

over to the population aged fifteen to sixty-four—is negatively associated with savings. In the study, each percentage-point increase in the elderly dependency ratio is estimated to raise consumption by 3 percentage points of GDP, suggesting that life-cycle factors do have a significant effect on the savings rate.

Figure 7-5 depicts the past and projected old-age dependency ratio for the Asian Tiger economies. We observe that, without exception, the elderly dependency ratio has been going up and is likely to climb further.[5] The hitherto high saving rates in these countries could partly be attributed to higher household saving as people prepare for retirement. More-developed financial sectors could thus help reduce the precautionary motive for saving. Looking ahead, we infer that ongoing changes in the age composition of the population in these countries are likely to increase the consumption-to-GDP ratio, notwithstanding bequest motives. Such adjustments are nonetheless likely to be gradual even as shifts in demographic profiles occur only slowly (Eichengreen 2006).

Role of Exchange-Rate Adjustment

How do fluctuations in the exchange rate affect the current account balance? A higher exchange-rate value makes local goods dearer in foreign currency terms and, at the same time, foreign goods cheaper in domestic currency terms. Hence

---

5. Demographic change in Singapore was supposed to produce one of the world's most rapidly aging populations. However, the transition toward an older population structure was slowed by large-scale immigration and importation of foreign talent and workers.

Figure 7-6. *Real Effective Exchange Rate and S-I Balance as Share of GDP, Asian Tigers, 2000–2012*

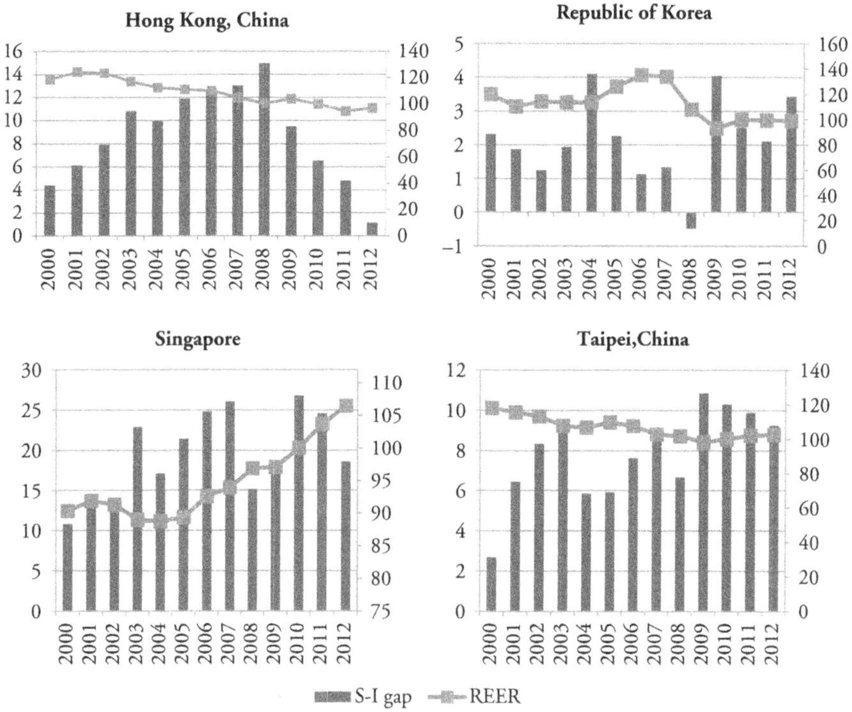

Hong Kong, China

Republic of Korea

Singapore

Taipei,China

S-I gap   REER

Source: Asian Development Bank, *Key Economic Indicators* database; Bank for International Settlements database.

an appreciation of the domestic currency is expected to dampen exports and boost imports, effectively reducing the trade surplus. Since net exports form the main component of the current account surplus of the Asian Tiger economies, a domestic currency appreciation would tend to narrow the positive S-I balance.

S-I Balance and the Exchange Rate

In this subsection, we investigate how developments in the S-I balance of the Asian Tiger economies relate to fluctuations in the value of their domestic currency. Figure 7-6 depicts the real effective exchange rate superimposed on the S-I balance from 1990 to 2009 for the individual economies.

A visual inspection of figure 7-6 suggests an apparent negative association between the level of the real effective exchange rate and the magnitude of the S-I balance. In general, a lower level of the real effective exchange rate tends to be associated with a higher level in the S-I balance. This negative relationship is particularly evident in the case of Hong Kong, China and Singapore and is discernible for the Republic of Korea. The figure reveals a persistent decline in the Hong Kong, China dollar in real effective terms over the past decade. During this period, the S-I balance in Hong Kong, China rose steadily. The real effective exchange rate of the Singapore dollar initially fell, reaching a trough in 2005, and then started to climb. Interestingly, the magnitude of the S-I balance in Singapore seems to mirror these movements in the exchange rate but with a lag. The strengthening of the Korean won in real effective terms picked up pace after 2004, accompanied by a lowering of the S-I balance in the recent period. Taipei,China is the only exception. We see from figure 7-6 that the depreciation in its real effective exchange rate does not appear to have a consistent relationship with the level of the S-I balance.

However, when considering the magnitude of response of the S-I balance to exchange-rate changes, the relevant relationship is not the one between the levels of the variables but that between the movements in these variables. For a tentative indication of the strength of linear association between changes in the S-I gap and changes in the real effective exchange rate, we examine the cross-correlation coefficients between the first differences of the two variables for the individual economies. First, we observe from figure 7-7 that the correlation coefficients at leads are in general not more significant that those at lags, implying that fluctuations in the real effective exchange rate do not exhibit a dominant leading relationship over changes in the S-I balance in all four economies. Second, the correlation coefficients occurring at lead time are not predominantly negative. These findings suggest that a depreciation of the real effective exchange rate in the Asian Tiger economies may not necessarily be linked to an increment in the S-I balance in the short run. We note that these cross-correlation coefficients are preliminary rough estimates as they are computed over a small number of time periods. In what follows, we carry out a more detailed econometric analysis of the impact of exchange-rate changes on the current account balance in the Republic of Korea.

Econometric Analysis of the Republic of Korea's Current Account

The Republic of Korea's current account seems to be correlated with major economic variables such as exchange rates, national GDP, and world GDP.[6] To determine the exact magnitude of the effects of these variables, we conducted econometric analyses using the dynamic ordinary least squares method. Specifically, we set up the following models for exports and imports. Equation 7-1 is for exports, where the real effective exchange rate and world GDP are the determinants. Equation 7-2 is for imports, where the real effective exchange rate and the Republic of Korea's GDP are the main determinants.

---

6. This subsection draws from Ha, Lee, and Sumulong (2010).

Figure 7-7. *Cross-Correlations between Changes in Real Effective Exchange Rate and Changes in S-I Balance, Asian Tigers, 2000–08*

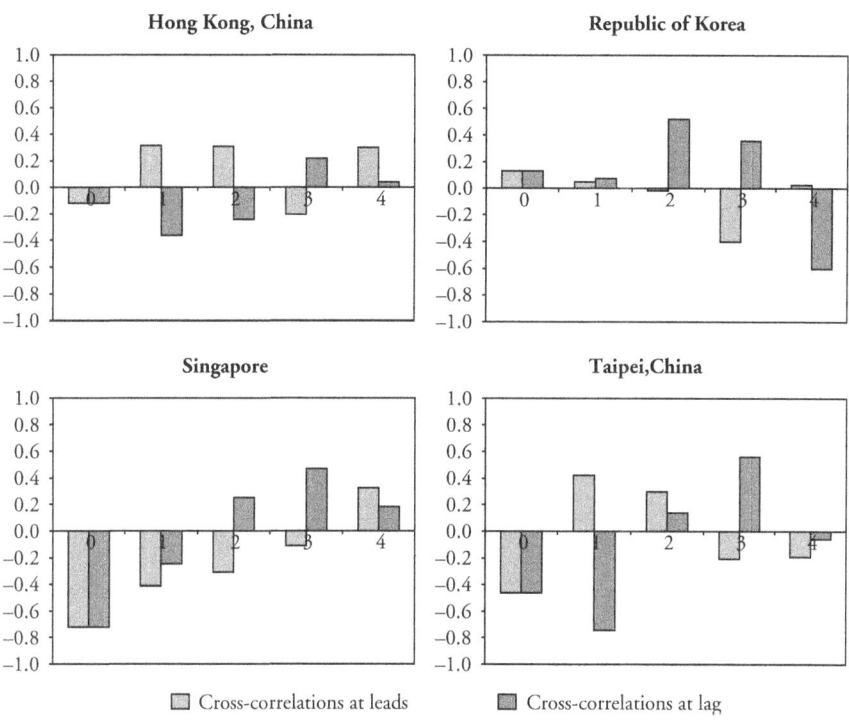

$$(7\text{-}1) \qquad ex_t = \alpha + \beta_1 reer_t + \beta_2 wgdp_t + \sum_{j=-p}^{p} \beta_{reer,j} \Delta reer_{t-j} + \sum_{j=-p}^{p} \beta_{wgdp,j} \Delta wgdp_{t-j} + u_t,$$

$$(7\text{-}2) \qquad im_t = \alpha + \beta_1 reer_t + \beta_2 gdp_t + \sum_{j=-p}^{p} \beta_{reer,j} \Delta reer_{t-j} + \sum_{j=-p}^{p} \beta_{gdp,j} \Delta gdp_{t-j} + u_t.$$

Here, *ex* is export volumes, *im* is import volumes, *reer* is real effective exchange rate, *wgdp* is world GDP, and *gdp* is the Republic of Korea's GDP. All variables are in natural logs and use quarterly data from various sources.[7] Equations 7-1 and 7-2 are estimated with $p = 2$.

7. The data for Korea's export volumes, import volumes, and GDP have been obtained from the Bank of Korea Economic Statistics System (http://ecos.bok.or.kr/EIndex_en.jsp). Real effective exchange rates for the Republic of Korea, Dubai crude oil prices, and world GDP growth rates have been obtained from Bloomberg, and real effective exchange rates for Japan from the International Monetary Fund, *International Financial Statistics* database.

Table 7-1. *Determinants of Exports, Republic of Korea, 1996–2007*[a]

Variable	Full sample		Noncrisis periods only	
	Coefficient	*t statistic*	*Coefficient*	*t statistic*
Constant	−11.74***	−28.54	−8.14***	−4.36
Real effective exchange rate	−0.16**	−1.97	−0.01	−0.02
World GDP	3.44***	49.65	2.52***	3.76
Adjusted R^2	0.9847		0.9838	
Sample (adjusted)	1996Q4–2009Q2		2000Q4–2007Q2	
N	51		27	

Source: Ha, Lee, and Sumulong (2010).
a. Coefficients on differences and lagged differences are not shown in the table.
***Significant at the 1 percent level.
**Significant at the 5 percent level.
*Significant at the 10 percent level.

The results for equation 7-1 are summarized in table 7-1. The first column is the specification for equation 7-1 with the full sample. The results show that the Republic of Korea's exports are significantly correlated with exchange rates and world GDP, as predicted by economic theory. However, the coefficient of the exchange rate, indicating the exchange-rate elasticity of exports, is much smaller (−0.16) than that of world GDP (3.44). This means that a 1 percent depreciation in the real effective exchange rate will increase the Republic of Korea's exports by 0.16 percent,[8] whereas a 1 percent increase in world GDP will increase the Republic of Korea's exports by 3.44 percent.

Overall, these results may have been influenced by drastic changes in the variables during the 1997–98 Asian financial crisis and the 2008–09 global financial crisis. If a stable period were considered, the same econometric model would give a totally different picture. The second column in table 7-1 shows the results for equation 7-1 for the noncrisis period covering 2000Q4–2007Q2. For this sample, the effect of the exchange rate on exports has virtually no significance, while world GDP has a strong effect.[9] During this noncrisis period, the won appreciated without reducing the pace of export growth.

Table 7-2 shows similar results for imports: while the real effective exchange rate and GDP are generally important determinants, the exchange-rate elasticity

8. While a depreciation in the real effective exchange rate increases real exports, the impact of the nominal exchange rate on exports would also depend on the magnitude of exchange-rate pass-through, that is, the extent to which exporters change export prices in response to the exchange rate.

9. We also considered the real effective exchange rate of the Japanese yen as an additional determinant of the Republic of Korea's exports. The coefficient of Korea's real effective exchange rate, *reer,* increased to −0.43 in the estimation with the full sample but remained insignificant in the noncrisis sample.

Table 7-2. *Determinants of Imports, Republic of Korea, 1996–2007*[a]

	Full sample (1)		Noncrisis periods only (2)	
Variable	*Coefficient*	t *statistic*	*Coefficient*	t *statistic*
Constant	−17.16***	−29.49	−19.47***	−10.97
Real effective exchange rate	0.59***	6.76	0.14	0.49
GDP	1.55***	43.66	1.91***	8.22
Adjusted R^2	0.9763		0.9516	
Sample (adjusted)	1996Q1–2009Q1		2000Q4–2007Q2	
No. of observations	53		27	

Source: Ha, Lee, and Sumulong (2010).
a. Coefficients on differences and lagged differences are not shown in the table.
***Significant at the 1 percent level.
**Significant at the 5 percent level.
*Significant at the 10 percent level.

is much smaller than the income elasticity. The first column corresponds to equation 7-2 with the full sample. The results show that a 1 percent appreciation in the Republic of Korea's real effective exchange rate raises imports by 0.59 percent, whereas a 1 percent increase in the Republic of Korea's GDP raises imports by 1.55 percent. Moreover, as seen in the second column of table 7-2, the effect of the exchange rate again becomes insignificant if one considers the noncrisis period.[10] During the noncrisis period, exchange-rate appreciation did not increase domestic demand; the share of private consumption declined continuously, regardless of the direction of the won's value.

These results suggest that exchange rates may not have a significantly meaningful impact on exports and imports in the Republic of Korea; however, immense shocks such as financial crises do affect net exports. Moreover, the magnitude of the exchange-rate elasticity is smaller compared with variables such as world GDP or the Republic of Korea's own GDP. These results are consistent with the findings of other research. For example, Y-I. Choi and J-R. Choi (2009) have shown that the effect of exchange-rate changes on exports and imports has diminished since 2000. This is partly owing to a significant weakening in the exchange-rate pass-through effect for export products, as more intermediate goods are outsourced globally. Similarly, Y-B. Kim and B-J. Kwark (2009) have shown that the effect of exchange rates on exports and investment has weakened significantly since the Asian financial crisis.

10. The Dubai crude oil price was also considered as an additional determinant of Korea's imports. The coefficient of the Republic of Korea's real effective exchange rate, *reer*, increased to 0.40 in the estimation with the full sample but remained insignificant in the noncrisis sample.

Table 7-3. *Pairwise Granger Causality Tests for Net Exports and Services Account Balance, Republic of Korea, 1980–2009*[a]

Sample: 1980M01–2009M11

Lags: 2

Null hypothesis:	Obs.	F statistic	Prob.
SERVICES does not Granger Cause NX	357	1.07212	0.3434
NX does not Granger Cause SERVICES		16.2723	2.E-07

Source: Ha, Lee, and Sumulong (2010).

a. SERVICES stands for services account balance; NX is net exports.

Why did the appreciation in the Korean won not reach levels where net exports would disappear? This can be partly explained by a kind of dollar-recycling mechanism that works as follows: the goods account surplus pushes up the value of the won, inducing Korean firms and households to buy more foreign services; this widens the services account deficit and keeps the value of the won from appreciating as much. There has been a clear shift in the composition of the current account balance. Before 1997–98, the goods and services accounts moved in the same direction. Shortly after the Asian financial crisis, however, the services account started moving in the opposite direction from the goods account. From 1999 to 2009, the accumulated goods account had a surplus of US$283.8 billion, while the services account had a deficit of US$117.3 billion. In other words, 41.34 percent of the goods account surplus has been offset by the services account deficit. Granger causality tests (table 7-3) confirm that the services account deficit follows the goods account surplus, and not the other way around.

What kind of services brought about the deficit in the services account? Travel and other business services account for most of the deficit. Travel includes not just tourism but also the money that goes to Koreans studying overseas. Other business services consist of merchant and other trade-related services; advertising; legal, accounting, and consulting services; and services between related enterprises.

The correlation between the goods account surplus and services account deficit may reflect a basic structural problem in the Korean economy: the weakness of the services sector, such as education and business services. If the services sector had been strong enough, domestic demand as a percentage of GDP would have been larger, and the Republic of Korea would not have had to rely so much on the external sector. The services account deficit would have been smaller, while the goods account surplus would not have been so large. This points to another kind of imbalance in the economy, that between the goods sector and the services sector. This imbalance is reflected not only in the external accounts but also in the internal imbalance in domestic industries, as discussed later in this chapter.

Targeting Final Demand in Regional Markets

The results of the empirical analysis in the previous section suggest that the potential role of the exchange rate in correcting current account imbalances is likely to be limited. In any case, exports have all along played a central role in the growth and development of the Asian Tiger economies. It is the export-oriented growth strategy that allowed the Asian Tiger economies to recover swiftly from the Asian financial crisis and facilitated their transformation into a surplus economy—that is, a net capital exporter. However, the very same strategy made the countries vulnerable to the 2008–09 global financial crisis. Overreliance on external demand made the Asian Tiger economies susceptible to a sharp fall in the industrial countries' appetite for imported goods. As mentioned earlier, huge declines in exports resulted in economic contraction in all four economies in the first quarter of 2009. In other words, though the export-led growth strategy adopted by these economies had for decades proved highly successful in delivering strong output growth, it has resulted in greater volatility in GDP growth rates. The challenge faced by policymakers in these countries is to dampen the business-cycle fluctuations that were accentuated by recurrent shocks from the external environment. A key way to increase the resilience of an economy against exogenous shocks is through the diversification of its export markets.

The Asian Tiger economies had long diversified their trading partners, as reflected by the myriad free trade agreements they had entered into. In particular, the Asian Tiger economies had steadily increased trade with regional partners over the past decade. It is well recognized that the increase in intraregional trade in Asia was spurred by the global integration of the PRC's economy.

Table 7-4 shows, for each Asian Tiger, the six most important trading partners based on bilateral exports trade data as well as the share of total exports each accounted for in 1990, 2008, and 2011. We observe from the table that, without exception, the regional economies, particularly the PRC, gained importance as trading partners of the Asian Tiger economies. However, the rise in intraregional trade can in large part be attributed to the growing intensity in vertical intraindustry trade in Asia. The Asian Tiger economies are well integrated in the regional production networks, which were strengthened by the emergence of the PRC as a manufacturing powerhouse. Specifically, these economies supply high-value intermediate components to the PRC for further processing and final assembly. The export profiles of the Republic of Korea, Singapore, and Taipei,China are similar—their export baskets weigh heavily on electronics components such as semiconductors and printed circuit boards bound for the PRC, the information technology assembly hub. In other words, trade flows with the regional countries are dominated by trade in parts and components rather than trade in final products.

Owing to the emergence of production networks, trade statistics no longer accurately reflect the dependence of Asian countries on extraregional demand. Gabor Pula and Thomas Peltonen (2009) used an updated Asian input-output

Table 7-4. *Key Export Markets as Share of Total Exports, Asian Tigers, 1990, 2008, and 2011*
Percent

	1990		2008		2011	
	Market	*Share*	*Market*	*Share*	*Market*	*Share*
Hong Kong, China	People's Republic of China	25	People's Republic of China	51	People's Republic of China	46
	United States	24	United States	11	United States	11
	Germany	6	Japan	4	Taipei,China	4
	Japan	6	Germany	3	Switzerland	3
	United Kingdom	4	United Kingdom	2	Singapore	2
	Singapore	3	Singapore	2	Japan	1
Republic of Korea	United States	29	People's Republic of China	25	People's Republic of China	24
	Japan	19	United States	11	United States	10
	Hong Kong, China	6	Japan	6	Japan	7
	Germany	4	Singapore	4	Hong Kong, China	6
	Singapore	3	Hong Kong, China	4	Singapore	4
	United Kingdom	3	Germany	3	Taipei,China	3
Singapore	United States	21	Malaysia	13	Malaysia	12
	Malaysia	13	Indonesia	11	Hong Kong, China	11
	Japan	9	Hong Kong, China	11	Indonesia	10
	Thailand	7	People's Republic of China	9	People's Republic of China	10
	Hong Kong, China	6	United States	7	United States	5
	Australia	2	Japan	4	Japan	4
Taipei,China	United States	32	Hong Kong, China	13	People's Republic of China	27
	Hong Kong, China	13	United States	12	Hong Kong, China	13
	Japan	12	Japan	7	United States	12
	Germany	5	Singapore	5	Japan	6
	Singapore	3	Republic of Korea	3	Singapore	6
	United Kingdom	3	Germany	2	Republic of Korea	0.4

Source: Asian Development Bank, *Key Economic Indicators* database, 1970–2010; 2011 data from respective countries' statistics databases.

table to show that Asia has not decoupled from the rest of the world.[11] In fact, a study by the Asian Development Bank (2007) estimates that only about a third of the final demand composition of Asia's exports in 2006 can be accounted for by the region. Hence, it is not surprising that the recent collapse in demand of the end markets was transmitted to these countries involved in the different stages of the production process, resulting in the synchronized fall in trade. Not unlike the other Asian economies, the Asian Tiger economies are still heavily dependent on U.S. and the European Union markets in terms of final demand. Consequently, the economic prospect of the Asian Tiger economies remains coupled to the upswings and downturns in the developed markets.

To reduce the vulnerability of export growth to demand shocks from the extraregional markets, the Asian Tiger economies need to gear their trade structure in terms of trade in final goods away from excessive dependence on the U.S. and eurozone markets toward regional markets. The aim would be to have intraregional trade based on trade in final products as an additional source of demand and growth for these economies. This means that intraregional trade should also be driven by consumption rather than by production alone. In this regard, the level of private consumption in Asia is likely to increase in view of rising affluence and standards of living in the fast-growing regional economies. In particular, the PRC offers some potential as a strong source of independent demand in view of the emergence of its large middle class with growing purchasing power.

An Asian Development Bank (2009) study provides evidence that domestic demand in the PRC is already starting to play a more prominent role in supporting exports from the Asian Tiger economies. In the study, total trade balance was decomposed into four major categories: basic products, construction materials, parts and components, and final goods. Since the figures for the first two categories are relatively small for the countries under consideration, we focus only on the last two categories in our analysis.

The PRC has been running current account surpluses with Hong Kong, China. This is not surprising given Hong Kong, China's role as a major transshipment center for the PRC's exports. Although the PRC also runs a trade surplus in final goods with Singapore, the magnitude is much smaller than the level of trade balance with the other three countries. By contrast, the PRC has been running current account deficits with the Republic of Korea and Taipei,China. Moreover, final goods are accounting for a growing share of the PRC's trade deficit with these two countries over time. The magnitude of these deficits is significantly higher for Taipei,China, reflecting its cross-strait trade integration with the PRC.

11. The same study found that Asia's exports account for only approximately one-third of its GDP, far below the 50 percent dependence indicated by trade data. The exaggerated export dependence is a result of the higher import content of exports that resulted from greater segmentation of the production process across the region.

Considering the probable shifts in the PRC toward a bigger consumption basket that is typical in a rapidly growing economy, trade in final goods will quite likely play a more important role in driving the increase in trade between the PRC and the Asian Tiger economies going forward.

Increasing Reliance on Domestic Demand

Is there any room for the Asian Tiger economies to reduce dependence on export-driven growth and to rebalance their economies toward more diversified sources of growth? After all, a key component of the transpacific rebalancing strategy is to implement structural policies that increase domestic demand. By examining the expenditure patterns in each country's growth, we can explore the prospect of adopting a new growth model for the Asian Tiger economies that leverages more on the domestic economy.

We note at the outset that the size of net exports does not indicate the importance of foreign demand relative to domestic demand in an economy, particularly when there is a high propensity to import. Each domestic expenditure category, namely private consumption (C), government consumption (G), and investment (I) (which comprises fixed capital formation as well as the increase in stocks), has its own import content. These import components are not shown separately but are aggregated and included in total imports (M), which is, in turn, subtracted from total exports (X) to produce net exports. Therefore, when considering drivers of growth, a better measure of the significance of external demand is the magnitude of total exports (rather than net exports) relative to the levels of domestic demand components.

To gauge the relative importance of foreign demand, we rewrite the standard national income accounting identity, $GDP = C + G + I + X - M$, as

$$(7\text{-}3) \qquad\qquad C + G + I + X = GDP + M.$$

The left- and right-hand sides of equation 7-3 represent total demand and total supply in the economy, respectively. We see from equation 7-3 that an increase in any of the components of total demand could suffer from import leakage. An increase in C, G, I, or X would not only lead to higher production in that country but also increase production elsewhere (as reflected by an increase in imports). Although imports in themselves do not generate income in an economy, they are necessary to allow the country to export. Of course, imports are also critical for restoring external imbalances.

These economies are highly dependent on export demand, and the reliance on foreign demand has grown over the past decade in all four countries. In 2008 external demand accounted for 70, 29, 76, and 45 percent, respectively, of total demand in Hong Kong, China; the Republic of Korea; Singapore; and

Taipei,China. In the case of Hong Kong, China and Singapore, external demand dominates domestic demand because reexports account for a significant portion of their total exports, exceeding 90 and 30 percent, respectively.

The extent to which the drivers of growth can be recalibrated depends on, among other things, the leverage each demand component exerts on output growth. For small open economies, a 1 percent increase in external demand is likely to have a greater impact on GDP than a corresponding 1 percent increase in, say, private consumption. After all, an exogenous increase in export demand will not only raise GDP in the current time period but will also have second-round effects of inducing growth in the domestic demand components in future time periods. Moreover, as explained earlier, an increase in any component of domestic demand in such economies would tend to suffer from high import leakage. Hiroshi Osada (1998) provides estimates of the marginal propensity to import for Hong Kong, China; the Republic of Korea; Singapore; and Taipei,China of 3.1, 0.4, 1.5, and 0.6, respectively.[12]

With the exception of the Republic of Korea, fluctuations in GDP growth are closely associated with changes in external demand rather than changes in domestic demand. For instance, the dip in domestic demand growth in Hong Kong, China in 2005 did not make a significant dent in its GDP growth in that year. Similarly, the upsurge in domestic demand in 2008 in Singapore—which is largely a result of a jump in government consumption—did not seem to have any discernible effect on its GDP growth in that year. In sharp contrast, movements in GDP growth in the Republic of Korea do not closely follow the fluctuations in external demand but are significantly influenced by developments in domestic demand. As for Taipei,China, there is insufficient deviation in the pattern of fluctuations between domestic demand and external demand, so that we are unable to distinguish which is dominating GDP growth.

These findings are not in the least surprising when we consider the population size of the two city-states Hong Kong, China and Singapore, which in 2008 are only 7 million and 4.8 million, respectively. In other words, added to the problem of high import leakage, domestic demand in both these economies lacks the scale to drive output growth. These observations seem to attest to the fact that a domestic-led growth model is clearly unsuited for ultra-small open economies such as Hong Kong, China and Singapore. In comparison, the 2008 populations of the Republic of Korea and Taipei,China are 48.6 million and 23 million, respectively. Hence, there is greater potential for these two larger economies to have domestic-led growth.

---

12. The marginal propensity to import exceeds unity for Hong Kong, China and Singapore owing to the high proportion of reexports. The propensity to import goods for domestic production or consumption in Singapore is estimated to be around 0.8 (Peebles and Wilson 2002), while the propensity to import in Hong Kong, China, calculated from retained imports using more recent data, is approximately 0.5.

Table 7-5. *Employment in Services and Manufacturing Sectors as Share of Total Employment, Republic of Korea, 1970–2010*

	1970	1980	1990	1995	2000	2005	2010
Services	34.3	38.6	47.7	54.8	61.2	65.2	57.7
Manufacturing	14.2	22.7	27.9	23.6	20.3	18.5	17.6
Other	51.5	38.7	24.4	21.6	18.5	16.3	24.7

Sources: Data from Organization for Economic Cooperation and Development (www.oecd.org/statistics/) and Korean Statistical Information Service (http://kosis.kr/eng/).

Addressing Imbalances in the Republic of Korea and Taipei,China

In comparison with Hong Kong, China and Singapore, the relatively large population sizes of the Republic of Korea and Taipei,China suggest more room for policy maneuvering with regard to increasing reliance on domestic demand in these two economies. Policy recommendations targeted at boosting domestic demand should be implemented to a greater extent in these two larger economies. Hence we focus our discussion in this section on the Republic of Korea and Taipei,China.

Republic of Korea: Internal Imbalances between Manufacturing and Services

As noted earlier, the imbalance between the manufacturing and services sectors is reflected in the behavior of the goods and services accounts.[13] The weakness in the services sector is also reflected in its labor productivity trends. Table 7-5 shows that the employment share of services in the Republic of Korea has been increasing over time—from 34.3 percent in 1970 to 65.2 percent in 2005. However, services' share of value added has not been increasing at the same rate, rising from 44.29 percent to only 58.96 percent during the same period.[14] This means that the labor productivity of the services sector has been decreasing over time. An analysis by Jong-Wha Lee (2005) has shown that while the manufacturing industry has enjoyed high productivity growth over the past few decades, Korean service industries, including the finance, insurance, real estate, construction, wholesale and retail trade, and restaurants and hotels sectors, have had little growth in productivity.[15] The weakness in the services sector can be attributed to both

13. This subsection draws from Ha, Lee, and Sumulong (2010).

14. These figures are for current prices. If constant prices are used, the changes in services' share become even smaller.

15. Lower productivity growth in the services sector relative to the manufacturing sector has been established since the seminal paper by Joe Baumol (1967). Increasingly unbalanced growth across sectors induces labor force reallocation toward stagnant sectors, which might eventually slow down aggregate GDP growth. That the Korean service industries have had relatively lower productivity growth is therefore not extraordinary. Nonetheless, the labor productivity growth differential between services and manufacturing has been much larger in the Republic of Korea than in other industrialized economies (see Lee 2005).

knowledge-intensive services—in particular, education and business services—and traditional services.

In education and business services, which are directly reflected in current account balances, the problem lies in the shortage and poor quality of supply. Although the shares of education and business services in value added have been increasing in nominal terms, these shares have actually been declining in real terms (that is, increases have resulted mainly from rising prices). From 1995 to 2008, education's share in value added increased from 4.94 percent to 6.52 percent in current prices but decreased from 6.97 percent to 5.80 percent in constant prices. Business services give a similar picture: value added in current prices increased from 3.98 percent to 5.42 percent but decreased from 4.97 percent to 4.87 percent in constant prices during the same period.

The Republic of Korea's education problem is complicated and goes beyond the scope of this paper. However, the huge number of Koreans studying abroad suggests that the Republic of Korea's education services cannot meet domestic demand. Korean students make up the bulk of overseas students in the United States (127,185 students in 2008, or 14.8 percent of the total), Canada (27,549 students in 2005, or 15.4 percent of the total), and the PRC (80,000 students). The story is similar in Australia, Japan, New Zealand, and the United Kingdom. Given the size of the Republic of Korea's population—about 50 million—these levels are rather surprising, and it is not difficult to guess how much money goes to these overseas students. Similarly, the supply of business services has been insufficient. In terms of value added, business services represented only 5.6 percent of GDP in 2005, compared with 11.5 percent in the United States and 7.7 percent in Japan. Employment in business services gives a similar picture: 6.8 percent of the Republic of Korea's workers are in the business services sector, compared with 11.7 percent in the United States and 10.5 percent in Japan.

By contrast, the supply of traditional services is more than sufficient. However, labor productivity in this sector is also relatively low. The productivity of the wholesale and retail trade sector and the restaurants and hotels sector was only 22 percent of producer services in 2003. The productivity of social and personal services was also low, amounting to only 43 percent of producer services. This is a result of too much supply and too little demand.

The excess supply of traditional services arose from efforts to restructure the economy after the financial crisis. Most of the workers who were laid off shifted to the services industry, opening small restaurants and laundry shops or becoming taxi drivers. For example, the employment share of the restaurants and hotels sector increased from 9.46 percent in 1995 to 10.6 percent in 2008, though its share in value added (in current prices) decreased from 2.65 percent to 2.39 percent. Meanwhile, the shortage of demand for traditional services has a lot to do with the declining income share of households. The share of households and private unincorporated enterprises in national income fell from

74.20 percent in 1996 to 64.09 percent in 2008. This drop of about 10 percentage points in household income has eroded the most important basis for domestic consumption.

Corporate savings have been rising in the Republic of Korea. Reducing corporate savings and raising the corporate investment rate, particularly in the services industry, may help reduce internal imbalances if these foster restructuring within the services sector and raise the sector's productivity. Although the services sector's share in the total economy has been gradually diminishing in real terms, it still remains the largest sector in the economy.

Nevertheless, the country remains heavily reliant on services imports. Since records have been kept, starting in 1980, surpluses in the services account have been recorded only twice, in 1982–89 and in 1998. Business services other than transportation and financial services account for the bulk of the deficits in the past few years. The Republic of Korea needs to further develop its services sector to shift to a domestically supported growth strategy. This issue is more complex than it seems, since the low productivity of the services industry is closely related to massive hidden unemployment created by economic restructuring after the Asian financial crisis. Moreover, raising the demand for traditional services will require improvements in the share of household income. Since 88 percent of workers were employed by small- and medium-size enterprises (SMEs) as of 2005, promoting investment in these businesses will be critical.

To raise investment rates, the productivity of investment will have to be improved. Raising the productivity of SME investment, particularly in the services industry, where about 70 percent of workers are employed, will be important to rebalancing the Korean economy both internally and externally. This will require a reduction in widespread entry barriers in knowledge services and reforms to address the inefficient structure of traditional services. Investments in knowledge services such as education and business services should focus more on how to cope with growing global competition, whereas investments in traditional services should focus primarily on industry restructuring and reallocating excess workers to productive sectors.

The emergence of a large and rapidly growing urban middle class will be crucial to increasing domestic demand. The expansion of the middle class will hinge on the dynamism of enterprises, especially SMEs. Increasing investment by SMEs will help reduce the internal imbalance between savings and investment. Further improvements in the investment climate are necessary to encourage greater investment and boost domestic demand. The upgrade in Korea's Doing Business (World Bank 2010) ranking for 2010 is largely owing to improvements in business startup procedures. Specifically, the number of procedures and the number of days required to start a business have been reduced. The minimum capital requirement and cost of starting a business have also been cut. The effects of these changes are expected to positively affect investment in the near term.

Taipei,China: Economic Integration with Mainland China

The Taipei,China economy, which grew at a rapid 9.2 percent year-on-year in the fourth quarter of 2009, has not only returned to precrisis growth levels but has also outperformed the other three Asian Tiger economies, whose corresponding growth figures are 2.6, 6.0, and 3.5 percent for Hong Kong, China; the Republic of Korea; and Singapore, respectively.[16] Interestingly, the PRC featured prominently in the rapid recovery of Taipei,China, even as exports of final goods to the PRC increased from 17.8 percent of total exports at the start of 2009 to 29.2 percent in January 2010. Exports for final consumption in the PRC have been accounting for a growing share of the PRC's trade deficit with Taipei,China over time. This reflects the increased penetration of Taipei,China's goods in the PRC's markets. Indeed, economic linkages between these two countries have proliferated since the 1990.[17] However, official figures tend to underestimate trade and investment flows between the two countries owing to various cross-border restrictions and political reasons. Taipei,China's trade with and investment in mainland PRC have all along been partly intermediated through third parties such as Hong Kong, China; Japan; and Singapore. For that matter, Hong Kong, China also serves as a key intermediary to the rest of the world for the PRC's external trade via reexports and offshore trade, as well as for raising international capital in the form of foreign direct investment, equity and bond financing, and syndicated loans to finance the PRC's economic boom.

Yin-Wong Cheung, Menzie D. Chinn, and Eiji Fujii (2003) assessed the degree of real and financial integration between Taipei,China and mainland PRC (as well as Hong Kong, China) by testing for real interest rate parity, uncovered interest rate parity, and real purchasing power parity. The authors found that these three parity conditions do hold over the long term, thereby providing empirical evidence of real and financial capital mobility as well as goods market integration between Taipei,China and the PRC, notwithstanding the presence of various forms of trade barriers and capital controls. As these impediments continue to be lifted, Taipei,China will gain economically through further integration of its economy with the PRC. Zhi Wang (2003) used a computable general equilibrium model to show the positive effects of a free trade area in the Greater China region, comprising mainland PRC; Hong Kong, China; and Taipei,China. Furthermore, Zhaoyong Zhang and Kiyotaka Sato (2007) found increasing structural symmetry among these three economies, which raises the potential of the region to become a candidate for monetary union. Taipei,China is likely to continue intensifying its economic integration with mainland PRC, which will concomitantly reduce its dependence on extraregional markets, thereby aiding in global rebalancing.

16. All the year-on-year growth rate figures are flattered by a low base effect.
17. See Zhang, Xu, and Bin (2003) for a discussion of these linkages from a dynamic economic and political perspective.

Policy Issues Pertaining to Rebalancing

We conclude this chapter by identifying policy options that apply in general to all the Asian Tiger economies attempting to rebalance their economies. It is important to note at the outset that boosting domestic demand through structural reforms in these economies would not necessarily require that they abandon the export-led growth strategy or turn back from economic openness. Rather, it is a policy imperative for the Asian Tiger economies to remain open to trade and capital flows for the following reasons: First, exports and output often mutually reinforce each other. For instance, exports are known to enhance long-run growth potential by accelerating the process of human capital accumulation, which in turn fosters growth (see Chuang 1998). Second, with reference to endogenous growth models, imports also tend to have a positive impact on labor productivity. It is well recognized that imports act as an important channel for foreign technology and knowledge (Grossman and Helpman 1991). Third, retaining a degree of openness would encourage foreign direct investment inflows that contribute to domestic economic growth through channels such as the injection of greater competitive forces, the introduction of managerial innovations, and the restructuring of underperforming firms.[18]

Notwithstanding the need to remain integrated with the world economy, it is in the interest of the Asian Tiger economies to increase their resilience against a possibly protracted period of subdued global demand conditions. After all, the unwinding of the huge global imbalances will quite likely require a prolonged period of adjustment to the global structure of supply and demand. The resolution of the imbalances does not imply that the Asian Tiger economies should all attempt to achieve balanced current accounts. Rather, what is required are policies that facilitate a more balanced structure of demand and growth within the economies. Given the mismatch between what the Asian Tiger economies produce and what they consume, such rebalancing will require major adjustments to their underlying economic structure. The rebalancing of growth toward domestic demand will thus be a complex structural process that is both difficult and time consuming (Adams and Park 2009). Nevertheless, there is scope for policy adjustments in the Asian Tiger economies in view of their strong economic fundamentals, fiscal latitude, and sound financial systems.

Furthermore, as pointed out by Li (2002), the erstwhile largely complementary economic relationship between the Asian Tiger economies and the PRC—in the form of the former supplying capital while the latter provides cheap labor—

18. See Organization for Economic Cooperation and Development (2002) for a review of empirical studies that show the positive impact of foreign direct investment on economic growth.

is likely to evolve into a more competitive relationship in the future as the PRC moves up the value chain and progresses to higher-value-added industries. This suggests the Asian Tiger economies would also need to identify new areas of comparative advantage as well as seek out new areas of complementarities, especially those that would help them reduce their reliance on extraregional demand.

As the income level in the PRC rises, there is a growing culture of consumerism, with shifts in spending patterns leading to higher consumption of luxury goods and services. For instance, strong demand from the PRC has been driving the recent recovery in the retail of branded watches and jewelry, while tourist arrivals in the Asian Tiger economies from the PRC have been growing rapidly (He, Cheung, and Chang 2007). In fact, this shift toward consumption whereby goods and services that had previously been regarded as luxuries are now viewed as necessities is also evident among the young urban generation in many traditionally thrifty societies in the region. The Asian Tiger economies should continue to position themselves to capitalize on such ongoing increases in intraregional demand by reorientating their economic structures to tap into the changing spending patterns of prospering Asian countries.

In this regard, the Asian Tiger economies could maintain their dynamic and niche-based competitiveness by focusing on services exports, particularly by building up ancillary capabilities. Services sector productivity in Hong Kong, China; the Republic of Korea; Singapore; and Taipei,China stands at approximately 84, 27, 58 and 53, respectively, on a scale of 1 to 100, where 100 represents the productivity level in the U.S. services sector. This suggests that there is ample room for further development of the services industry, and there is a need to eradicate existing policy distortions that favor the manufacturing industry.

Regulatory reforms in the services sector of the Asian Tiger economies would not only boost productivity in this sector but would also generate large gains in overall economic growth. Policy initiatives such as funding the upgrading of workers' skills and expertise would result in a more knowledgeable and experienced workforce that would enhance the quality of services. Moreover, policies that induce firms to innovate in their work processes and incorporate the use of technology would lead to the improvement of work practices. Business investments targeting higher-value-added exportable services industries, such as financial services, medical tourism, and tertiary education, should also be encouraged, perhaps by offering tax breaks and incentives for regional expansion.

Apart from tradable services, service sector companies in the Asian Tiger economies that provide lower-value homegrown services such as retail, food and beverages, and personal grooming should also be granted greater tax incentives and a reduction in start-up costs. These industries are important for the stimulation of local consumption, as they generate employment and income for the majority of the unskilled population. It follows that the long-held bias in favor of the production of tradables over nontradables in these economies has to be reduced to bring about an increase in domestic consumer demand.[19]

Meanwhile, demand-side policies for reducing the imbalance between output and demand structures should aim at narrowing the income gap or at least arresting any further worsening of the income distribution.[20] In particular, wage levels at the lower end of the income scale should be raised to alleviate the financial insecurity felt by local residents. Of course, this should be matched by an increase in their productivity such as through retraining efforts. For instance, in the case of Singapore, the authorities have begun to slow the upsurge of low-skilled migrant workers as their hitherto easy availability removes the incentives for companies to upgrade and places downward pressure on wages of the lower-skilled domestic workforce.

A rise in household consumption brought about by a reduction in precautionary saving could also be induced through further development of the financial markets in Asian Tiger economies. For instance, a wider array of financial products could be offered to provide investment opportunities that give better rates of return. The provision of high-yielding saving vehicles would help raise household incomes. Moreover, the introduction of annuity products, health insurance schemes, and financial assistance programs for education would help ease the requisite level of saving for retirement, medical, and education purposes. Nevertheless, we note that in response to financial sector reforms in the aftermath of the Asian crisis, consumer credit expanded rapidly—particularly in the Republic of Korea and to a lesser extend in Taipei,China—leading to a jump in household delinquencies and nonperforming loans (IMF 2006a). Hence it is vital for the supervisory authorities to keep pace with new developments in the financial markets and to impose regulatory curbs on excessive consumer lending to ensure financial stability.

The economic integration of the Greater China economies is already taking place and is likely to intensify. In a similar vein, a way forward to advance transpacific rebalancing is to establish a common market within the region over the long term, as this will raise intra-Asian demand and investment (Kawai 2009). Combining markets in the region could prove to be an effective strategy, given that the Asian economies, with few exceptions, do not individually have the scale to transition from externally driven to internally driven growth. The market enlargement would also induce growth through greater competition among firms, which will lead to productivity gains, and through efficiency gains for

19. However, we are not advocating that the Asian Tiger economies adopt a new growth model whereby domestic demand consistently grows faster than output, as this would in the long term lead to unsustainably large trade deficits.

20. According to a study by the International Monetary Fund (2006b), the Gini coefficients for Hong Kong, China; the Republic of Korea; Singapore; and Taipei,China rose between 1995 and 2005, reaching 51.4, 33.1, 48.1, and 33.9 respectively in 2005.

consumers (both final and intermediate), owing to an increase in the range of product choice. Drawing on the European experience with the 1992 European Single Market Programme, measures that would need to be taken include the adoption of a trade liberalization program,[21] a lowering of the barriers to cross-border public procurement, enforcement of competition policy in all sectors, and elimination of hindrances to free movement of labor, capital, and services across member countries. Clearly, these initiatives will present many hurdles, such as historical legacy issues, territorial disputes, structural and institutional hetero-geneity, and economic diversity. Nonetheless, the probable muted recovery in the advanced industrialized countries might just provide the necessary impetus to overcome the political, economic, and institutional challenges and accelerate efforts to establish a common market within Asia. Indeed, the Asian countries should make greater efforts to advance the establishment of a common market to better position themselves to benefit from the growing consumer and service demand in their own prospering region.

References

Adams, Charles, and Donghyun Park. 2009. "Causes and Consequences of Global Imbalances: Perspectives from a Developing Asia." *Asian Development Review* 26, no. 1: 19–47.

Asian Development Bank. 2007. "Uncoupling Asia: Myth and Reality." In *Uncoupling Asia: Myth and Reality.* Manila: Asian Development Bank.

———. 2009. "Broadening Openness for a Resilient Asia." In *Asian Development Outlook 2009 Update*, pp. 35–80. Manila: Asian Development Bank.

Baumol, William J. 1967. "Macroeconomics of Unbalanced Growth: The Anatomy of Urban Growth." *American Economic Review* 57, no. 3: 415–26.

Blanchard, Olivier J., and Gian M. Milesi-Ferretti. 2009. "Global Imbalances: In Midstream?" Staff Position Note SPN/09/29. Washington: International Monetary Fund (December).

Cheung, Yin-Wong, Menzie D. Chinn, and Eiji Fujii. 2003. *China Economic Review* 14, no. 3: 281–303.

Choi, Y-I., and J-R. Choi. 2009. "The Effect of Exchange Rate Changes on the Trade of Goods and Services." *Monthly Bulletin,* September. Seoul: Bank of Korea.

Chow, Hwee K. 2010. "Asian Tigers' Choices: An Overview." Working Paper 238. Tokyo: Asian Development Bank Institute.

Chuang, Yih-Chyi. 1998. "Learning by Doing, the Technology Gap, and Growth." *International Economic Review* 39, no. 3: 697–721.

Eichengreen, Barry. 2006. "Global Imbalances: The Blind Men and the Elephant." *Issues in Economic Policy,* no. 1. Brookings (January).

Grossman, Gene M., and Elhanan Helpman. 1991. *Innovation and Growth in the Global Economy.* MIT Press.

Ha, Joonkyung, Jong-Wha Lee, and Lea Sumulong. 2010. "Rebalancing Growth in the Republic of Korea." Working Paper 224. Tokyo: Asian Development Bank Institute.

---

21. At the current juncture, the PRC, Japan, and the Republic of Korea have each arranged a free trade agreement with the whole of ASEAN; the proposal here is to merge these bilateral arrange-ments into a regionwide free trade agreement.

He, Dong, Lilian Cheung, and Jian Chang. 2007. "Sense and Nonsense on Asia's Export Dependency and the Decoupling Thesis." Working Paper 03/2007. Hong Kong, China: Hong Kong Monetary Authority.

International Monetary Fund (IMF). 2005. "Global Imbalances: A Saving and Investment Perspective." In *World Economic Outlook,* September. Washington: International Monetary Fund.

————. 2006a. "The Consumer Finance Boom: Is It a Problem?" In *Regional Economic Outlook: Asia and Pacific,* May. Washington: International Monetary Fund.

————. 2006b. "Rising Inequality and Polarization in Asia." In *Asia and Pacific Regional Economic Outlook: Asia and Pacific,* September. Washington: International Monetary Fund.

————. 2009. "Asia's Recovery in the Global Context." In *Regional Economic Outlook: Asia and Pacific,* October. Washington: International Monetary Fund.

————. 2014. "Country and Regional Perspectives." In *World Economic Outlook,* April. Washington; International Monetary Fund.

Kawai, Masahiro. 2009. "The Global Financial Crisis and Asia's Rebalancing Agenda." Paper presented in the Plenary Session on Asia after the Global Financial and Economic Crisis. Singapore Economic Review Conference, Singapore, August.

Kim, Y-B. and B-J. Kwark. 2009. "The Effect of Exchange Rate Changes on the Real Sector: Focusing on Export, Import, and Investment." Working Paper 378. Seoul: Bank of Korea.

Lee, Jong-Wha. 2005. "Human Capital and Technology for Korea's Sustained Growth." *Journal of Asian Economics* 16, no. 4: 663–87.

Lee, Jong-Wha, and Warwick J. McKibbin. 2006. "Domestic Investment and External Imbalances in East Asia." *Brookings Discussion Papers in International Economics,* no. 172. Brookings (January).

Li, Ku-Wai. 2002. *Asia-Pacific Development Journal* 9, no. 1: 109–20.

Loayza, Norman, Klaus Schmidt-Hebbel, and Luis Servén. 2000. "Saving in Developing Countries: An Overview." *World Bank Economic Review* 14, no. 3: 393–414.

Organization for Economic Cooperation and Development. 2002. *Foreign Direct Investment for Development: Maximising Benefits, Minimising Costs.* Paris.

Osada, Hiroshi. 1998. "Deepening Economic Interdependence in the APEC Region–Boom and Vulnerability through Trade Linkages." In *The Deepening Economic Interdependence in the Pacific Region,* edited by Keiji Omura, pp. 21–46. Tokyo: Institute of Developing Economies.

Peebles, Gavin, and Peter Wilson. 2002. *Economic Growth and Development in Singapore: Past and Future.* Cheltenham, U.K.: Edward Elgar.

Pula, Gabor, and Thomas A. Peltonen. 2009. "Has Emerging Asia Decoupled? An Analysis of Production and Trade Linkages Using the International Input-Output Table." Working Paper 993. Frankfurt am Main, Germany: European Central Bank.

United Nations Secretariat. 2008. *World Population Prospects: The 2008 Revision.* Department of Economic and Social Affairs, Population Division. New York.

Wang, Zhi. 2003. *China Economic Review* 14, no. 3: 316–49.

World Bank. 2010. "Doing Business." International Finance Corporation (www.doing business.org).

Zhang, Zhaoyong, and Kiyotaka Sato. 2008. "Whither a Currency Union in Greater China?" *Open Economies Review* 19, no. 3: 355–70.

Zhang, Zhaoyong, Xin Xu, and Wei-Bin Zhang. 2003. *Papers in Regional Science* 82, no. 3: 373–88.

8

ASEAN's Need to Rebalance: More Regional than Global?

IWAN J. AZIS AND MARIO B. LAMBERTE

The Association of Southeast Asian Nations (ASEAN) is facing a large current account surplus.[1] To address the problem, member nations need to rebalance their economies not only to be in line with the goal of lowering the current imbalances in the global economy but, more important, for the region's own interests. What ultimately matters is the welfare of each country's population, and as has been observed in many countries, positive achievements in macro indicators, irrespective of the imbalances, do not guarantee a real welfare improvement. The relatively good macroeconomic performance of ASEAN has been accompanied by some undesirable trends, such as worsening income inequality and falling employment elasticity. These are far more serious problems than the imbalances per se, and they are a more important challenge than the current account surplus and excess savings.

The Golden Rule savings rate is the rate of savings which optimizes the level or growth of consumption. In a standard Golden Rule setting—which depicts an inverted U relationship between savings rate and consumption, the position of ASEAN as a group is generally on the right side of the curve, suggesting there is still room for transforming savings into consumption. The policy direction to

The authors are deeply indebted to Damaris L. Yarcia, Asel Karamuratova, and Mara Claire C. Tayag for excellent research support and data processing.

1. The ten ASEAN member nations are Brunei Darussalam, Cambodia, Indonesia, the Lao People's Democratic Republic, Malaysia, Myanmar, the Philippines, Singapore, Thailand, and Viet Nam.

reach the Golden Rule equilibrium is therefore to increase spending (particularly in investments for most ASEAN countries) and to lower savings. Although exports exceed imports in some member countries and imports exceed exports in others, ASEAN as a group faces a current account surplus, consistent with the region's excess saving. Such a trend emerged particularly after the Asian financial crisis of 1997–98. Although the size of the region's imbalances is too small to make a significant contribution to the global imbalances, it is necessary for ASEAN to rebalance its economies for its own welfare improvement.

Trend in Imbalances and Capital Flows

As a group, the ASEAN economies moved from a US$8.7 billion current account deficit in 1990 to a US$109.1 billion surplus in 2010—although it has since declined to reach an estimated $55 billion surplus in 2013. This, however, is dwarfed by the rise in the People's Republic of China's (PRC) current account surplus, which, over the same period, rose from US$12.0 billion to US$237.8 billion in 2010, before declining to US$182.8 billion by end-2013. From 1990 to 2010, the U.S. deficit worsened, moving from US$79.0 billion to US$470.9 billion, albeit narrowing since the onset of the global financial crisis (2007–08) and has settled at $379.3 billion in 2013. Expressed as a percentage of gross domestic product, ASEAN's current account deficit before the Asian financial crisis (1997–98) was around 2 percent, and during the 1997–2001 period, the current account surplus reached 5.7 percent, higher than surpluses in the PRC and the newly industrializing economies. The current account balance slipped slightly after the global financial crisis, but it remained higher than other comparator regions (see figure 1-1 in chapter 1).

Most ASEAN countries underwent a transition from a current account deficit to a surplus, except Cambodia, Lao People's Democratic Republic (PDR), and Viet Nam, where the current account continues to register a deficit, and Singapore and Brunei Darussalam, where huge surpluses persist. In the post–global financial crisis period (2008–2013), the current account surplus as a percentage of GDP declined in Brunei Darussalam, Malaysia, Singapore, and Thailand; and shifted to a deficit in Indonesia and Myanmar; while the current account deficit worsened in Cambodia and Lao PDR. Only the Philippines and Viet Nam saw an improvement in the current account balance (figure 8-1).

A similar trend is exhibited in the saving-investment (S-I) gap, with the ASEAN region as a whole generating excess savings after the Asian financial crisis at a rate higher than that of the newly industrializing economies, the PRC, Japan, the eurozone, and the United States. After the collapse of Lehman Brothers, however, the region's excess savings fell and were overtaken by the PRC.

Among ASEAN member countries, Singapore had the largest excess saving. Indonesia, Malaysia, the Philippines, and Thailand had negative S-I gaps before

Figure 8-1. *Current Account Balance as Share of GDP, ASEAN Member Countries, 1990–2013*[a]

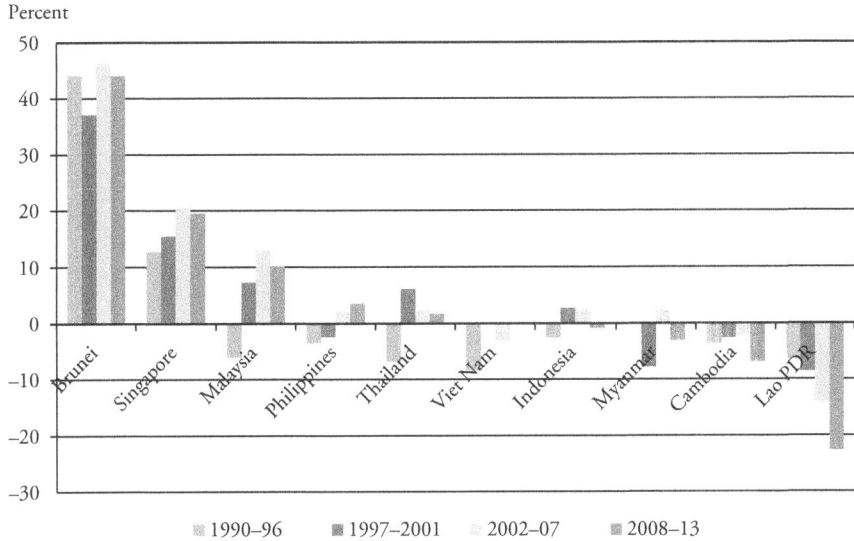

Percent

■ 1990–96 ■ 1997–2001 ░ 2002–07 ■ 2008–13

Source: International Monetary Fund (IMF), *World Economic Outlook* database, April 2014 (1990–2013).

a. Data for Myanmar start in 1998. IMF estimate for 2013 is used for Brunei Darussalam, Cambodia, Lao PDR, Myanmar, and Philippines.

the Asian financial crisis but improved their positions afterward. The S-I surplus continued during and after the global financial crisis for all ASEAN countries except Indonesia (figure 8-2). Of the four countries that transitioned from a negative S-I gap to a positive S-I gap after the Asian financial crisis, a rise in the saving rate characterizes the Philippines, while a fall in the investment rate is reported for Malaysia, Indonesia, and Thailand (figure 8-3). A prolonged fall in the investment rate has implications for a country's capacity utilization. For example, between 1997 and 2006, the capacity utilization in Thailand remained well below the precrisis level of about 75 percent (Azis 2008; Sussangkarn and Nikomborirak 2011). Because investment has long-term implications for future growth, such a trend may hamper the country's growth prospects. However, the case of Thailand is different since the fall in the investment rate reflects a trend back to normal, given the excessively high rate of investment (overinvestment) before the Asian financial crisis. In fact, Thailand's rate of investment after the Asian financial crisis and before the global crisis exceeded that of all other ASEAN countries with the exception of Viet Nam.

A look at the trade balance confirms the changing patterns within ASEAN since the dramatic events of 1997. From 1993 to 1996, the region was a net importer; after the Asian financial crisis it became a net exporter. Of the five

Figure 8-2. *Saving-Investment Gap as Share of GDP, ASEAN Member Countries, 1990–2013*[a]

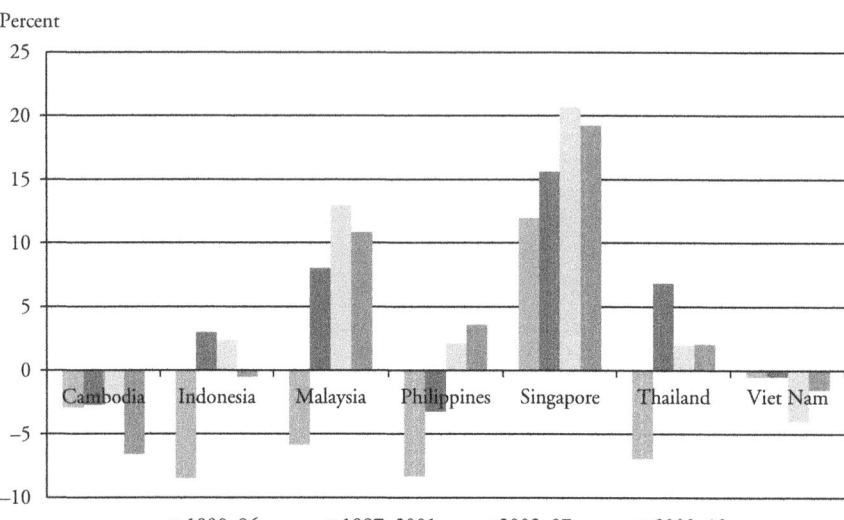

Percent

net exporters, Brunei Darussalam, Indonesia, and Malaysia are oil- and natural resource–exporting countries, while Singapore is a major entrepôt for the region. Cambodia, the Lao PDR, the Philippines, and Viet Nam register trade deficits (figure 8-4).

Aside from the generally high domestic saving rate, the high investment rate in the region has also been spurred by capital inflow and lending booms.[2] With a relatively low level of capital outflow in the early 1990s, net capital inflow as a percentage of GDP was close to double digits. A considerable portion of the inflows took the form of foreign debt, which was largely short term and unhedged and was used to finance many long-term and unproductive investments. It was precisely this double mismatch that eventually brought down the region into crisis in 1997–98, resulting in massive capital outflows. As figure 8-5 shows, the net capital inflow as a percentage of GDP plunged after the Asian financial crisis, and it did not return to positive levels until 2010, thirteen years after the crisis. It should be noted, however, that capital inflow actually began to recover in 1999 and continued to increase until it reached its peak right before the global financial crisis

2. Note that ASEAN's investment rate before the Asian financial crisis was at par with the rate in the PRC and higher than in newly industrializing economies.

Figure 8-3. *Saving and Investment Rates as Share of GDP, ASEAN Member Countries, 1990–2013*[a]

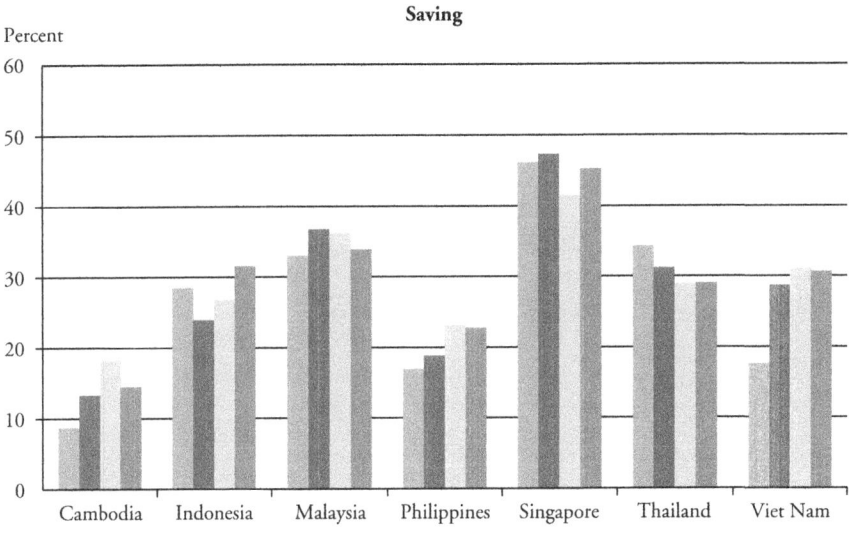

Saving

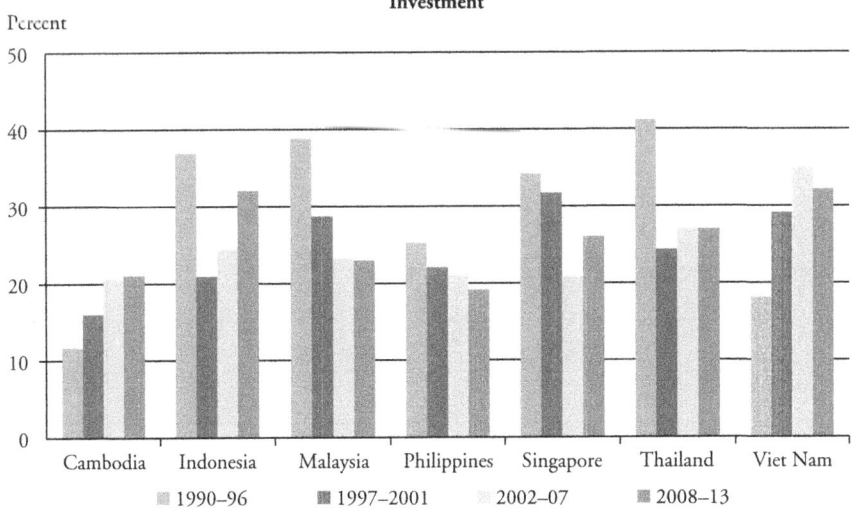

Investment

Source: International Monetary Fund, *World Economic Outlook* database, April 2014 (1990–2013).
a. No historical data for Brunei Darussalam, Lao PDR, and Myanmar.

Figure 8-4. *Trade Balance as Share of GDP, ASEAN Member Countries, PRC, United States, and Eurozone, 1990–2013*[a]

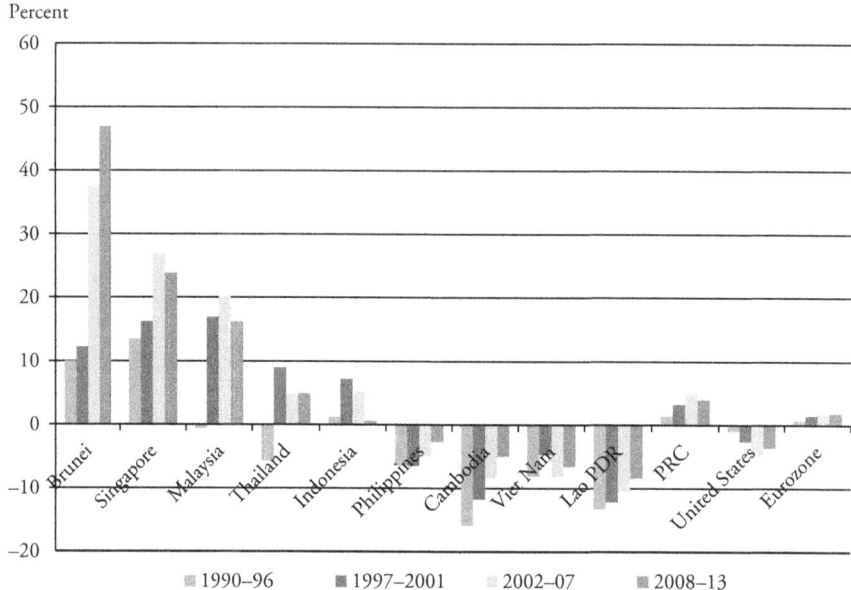

Percent

■ 1990–96   ■ 1997–2001   ■ 2002–07   ■ 2008–13

Source: World Bank, *World Development Indicators,* 1990–2013.
a. Data for Cambodia start in 1993 and end in 2011; for the United States and Viet Nam data end in 2012. Data for Myanmar are unavailable. Trade balance is computed as the difference between exports and imports of goods and services (as percent of GDP).

Figure 8-5. *Financial Capital Flows as Share of GDP, ASEAN, 1990–2011*[a]

Percent

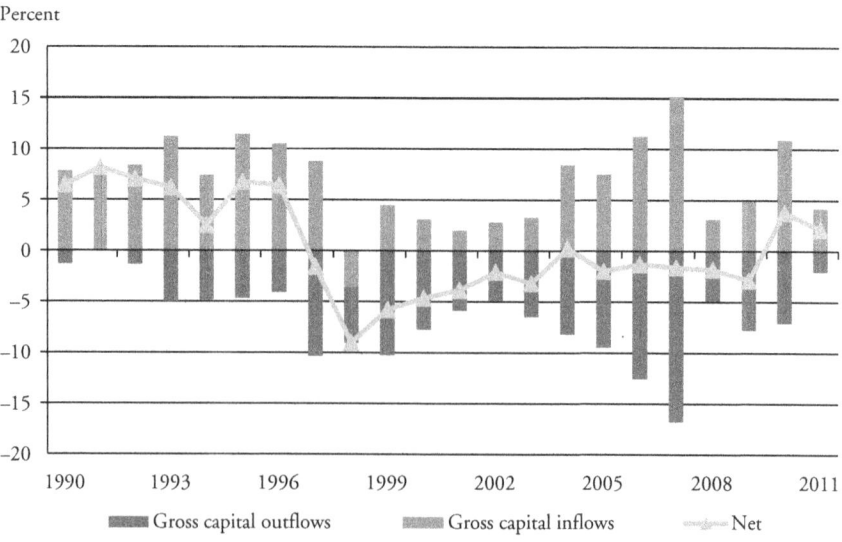

■ Gross capital outflows   ■ Gross capital inflows   — Net

Source: International Monetary Fund, *International Financial Statistics* database and *World Economic Outlook* database, April 2014.
a. Indonesia, Malaysia, Philippines, Singapore, Thailand, and Viet Nam. Data for Viet Nam start in 1996. Malaysia not included in 2010 and 2011 as inflow-outflow breakdown for portfolio and other investment is unavailable. Singapore and Thailand not included in 2011 as data are unavailable.

began in 2008. Thus it was outflow exceeding inflow that occurred in ASEAN countries during the period.

Foreign direct investment in ASEAN remained strong during the first decade of this century. Early in the decade, other investments made up the greater share of outflow, while foreign direct investment made up the greater share of capital inflow. From about 2005 to 2008, before the Lehman Brothers collapse, capital inflow included large amounts of portfolio investments. The response of the capital markets to the global financial crisis came in the form of net outflow of portfolio investments immediately after the crisis. But beginning in late 2009, with the persistently low interest rate policy and the introduction of quantitative easing (QE) in the United States, the ASEAN countries as a group registered a net inflow of portfolio investments (Azis & Shin 2013).

Along with other emerging market economies, ASEAN has benefited from a windfall effect of the economic slowdown in the United States and Europe. The region has been perceived as the new safe haven. It is important to note, however, that relative to its economic size and situation before the Asian crisis, capital flow in the region remained low, especially in comparison with other economies such as the PRC, the United States, and countries in the eurozone.

Capital flow provide liquidity, but they can also create vulnerability. The current account can deteriorate owing to the resulting stronger currency, and a sudden stop phenomenon can occur caused by bubbles and asymmetric information.[3] ASEAN policymakers faced this policy challenge during the period of strong capital inflow following the global financial crisis, prompting many of them to introduce various forms of prudential regulatory measures affecting capital flow and foreign exchange positions (Azis and Shin 2014; Kawai, Lamberte, and Takagi 2012). The lesson of the Asian financial crisis of 1997–98, however, has been instrumental in making the region's financial sector stronger and more resilient to shocks, and this has played an important role in the region's ability to avert crises.

However, when the eurozone crisis emerged in the summer of 2011, fear of another crisis surfaced as a considerable size of capital outflow occurred in some of the region's countries. The huge fluctuations of flow had some adverse effects on the region's economy as financial indicators, including the exchange rate, became volatile. In countries such as Indonesia and Malaysia, where the share of foreign capital in the domestic capital market is large, the effect of the pullout of capital resulting from deleveraging by European banks has been quite significant, exposing these countries' vulnerability to external shock. Fortunately, the impact on the credit market through the banking sector has not been severe, owing to ASEAN's limited exposure to bank credits from the United States and Europe. By mid-2011, the percentage of bank loans from these countries in total domestic

---

3. The sudden stop phenomenon is characterized by large reversal of capital inflows and current accounts, deep recessions, and collapses in asset prices (Mendoza and Smith 2002).

credit was around 4 and 11 percent, respectively. There has been also an increase of lending to the region by Japanese and Australian banks.

Looking ahead, as far as ASEAN's imbalances and the associated capital flow are concerned, we expect that the size of imbalances will continue to narrow down but the net capital inflow will continue to rise, at least as long as the economic growth and interest rates differential with advanced economies remain low. Although the region is less likely to face a serious liquidity problem, however, it will continue to face the major challenge of how to convert the liquidity into real investments and more productive infrastructure, which the region badly needs. Volatility may also return if the interest rates in the US reverse and the QE policy ends. This link between imbalances and development issues is taken up later when we use flow-of-funds data to analyze the use of the excess savings in ASEAN countries.

Rebalancing and the Role of Exchange Rates

Measured by the ratio of trade to GDP, many ASEAN countries are trade dependent, with ratios greater than 50 percent, while in Singapore, Malaysia, Viet Nam, Thailand, and Cambodia, the ratio exceeds 100 percent. Combined with the low but positive net exports to GDP, the region's trade is clearly heavily import dependent. The evidence from 1997 cannot be overemphasized: during the Asian financial crisis, exports grew only slowly, despite a sharp fall in the exchange rates in many countries during the time. The region's dependence on imports continues to be strong, if not stronger, especially since many of its countries became involved in the growing production network in Asia.

One can also look at the contribution of net exports to GDP growth to evaluate the region's efforts to rebalance. In particular, a small (or large) contribution indicates a large (or small) role of domestic demand. The latter is of course an important component of rebalancing. Looking at the trend, the contribution of net exports to GDP growth in most ASEAN countries is low. It is only substantial in some countries in some years, such as Brunei Darussalam and Singapore in 1996 and 1997, while for the rest of the region, the share of net export falls below 1 percentage point. Taking the case of the ASEAN4 (Indonesia, Malaysia, the Philippines, and Thailand), for example, net exports contributed only 0.5 percentage points toward the 5.1 percent average growth in GDP from 2006 to 2013. Exports alone contributed 2.9 percentage points, higher than the share of consumption (2.6 percentage points), but imports accounted for 2.4 percentage points. This is a sign of import-dependent countries, and the ASEAN4 depends particularly on imports of high-technology capital goods.

The low contribution of net exports to GDP growth indicates that domestic demand has been the primary driver in the region's growth. This is unlikely to change in the current global economic climate, where external demand in

Table 8-1. *Share in Total Exports, 2000, 2010, and 2013*
Percent

| | \multicolumn{6}{c}{Destination} | | | | | |
Exporter	ASEAN	PRC	India	Japan	European Union	United States
2000						
ASEAN	23.1	3.9	1.5	13.4	13.9	19.2
PRC	7.0	—	0.6	16.7	15.4	20.9
India	6.3	1.7	—	4.3	20.7	22.0
Japan	14.3	6.3	0.5	—	15.6	29.7
European Union	1.7	1.0	0.4	1.8	57.4	9.5
United States	6.1	2.1	0.5	8.4	19.6	—
2010						
ASEAN	25.1	10.8	3.5	9.5	10.0	9.6
PRC	8.8	—	2.6	7.7	18.2	18.0
India	10.4	7.9	—	2.2	16.4	10.7
Japan	14.7	19.4	1.2	—	10.1	15.6
European Union	1.7	3.2	0.8	1.2	53.6	6.7
United States	5.5	7.2	1.5	4.7	16.6	—
2013						
ASEAN	27.2	12.1	3.4	9.7	8.0	8.1
PRC	11.0	—	2.2	6.8	14.1	16.7
India	11.3	4.9	—	2.2	14.5	12.5
Japan	15.5	18.1	1.2	—	9.0	18.8
European Union	1.9	3.5	0.7	1.3	51.0	6.8
United States	5.0	7.7	1.4	4.1	14.4	—

Source: Data from United Nations Commodity Trade (UN Comtrade) database.

major trade partners like the United States, Europe, and Japan is weak. Pursuing an export-led growth strategy as a way out of addressing any external imbalances will be difficult unless alternative markets for exports are found. What is the trend so far?

A look into trade statistics shows that trade among ASEAN countries as well as trade with other emerging markets has been gaining ground. From US$96.3 billion in 2000, intra-ASEAN trade rose to US$305.3 billion in 2013. It also rose in terms of share of total trade, from 23.1 percent to 27.2 percent (table 8-1). In terms of ASEAN's exports to its major trading partners, the PRC showed the biggest increase, from 3.9 percent in 2000 to 12.1 percent in 2013; but ASEAN's exports to Japan declined from 13.4 percent to 9.7 percent during the same period. Since 2000, the ASEAN region has been in a trade deficit with the PRC, Japan, and the Republic of Korea and in trade surplus with India, the European Union, and the United States. As of 2013, this trade structure has not changed

Table 8-2. *Intermediate Goods Exports, 2000, 2010, and 2013*[a]
Billions of US$

	Destination					
Exporter	ASEAN	PRC	India	Japan	European Union	United States
2000						
ASEAN	73.4	13.4	5.0	37.3	31.5	38.2
PRC	10.5	—	1.3	14.0	12.5	13.3
India	1.9	0.6	—	1.0	3.5	4.6
Japan	46.7	22.3	1.8	—	32.2	59.1
European Union	22.0	12.2	6.5	15.7	619.0	101.6
United States	34.1	9.6	2.2	35.9	87.0	—
2010						
ASEAN	192.0	89.7	29.5	69.9	57.2	41.3
PRC	74.9	—	26.4	48.0	101.7	78.6
India	16.1	16.8	—	4.0	20.8	12.3
Japan	79.6	99.4	6.0	—	40.3	53.5
European Union	44.6	78.7	22.1	24.5	—	162.3
United States	46.2	64.5	13.7	32.3	105.7	—

Source: Data from United Nations Commodity Trade (UN Comtrade) database.

a. Intermediate goods include primary goods, parts and components, and processed goods for industry. Data are based on UN Comtrade's Broad Economic Categories classification.

except with the European Union, which turned into a trade deficit in 2013. If anything, with the slowing down of growth in the United States and Europe, intraregional trade in Asia and trade among emerging markets in general are likely to intensify.

It is important to note, however, that the increase in intraregional trade has mostly been from trade in intermediate goods. Of the US$120 billion increase in goods exports to the PRC from 2000 to 2013, for example, US$100 billion (over 80 percent) came from intermediate goods (tables 8-2 and 8-3). The bulk of the increase in exports within ASEAN, and to India, Japan, and the European Union, are also in the form of intermediate goods. In the United States, the main source of increase is final goods until 2012, despite the economic slowdown in the United States. In 2013, however, this has shifted to intermediate goods, given the fact that the share of Asian trade with the United States has declined since the Asian financial crisis, and the fall has intensified since the global financial crisis in 2008.

In 2000 ASEAN trade in intermediate goods was in surplus with the PRC, India, the European Union, and the United States and in deficit with Japan. By 2013, it was in deficit with the PRC, the European Union, and the United States; and turned into a surplus with Japan. In terms of final goods, ASEAN was in

Table 8-3. *Final Goods Exports, 2000 and 2010*[a]
Billions of US$

Exporter	Destination					
	ASEAN	PRC	India	Japan	European Union	United States
2000						
ASEAN	22.0	2.6	1.3	18.2	26.2	41.3
PRC	6.8	—	0.3	27.6	25.8	38.9
India	0.7	0.2	—	0.8	5.0	4.3
Japan	18.7	7.3	0.6	—	40.0	77.9
European Union	12.0	8.3	2.1	22.0	573.2	95.5
United States	11.8	5.7	1.3	27.5	60.2	—
2010						
ASEAN	60.1	20.3	6.6	26.7	40.3	57.0
PRC	62.9	—	14.4	71.9	185.3	205.1
India	6.1	0.6	—	0.8	15.1	11.1
Japan	28.2	42.5	2.7	—	32.8	61.1
European Union	30.7	64.0	11.7	28.8	1,046.6	134.5
United States	15.0	20.3	4.0	21.5	73.1	—
2013						
ASEAN	71.1	21.0	5.1	26.6	34.7	46.7
PRC	110.4	—	18.7	92.5	208.3	260.0
India	10.7	1.1	—	1.3	20.0	17.7
Japan	28.2	33.6	2.1	—	26.3	68.5
European Union	43.3	85.5	12.0	38.5	1,150.5	170.4
United States	18.5	31.9	5.4	24.7	79.6	—

Source: Data from United Nations Commodity Trade (UN Comtrade) database.

a. Final goods include capital goods and consumption goods. Data are based on UN Comtrade's Broad Economic Categories classification.

deficit with the PRC and Japan and in surplus with India, the European Union and the United States in 2000. By 2013, it shifted into a deficit with India and the European Union.[4] Along with the growing production network and the trend of capital flows, the development of the exchange rate explains the above trade patterns as well as the development of the intraregional trade.

The exchange rate in ASEAN countries in the period following the Asian financial crisis has been more market determined than in the period preceding it. Yet authorities in the trade-dependent region tend to intervene in the foreign exchange market when the movements of the exchange rate affect their countries'

4. The United States remains the largest importer of final goods from ASEAN, though its share in total ASEAN final goods exports slid by half from 2000 to 2013.

export competitiveness. The current account is quite sensitive to the exchange rate.[5] However, the sensitivity of the region's exchange rate to the movements of major currencies has also changed, shifting away from sole reliance on the U.S. dollar toward reliance on a basket of currencies, especially after the Asian and global financial crises.

The sensitivity of the region's exchange rate to movements of major currencies after 1998 has been discussed in great detail by Azis and Puttanapong (2008). Here, we want to highlight the changing sensitivity in the more recent period by using the global financial crisis as the reference point. Before the crisis hit, the Brunei dollar, the Korean won, the Singapore dollar, the NT dollar, and the Thai baht were more sensitive to the yen, but in the postcrisis period, most ASEAN currencies became more sensitive to the movements of the euro. This is most evident in the case of the Brunei dollar and Singapore dollar and, to a certain extent, the Malaysian ringgit, the Philippine peso, and the Thai baht.

The yuan is also rising as an international medium of exchange.[6] Given the region's increasing trade with the PRC, the yuan's impact on regional currency has risen, particularly in the postcrisis period. The Cambodian riel, the Myanmar kyat and the Vietnamese dong remain predominantly driven by the U.S. dollar, whereas the Indonesian rupiah, the Malaysian ringgit, the Philippine peso, the Singapore dollar, and the Thai baht have become more sensitive to the yuan since 2007.

This tells us that when looking at the exchange-rate volatility, one needs to take into account the fluctuations of ASEAN exchange rates with respect to a basket of currencies and not just the U.S. dollar. This prompts the question, what basket of currencies should be used? Adopting the concept of a currency basket based on the Asian currency unit to examine the link between exchange-rate stability (both over time and with respect to Asian currency units) and intraregional trade, Azis and Puttanapong (2008) found a negative relationship between the two variables. As the volatility of the exchange rate increases, intraregional exports decline. Although this calculation is based on a large number of countries in Asia, we believe that a similar pattern holds for the ASEAN region as well.[7] To the extent that a growing intraregional trade is to be pursued in response to the decline in demand from the United States and Europe, and that diversifying the

5. Thorbecke and Komoto (2010) found that the exchange-rate elasticity of Thailand's imports, estimated at 0.38, is much smaller than that of exports, which is estimated to be 0.69. Thus a real depreciation of the baht in response to a balance of payments pressure leads to a significant improvement in the current account balance.

6. Malaysian companies, for example, now have the option to settle their trade transactions with their counterparts in the PRC in yuan.

7. Tang (2011) found the same negative relationship between intraregional exchange-rate volatility and intraregional exports in Asia, where the adverse impact of volatility is pronounced in the subregion of the ASEAN plus the PRC; Hong Kong, China; Japan; the Republic of Korea; and Taipei,China, and especially among intermediate and equipment exports. This impact is further magnified if smaller ASEAN economies are excluded from the subgroup.

direction of trade is an important part of the rebalancing process, maintaining stability of the intraregional exchange rate should be pursued. Whether or not this stability will be secured through formal exchange-rate cooperation depends on how leaders of ASEAN perceive the need for such cooperation.

Uses of Excess Saving and Implications

We have been arguing that for ASEAN, rebalancing is important for the region's own interests, even though its share in the global imbalances is small. For any policy and strategy, ultimately one needs to look at the implications of rebalancing for overall welfare. For this purpose, one needs a better understanding of the complex transmission mechanisms that relate imbalances to welfare indicators. We attempt to do this by looking at the breakdown of the excess saving according to institutions and account types and trace where these excess savings go. This can be done only by using information from the flow-of-funds data.[8] In particular, we focus on the saving and investment behaviors of three institutions: firms or the nonfinancial corporate sector, financial institutions, and households. Owing to data limitations, however, we look at the case of only three ASEAN countries: the Philippines, Thailand, and Indonesia.

Based on these countries' flow-of-funds data, household saving in the Philippines constitutes the bulk of domestic saving, whereas corporate saving makes up the biggest share of Thailand's total domestic saving.[9] In the case of Indonesia, saving went up for the household and business sectors but fell for the public and financial sectors in the period following the Asian financial crisis (figure 8-6). In the Philippines, the average household saving rate continued to increase throughout the 1990s to 2011 (the last year for which we have data). Nonfinancial corporations also increased their savings in response to the crisis, whereas financial corporations reduced their saving. Similar to the case of Indonesia, the government sector in the Philippines responded to the crisis by raising government spending, which effectively reduced government saving. In the case of Thailand, households saved less after the Asian financial crisis, and the same is true with the financial and public sectors. Only the nonfinancial corporations increased their savings. Hence in general, the response of household saving to the crisis was mixed, whereas the financial and government sectors responded by reducing their savings.

---

8. The International Monetary Fund's *International Financial Statistics* presents a number of accounts commonly used in macroeconomic and financial analysis, for example, the balance of payments, the banking sectors, and the government sector. All these accounts can be arranged into a flow-of-funds system, whereby the saving and investment allocation of each sector (institution) in different financial instruments is presented in a fairly detailed way.

9. Similar analysis for Indonesia is not possible because there is no disaggregation of saving between households and businesses.

Figure 8-6. *Savings by Institution as Share of GDP, Indonesia, Philippines, and Thailand (1990–2012)*[a]

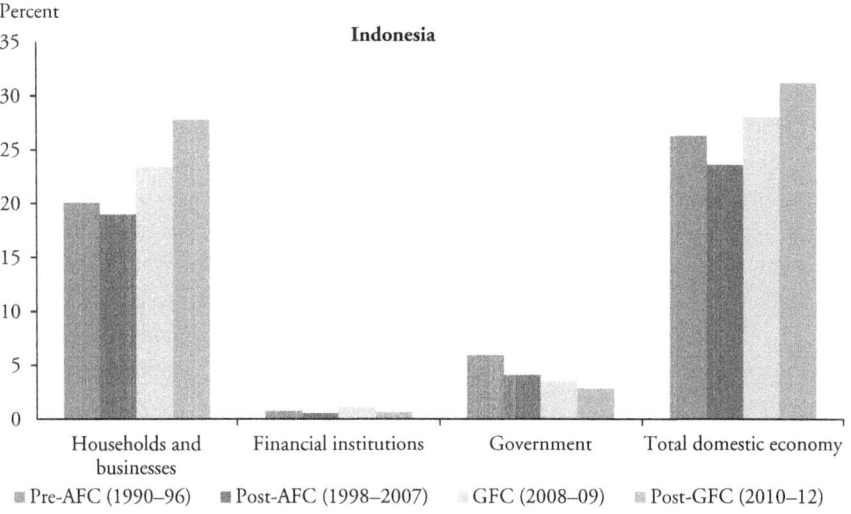

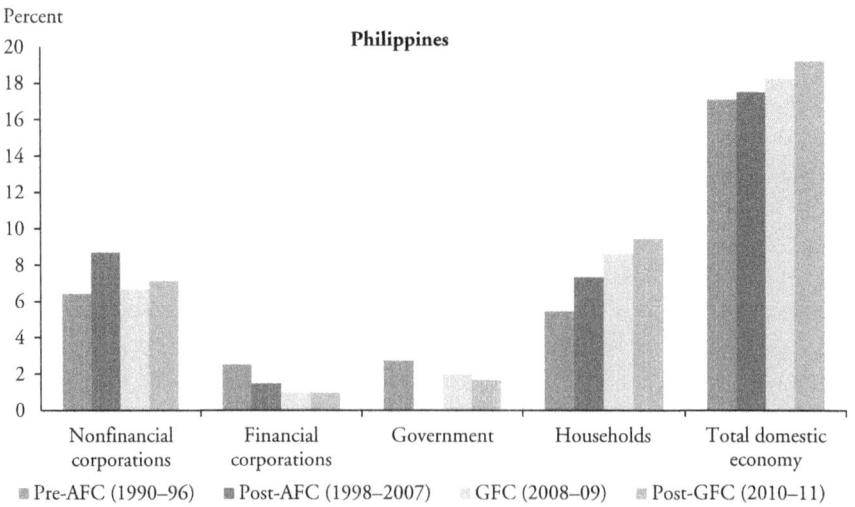

Figure 8-6. *(Continued)*

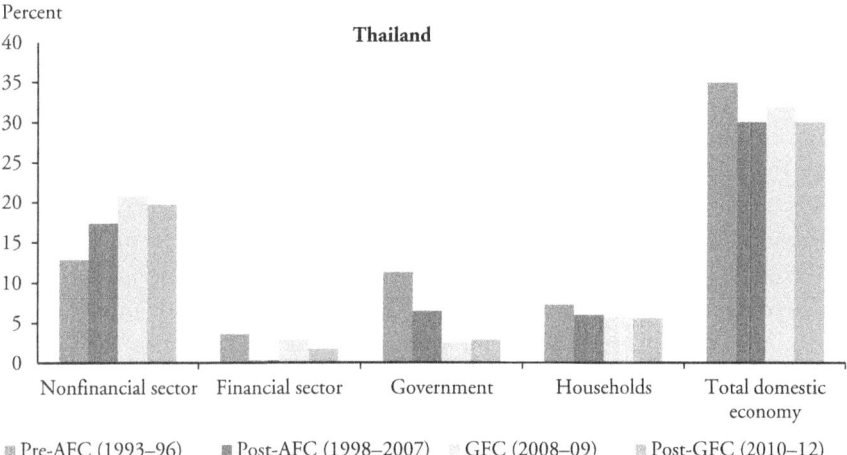

Source: Flow of Funds data from Statistics Indonesia, Bankgo Sentral ng Pilipinas, and Bank Negara Malaysia; and International Monetary Fund, *World Economic Outlook* database, April 2014, for GDP data.

a. AFC = Asian financial crisis, GFC = global financial crisis. Financial institutions consist of the central bank and domestic money banks. Pre-AFC pertains to 1996 data only for government and total domestic economy.

ASEAN corporate savings are relatively high for a number of reasons, one of which is the economic and financial structure that lowers the costs of inputs and permits oligopolistic profit. Inaccessibility of funds and various forms of uncertainty drive firms to rely more on retained earnings for their current and future investments and thereby increase their savings. Household saving generally responds more to demographic factors.[10] However, what is more important for our analysis is where the excess savings go.

Philippines

In the Philippines, excess saving in the financial sector fell from an annual average of Php693 billion in 1995–96 to Php504 billion in 2002–07, before making a strong recovery following the global financial crisis, as the sector's total resources reached Php1,605 billion by 2010–11. This was financed mainly by currency and deposits. Shares, other equity, and claims constituted the second major source of

---

10. The age of household head and the retirement age can determine the saving rate (Bersales and Mapa 2006; Prasad 2012). Horioka and Terada-Hagiwara (2010) argue that generally demographic transition matters in developing Asia, where the aging of population will play an important role in determining future domestic saving. For further explanations on the region's excess savings, see Azis and Yarcia (2014).

excess savings before the Asian financial crisis but were subsequently replaced by securities, other shares, and other accounts payable during and after the global financial crisis. Before the Asian financial crisis, the financial sector used its excess saving mainly to issue loans, but by 2008–09 it was used primarily to issue securities and cash, although loans and other accounts receivable also received a fair share. Excess saving in the Philippines' corporate (nonfinancial) sector fell from Php415 billion in 1995–96 to Php258 billion in 2002–07 and then rose back up to Php513 billion in 2008–09. Before the Asian crisis, the Philippines' corporate sector sourced most of its funds from securities and other shares. Its major source of financing was other accounts payable during the period 2002–09, followed by shares, other equity, and claims between 2002 and 2007 and by loans and securities, other than shares, during and after the global financial crisis. Before the Asian financial crisis, the corporate sector divided its funds almost equally among five financial assets, but by 2002–07 this was largely spent on other accounts receivable and currencies, and by 2008–09 on other accounts receivable, loans, and shares other than equity and claims. And by 2010–11 the corporate sector kept most of its funds as currencies while loans turned negative.

In the household sector, loans were the major source of funds. Accounts payable also provided funds for households before the Asian crisis, although this was reduced by some unclassified items. We also observe that households in the Philippines had a high level of investment in securities before the crisis, which were greatly reduced after the Asian financial crisis had passed; but later on increased after the global crisis. In the latter period, the sector instead increased investments on some unclassified items and insurance technical reserves.

Thailand

The excess saving in Thailand's financial corporation went down from an annual average of B934 billion in 1993–96 to B572 billion in 2002–07 before rising again to B947 billion in 2008–09 and to B2,771 billion in 2010–12. This was financed mainly by currency and deposits, while loans and securities were the other major sources of financing before the Asian financial crisis. However, other accounts payable, insurance technical reserves, and shares and other equity became the other major sources of financing immediately after the crisis, while securities had a negative contribution to financial assets.

The financial sector invested its financial assets mainly in loans and securities, with the latter having the biggest share in the period before the global financial crisis. After the global financial crisis, the financial sector divested itself of its currency and deposits and increased its loan issuances.

Financial assets of the Bank of Thailand before the Asian crisis came almost solely from currency and deposits, but in 2002–07 securities became the biggest source of financing, while loans dominated in 2008–09. Post-GFC, securities returned as the biggest source of financing, while loans turned to negative.

The bank used this excess saving on monetary gold and special drawing rights (SDRs), cutting back its loan issuances in 2008–09. Monetary gold and SDRs, however, declined sharply in 2010–12 while loans increased.[11]

Excess saving in the business sector dropped from B1.2 trillion in 1993–96 and settled at an average of around B680 billion from 2002–09, and increased further to B1.4 trillion in 2010–12. Most of the excess saving before the crisis in Asia had been funded by loans and some shares and securities. Businesses used it to lend, to buy securities, and to hold cash. In the period between the Asian and global financial crises, their financial assets had been funded by shares, equity, and securities. Investment on other accounts payable rose after the Asian financial crisis, along with higher levels of loans, securities, and shares. The country's business sector kept a significant share of cash throughout the period, presumably as a precautionary measure. The extent to which the financial and business sector in Thailand has been active in the securities market is also demonstrated by the fact that in addition to using currency and deposits they are holding, the country's financial sector has been drawing from shares and other equity sources, as well as insurance reserves, to finance lending and to purchase securities and shares.

Thai households received some funds from securities during the same period. Similar to the case of the Philippines, households in Thailand also reduced their saving after the Asian crisis, albeit not by as much. The saving rate picked up during the global financial crisis. The household sectors in both countries maintained a substantial amount of currency on hand, although Thai households were more conservative, keeping a greater part of their excess saving in the form of currency in 2008–12. They also had a relatively higher investment in shares and other equity. In short, as was the case in the Philippines, funding for Thai households came largely from loans, presumably from the banking sector, and a substantial portion of it was stored in the form of currency and also invested in securities and shares and other equity.

Indonesia

Excess saving of monetary authorities in Indonesia rose sharply from Rp4.0 trillion in 1996 to Rp68.8 trillion in 2009–12, primarily driven by the increase in interbank claims, which they used mainly in acquiring foreign exchange reserves and other foreign claims. Bank assets, on the other hand, were mostly funded by currency and deposits, except in 2002–07, when miscellaneous accounts became a substantial source of funding and negative equity significantly pulled down net financing. Before the Asian financial crisis, banks used their assets mainly in lending activities, but afterward, they also used them to pay off interbank claims.

11. Sussangkarn and Nikomborirak (2011) note that gross official reserves rose sharply from US$39 billion at the end of 1996 to US$143 billion at the end of 2009.

Securities made a negative contribution to bank investments in 2002–07, but turned positive during 2009–12.

To summarize, though the saving and investment behaviors of the corporate, financial, and business sectors from the three countries differ, the following common trend stands out:

—Currency and deposits remain the biggest source of financing in the financial sector, but there is an increasing dependence on accounts payable and securities.

—Despite having large saving, the region's corporate sector tends to borrow to finance further lending activities.

—Investment in securities has been on the rise.

In the case of households, their excess savings in recent years have been spent mostly on lending, but they are also increasingly investing in financial assets such as securities, shares, and equity.

Investing a considerable amount of saving in financial assets and investing the excess liquidity in much-needed productive infrastructure clearly have different impacts on a region's economy. Aside from the macroeconomic repercussions, we argue that the region's excess savings also produce a negative effect on the region's socioeconomic conditions.

Although the financial sector in ASEAN countries remains underdeveloped compared with that of industrial countries and other emerging economies, it has been developing relatively quickly after being substantially liberalized. This has contributed to a growing middle class that has access to the growing financial sector. This segment of society is able to accumulate wealth through consuming and saving more by riding on the continued growth of the financial sector, but the bulk of the population has limited or no access to financial services and cannot enjoy the gains of financial development. As a result, income inequality widens. This situation is worse when analyzed in a dynamic context, because the lack of investment in the real sector curtails the capacity of the economy to generate employment, hence aggravating the problem of income disparity over time.

Indeed, income inequality across many countries has worsened, not only in the ASEAN region but also in many economies across Asia. Declining capacity of the economy to generate employment (falling employment elasticity) is also observed across countries, despite the fast growth rate of the financial sector, which is even exceeding the GDP growth rate.

To the extent that the effect of massive capital inflows on the domestic economy has not always been positive, owing to the negative repercussions on the exchange rate and other vulnerabilities, our analysis reinforces the following argument: from the perspective of the saving-investment gap, the region's efforts to rebalance are necessary not primarily to help resolve the problems of global imbalances but to improve overall development in the region.

Concluding Remarks and Policy Implications

ASEAN's imbalances in the current account and saving-investment rates are too small to have a meaningful effect on the global imbalances. The collective current account surplus and excess saving are declining, growth has been driven by domestic demand, and trade among ASEAN countries as well as with other Asian and emerging markets is gaining ground, compensating for the slow demand from the United States and Europe. The resulting net capital flows, however, have been strong owing to the region's healthy growth prospect, open capital account, and low interest rates in advanced economies. We are inclined to believe that the ASEAN imbalances will continue to shrink, while portfolio inflows will continue to increase, albeit they will be more volatile. FDI flows are likely to go up, especially from other Asian countries such as the PRC, Japan, and the Republic of Korea. The region will be less likely to face a serious liquidity problem in the years to come.

The major challenge, though, is to convert the liquidity into productive investment and infrastructure, which the region badly needs. This will be necessary to sustain growth as well as to help improve the overall welfare by lowering income inequality and strengthening the capacity to generate employment. It is in this context that rebalancing should be seen as an important policy to pursue for ASEAN's own interest. For this to happen, the overall business climate ought to be improved to alter the incentive structure. The service sector, in particular, needs to be exposed to greater competition by opening up the sector to foreign players and by formulating and enforcing competition law.

Furthermore, regional liberalization of trade in final goods will open up vast market opportunities for member countries. Thus it is important for ASEAN to exert greater effort to achieve the aims of transforming the region into a highly competitive, single market and production base as detailed in the ASEAN Economic Community Blueprint (ASEAN Secretariat 2008). To enhance the intra-regional trade and cross-border capital flows, the region needs to strengthen harmonization, standardization, and technical infrastructure such as trade facilitation, customs clearance, and payments and settlement systems. In addition, it needs to remove other remaining impediments that reflect behind-the-border obstacles, as well as to ensure intraregional exchange-rate stability.

The supply-side factors are no less important. The quality of human resources holds the key to improving product quality for both intermediate and final goods, which is critical for developing a global-production value chain and for maximizing the benefits of regional free trade agreements. High product standards can also help to differentiate domestic products from lower-quality imports, providing domestic companies with an opportunity to maintain their domestic market share while capturing a global market share.

By strengthening these demand- and supply-side factors, the role of domestic demand in driving ASEAN growth will be further enhanced, while intraregional trade and the production network with other Asian countries are likely to be strengthened as goods and services being traded are higher in both value and quality. Stimulating domestic demand and intraregional trade that will ensure welfare improvement is the essence of rebalancing for the ASEAN region.

References

ASEAN Secretariat. 2008. *ASEAN Economic Community Blueprint.* Jakarta, Indonesia: ASEAN Secretariat.

Azis, Iwan J. 2008. "Macroeconomic Policy and Poverty." Discussion Paper 111. Tokyo: Asian Development Bank Institute. July.

Azis, Iwan J., and Nattapong Puttanapong. 2008. "A Regional Trend towards a Basket Peg System." *International Journal of Trade and Global Markets* 1, no. 2: 144–62.

Azis, Iwan J., and Hyun Song Shin. 2013. *How Do Global Liquidity Phases Manifest Themselves in Asia?* Mandaluyong City, Philippines: Asian Development Bank.

Azis, Iwan J., and Hyun Song Shin, eds. 2014. *Global Shock, Asian Vulnerability and Financial Reform.* Cheltenham, UK: Edward Elgar.

Azis, Iwan J., and Damaris Lee Yarcia. 2014. "How Capital Flows Affect Economywide Vulnerability and Inequality: Flow-of-Funds Analysis of Selected Asian Economies." Regional Economic Integration Working Paper 136. Mandaluyong City, Philippines: Asian Development Bank.

Bersales, Lisa Grace S., and Dennis S. Mapa. 2006. *Patterns and Determinants of Household Saving in the Philippines.* Report. Manila: USAID/Philippines Office of Economic Development and Governance.

Horioka, Charles Y., and Akiko Terada-Hagiwara. 2010. "Determinants and Long-Term Projections of Saving Rates in Developing Asia." Economics Working Paper 228. Mandaluyong City, Philippines: Asian Development Bank. October.

Kawai, Masahiro, Mario B. Lamberte, and Shinji Takagi. 2012. "Managing Capital Flows: Lessons from the Recent Experiences of Emerging Asian Economies." In *Regulating Global Capital Flows for Long-Run Development,* edited by Kevin P. Gallagher, Stephany Griffith-Jones, and Jose Antonio Ocampo, pp. 35–46. Boston: Frederick S. Pardee Center for the Study of the Longer-Range Future. March.

Mendoza, Enrique G., and Katherine A. Smith. "Margin Calls, Trading Costs, and Asset Prices in Emerging Markets: The Financial Mechanics of the 'Sudden Stop' Phenomenon." NBER Working Paper No. 9286. Cambridge, Massachusetts: National Bureau of Economic Research. October.

Prasad, Eswar S. 2012. "Growth Patterns in Asian Emerging Markets: Implication for Global Rebalancing." In *The Global Financial Crisis and Asia: Implications and Challenges,* edited by Masahiro Kawai, Mario B. Lamberte, and Yung Chul Park, pp. 262–91. Oxford University Press.

Sussangkarn, Chalongphob, and Deunden Nikomborirak. 2011. "Trans-Pacific Rebalancing: Thailand Case Study." Working Paper 273. Tokyo: Asian Development Bank Institute. March.

Tang, Hsiao-Chink. 2011. "Intra-Asia Exchange Rate Volatility and Intra-Asia Trade: Evidence by Type of Goods." Working Paper on Regional Economic Integration 90. Mandaluyong City, Philippines: Asian Development Bank Institute. December.

Thorbecke, Willem, and Ginalyn Komoto. 2010. "Investigating the Effects of the Exchange Rate Changes on Transpacific Rebalancing." Working Paper 47. Tokyo: Asian Development Bank Institute. September.

9

Crisis, Imbalances, and India

RAJIV KUMAR AND PANKAJ VASHISHT

After a year of sharp contraction, advanced economies have shown some signs of economic revival. A boom in United States retail sales in late 2009 and strong growth in the fourth quarter of 2009 and the first quarter of 2010, coupled with positive gross domestic product growth in Japan, Germany, and France in the second half of 2009, suggests that the crisis has bottomed out and recovery is on its way. These positive developments have provided great relief to policymakers across the globe who implemented the largest coordinated fiscal stimulus in history and a liquidity infusion to prevent the recession from becoming a depression. Fortunately, they succeeded, despite some concerns that with the tapering off of the stimulus in mid-2010, U.S. economic growth could weaken significantly and pull the global economy down with it. The possibility of a double-dip recession, stagnating unemployment levels, and fears of sovereign defaults in Europe have forced policymakers to consider how and when to roll back the fiscal stimulus and other measures needed to achieve more balanced global economic growth in the future. With an unsettled debate on the likely shape of the recovery, the issue of exit policy has recently gained purchase among policy discussions in mature economies.[1]

1. Relying on traditional economic dynamics (a steep downturn producing a sharp rebound), some economists, led by Michael Mussa (2009), are predicting a strong V-shaped recovery. They argue that businesses have cut their workforces disproportionately to the decline in customer demand and are significantly understaffed. Therefore, a reemployment process is inevitable and will be much faster than in past recessions. According to these economists, the reemployment process will boost consumer demand; given its extremely low level, even a small increase in demand would ensure a strong V-shaped recovery. This hypothesis has been severely criticized by some renowned

Table 9-1. *Components of GDP Growth, PRC and India, 1995–2011*
Percent

	People's Republic of China			India		
	1995–2000	2001–07	2008–11	1996–2001	2001–07	2008–11
Final consumption expenditure	66.1	38.3	46.8	76.9	53.2	102.6
Gross capital formation	27.1	48.3	60.1	20.4	57.3	26.3
Net exports	6.8	13.4	−7.6	2.7	−10.5	−8.8
Total	100	100	100	100	100	100

Source: Data from Government of India (2013) and National Bureau of Statistics of China (2012). Authors' compilation.

Although India, like other Asian economies, suffered only an indirect impact from the global financial crisis, its current policy challenges appear to be different from those facing the People's Republic of China (PRC) and other East Asian economies, which have relied heavily on external demand and access to the U.S. market for their growth momentum. India had a negative contribution of net exports to GDP growth from 2001 to 2011 (see table 9-1), and its foreign exchange reserves are a mere one-ninth of the PRC's. Therefore the issue of transpacific rebalancing of economic growth does not have the same connotations for India as it might for other East Asian economies. However, given its large domestic market, India could help other East Asian economies in their efforts to achieve greater export diversification and rebalancing of growth.

Impact of the Global Financial Crisis on the Indian Economy

The Indian economy appeared to be relatively insulated from the global financial crisis that started in August 2007 when the subprime mortgage crisis first surfaced in the United States. In fact, the Reserve Bank of India was raising interest rates until August 2008 with the explicit objective of bringing down the GDP growth rate, which had visibly moved above the rate of potential output growth and was contributing to the expansion of inflationary pressures.[2] But when the

economists, including Joseph Stiglitz and Nouriel Roubini. Citing the low level of final demand as the principal reason, Roubini (2009) has predicted a weak U-shaped recovery. He attributes the recent upturn in assets markets to excess liquidity that has resulted from government and central bank initiatives to arrest the downturn. He further warns that if policymakers fail to work out a proper exit policy, the global economy may head toward a double-dip recession.

2. Several observers, led by Surjit Bhalla (2008), have been pointing out since May 2008 that inflation, which rose as high as 12.3 percent at the end of June 2008, was largely imported and a result of global commodity price hikes. Therefore, inflation had little to do with India's own rate of economic growth, which started to slow down in the third quarter of FY2007–08 after reaching the highest level, 10.6 percent, in the second quarter of the same fiscal year.

collapse of Lehman Brothers on September 23, 2008, morphed the U.S. financial meltdown into a global economic downturn, the impact on the Indian economy was almost immediate. The impact can broadly be divided into two parts: the immediate or direct impact on its financial sector and the indirect impact on economic activities.

India, like most of the emerging economies, was lucky to avoid the first round of adverse effects because its banks were not overly exposed to subprime lending. Only one of the larger private sector banks, the ICICI (formerly the Industrial Credit and Investment Corporation of India), was partly exposed, but it too managed to avoid a crisis because of its strong balance sheet and timely action by the government. The banking sector as a whole remained financially sound. In fact, during the third quarter of FY2008–09, which was a nightmare for many large global financial institutions, banks in India announced encouraging results and witnessed an impressive jump in their profitability (Kumar and Vashisht 2009).

However, the indirect, or second-round, impact of the crisis affected India quite significantly. The liquidity squeeze in global markets following the collapse of Lehman Brothers had serious implications for India: it not only led to massive outflows of foreign institutional investment but also compelled Indian banks and corporations to shift their credit demand from external sources to the domestic banking sector. These events put considerable pressure on liquidity in the domestic market and consequently provoked a credit crunch. The credit crunch, coupled with a general loss of confidence, increased the risk aversion of Indian banks, thereby eventually hurting credit expansion in the domestic market.

On top of that, given the recessionary conditions in many advanced economies, the demand for India's exports in its major markets almost collapsed. Merchandise exports shrank by more than 17 percent from October 2008 to May 2009. Similarly, exports of services also faced a steep downturn. During the third quarter of FY2008–09, growth in services exports declined to a mere 5.9 percent, compared with 34 percent in the corresponding period the previous year. Earnings from travel, transportation, insurance, and banking services also suffered sharp contractions, while the growth of software exports declined by more than 21 percentage points. Yet the real shock came in the fourth quarter of FY2008–09, when services exports witnessed a contraction of 6.6 percent over the same period in the previous year (Kumar and Vashisht 2009). This was the first quarterly decline in services since the fourth quarter of FY2001–02.

The impact of the global crisis on the real economy became even more evident in the second half of FY2008–09, when, contrary to the optimistic official pronouncements, the Indian economy registered modest growth of 5.8 percent, significantly lower than 9.0 percent achieved in the corresponding period in FY2007–08 and GDP growth of 7.8 percent in the first half of FY2008–09. However, this slump in the GDP growth rate was much lower than the decline in several East Asian economies. Apart from the low trade-to-GDP ratios and a negative contribution of net exports to GDP growth, the relative importance of

Figure 9-1. *Year-on-Year Quarterly GDP Growth Rate, by Sector, 2004–13*

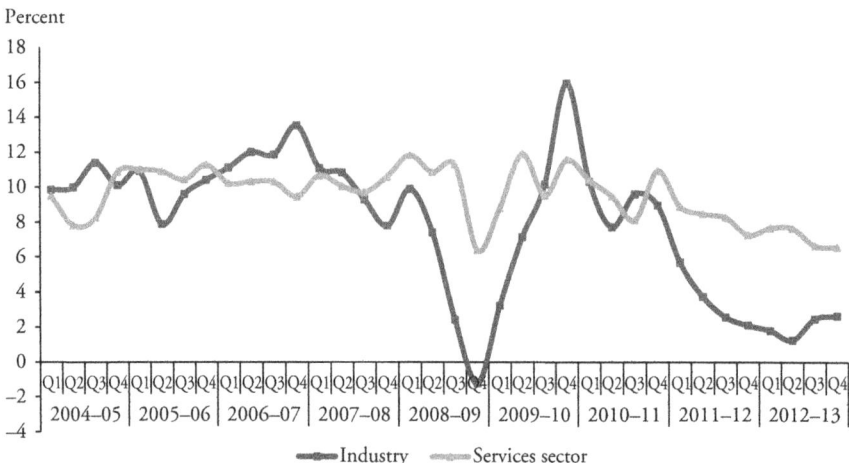

Source: Government of India (2013).

services, both in terms of their contribution to GDP and trade, differentiated India from most East Asian economies. It could be argued that since a large number of services are of a nontradable nature, they are less vulnerable to an external crisis. Moreover, even in the case of tradable services, the impact of external shocks is expected to be relatively low as the demand for traded services is less cyclical (because they are not storable) and their production is less dependent on external finance (Borchert and Matto 2009). This hypothesis was well corroborated by the performance of India's service sector during the recent crisis, when India showed a remarkable resilience and maintained a growth rate of more than 8 percent (see figure 9-1), which, though historically low by India's standards, was still fairly robust.

However, similar resilience was not observed in some East Asian economies—such as Japan, Singapore, the Republic of Korea, and the Philippines—where the services sector had an equal or even larger share of GDP. One possible explanation could lie in the different composition of the services sectors in these countries. Owing to the higher level of merchandise trade, the services sectors in the above-mentioned economies have largely been dominated by foreign trade–related services, such as trade, transportation, and storage, and other trade-related financial services, such as foreign trade financing and insurance. For example, in Singapore, where merchandise trade is as high as 386 percent of GDP, trade-related services account for more than 75 percent of total value added in the services sector (see table 9-2). With this high dependence of services on merchandise trade, the sector suffered along with merchandise trade in the face of a collapse in external demand.

Table 9-2. *Components of Services Sector, India, 2011, and Singapore, 2012*

Percent

Sector	Singapore	India
Trade, transportation, and storage	51.88	28.26
Hotels and restaurants	3.50	2.41
Information and communications	7.34	16.38
Financial and business	24.75	30.99
Other	12.53	21.96

Source: Data from Government of India (2013) and Singapore Department of Statistics (www.singstat.gov.sg/statistics/browse_by_theme/services.html).

In contrast, the dependence of the services sector on foreign trade–related services in India is much lower, at around 59 percent.[3] A disaggregated analysis of services sector growth shows that this lower dependence on merchandise trade has been critical in maintaining growth. As anticipated, trade-related services registered a significant decline during the period of crisis, while other services—including community, social, and personal services (17.5 percent) and financial, real estate, and business services (8.9 percent)—continued to grow at a healthy rate (see table 9-3).

In India, as in other emerging economies, manufacturing bore the real brunt of the crisis. In the wake of a decline in domestic and export demand, the manufacturing sector witnessed a contraction of 0.25 percent in the second half of FY2008–09, while growth in mining and quarrying slowed from 4.15 to 3.25 percent.

Policy Responses to the Crisis

Fiscal Stimulus Measures

The Indian economy received a major fiscal stimulus as early as February 2008, when an election-oriented budget for FY2008–09 was announced. The electoral cycle, often criticized for its deleterious effects on reforms and economic performance, on this occasion helped India to anticipate the global crisis and take advance action. The budget included massive increases in public outlays in support of employment guarantee schemes, farm loan waivers, pay hikes to government employees, and increases in food and fertilizer subsidies (Kumar

3. It should be noted that the financial and business services also include software and business process outsourcing services, which are not related to merchandise trade. In India, these services have grown rapidly. If we remove these services (which we were unable to do, owing to the lack of disaggregated data), the share of merchandise trade–related services would most likely decline significantly.

Table 9-3. *Biannual Estimates of GDP Growth, by Sector, 2007–10*
Percent

Sector	2007–08			2008–09			2009–10
	First half	*Second half*	*Annual*	*First half*	*Second half*	*Annual*	*First half*
Agriculture, forestry, and fishing	4.1	5.15	4.9	2.85	0.95	1.6	1.65
Mining and quarrying	1.95	4.45	3.3	4.15	3.25	3.6	8.7
Manufacturing	9.1	7.45	8.2	5.3	−0.25	2.4	6.3
Electricity, gas, and water supply	6.4	4.2	5.3	3.25	3.55	3.4	6.8
Construction	12.2	8.3	10.1	9	5.5	7.2	6.8
Trade, hotel, transport, and communication[a]	12	12.75	12.4	12.55	6.1	9	8.3
Finance, real estate, and business services	12.5	11.1	11.7	6.65	8.9	7.8	8.25
Community, social, and personal services	5.8	7.5	6.8	8.6	17.5	13.1	9.75
GDP	9.1	9.0	9.0	7.8	5.8	6.7	7.0

Source: Government of India (2009–10).

a. It should be noted that during the period of crisis, the communication sector continued to grow at a reasonable rate. This was the period when the number of mobile phone subscribers was growing at a reasonably high rate. Therefore, the real slump was in trade and transportation services.

and Vashisht 2009). This preelection fiscal splurge resulted in an increase in the revenue deficit from 1.1 percent of GDP in FY2007–08 to 4.5 percent in FY2008–09. Yet it also ensured that domestic aggregate demand did not slacken in the aftermath of the Lehman meltdown, compensated for the collapse in external demand, and, as described above, helped sustained overall GDP growth at a reasonable 5.8 percent. Having inadvertently anticipated the crisis, the government found that it did not have much fiscal space to take further steps to counter the impact of the global downturn.

However, some fiscal stimulus was still provided, primarily as a response to the global call for coordinated action by the G-20 summits. Three fiscal stimulus packages—one in December 2008, following the Washington G-20 summit, and one each in January and March 2010, just preceding the London summit—were announced. These stimulus packages were in large measure focused on optics to try to convey the impression that the government was taking strong action while not increasing fiscal outlays substantially. The measures announced included the full value of staggered outlays, and not just the new expenditures, on infrastructure, reduction in indirect taxes, and some assistance for export-oriented industries. To boost spending on infrastructure, clearly the most desirable modality for delivering the fiscal stimulus, the Indian government announced an increase of US$4 billion in planned spending and allowed the state governments an additional US$6 billion in market borrowing. Apart from this, the India Infrastructure Finance Company, established in 2007, was allowed to issue interest-free bonds worth US$6 billion for refinancing long-term loans for infrastructure projects.

A real push for demand came from a rate reduction in central excise duties from 14 to 8 percent and a lowering of the services tax rate from 12 to 10 percent. Exporters were given relief by reducing their interest costs by up to 2 percent, subject to a minimum rate of 7 percent a year. Another US$240 million was allocated for a full refund of terminal excise duty or central sales tax, wherever applicable, and US$80 million for beefing up various export incentives schemes. In aggregate, the fiscal stimulus, under all three packages, came to about 2 percent of total GDP. This figure looks rather small compared with the size of the stimulus in some other economies, such as the PRC or the United States. However, if the stimulus provided in the FY2008–09 budget is included, the size of the fiscal stimulus in FY2008–09 can be estimated at around 6 percent of GDP, comparable to the efforts made by other governments.

Monetary Policy Response

Joining the global trend, the Reserve Bank of India has, since October 2008, injected considerable liquidity into the economy through a series of policy rate cuts. The cash reserve ratio was brought down from 9 to 5 percent, and the repurchase rate by 425 basis points. Furthermore, to discourage banks from parking overnight funds with the Reserve Bank of India, the reverse repurchase rate was reduced from 6.0 percent in November 2008 to 3.25 percent in April 2009. The statutory liquidity ratio was also lowered by 1 percentage point from 25 to 24 percent. Apart from this, some special refinancing schemes were announced to improve liquidity for certain sectors (Kumar and Vashisht 2009). The cash reserve ratio has been reduced 400 basis points since September 2008; that alone resulted in a liquidity injection of US$32.7 billion. In addition, another sum of US$12.9 billion was injected by unwinding the market stabilization scheme. As of April 2009, nearly US$80 billion had been pumped into the system.

As a result of these policy rate cuts, the prime lending rates of commercial banks came down from 13.75–14.0 percent in October 2008 to 12.0–12.5 percent in January 2009. They softened further during 2009 as the demand for commercial bank credit fell owing to the slowdown in growth. Several banks ended up with huge liquidity overhangs and parked liquid funds with the Reserve Bank of India in overnight deposits that earned them low returns of 3–3.5 percent, depending on the reverse repurchase rate at the time. The call money rates have also remained stable at low levels, and the overnight money market rate has remained within the liquidity adjustment facility corridor.[4]

To attract foreign capital, the Reserve Bank also liberalized the norms governing external commercial borrowings and foreign institutional investment. The limit on foreign institutional investment in corporate bonds was increased from US$6 billion to US$15 billion. At the same time, real estate developers were permitted to raise external commercial borrowings for integrated township projects, while nonbanking financial companies dealing exclusively with infrastructure financing were allowed to access external commercial borrowings from either multilateral or bilateral financial institutions.

The three fiscal stimulus measures and other monetary policy measures reinforced the significant fiscal expansion undertaken in the FY2008–09 budget. However, in hindsight, it is clear that the fiscal measures, which effectively transferred substantial purchasing power to the rural sector, were more effective in shoring up aggregate demand than were monetary policy measures, whose traction has been evidently weak. Perhaps monetary policy measures were less effective because of underutilized capacities and the uncertain external demand conditions, both of which kept investment demand rather subdued until September 2009, when demand began to rise as reflected in the upturn in capital goods imports and growth in commercial bank credit. The expansionary budget of February 2008, together with subsequent policy measures, ensured that the downturn in GDP growth was not as steep as that experienced by some of the

---

4. With the economy picking up in the second half of 2009, the situation began to change, and the nonfood credit off-take improved significantly in the first three months of 2010, rising to 16.9 percent by the end of March 2010.

advanced and major emerging economies, ultimately suggesting that the economy could be brought back to its potential growth path in the short term.

Short-Term Growth Outlook

The Indian economy recovered fairly quickly from the downturn that saw the GDP growth slump to 5.8 percent in both the third quarter of FY2008–09 (October to December 2009) and the fourth quarter of FY2009–10 (January to March 2009; see table 9-3). It achieved 6.1 percent growth in the next quarter and was growing at 7.9 percent in the second quarter of FY2009–10. This was in line with global trends and clearly a result of the expansionary fiscal and monetary policy measures taken in the wake of the global recession. The government's advanced estimate for economic growth for FY2009–10 (April 2009 to March 2010) was 7.2 percent (Government of India 2009). The growth momentum is likely to continue in the current year (FY2010–11) as well, with both the government and the Reserve Bank of India now estimating GDP growth in FY2010–11 to be around 8 percent. The key question is whether GDP growth can be maintained in the face of strong prevailing inflationary pressures and without a further worsening of the fiscal and current account deficits.

We made our own forecasts for the nonagriculture sector GDP growth in FY2010–11 on the basis of an index of leading economic indicators (LEIs).[5] Using this index to forecast GDP growth, we found that the LEI with a five-quarter lag explains the variation in nonagriculture GDP growth most precisely.[6] However, since the selected leading indicators do not capture the impact of external shocks such as the information technology boom and bust in FY2000–01 and the recent U.S. financial meltdown, both of which directly and indirectly affected the Indian economy, we used a dummy variable to capture their impact.

---

5. Leading economic indicators are variables that are considered to have significant influence on the future level of economic activity in the country. These indicators give advance signals about the likely future growth rate. Generally, they are used to identify inflection points in the business cycles, which can be done with some accuracy as the change in direction of the principal leading indicators would result in a similar directional change in the overall economic activity. The predictive quality of these indicators has led them to be called "leading" indicators. For constructing the leading indicators' index, the following nine indicators have been selected, after testing their correlation with and predictive quality for overall economic activity: production of machinery and equipment, nonfood credit, railway freight traffic, cement sales, net sales of the corporate sector, fuel and metal prices, real rate of interest, the Bombay stock exchange's Sensex, and export growth. A composite index has been constructed for the period 1997–2008 with the quarterly series of growth of these variables (except for the real rate of interest, for which the level, and not the growth, has been used) using the principal component index method.

6. We have been using the LEI index for GDP forecasting for three years. Using LEI methodology, for example, we predicted growth of GDP at 9.2 percent for 2007–08 in November 2007. Most other agencies had predicted a lower growth rate of 8.5 percent or below for that year as against the actual growth rate of 9 percent.

Figure 9-2. *Actual and Forecast Nonagricultural GDP Growth*

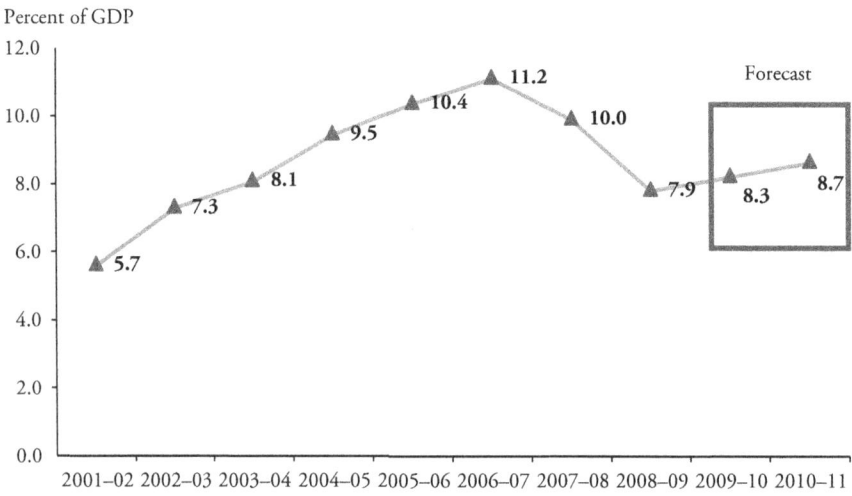

Source: Government of India (2009). Authors' estimates.

The LEI with a five-quarter lag and the shock represented by a dummy variable (equal to 1 with shock and 0 without) are used to forecast India's nonagriculture GDP growth. The estimated equation for forecasting nonagriculture GDP (given below) is satisfactory with an adjusted R^2 value of 0.55 and all the coefficients being statistically significant at a 99 percent confidence level.

$$GRNon\text{-}agriGDP_t = 8.72 + 1.54 \, LEI_{t-5} - 3.13 \, Dummy.$$

$$(5.67) \qquad (-5.72)$$

Based on this model, the LEIs suggest that perhaps the Indian economy bottomed out in the first quarter of FY2009–10 and economic activity has since been on the upturn. According to this model, the nonagriculture GDP will grow by 8.3 percent in FY2009–10 and rise by 8.7 percent in FY2010–11 (see figure 9-2). Thus the recovery seems to be well under way. And if macroeconomic stability can be achieved in India, the economy could be on its potential growth trajectory by FY2011–12.

The economic downturn in India lasted for two years, FY2008–09 and FY2009–10, when the GDP growth rate fell to 6.7 and 7.2 percent, respectively, from the average rate of 9 percent achieved in the previous five years. The slowdown in FY2008–09, as discussed earlier, was a result partially of policy tightening (until August 2008) and partially of the second-round effects of the global recession. Recovery in FY2009–10 was hampered by the monsoon, which affected the main *kharif* (winter) crop and is expected to bring down the rate of growth of agriculture GDP to about negative 2–4 percent. On the basis of their estimate for agriculture growth, Mathew Joseph and Karan Singh (2009) forecast the FY2009–10 GDP growth at 6.8 percent. Other development organizations— the International Monetary Fund, the World Bank (2010), and the Asian Development Bank (ADB 2009), among others—have also estimated Indian GDP growth in FY2009–10 at similar levels (7.0 percent) in their latest forecasts.

With stronger industry growth being indicated for FY2010–11 and a better external environment, we might expect higher GDP growth in FY2010–11. According to our LEI index nonagriculture sector GDP growth for FY2010–11 is likely to be 8.7 percent. From all accounts, monsoons are expected to be normal this year. With the advantage of a low base and a normal monsoon season, agriculture growth in FY2010–11 is expected to be about 4 percent. This will yield an overall GDP growth rate of nearly 8 percent for FY2010–11—an estimate similar to that made recently by the Reserve Bank of India (2010).

There are three potential risks to this growth forecast for FY2010–11. The first is the continuing inflationary pressure in the economy, with the wholesale price index rising to 9.9 percent by the end of March 2010 and expected to remain in double digits until October 2010. Although it is expected to decline to 5–6 percent by March 2011, that expectation is premised on a normal monsoon season, stability in global commodity and oil prices, and significant improvement in food availability.[7] Moreover, even if the reduction in the fiscal deficit as announced in the FY2010–11 budget is achieved, the government's borrowing program still remains large and has to be financed almost fully by issuance of new securities, which will require the Reserve Bank of India to keep the liquidity at comfortable levels if the market interest rates are not to shoot up. This will also add to inflationary pressures.

Second, FY2009–10 is expected to end with an external sector imbalance reminiscent of the crisis years of 1990–91, when the country faced an external payments default. The current account deficit is expected to be nearly 4 percent of GDP in FY2009–10 compared with only 2.4 percent in the previous year and 3.1 percent in 1990–91. This may also prompt the Reserve Bank of India to raise interest rates in an effort to dampen investment demand and slow the rise in imports, which increased by 66 percent in February 2010—pushed up, to a large extent, by capital goods imports. Additional complications may arise from the appreciation in the Indian rupee's exchange rate owing to higher capital inflows, which may further worsen the current account deficit. An appreciating Indian rupee also means that the economy may not be able to benefit from an increase

7. As mentioned here, GDP growth came down to about 5 percent for both 2012–13 and 2013–14. This was at a time when global recovery had started, but Indian policymakers continued to give global conditions as the cause for this slowdown rather than take corrective actions focusing on domestic policy measures.

in export demand. Finally, the global economic recovery, it is argued, could falter as the expansionary effects of the fiscal stimulus begin to wear off mid-year. This could mitigate the U.S. rebound and, in the event the eurozone and Japan experience a sluggish recovery, further dampen external demand. Overall, therefore, we tend to believe that the 8 percent GDP growth rate has a downward bias rather than an upward one, as stated by the Reserve Bank of India (2010) in its recent macroeconomic policy review.

Assessment of the Policy Responses and Issues of Exit Policy

The Indian fiscal policy response to the crisis can best be summarized as having been preempted by political considerations. This resulted in a fiscal expansion ahead of the global crisis. While clearly inadvertent, it proved to be a master stroke, as it effectively anticipated the crisis and prevented the collapse of domestic and specifically rural demand at a time when external demand had virtually disappeared. But with the combined fiscal deficit of the central (federal) government and the states (the regional or provincial governments) reaching 8.5 percent of GDP, it left only limited fiscal space to respond in the aftermath of the crisis. This is reflected in the size of the post–December 2008 fiscal stimulus packages. Being smaller than expected, the burden fell largely on monetary policy.[8] The postcrisis fiscal stimulus, though small in size compared with other countries', worsened the fiscal deficit, increasing it to 9.4 percent of GDP in FY2009–10 (see table 9-4). This implied a significant expansion in government borrowing, which increased from Rs126,912 crore (US$25.3 billion) in FY2007–08 to Rs284,396 crore (US$63.1 billion) in FY2008–09 and further to Rs419,622 crore (US$93.1 billion) in FY2009–10. Debt servicing, which accounted for about 50.8 percent of total revenue receipts in FY2008–09, went up to 54.5 percent in FY2009–10 and is expected to be around 56 percent in FY2010–11. The rise in the fiscal deficit could have engendered a significant downgrading of India's sovereign credit.[9] However, the risk of the downgrade was averted as government brought down the fiscal deficit to 6.9 percent in FY 2010–11.

The monetary policy response was more robust and aggressive than the constrained fiscal policy response, as the authorities had significant policy space created by the monetary policy tightening undertaken since October 2005. The

8. It is argued by some observers that the policy response was delayed because the government was initially in a state of denial, believing that the global crisis would not affect the Indian economy since its banking sector was not at all affected. It was argued that the net contribution of trade-to-GDP growth is negative and hence the turmoil in the global market would not have any major impact on India. However, a sharp deterioration in some key sectors soon changed this perception, and the government's policy response started in December 2008.

9. Because of the deteriorating fiscal position, leading credit rating agencies like Standard & Poor's (S&P) and Moody's put India on a negative watch list in March 2009.

Table 9-4. *Key Fiscal Indicators as Share of GDP, 2007–13*
Percent

Year	Fiscal deficit			Debt-to-GDP ratio		
	Center	State	Combined	Center	State	Combined
2007–08	2.5	1.5	4.1	58.9	26.6	85.5
2008–09	6.0	2.4	8.4	58.6	26.1	84.7
2009–10	6.5	2.9	9.4	56.3	25.5	81.7
2010–11	4.8	2.1	6.9	52.1	23.5	75.5
2011–12[a]	5.7	2.3	8.1	51.9	22.3	74.2
2012–13[b]	5.2	2.1	7.3	51.9	22.2	74.1

Source: Reserve Bank of India (2013).
a. Revised estimates.
b. Budget estimates.

Reserve Bank of India brought down the repurchase and reverse repurchase rates by 4.25 and 2.75 percentage points, respectively, between October 2008 and April 2009, and reduced the cash reserve ratio by 4 percentage points. However, the sharp increase in government borrowing to finance the high fiscal deficit has generated an upward pressure on market interest rates. This is also reflected in the rise of the ten-year bond yield rate (Kumar and Vashisht 2009). The monetary policy's impact has been limited not only by the government's large borrowing requirement, which has kept market interest high, but also because domestic credit markets are fragmented and a large part of the economy still operates outside the formal banking system. As a result, policy rate cuts have not filtered down to the retail credit market, with commercial bank lending rates coming down by only about 200 basis points despite the Reserve Bank of India's having slashed its repurchase rate by as much as 450 basis points. Consequently, the growth in nonfood credit, a leading and significant indicator of investment demand, remained significantly below past trends—at least until the last quarter of FY2009–10, when it picked up to reach almost the FY2008–09 level (16.9 percent compared with 17.3 percent) but still noticeably lower than the 22 percent growth in FY2007–08. In the Indian context, where there is apparently a relatively high structural floor to the fiscal deficit and where monetary policy has limited impact, macroeconomic policy measures can be expected to have a somewhat limited capacity to sustain rapid growth along with macroeconomic stability. Unlike the PRC, which has been able to achieve both rapid growth and stable prices, India seems to run rapidly into the trade-off between rapid growth and macroeconomic stability. Thus cyclical upswings are fairly short lived. The longest upswing between FY2003–04 and FY2007–08 was largely a result of the most benign and expansionary global economic conditions. For the future, India must focus on completing its program of structural economic reforms to sustain rapid and inclusive growth along with macroeconomic stability.

Asian Economic Integration and India's Potential Role

The economic rise of Asia is one of the most noticeable facts of the past few decades. First, the impressive growth of East Asian economies—mainly the so-called Asian Tigers in the late 1960s and 1970s and the phenomenal rise of the People's Republic of China (PRC), followed more recently by India—has ensured Asia's emergence as perhaps the principal engine of global growth.[10] Noticeably, all successful Asian economies, excluding India, have used an export-oriented growth model, which, though it generated higher growth rates for these econo-mies, also increased their dependence on access to advanced economy markets for absorbing these exports, in turn making them more vulnerable to any nega-tive development in these economies. The People's Republic of China has clearly emerged as the major production hub within Asia, with the ASEAN economies providing the necessary intermediate inputs and components and the euro-zone and North America representing the major markets for the final products. These two markets had absorbed nearly US$1.03 trillion in exports from this Asian production system just before the Lehman crisis—about 33 percent of the total exports from the PRC and the ASEAN economies. The region had clearly become vulnerable to any downturn in these markets, as demonstrated rather spectacularly in the post-Lehman period. The need to reduce the region's dependence on external demand and achieve more balanced growth has become evident. The rather sharp recoveries in the PRC and in other Asian economies in 2009 suggest that efforts to raise the share of indigenous demand in sustaining the region's growth may already be yielding the desired results. This process of reducing Asia's dependence on external markets can be further strengthened with the expansion of the production networks and markets beyond East and South-east Asia to South Asia.

Given its potentially large domestic market, ample supply of skilled labor at relatively low wages, and dynamic entrepreneurial class, India can play an important role in the rebalancing of Asia Pacific economic growth in future. Until recently, India's interaction and integration with the South and East Asian economies has not been substantial. However, this changed with the launch-ing of India's Look East Policy in 1992, with the avowed goal of achieving far greater integration with its dynamic neighbors in East and Southeast Asia. Major initiatives included a free trade agreement with Thailand, a comprehensive eco-nomic partnership agreement with Singapore and the Republic of Korea, and a recently concluded free trade agreement between India and ASEAN, which, for

10. The success of the Asian Tigers not only highlighted Asia on the global map but also brought a radical change in economic policies worldwide. Until 1965, structural schools of thought, which put great emphasis on import protection, dominated policy circles. However, since the success of East Asian economies was based on an open-economy model, it gave a great boost to the neoclassical schools of thought.

Table 9-5. *India's Two-Way Trade with Selected Asian Economies, 2001–12*
US$ billions

	ASEAN		SAARC[a]		PRC		Japan		Korea	
	Value	Share	Value	Share	Value	Share	Value	Share	Value	Share
2001	6.7	7.5	2.7	3.0	2.8	3.1	3.3	3.7	1.6	1.8
2002	8.0	7.7	2.9	2.8	4.2	4.0	3.9	3.8	1.9	1.8
2003	9.9	7.8	4.5	3.6	6.2	4.9	4.0	3.2	3.1	2.4
2004	13.6	8.2	5.5	3.3	10.1	6.1	4.8	2.9	4.3	2.6
2005	17.9	7.8	6.8	3.0	17.3	7.6	6.1	2.7	5.9	2.6
2006	25.1	8.8	7.7	2.7	23.5	8.2	7.5	2.6	7.2	2.5
2007	30.0	8.6	9.6	2.8	34.0	9.8	9.0	2.6	7.9	2.3
2008	39.7	8.3	12.3	2.6	41.7	8.7	11.4	2.4	12.1	2.5
2009	41.9	9.4	8.9	2.0	41.0	9.2	9.9	2.2	12.0	2.7
2010	52.6	9.2	13.2	2.3	58.7	10.3	13.1	2.3	13.6	2.4
2011	74.8	9.8	15.4	2.0	72.2	9.5	16.8	2.2	16.9	2.2
2012	75.0	9.6	16.0	2.1	68.9	8.8	18.8	2.4	17.8	2.3

Source: United Nations, UN Comtrade database (http://comtrade.un.org/db/default.aspx).
a. South Asian Association for Regional Cooperation.

the time being, is limited only to goods. The positive outcome of these initiatives is reflected in a sharp increase in bilateral trade between India and the PRC and ASEAN economies (see table 9-5). However, somewhat paradoxically, India's trade has increased most rapidly with the PRC, which does not have any trade agreement with India. The two-way trade between India and the PRC rose from US$2.7 billion in 2001 to US$41.7 billion in 2008, and trade between India and ASEAN increased from US$6.7 billion to US$39.6 billion during the same period. Within ASEAN, India's trade has increased substantially with Singapore and Thailand, which have signed trade pacts with India. Similarly, India's trade with the eight countries of the South Asian Association for Regional Cooperation (SAARC), Japan, and the Republic of Korea has also increased, though at lower rates. India is increasingly becoming integrated with Asia, which has emerged as its major trade partner, replacing the erstwhile dominant role of the United States and Europe in India's external linkages.

Despite the recent growth, India's current trade with the above-mentioned economies is far below potential. In an empirical investigation, Prabir De (2009) found that India's trade with the PRC, Singapore, Thailand, Malaysia, Indonesia, Viet Nam, and Myanmar is 5–15 percent lower than its potential; for the Philippines, Brunei Darussalam, Cambodia, the Lao People's Democratic Republic, Bangladesh, and Pakistan, the gap between actual and potential trade is much wider, ranging from 53 percent to 93 percent. Thus there is sufficient scope for India to continue with its efforts to integrate more closely with its Asian partners.

In line with growing trade, India's investment relations with Asia have also recently improved. Foreign direct investment from Asia to India, which was just

Table 9-6. *Value and Share of Asia in India's Cumulative Inbound and Outbound Foreign Direct Investment, 1991–2012*
US$ billions

	Inbound FDI from Asia		Outbound FDI to Asia	
	Value	*Share in total*	*Value*	*Share in total*
2001	10.94	15.1	1.5	23.2
2012	54.91	20.7	40.6	31.6

Source: Data from Ministry of Commerce (2007, 2013), Export-Import Bank of India (2014), and Ministry of Finance (http://finmin.nic.in/the_ministry/dept_eco_affairs/icsection/Annexure_5.html).

US$10.94 billion in 2001, increased to US$54.91 billion in 2009 (see table 9-6). Similarly, foreign direct investment from India to Asia has also increased from US$1.5 billion in 2001 to US$31.6 billion in 2012, thereby increasing Asia's share in total Indian outbound foreign direct investment from 23.2 percent to 31.6 percent during the same period.

India has recently emerged as one of the fastest-growing Asian economies, with a growth model that is quite distinct from the export-oriented strategy adopted by other rapidly growing Asian economies. Although all East Asian economies have derived a predominant part of their growth from external sources, both in terms of foreign capital and export markets, India's growth has mostly come from its internal sources. This is shown rather dramatically by comparing the contribution of net exports with GDP growth in the PRC and India (see table 9-1). India has managed to grow at a reasonably high rate despite consistently generating a large trade deficit, which has been made up principally of the surplus on the invisibles account. This highlights the role that services exports, principally software exports, have played in maintaining an external sector balance for India and in sustaining high GDP growth rates as well.

The overall current account deficit has been managed at fairly low levels, ranging from 1.5 to 2.5 percent of GDP, except in certain years. This implies that the gap between domestic savings and investment has been kept at low levels and that India has managed to finance a predominant part of its capital formation from domestic savings (see figure 9-3). At the same time, unlike the PRC, India has not generated excessive savings that then need to be invested abroad in foreign country bonds or absorbed in a continuous buildup of foreign exchange reserves. This phenomenon is reflected in a country running a current account surplus as in the case of China. The Indian savings rate, though high, has been fully absorbed in domestic investment, which has also made use of the inflow of foreign savings as reflected in India's current account deficit.

Taken together, a small current account deficit and only a modest level of foreign exchange reserves until 2002 implies a rather limited inflow of foreign

Figure 9-3. *Domestic Savings and Investment as Share of GDP, 1950–2011*

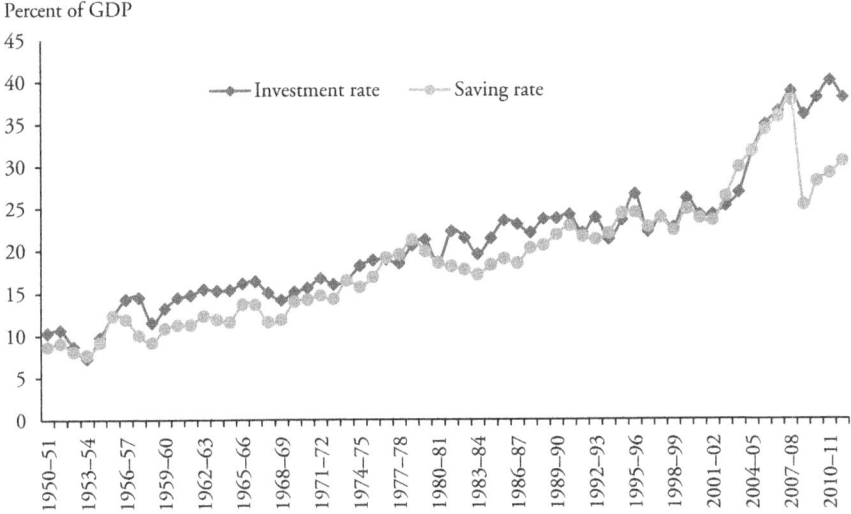

Percent of GDP

Source: Reserve Bank of India (2013).

capital into India. As table 9-7 shows, foreign capital inflows, both portfolio and direct equity varieties, ranged from US$103 million to US$6.62 billion between 1991 and 2001. These were hardly a fraction of the foreign direct investment and portfolios that the PRC managed to attract during the same period. However, this changed significantly in 2003, when the combined foreign direct investment and portfolio capital inflows jumped up to US$15.7 billion and marked the beginning of an upward trend. Given the low current account deficit during these years (and a small surplus in 2002–03), these enhanced capital inflows have enabled India to build up sizable foreign exchange reserves, As shown in table 9-7, these were US$279.1 billion at the end of FY2009–10, a level that is still only a fifth of the PRC's reserves but affords India ample insurance against external shocks. India's reserves represent 121 percent of its total foreign debt and 73 percent of its total annual current account liabilities.

There has been a major debate about the beginning of India's high growth trajectory.[11] This debate, in our view, is somewhat misdirected because, irrespective of when India's high-growth phase started, it could not have been sustained without the major structural reforms undertaken by the Narasimha Rao government from 1991 to 1995. These reforms significantly increased India's

11. Some economists, such as Subramanian (2008), argue that the foundation of India's high growth was laid in the 1980s, and perhaps even earlier, when India acquired a skilled workforce and industrial experience. However, Panagariya (2008) attributes India's success entirely to the market-friendly reforms of the 1990s.

Table 9-7. *India's Foreign Capital Inflows and Foreign Exchange Reserves,*
1999–2013
US$ millions

Year	Direct investment (1)	Portfolio investment (2)	Total (1 + 2)	Foreign exchange reserves
1990–91	97	6	103	5,834
1991–92	129	4	133	9,220
1992–93	315	244	559	9,832
1993–94	586	3,567	4,153	19,254
1994–95	1,314	3,824	5,138	25,186
1995–96	2,144	2,748	4,892	21,687
1996–97	2,821	3,312	6,133	26,423
1997–98	3,557	1,828	5,385	29,367
1998–99	2,462	−61	2,401	32,490
1999–2000	2,155	3,026	5,181	38,036
2000–01	4,031	2,590	6,621	42,281
2001–02	6,125	1,952	8,077	54,106
2002–03	5,036	944	5,980	76,100
2003–04	4,322	11,356	15,678	112,959
2004–05	5,987	9,287	15,274	141,514
2005–06	8,901	12,494	21,395	151,622
2006–07	22,739	7,060	29,799	199,179
2007–08	34,729	27,433	62,162	309,723
2008–09	41,737	−14,031	27,706	251,985
2009–10	33,107	32,396	65,503	279,057
2010–11	29,029	30,293	59,322	304,818
2011–12	32,957	17,171	50,128	294,398
2012–13	26,953	26,891	53,844	292,046

Source: Reserve Bank of India (2013).

openness to the global economy and reduced the level of government controls and licenses, which have clearly become dysfunctional (Pursell, Kishor, and Gupta 2007; Panagariya 2008). By lowering policy-induced entry barriers, the reforms also greatly increased the level of competition in domestic markets and encouraged the import of new and much-needed technology. The growing openness, increasing domestic competition, and greater space for private sector activity in the manufacturing and services sectors virtually redefined the macroeconomic fundamentals of the economy and put India on a new growth trajectory essentially by raising the rate of growth of its potential output. After the reforms of the early 1990s, India was able to achieve much lower rates of inflation and significantly higher rates of domestic savings, which increased from 21 percent of GDP in FY2001–02 to 33 percent in FY2007–08, and consequently a higher level of investment as well (see figure 9-3). An improved domestic savings rate, coupled with increased inflow of foreign capital, both in terms of foreign direct investment and external commercial borrowings, eased the domestic cost of capital,[12] which declined in nominal terms from 19 percent in 1993 to 11.75 percent in 2006. These changes have been the fundamental basis for India's higher sustained GDP growth in the postreform period.

If sustained, the reforms will help to raise India's rate of growth of potential output and may even enable the country to catch up with the People's Republic of China in the coming decades. To demonstrate the average annual growth rate of the two countries, we take 1978 as the initial year for the PRC's reforms and 1991 for India.[13] The trend growth rate achieved by India in its shorter postreform period is not much different from the PRC's. This holds out the hope that even following the rather distinctly domestic demand–driven growth strategy, India could achieve a sustained rapid growth that could match the PRC's in the coming years.

The post-1991 high rate of GDP growth has largely been attributed to the spectacular performance of the services sector, especially the software and information technology–enabled services sector, in India.[14] The relative success of India's services sector, at least before 1980, can be entirely attributed to its education system, which until recently was biased toward secondary and higher education. The bias toward higher technical education proved fortuitous, as it provided India with a first-mover advantage in the U.S. software market when it opened up significantly during the mid-1990s and faced a huge manpower shortage as the U.S. completed the transition of its information technology–based equipment to the new century, which required a massive effort to rewrite existing software.

This was also reflected in the services sector's success in attracting foreign direct investment (see figure 9-4). The surge in foreign direct investment in services ensured a wholesale movement in technological upgrading. The surge in software and services growth, premised as it was on technological breakthroughs, was greatly facilitated by the major reforms in the telecommunications sector. Before the reforms of the 1990s, the telecom sector was a dysfunctional government monopoly, unable to satisfy the rising demand, as reflected in the country's abnormally low teledensity level of 0.8 percent in 1992. The sector was characterized by extensive rationing and the generation of rents and high tariffs. But with the economic reforms of the 1990s, specifically privatization and the entry of foreign players, the communication sector became the fastest-growing sector of the Indian economy. Since then, teledensity has increased to nearly 50 percent, and

12. Prime lending rate (maximum).

13. 1978 was the year that the PRC started its process of liberalization. In the same way, India embarked on the path of liberalization in 1991.

14. Although the Indian services sector hogged the limelight after the economic reforms of the 1980s and 1990s, its relative success can in fact be traced back to the preindependence period. In an interesting analysis, Broadberry and Gupta (2008) compared the productivity gap between Britain and India for all three sectors—agriculture, industry, and services—and found it to be smaller in services than in industry or agriculture since World War I.

Figure 9-4. *Sectors with Highest Level of Foreign Direct Investment: Percent Share in Total Foreign Direct Investment*

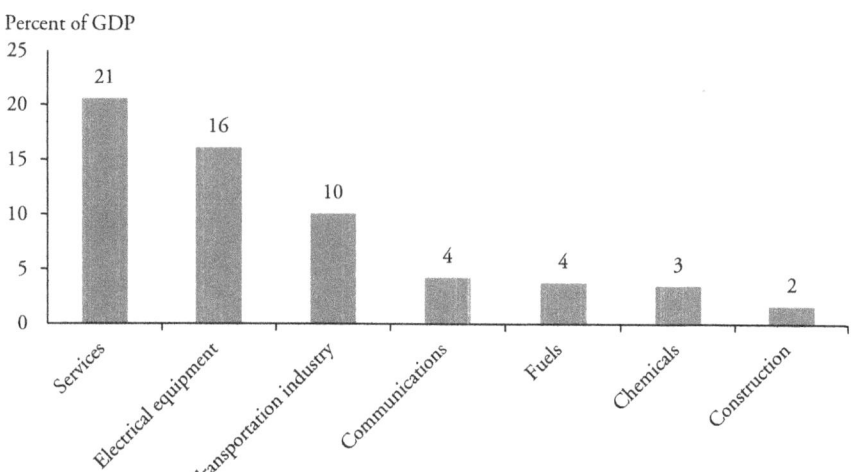

Percent of GDP

Source: CEIC database.

India has emerged as the fastest-growing market for mobile phones, with new connections increasing at a phenomenal rate of more than 12 million a month. The sector also emerged as a major contributor to GDP growth, with its average contribution rising to 6.13 percent in 2001–10 (see table 9-8). In a similar manner, other services sectors—such as the financial and nonfinancial sectors, which have received a large amount of foreign direct investment—have also contributed significantly to GDP growth.

The positive contribution of the services sector to India's GDP growth rate in the past two decades is unequivocal. The question is whether this rather unbalanced growth, which has seen the manufacturing and agriculture sectors lag behind significantly (as reflected in their stagnant and declining shares in GDP), can help India achieve the necessary growth rate in employment and sustain its overall rate of economic activity. It is estimated that for all its burgeoning exports and rapid expansion, the software and information technology–enabled services sector has generated only 1.63 million employment opportunities (Illiyan 2008). This is clearly inadequate for a country in which 65 percent of its population is below the age of twenty-five and whose workforce expands annually by more than 12 million people. A growth model that does not generate sufficient employment opportunities cannot be sustained. Evidently, India has to undertake a form of rebalancing of its growth strategy by making the sources of growth more broadly based so that more employment is generated and inequalities are not allowed to increase. India's democratic, diverse, and pluralistic society will

Table 9-8. *Sectoral Contribution to GDP, 2001–10*

Sector	Average contribution to growth	Average share in GDP
Agriculture, including livestock	6.06	15.76
Forestry and logging	0.43	2.02
Fishing	0.47	0.92
Mining and quarrying	1.59	2.69
Registered	12.22	10.12
Unregistered	4.60	5.42
Electricity, gas, and water supply	1.76	2.08
Construction	10.18	7.47
Trade	17.04	14.56
Hotels and restaurants	1.86	1.48
Railways	1.00	0.98
Transport by other means	6.41	5.45
Storage	0.05	0.07
Communication	6.13	1.95
Banking and insurance	10.16	6.40
Real estate, ownership of dwellings	9.56	9.04
Public administration and defense	4.49	5.86
Other services	6.73	7.73
Total	100	100

Source: Government of India (2013).

not be able to sustain unbalanced and jobless growth. To achieve the necessary balance, India needs to concentrate its policy attention on completing the next phase of structural reforms.

Restructuring and Reforms for Sustainable Growth

Although India has so far managed to grow without a rapid expansion of its manufacturing sector, such growth is certainly not a viable option in the long run. Given the vast pool of unskilled labor and the inability of the services sector to generate adequate employment opportunities, a strong and dynamic manufacturing sector is a prerequisite for sustainable growth. The failure of the manufacturing sector in generating employment could exacerbate the growing economic inequalities, which are already causing considerable social stress. With wage rates beginning to rise in the PRC, India has a fair chance of attracting foreign investment in labor-intensive industries. However, for this to happen, India urgently needs to initiate another round of structural reforms that will improve the investment climate; continue to improve its physical infrastructure, as has been done over the past ten years; remove the impediments for the growth of small- and medium-size enterprises; expand enrollment in secondary, vocational, and higher education; and improve the quality of education at all levels.

Being concentrated in labor-intensive and often in export-oriented industries, small- and medium-size enterprises have borne the brunt of the collapse in external demand during the most recent crisis. They presently face a plethora of official procedures and licensing and regulatory requirements that raise their transaction costs significantly, making them uncompetitive in global markets and unable to withstand import competition in domestic markets. The government will do well to review all the policies that have an impact on doing business in India with the clear objective of improving the investment climate, specifically for small- and medium-size enterprises.[15]

The other major area in need of structural reform is the education sector. The sector is presently characterized by massive capacity constraints, an acute shortage of adequately trained teachers, and poor curriculum quality. Investment is constrained by extensive entry barriers, dysfunctional institutions, and pervasive rent seeking owing to the license-permit raj.[16] Quality is confined to the top few institutions; in the remaining schools, curriculums are outdated, pedagogical skills are deficient, facilities are poor, and there is a singular student focus on passing examinations. The sector needs policy attention as urgently as the industry and trade sectors did at the end of the 1980s. Without these reforms, India will miss the oft-touted demographic dividend. Without reform, the addition of ill-trained and unemployable entrants to the workforce every year could create the conditions for major social conflict and unrest.

India cannot hope to compete effectively in the emerging global knowledge economy if the country's education sector remains underdeveloped (see Dahlman and Utz 2005). A comparison with the People's Republic of China is instructive. India's adult literacy is 61 percent, compared with the PRC's 91 percent (World Bank 2008). Expenditures on education represent 10.7 and 12.8 percent, respectively, of total public expenditure in India and the PRC. The latter has 708 researchers per million people as compared with 119 in India. In 1985 the number of doctoral degrees in science and engineering was 4,007 in India and just 125 in the PRC; but by 2004 the PRC had 14,858 doctorates, while India had increased its number to only 6,318. In 2007 Indians filed 35,000 patents, compared with 245,161 patents by the Chinese. The PRC allocated 1.34 percent of its GDP in 2005 to R&D (which, incidentally, is well below the 3.6 percent allocated in the Republic of Korea), compared with barely 0.61 percent in India. The country has only 12,000 vocational training institutes compared with nearly 500,000 in the PRC, which sends more than 19 percent of its youth on to higher education. In India, on the other hand, just 11–12 percent of students attend colleges and universities (Guruswamy and Singh 2010).

---

15. The evidence for this would be best reflected in an improvement in India's rankings in the World Bank's Doing Business surveys this coming year.

16. *Raj* is a local word that means regime.

Reforms are long overdue. India must ensure that education is accessible to all by multiplying the number of scholarships a hundredfold and, more important, making commercial bank credit for all levels of education more readily available. In short, a social movement may be necessary to ensure that the right to education is actually achieved. If successful, India will be on a sustainable path of rapid growth. Governance reforms, discussed above in the context of small- and medium-size enterprises, and an overhaul of the education sector are perhaps the two most critically needed structural reforms. The payback on them could well be even higher than those from industrial and tariff or telecom sector reforms.

The agriculture sector, which employs up to 50 percent of the working population but contributes less than a fifth of GDP, is lagging behind the rest of the economy. There is a growing gap between rising per capita incomes and per capita availability of food grains (Kumar and others 2010). This could make inflation sticky and macroeconomic stability more difficult to achieve. Inadequate availability of consumer goods (food and other essential commodities) could lower the potential growth rate, as monetary policy will have to remain tight in the face of inflationary expectations. Inflation, being an insidious tax on the poor, is also a politically sensitive issue. Urgent attention is needed to address the structural constraints that currently afflict Indian agriculture. In short, the agriculture sector needs to be modernized with the infusion of new technologies, modern cultivation practices, and more efficient logistics chains to move food from the farm gate to consumers with minimal waste and higher incomes for the farmers. This can only happen if private capital is attracted to agriculture and brings in new technology for raising yields. This calls for a new approach to the agriculture sector that will make it far less dependent on government subsidies, support prices, and other government interventions, which are currently pervasive in the sector. Government policy may be directed toward creating a set of incentives for attracting private investment to the sector both in production and logistics. The experience of contract farming, which is essentially an attempt to overcome the fragmented nature of agriculture holdings, should be reviewed and lacunae identified and addressed. The modernization of retail trade, with its extensive backward linkages to agriculture, should also be considered as a way to give farmers a higher return and as an instrument for the introduction of new technologies and infrastructure in agriculture.

The other major area for reform is the delivery of public services, starting with law and order and including primary health, urban facilities, and better connectivity in the rural sector. This would essentially depend on success in undertaking governance reforms and making public administration more accountable. India's Right to Information Act, enacted in 2005, could play an important role in improving accountability, as it allows the potential beneficiaries to follow the trail of public expenditure and ensure its efficient utilization. Accountability would also be increased by empowering local rural and urban governments, as is being

RAJIV KUMAR AND PANKAJ VASHISHT

attempted under the provisions of the Panchayti Raj (local rural government) bill that is now eighteen years old. A further impetus for public sector accountability could come from moving to a well-designed performance-based or outcome-based budgetary process[17] and the creation of a unified, all-India economic space by implementing the generalized services and goods tax as recommended by the Kelkar task force and more recently by the Thirteenth Finance Commission. This would reduce the tax burden, thereby generating higher demand and allowing for an easier flow of capital and labor across the country—in turn reducing transaction costs and encouraging a more rational allocation of investment. This set of second-generation reforms is crucial if India is to accomplish the necessary rebalancing of its economic activity so that it can achieve rapid but also inclusive and sustainable growth in the coming period.

References

Asian Development Bank. 2009. "Asian Development Outlook 2009: Rebalancing Asia's Growth." Asian Development Bank, Manila (www.adb.org/publications/asian-development-outlook-2009-rebalancing-asias-growth).

Bhalla, Surjit S. 2008. "Inflation Control Chokes Growth." *Business Standard,* October 17 (www.business-standard.com/article/opinion/surjit-s-bhalla-inflation-control-chokes-growth-108101701085_1.html).

Borchert, Ingo, and Aaditya Mattoo. 2009. "Resilience of Services Trade." Policy Research Working Paper 4917. Washington: World Bank.

Broadberry, Stephen, and Bishnupriya Gupta. 2008. "The Historic Roots of India's Booming Services Economy." Vox, May 9 (www.voxeu.org/article/historical-roots-india-s-booming-service-economy).

Dahlman, Carl, and Anuja Utz. 2005. *India and the Knowledge Economy: Leveraging Strengths and Opportunities.* Washington: World Bank.

De, Prabir. 2009. "Global Economic and Financial Crisis: India's Trade Potential and Future Prospects." Working Paper 64. Bangkok: Asia-Pacific Research and Training Network on Trade.

Export-Import Bank of India. 2014. *Outward Foreign Direct Investment from India: Trend, Objects and Policy Perspectives.* Occasional Paper 165. New Delhi (www.eximbankindia.in/sites/default/files/Full%20OP/ODI%20OP.pdf).

Government of India. 2009. *National Account Statistics.* New Delhi: Central Statistical Office.

———. 2009–10. Press Release on India's GDP Growth, May 2009–February 2010. New Delhi.

———. 2013. *National Account Statistics.* New Delhi: Central Statistical Office.

Guruswamy, Mohan, and Zorawar D. Singh. 2010. *Chasing the Dragon: Will India Catch up with China?* New York: Pearson.

17. A start was made in this direction by Finance Minister P. C. Chidambaram, who mandated the establishment of certain performance criteria for all the line ministries of the government and compiling them together in an "outcome budget." However, the outcomes themselves were simply the targets the ministries wanted to achieve, and there was no attempt to monitor or audit the progress toward achieving these targets and relate budgetary allocation to them. Rather than build on this admittedly modest stratum, unfortunately, the process has since been abandoned.

Illiyan, Asheref. 2008. "Performance Challenges and Opportunities of India Software Export." *Journal of Theoretical and Applied Information Technology* 4, no. 11: 1088–106.

Joseph, Mathew, and Karan Singh. 2009. "The Impact of Monsoon Failure on GDP Growth, 2009–10." Macro Perspective and Updates. New Delhi: Indian Council for Research on International Economic Relations.

Kumar, Rajiv, and Pankaj Vashisht. 2009. "Global Economic Crisis: Impact on India and Policy Response." Working Paper 164. Tokyo: Asian Development Bank Institute.

Kumar, Rajiv, Pankaj Vashisht, and Gunajit Kalita. 2010. "Food Inflation: Contingent and Structural Factors." *Economic and Political Weekly* 14, no. 10: 16–19.

Mussa, Michael. 2009. "Global Economic Prospects as of September 2009: Onward Economic Recovery." Paper presented at the Sixteenth Semiannual Meeting on Global Economic Prospects. September 17, 2009 (www.iie.com/publications/papers/mussa0909.pdf).

National Bureau of Statistics of China. 2012. *China Statistical Year Book.* Beijing.

Panagariya, Arvind. 2008. *The Emerging Giant.* Oxford University Press.

Pursell, Garry, Nalin Kishor, and Kanupriya Gupta. 2007. "Manufacturing Protection in India since Independence." Working Paper 2007/07. Canberra: Australia South Asia Research Centre.

Reserve Bank of India. 2013. *Handbook of Statistics on Indian Economy, 2012–13.* Mumbai.

Roubini, Nouriel. 2009. "The Road Ahead for the Global Economy." EconoMonitor, July 23 (www.economonitor.com/nouriel/2009/07/23/the-road-ahead-for-the-global-economy/).

Subramanian, Arvind. 2008. *India's Turn: Understanding the Economic Transformation.* Oxford University Press.

World Bank. 2008. *World Development Indicators.* Washington.

———. 2010. *Global Economic Prospects.* Washington.

Contributors

Iwan J. Azis
*Head, Office of Regional Economic
Integration, Asian Development Bank*

Barry Bosworth
*Robert Roosa Chair for International
Economics, Brookings Institution.*

Hwee Kwan Chow
*Professor of Economics and Statistics
(Practice), Singapore Management
University*

Susan M. Collins
*Joan and Sanford Weill Dean of Public
Policy, Gerald R. Ford School of
Public Policy, University of Michigan*

Barry Eichengreen
*George C. Pardee and Helen N. Pardee
Professor of Economics and Political
Science, University of California,
Berkeley*

Yiping Huang
*Professor of Economics, National
School of Development, Peking
University.*

Masahiro Kawai
*Professor, Graduate School of Public
Policy, University of Tokyo and,
previously, Dean and CEO, ADBI*

Ginalyn Komoto
*Former Junior Consultant and Research
Associate, Asian Development Bank
Institute*

Rajiv Kumar
*Senior Fellow, Centre for Policy
Research, New Delhi*

Mario B. Lamberte
*Team Leader, COMPETE Project, The
Asia Foundation*

Gisela Rua
Economist, Division of Research and
Statistics of the Board of Governors,
Federal Reserve System

Shinji Takagi
Assistant Director, Independent
Evaluation Office, International
Monetary Fund

Kunyu Tao
Assistant Professor, School of Finance,
Central University of Finance and
Economics, Beijing

Willem Thorbecke
Senior Fellow, Research Institute of
Economy, Trade, and Industry, Tokyo

Pankaj Vashisht
Research Associate, Indian Council for
Research on International Economic
Relations, New Delhi

Index

Abe, Shinzo, 16, 142–43

Access to financial services, 20, 21, 24, 228

Advanced economies: concerns about global recovery prospects and, 2–3; differing perspectives on rebalancing strategies for, 27; modeling current account surplus reversals in, 41–54, 44*t*, 51*t*, 52; recovery from 2008 financial crisis, 1, 184, 231

ASEAN countries: access to financial services in, 20, 21; consumption patterns and trends in, 20; corporate saving in, 20; current and projected economic performance of, 229; economic challenges for, 211; evolution of capital flows in, 214–18, 216*f*; evolution of external imbalances in, 212–213, 213*f*; evolution of savings-investment gap in, 20, 212–13, 214*f*, 215*f*; evolution of trade balances in, 213–14, 216*f*, 218–21, 219*t*, 220*t*,

221*t*; exchange rate policies and patterns in, 21, 221–23; export and import elasticities, 12; export markets, 21; financial sectors of, 228; goals for economic community, 20, 21; implications of rebalancing for economies of, 223, 229–30; income inequality in, 20; India's trade with, 244–45, 245*t*; infrastructure spending, 21, 24; member countries, 20 (*see also specific country*); projected current account balances in, 218; rationale for regional economic integration, 244; savings patterns and trends in, 20, 223–25, 224–25*f*; size of economy of, 20; small- and medium-sized enterprises in, 24; strategies for rebalancing in, 20–21, 24, 211–12, 229–30; trade policy, 21.

Asia: capital goods trade in, 77; consumption goods trade in, 77–78; currency appreciation to foster

Asian Development Bank Institute

The Asian Development Bank Institute (ADBI), located in Tokyo, is the think tank of the Asian Development Bank (ADB). ADBI's mission is to identify effective development strategies and improve development management in ADB's developing member countries. ADBI has an extensive network of partners in the Asia and Pacific region and globally. ADBI's activities are aligned with ADB's strategic focus, which includes poverty reduction and inclusive economic growth, the environment, regional cooperation and integration, infrastructure development, middle-income countries, and private sector development and operations.

Brookings Institution

The Brookings Institution is a private nonprofit organization devoted to research, education, and publication on important issues of domestic and foreign policy. Its principal purpose is to bring the highest quality independent research and analysis to bear on current and emerging policy problems. The Institution was founded on December 8, 1927, to merge the activities of the Institute for Government Research, founded in 1916, the Institute of Economics, founded in 1922, and the Robert Brookings Graduate School of Economics and Government, founded in 1924. Interpretations or conclusions in Brookings publications should be understood to be solely those of the authors.